THE ILLUSTRATED ENCYCLOPEDIA OF
CATHOLICISM

THE ILLUSTRATED ENCYCLOPEDIA OF
CATHOLICISM

A COMPREHENSIVE GUIDE TO THE HISTORY, PHILOSOPHY AND PRACTICE OF
CATHOLIC CHRISTIANITY, WITH MORE THAN 500 BEAUTIFUL ILLUSTRATIONS

CONSULTANT: REVEREND RONALD CREIGHTON-JOBE

MARY FRANCES BUDZIK • MICHAEL KERRIGAN • CHARLES PHILLIPS

LORENZ BOOKS

CONTENTS

Above *Detail from* The Presentation in the Temple *by Fra Angelico, 1442.*

Above *A 5th-century carved ivory relief illustrating the Resurrection of Christ.*

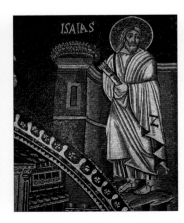

Above *A 6th-century mosaic of the prophet Isaiah, San Vitale Basilica, Ravenna, Italy.*

Above *Pope John Paul II celebrating Mass in Knock, Ireland, in 1979.*

Above Christ refusing the banquet offered by Satan, by William Blake, c.1816–18.

Above A Roman legionary killing a barbarian from a 3rd-century marble sarcophagus.

Above A 15th-century French depiction of the capture of Antioch in the First Crusade.

Above The interior of the 13th-century Notre-Dame Cathedral, Reims, France.

INTRODUCTION

Catholicism is the oldest and the largest of the Christian churches and has become one of the world's largest religions. More than half of the world's Christians take their leadership from the pope in Rome. In 2006, indeed, the number of Catholics stood at 1.31 billion people – 17.4 per cent (about one-sixth) of the planet's population. (Islam, if all its branches are taken together, just tops that total; none of the other creeds comes close.) One of the world's biggest and most formidably organized institutions, the Church can call on around 136,000 priests and 750,000 nuns – along with a multitude of loyal lay supporters. It is too important a moral force to be ignored, and is capable of exerting an influence on public policy and international affairs. Its teachings shape many millions of lives.

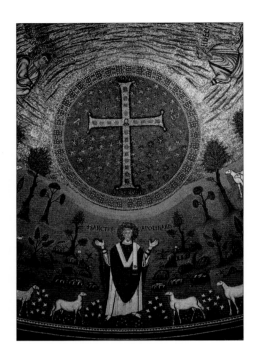

Above *Moses and Elijah look on as St Apollinare tends his flock. Ravenna's first bishop was buried in the 6th-century basilica that contains this painting.*

HEAVEN AND EARTH

The Catholic Church would be nothing if it were only an earthly institution – "My kingship is not of this world," its founder Jesus stated (John 18: 36). Looking beyond this life to the hereafter, the Church views humankind's existence in an eternal perspective: the living and departed come together in the Communion of Saints. As this book sets out to demonstrate, Catholicism offers its followers an account of God's Creation, of life and death – along with the possibility of salvation for devout Catholics, with everlasting joy in heaven.

Below *This demographic map illustrates the percentage of the Roman Catholic population around the world. It is increasing fastest in Africa and Asia, and although 25 per cent of Catholics live in Europe, it has the slowest growth rate.*

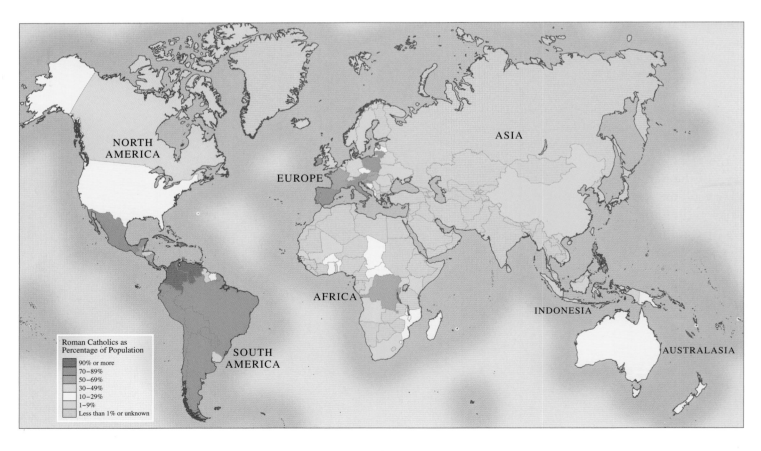

NORTH AMERICA

ASIA

EUROPE

AFRICA

INDONESIA

SOUTH AMERICA

AUSTRALASIA

Roman Catholics as Percentage of Population
- 90% or more
- 70–89%
- 50–69%
- 30–49%
- 10–29%
- 1–9%
- Less than 1% or unknown

AN EVENTFUL HISTORY

The first part of this book, "Catholic History", shows how eventful and exciting the story of the Church has been – and at times how complex, even contradictory. Catholicism's truths might be eternal, yet they took many centuries to articulate. Although Catholicism's inspirations might be divine, many of its practitioners have been all too human.

At key turning points in its history, the Church was able to grow in strength even through suffering and struggle; however, at other moments, it persecuted those who stood against it. An inspiration to creativity, Catholicism has played a central role in the Western artistic tradition, though at times it has arguably been too involved in acquiring these splendours. The papacy has provided vital leadership, yet an absolute authority it was endowed with by Christ himself has not always been wielded as conscientiously as it should have been.

DIVINE DOCTRINES

The second section of the book, "Catholic Doctrine" looks at the various different teachings that constitute Catholic belief. It considers beliefs on the eternal truths of existence as well as those that goven the everyday dilemmas of social and personal morality. From the Trinity to the transubstantiation, from the status of the Scriptures to the significance of the saints, the complete range of the Church's teachings are examined here. Among the questions explored are: What is sin? What does Christ's redemption mean? How are we to understand the concepts of salvation or damnation?

Right St Peter's Basilica, in the Vatican within Rome, Italy, is both the historic centre of an ancient Catholic Church and at the heart of the modern world. Catholicism continues to flourish amid changing times.

LIVING THE FAITH

The third section of the book, "Practising Catholicism" shows how these doctrines find expression in the everyday life of the Church: in its institutions, its rituals and its festivities. The administrative structures of the Church are examined, from the Vatican down to parish level, and the functions of its different offices are explained. The varieties of religious life are looked at: the contemplative, the charitable and the missionary vocations; the duties performed by the different sorts of priests and nuns; and the vows such men and women take, along with the reasoning behind them.

The seven sacraments are the heart and soul of Catholic observance. Each is described in detail, with its rituals and what they mean. From baptism to the anointing of the sick, these mark out the landmark moments in the life of the believer, from birth to death: the development of reason, full communion with God and, of course, the partnership of marriage – which is a sacred state in the Catholic scheme. The Church has attracted both admiration and opprobrium for its stands on a number of issues of sexual morality and medical ethics. Often misunderstood, the principles behind them are explored here.

The place of prayer is also considered, along with that of such special devotions as the Stations of the Cross and the rosary – spiritual disciplines that may bring the Catholic into a closer relationship with God. There is coverage, too, of the main holy days and feasts of the Catholic year, their spiritual meaning and the often colourful customs associated with them.

Catholicism is a complex creed and the Church a vast and venerable institution. The hope is that by offering a factual account of the Church's achievements and theology and by demonstrating the beauties of its rituals, this book will help to bring an understanding of Catholicism and its teachings to its readers.

TIMELINE

THE CATHOLIC CHURCH HAS A LONG HISTORY. THE TIMELINE BELOW LISTS SOME OF THE MAJOR EVENTS THAT HAVE AFFECTED IT.

1ST CENTURY BC
- Romans conquer Judaea, 63 BC.
- Herod the Great begins renovations on the Temple of Jerusalem, *c.*19 BC.

1ST CENTURY AD
- *Anno Domini* – by tradition, the year of Christ's birth.
- Saul witnesses the martyrdom of St Stephen, *c.*AD 35.
- Council of Jerusalem convened by St Peter, the first pope, *c.*AD 50.
- Nero launches the first persecution of Rome's Christians in AD 64.

2ND CENTURY
- Monumental shrine erected around St Peter's tomb in Rome, *c.*150.

3RD CENTURY
- Persecution of Valerian, 253-60.

4TH CENTURY
- Diocletian's "Great Persecution", 303–11.
- Emperor Constantine converts to Christianity in 312.
- Constantine calls the Council of Nicaea in 325.
- Proclamation of the Nicene Creed, 381.
- St Jerome begins work on his Latin "Vulgate" Bible, 382.

5TH CENTURY
- St Augustine starts writing his great work, *The City of God*.
- Leo the Great centralizes power in the papacy, 440–61.

6TH CENTURY
- St Benedict of Nursia establishes his monastic rule.

Above Detail from a fresco showing Pope Gregory the Great (540–604), from Vezzolano, Italy.

- Reforming papacy of Gregory the Great begins in 590.

7TH CENTURY
- Muhammad begins receiving his revelations of Islam in 610.
- Arab armies occupy Jerusalem in 638.

8TH CENTURY
- The Church is given temporal authority over Rome and its environs under the "Donation of Pepin", 754.

9TH CENTURY
- The legendary "Pope Joan" supposedly succeeds to the papacy in 853.

10TH CENTURY
- The reformist abbey of Cluny is founded in eastern France, 910.

11TH CENTURY
- The Cistercian order tries to take monasticism back to its first Benedictine principles.
- The Eastern Orthodox Church formally parts company with Rome, 1054.
- Urban II calls the First Crusade in 1095. Jerusalem is taken four years later.

Above Worshippers gather outside the entrance to the Church of the Holy Sepulchre, Jerusalem, Israel.

12TH CENTURY
- The beginning of the Gothic movement in religious architecture.
- The Second Crusade of 1145 breaks down in chaos.
- The Third Lateran Council begins in 1179.
- Saladin recaptures Jerusalem for the Muslims in 1187. The Third Crusade that follows is a failure.
- Peter Waldo denounces the wealth of the Church from 1177.

13TH CENTURY
- The forces of the Fourth Crusade (1202–4) sack Christian Constantinople.
- Innocent III proclaims the Albigensian Crusade against the heretical Cathars in 1208.
- St Francis of Assisi begins his ministry in 1209.
- Thomas Aquinas writes the *Summa Theologica*, 1266–74.

14TH CENTURY
- Clement V transfers the papacy to Avignon in France, 1309.
- Gregory XI makes Rome the centre of papal power again in 1377 – but rival popes continue in opposition in Avignon after his death in 1378.

15TH CENTURY
- The Council of Pisa (1408) fails to resolve the Western Schism. A solution is found in 1417.
- Czech heretic Jan Hus is burnt at the stake in 1415.
- The Spanish Inquisition is at its height, encouraged by the "Catholic Monarchs", Ferdinand and Isabella.
- The Reconquista is complete, with the expulsion of the Moors from Granada in 1492. That same year Columbus starts opening up an empire for Spain in the Americas.

16TH CENTURY
- The reconstruction of St Peter's Basilica, Rome, begins in 1505.
- Martin Luther nails his "95 Theses" to the door of the cathedral in Wittenberg, Germany.
- Clement VII is taken prisoner by German forces during the Sack of Rome, 1527.
- The Ottoman Siege of Vienna is successfully repulsed in 1529.
- Henry VIII announces that he and his successors will henceforth be heads of the Church of England, 1534.
- Ignatius Loyola founds the Society of Jesus in 1534.

- Copernicus' theories are published after his death in 1543.
- St Francis Xavier undertakes his mission to the East, 1542–52.
- The Council of Trent gets under way in 1545. Church leaders resist the Reformation.
- Turkish naval power is defeated by the Christian fleet at the Battle of Lepanto, 1571.

17TH CENTURY
- Galileo is forced to recant his claims for Copernican astronomy.
- A Congregation for the Evangelization of Peoples is founded to co-ordinate missionary endeavours, 1622.
- The Thirty Years' War ends in 1648, with Europe divided along religious lines.

18TH CENTURY
- Denis Diderot and friends begin work on their secularizing *Encyclopédie* in 1750.
- Revolution convulses France from 1789.

19TH CENTURY
- Pius IX denounces modern liberalism in his *Syllabus of Errors*, 1864. Papal infallibility will be proclaimed six years later.

- The "White Fathers" are at work evangelizing in Africa, from 1868.
- Papal rule in the city of Rome is brought to an end in 1871.
- Leo XIII throws the Church's weight behind the cause of workers' rights in *Rerum Novarum*, written in 1891.

20TH CENTURY
- The Lateran Treaty of 1929 sees the Church enter into partnership with Mussolini's Fascist state.
- A Concordat is signed with Nazi Germany in 1933.
- Pius XI condemns anti-semitic violence in Germany, 1937.
- John XXIII calls the Second Vatican Council in 1962.
- Liberation theology takes root in Latin America from the 1960s. Its followers play a leading role in the Nicaraguan Revolution of the 1980s.
- Pope John Paul II is elected by an enclave in 1978.

21ST CENTURY
- Protestant Pentecostalism is on the rise in Latin America.
- Pope John Paul II makes the first papal visit to Israel, in 2000. That same year he becomes the first pope to pray in a Muslim mosque.

Above The striking Gothic façade of the 14th-century Duomo di Milano, or Milan Cathedral.

Above An 18th-century Peruvian painting of St Francis Xavier. He is the patron saint of all missions.

Above John Paul II (served 1978–2005), an influential pope, was the second longest-serving pope to rule in Rome.

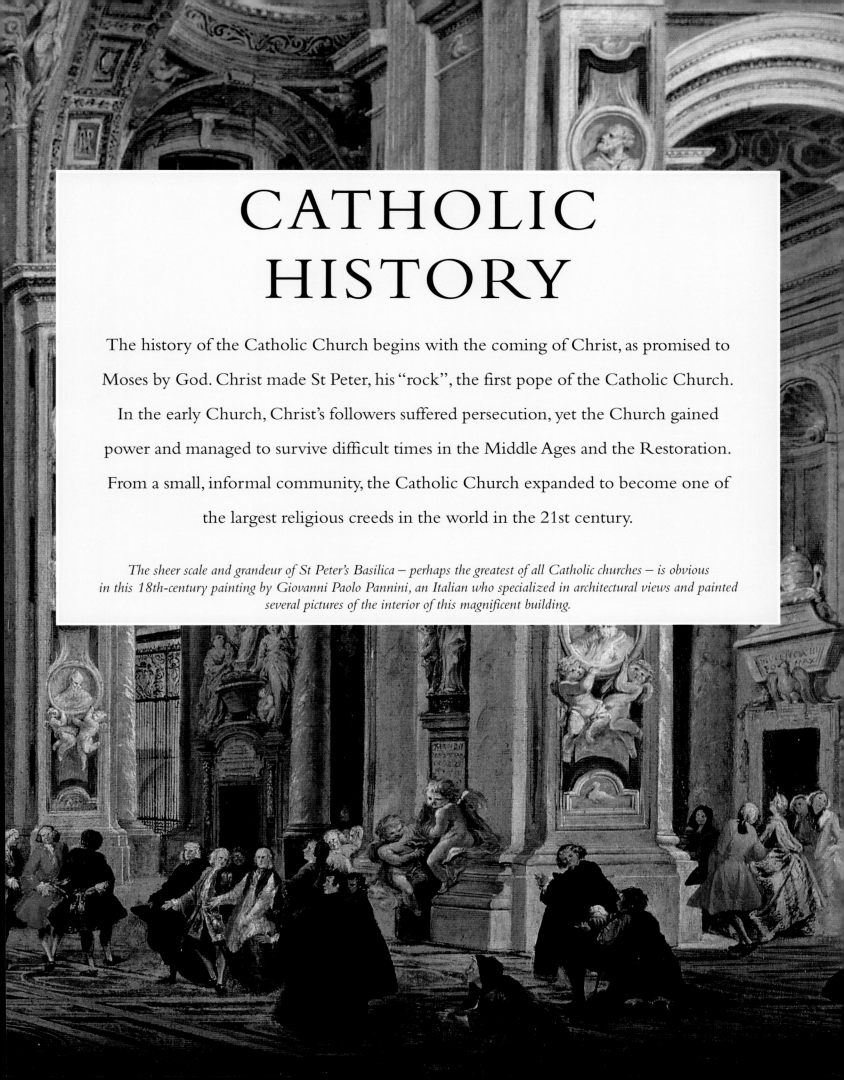

CATHOLIC HISTORY

The history of the Catholic Church begins with the coming of Christ, as promised to Moses by God. Christ made St Peter, his "rock", the first pope of the Catholic Church. In the early Church, Christ's followers suffered persecution, yet the Church gained power and managed to survive difficult times in the Middle Ages and the Restoration. From a small, informal community, the Catholic Church expanded to become one of the largest religious creeds in the world in the 21st century.

The sheer scale and grandeur of St Peter's Basilica – perhaps the greatest of all Catholic churches – is obvious in this 18th-century painting by Giovanni Paolo Pannini, an Italian who specialized in architectural views and painted several pictures of the interior of this magnificent building.

THE EARLY CHURCH

The gospels tell an inspirational story. "The word became flesh," says John's Gospel, "he lived among us and we saw his glory." The coming of Christ was the fulfilment of a promise. His remarkable life and death, and above all his Resurrection, made good God's undertaking to both Moses and Abraham. It realized the predictions of the prophets and renewed humanity's hope.

However, inspiration was not enough: as Christ incarnated the word of God, so his message had to be embodied in the institutions and practices of a living, working Church. Catholicism's structures evolved slowly, sometimes painfully, over centuries. Tried in the fire of persecution and torn by dissension – and, ultimately, division – the Church faced many difficulties as it developed. Christian theology was still comparatively new and unexplored, and it had to be systematized by learned scholars.

There were also the difficulties that come with success. The bigger and more secure Catholicism became as a worldwide institution, the greater the political pressures. The emergence of the papacy as a seat of spiritual authority and political power was a temptation as well as a triumph for the Church. Even so, as the 1st millennium came to an end, the faith was the dominant spiritual and cultural force across much of Europe. Catholicism had come a long way in its first thousand years.

Above The Greek letters Iota (for Iesu, or "Jesus"), Chi (for Christos, or "Christ") and Theta (for Theou, or "Saviour") spell Ichthus, Greek for "fish". The fish, as seen in this 4th-century Italian mosaic, became a Christian emblem.

Left In this 1485 painting The Life of Mary by the Master of Aachen, the old priest Simeon blesses the baby Jesus on his presentation in the Temple.

IN THE DAYS OF KING HEROD

THE COUNTRY IN WHICH THE CHRISTIAN STORY STARTED WAS A TERRITORY OF THE ROMAN EMPIRE, ALTHOUGH THE ROMANS WERE JUST THE LATEST IN A LONG SUCCESSION OF INVADERS.

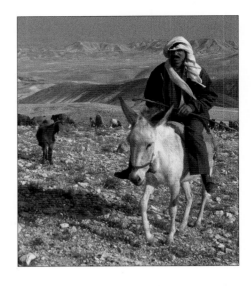

Jesus' birthplace, Bethlelem, and the surrounding regions have an ancient history. Christ was born among the Jews, who saw themselves as the "Chosen People" of Jehovah. However the "Holy Land" that was so important to the Jews was one of the less significant corners of the world at the beginning of the first millenium.

Judaea and Israel, its neighbour to the north, had been brought together under King David from *c.*1007 BC. The state he created, with its capital in Jerusalem, had come to prominence under his son, Solomon, in the 10th century BC. Though known for his legendary wisdom, Solomon had in reality all but ruined his kingdom; the construction of his celebrated Temple had bankrupted the state. Eventually, the country disintegrated and was conquered by the Assyrians in 841 BC.

UNDER OCCUPATION

The Jews never accepted their subject status, despite being subjugated for centuries, first under the rule of the Assyrians, then the Babylonians. In the 6th century BC, leading Jews were taken from their country to the imperial capital in what is known as the "Babylonian Captivity", but this failed to break their spirit of resistance.

Persian power proved more benign: after conquering Babylon in 539, Cyrus the Great of Persia let the exiles return to Israel. (He even ordered the reconstruction of the Temple, which had been sacked by Babylon's King Nebuchadnezzar after a Jewish uprising in 587 BC.) The Persians, however, were swept aside by the eastward march of Alexander the Great, who came with his Greek army in 332 BC. After Alexander's death, his vast empire was fought

Above A Bedouin tends his flock in the rocky Judaean Desert, just as Jewish shepherds would have done 2,000 years ago.

over by his surviving generals. Along with much of the Middle East, Israel fell to Seleucus, a boyhood friend and comrade-at-arms of Alexander. His descendants reigned after him, in what is known as the Seleucid line.

A TASTE OF FREEDOM

Attempts by the Seleucid ruler Antiochus IV to suppress the religious rituals of the Jews sparked a revolt in 167 BC. Simon

HEROD..."THE GREAT"?

Herod's honorific title, "the Great", strikes modern Christians as strange, given his client-king status – and the part he played in the Gospel account of Jesus' birth. The Magi, wise men who had journeyed from the east by following a star to where they had been told a new king of the Jews would be born, went to Herod and sought his assistance in finding the infant. He was horrified to hear of a rival's birth. However, he begged his visitors to tell him when they found the boy, so that he, too, could pay him homage. Warned by an angel not to tell Herod anything, the Magi instead returned home by another route, whereupon the enraged king had all the infant boys in Israel – the "Holy Innocents" – massacred. This is a cruel and ignominious role in the Christian Scriptures, but

Jewish tradition and mainstream history have judged Herod more kindly. He is called "Herod the Great" on account of his reconstruction of the Temple.

Below A 14th-century Italian mosaic shows King Herod enjoying a lavish banquet.

Above Herod lives in Jewish memory as the rebuilder of the Temple, shown here in a 19th-century painting by James Jacques Tissot (1836–1902).

Maccabaeus' Hasmonean Dynasty took power and Jewish sovereignty was restored. Jewish rule lasted until 63 BC, when the country was conquered once again – this time by the Roman general Pompey. He let the Hasmoneans stay in office, but as client-kings of what was now named Judaea. They reigned at the beck and call of the Roman emperors, but in return their subjects could still find some comfort in the fact that their country was a kingdom, rather than a mere province.

That the Jews were allowed this degree of autonomy indicates the strength of their identity – however, it also reflects the comparative irrelevance of a people living on the margins. The main centres of wealth and civilization in the ancient world were to the east in Mesopotamia (modern–day Iraq) and Persia, and to the west in the Mediterranean. Palestine was peripheral to both these spheres. Regardless, as insignificant as they were, the Jews had been allowed considerable freedom to live and worship God in the way they had for generations. This freedom was a dangerous thing: many Jews were in no way reconciled to their subjection and were eager to shake off the Roman yoke.

KING OF THE JEWS

For the moment, Rome was firmly in charge and King Herod was the Empire's servant. He had been appointed by the Romans as King of Judaea in 37 BC and was given the title "King of the Jews". In return for his loyalty, Herod won certain privileges for the Jews, and the Romans made no objections to his request when, in 19 BC, he renovated the Temple.

Above "No foreigners shall enter…" reads the tablet King Herod placed in the Temple. Christ, by contrast, was to reach out to all people.

AND IT CAME TO PASS…

THE JEWS HAD BEEN EXPECTING A MIGHTY KING AS A SAVIOUR, BUT INSTEAD CHRIST WAS BORN IN A LOWLY STABLE IN BETHLEHEM. COULD THIS REALLY BE THE MESSIAH THEY HAD BEEN WAITING FOR?

Jewish scriptural tradition had long foreseen the coming of a "Messiah" – whom the Book of Daniel (9:24) referred to as the "anointed one" or "prince". "The people who lived in darkness have seen a great light," prophesied Isaiah (9:2–9). As a king descended from the House of David, it was believed that the Messiah would introduce an eternal era of justice and peace.

Most Jews expected a king to come in glory, but there were Old Testament writers with another vision. Zachary's Messiah (9:9) was envisaged as "lowly, and riding on a donkey". In a chapter of Isaiah (53:3–6), there is a foreshadowing of how the Christian

Below "Behold the handmaid of the lord…", begins the Latin inscription beneath this Annunciation by the Italian painter Filippo Lippi, c.1440.

servant-saviour was received: "despised, and rejected by men… he was wounded for our transgressions…and with his stripes we are healed."

A VISIT FROM AN ANGEL

"Behold, a virgin shall conceive," promises Isaiah (7:14), "and bear a son, and shall call his name Immanuel." That prophecy found fulfilment in the gospel account (Luke, Chapter 1) in which the archangel Gabriel announced to the astonished Virgin Mary the miraculous part she had been appointed to play as the Messiah's mother. The angel's words were later to form the first line of the prayer that is still repeated daily by many Catholics: "Hail Mary, full of grace, the Lord is with thee."

The angel also told Mary that her much older relative Elizabeth was pregnant, despite years of

Above The Messiah was expected to renew the reign of King David, writer of the Psalms, shown in this c.1500 painting by the Master of Riofrio.

childlessness, so the Blessed Virgin went to see her in the "Visitation". Elizabeth greeted Mary with the words that became the second line of the Hail Mary: "Blessed art thou amongst women, and blessed is the fruit of thy womb."

THE ANGELUS

Although the custom has fallen victim to the mounting pressures of modern life, for centuries, throughout the Catholic world, the rhythm of the day was set by the sound of the angelus bell. Three sets of three slow, solemn strokes rang out at 6 a.m., 12 noon and 6 p.m. as a signal to the faithful to stop whatever they were doing to meditate on the Annunciation and what it meant. The call-and-response devotion that followed re-enacted the abrupt arrival of the angel in the Virgin Mary's presence and Christ's conception by the power of the Holy Spirit.

Mary's reply ("Behold the handmaid of the Lord...Be it done to me according to thy word") is also recollected in the angelus, as are John's words (1:14) on the Incarnation of Our Lord ("And the word was made flesh, and dwelt amongst us").

THE NATIVITY

Mary, though a virgin, was betrothed to Joseph, whose occupation as a carpenter has made him the patron saint of working men. However, the Gospels of Matthew and Luke are at pains to make the point that he is also a descendant of the House of David: as his son, then, Christ is from Israel's royal line. Yet his is anything but a kingly birth.

At the time when Mary was due to deliver her child, she and her husband were in Bethlehem. The Romans were conducting a census in Judaea and all families had been ordered to go to the ancestral home of the father to be counted. There was no room for them at the inn, so Mary had to give birth in a stable and lay her baby in a manger.

The baby was attended, not by great Jewish dignitaries, but by shepherds from the surrounding hillsides. Although the Magi, "kings" or "wise men", had come to honour the newborn, they were outsiders, summoned from afar. The manner of Jesus' arrival

Above The most momentous of events, Christ's Nativity in the stable was painted by Hans Leonhard Schaufelein in the 16th century.

Below The Holy Family fled to Egypt when they learned that Herod had ordered the slaughter of all male babies, as shown here in this late 15th-century manuscript.

in the world anticipates his later remark (Matthew 13:58) that "a prophet is not without honour except in his own country". By the same token, the coming of the Magi may be seen as a signal that Christ will ultimately find most of his followers abroad.

ANNO DOMINI

The "Year of the Lord" – from the Latin *anno domini* (which is commonly abbreviated to AD) – has been taken as a chronological starting point in western tradition. Supposedly, it was the year in which Christ was born. But was it really? Luke's account has the holy family travelling to Bethlehem to take part in a census ordered by the Romans. This could only refer to the survey conducted by Quirinius, Rome's governor in Syria, which is known to have taken place in AD 6–7. However, Matthew implies an earlier date, and some scholars believe that the Nativity might have taken place in 8 BC.

"YOU ARE MY SON, THE BELOVED..."

JESUS GREW UP QUIETLY IN NAZARETH, A LITTLE TOWN IN GALILEE. NO ONE GUESSED THAT THE BOY THEY SAW HELPING OUT IN HIS FATHER'S WORKSHOP WAS ACTUALLY THE MORTAL SON OF GOD.

Christ may have been born, but "Christianity" was as yet unheard of, and Jesus was raised by his parents in the traditions of Judaism. Like any other Jewish baby boy, he was circumcised at eight days old and, on the 40th day after his birth, Jesus' mother took him to the Jewish Temple for his presentation. Tradition demanded not only that the mother herself should be ritually "purified" after giving birth but that the baby should be formally presented. Jewish law decreed that the Temple had the right to claim any

Below Simeon, an elderly priest, sees the Messiah during his presentation in this 15th-century painting by Giovanni Bellini.

firstborn boy for the priesthood, unless he was redeemed with a token payment.

SEEING SALVATION

The Gospel of Luke (2:29–31) describes how Simeon, an old priest who had prayed to God to let him live long enough to see the Messiah, finally saw the infant saviour during his presentation and realized that God had answered his prayers. "Now master you are letting your servant go in peace," he said in gratitude, "for my eyes have seen the salvation which you have made ready in the sight of the nations." The child was destined to be the deliverance of his people, though he would also face great opposition from

Above The adolescent Jesus is shown astonishing the elders of the Temple with his knowledge in this early 19th-century Russian icon.

them and others. Simeon also warned Mary, "a sword will pierce your soul, too" (2:35).

A SPECIAL BAPTISM

At 12 years old, Jesus disappeared during a pilgrimage his family was making to Jerusalem. His frantic mother found him in the Temple talking to the elders. These experienced scholars were in raptures at his knowledge and insight.

Above Jesus is determined to be
purified through baptism, like any
sinner, in this early 14th-century
painting entitled The Baptism of
Christ *by Giotto.*

The boy – a little impatiently –
dismissed his mother's reproaches:
"Why were you looking for me?"
he asked (Luke 2:49). "Did you
not know that I must be in my
father's house?" Though his parents did not understand what their
son was saying, this is a clear indi-
cation that Jesus' own mind was
already on his heavenly kingdom
and his earthly mission.

The gospels agree that it was
not until many years later, when
Jesus was about 30 years of age,
that he left home and made his
way into the desert beside the
River Jordan. There he found
John – Elizabeth's son and his
relative. Known as John the
Baptist, he had already embarked
on his own sacred ministry, living
simply in the wilderness and
preaching to the people, calling on
them to change their lives. He
baptized the repentant and prophesied the coming of a saviour.

When Jesus appeared, John
pointed him out as the one who
was to come. John was perplexed

Right Christ is tempted by the devil
in the desert, shown here in this
c.1225 stained-glass scene in Troyes
Cathedral, in France.

THE INFANCY GOSPELS

The gospels say little about Jesus' boyhood, so perhaps it is inevitable that
popular folklore has made up the shortfall. Among the many Apocrypha
(purported scriptural writings of dubious origin) produced in the early
centuries after Christ's death and Resurrection were what is known as
the Infancy Gospels. These offer more details on Jesus' boyhood, but
they view him like a fairytale hero with "magical" powers. Some of his
supposed deeds, indeed, could hardly be seen as Christ-like. In one story,
for instance, he reacted to an insult by cursing the boy who delivered it
so he died; then when the boy's parents complained, Jesus blinded them.

when the man he regarded as the
Messiah asked to be baptized like
any sinner, but Jesus was adamant,
and John agreed. As Christ arose
from the water, the heavens parted
and the Holy Spirit descended in
the form of a dove. A voice rang
out, saying "You are my Son, the
Beloved; my favour rests on you"
(Mark 1:11).

THE TEMPTATION

After his baptism, Matthew tells
us, Jesus went into the wilderness
alone to fast and pray in preparation for the task that awaited him.
He spent 40 days and 40 nights in
the desert, with his solitude being
interrupted only by the devil, who
had come to test his resolve.

Satan appeared three times to
tempt Jesus. First he offered Jesus
all the kingdoms of the world if he
would bow down and worship
Satan. Then he challenged Jesus to
turn stones into bread to satisfy his
hunger. Finally, Satan took Jesus to
the highest point on the Temple
and dared him to jump off (the
angels will make sure you are not
hurt, he said). Christ refused to rise
to these provocations. Dismayed,
the devil left and angels arrived
with bread to ease Jesus' hunger.

"BLESSED ARE THE POOR IN SPIRIT"

IT IS UNCLEAR WHETHER CHRIST'S MINISTRY LASTED FOR WEEKS OR YEARS. EITHER WAY, HE HAD TIME TO PERFORM MIRACLES AND PROCLAIM THE MOST REMARKABLE MESSAGE EVER HEARD.

Above Christ cures a blind man in this warm and intimate scene by an 11th-century Italian artist.

Jesus first performed a miracle at his mother's urging during the Wedding Feast at Cana. Supplies were running low, so he turned jars of ordinary water into wine. Once his ministry got under way in earnest, Jesus cast out demons and healed the sick – and, in the case of Lazarus, he even gave life back to the dead.

From a modern perspective, the early miracles appear to have established Christ's credentials as the Messiah. Certainly, when the apostles saw him walking across the waters of the Sea of Galilee toward their boat, they were left in no doubt of his divinity (but Peter's own faith faltered as he attempted to walk out to meet his Lord).

A DIVINITY KEPT SECRET

Jesus himself did not necessarily want his divinity known to others. At a number of points, in the Gospel of Mark especially, he urged his hearers to keep what is called the "Messianic Secret". Even when his apostles witnessed him standing on a high mountain in the episode known as the "Transfiguration", blazing forth in all his godly radiance, they were urged to not tell others what they had witnessed.

After one of his first miracles, the healing of a leper (Mark 1), Christ gave the man strict orders that he should tell no one of his cure. However, in his exhilaration, the man ignored this injunction and told everyone he met what Jesus had done for him. Crowds came from far and wide to see this marvellous miracle worker. Some came in hopes of being cured themselves; some to witness miracles or to hear what this new prophet had to say.

THE BEATITUDES

Christ's teachings have their single, most sustained exposition in the extraordinary episode known as the Sermon on the Mount – although on which particular mount the discourse was delivered is unclear. Wherever it occurred, it was during this sermon that Jesus formulated the Beatitudes (literally, Blessednesses), as is recorded in Matthew 5:3–12:

Left Jesus is surrounded by his followers as he gives his Sermon on the Mount. He is standing in this painting by James Jacques Tissot, but traditionally Jesus is shown sitting – rabbis often sat while teaching.

- *How blessed are the poor in spirit; the kingdom of heaven is theirs.*
- *Blessed are the gentle; they shall have the earth as inheritance…*
- *Blessed are the merciful; they shall have mercy shown them…*
- *Blessed are the peacemakers; they shall be recognized as children of God…*

These blessings gave encouragement to his listeners. However, there were many other components to this thought-provoking sermon, including the Lord's Prayer and what are considered by many people to be the central tenets of Christianity. The convention is that Jesus' life and death created a "new covenant" between God and humankind. This was a merciful reaching out, a second chance for the fallen descendants of Adam and Eve.

This interpretation is true enough, but at the same time, for all the generosity and love it represented, the "deal" Jesus offered was extremely exacting. Those who followed his way, he warned, could expect to endure abuse and persecution. Harder than the insults and violent treatment they were to expect, would be the duty they would have to respond to their oppressors with friendship and forgiveness: rather than retaliate if anyone hit them, they must offer them the other cheek (Matthew 5:39). They should love their enemies, do good to those who wish them harm, and treat others as they would hope to be treated themselves.

NOT ONLY FOR THE JUST

Jesus found his first followers when, walking by the Sea of Galilee, he met the fishermen Simon (whom Jesus promptly renamed Peter) and his friend Andrew, along with two brothers, James and John. Other "apostles" followed: 12 in all, including Philip, Bartholomew and Thomas. None was rich or learned; they represented the working poor rather than the priestly elite. Matthew, a tax collector, was a member of a despised class. But Christ had come to call sinners, he said. His later friendship with Mary Magdalene, the repentant prostitute, underlined his concern that his redemption was for all, not just the traditionally pious.

Right Jesus dismisses the disapproving stares of his pious companions as Mary Magdalene prostrates herself at his feet in this 16th-century painting attributed to the French School.

TEACHING TALES

Arriving as he did to bring God's Word to the poor and uneducated, Christ made his message as vivid as he possibly could. Rather than setting out an abstract code of instructions, he expressed his teachings in strikingly human terms. He spoke of the Sower whose seed fell largely on stony ground; the Samaritan who remembered his charitable duty when his "betters" forgot theirs; and the Prodigal Son, welcomed home from his wanderings by his joyful father. Such parables demonstrated, more strongly than any commandments could, what it might mean to follow in the way of Christ.

Right Christ's parable of fishermen making an abundant catch but only keeping the best fish is recalled in this c.1530 illustration for medieval readers.

THE WAY OF THE CROSS

CHRIST MAY HAVE COME TO BRING HUMANITY EVERLASTING LIFE, BUT FIRST HE HAD TO SUFFER AND DIE. THE AGONIES OF HIS CRUCIFIXION WERE THE PRICE HE PAID FOR MAN'S REDEMPTION.

The climax of Christ's ministry occurred when he made his triumphal entrance into Jerusalem. He did not do so in a chariot or on a noble stallion but mounted on a donkey. This is kingship in the humble spirit of the Beatitudes. The huge crowd cheered the Messiah through the streets, scattering palm leaves before him as he went. The crowd cried out the words of Psalm 118, "Hosanna! Blessed is he who is coming in the name of the Lord!"

However, he received a decidedly cooler welcome from his country's religious establishment. The Christ who had come to call sinners had already alienated both the learned scribes and the self-consciously pious Pharisees. Their devotion, he said, was to the letter of the law, while his was to its spirit. In Jerusalem, it became clear just how radical a reformer he was prepared to be. He was even willing to violate the peace of the Temple, driving out the moneychangers from its sacred precincts. For Jesus, they had turned the house of God into a den of thieves.

THE LAST SUPPER

Jesus had journeyed to the capital to join the celebrations for the Passover feast. As a good Jew, he wanted to take the traditional supper of lamb and unleavened bread with his apostles, but he gave the occasion a new and

Above Christ's entry into Jerusalem, with palm leaves spread before him, has been captured in this 15th-century fresco by an unknown artist.

very special slant. Breaking the bread, he gave it to his friends, telling them solemnly, "This is my body". He offered them wine, telling them to drink it and saying, "This is my blood". What was to be his "Last Supper" with his apostles thus became a foreshadowing of the sacrifice he was so soon to be making on Calvary, and, of course, the Catholic sacrament of the Eucharist.

When the meal was over, Jesus and his apostles withdrew to the Garden of Gethsemane to pray in seclusion. Jesus felt all-too-human fear and panicked at the thought of what he was about to face. Men sent by the Sanhedrin – the sacred judges of the Jews – arrived to arrest him, away from the public eye. He was pointed out by his own apostle Judas, who betrayed him for 30 pieces of silver.

ON TRIAL

Jesus' captors accused him of blasphemy, although the evidence against him proved exasperatingly slight, until he told them that he was Christ, the son of God. His guilt established to their own satisfaction, the judges handed

Below Jesus feared death, as any mortal would. In the Agony in the Garden, *painted by Giovanni Bellini c.1465, he prays for help.*

Above The Crucifixion, and the sign of the Cross, became emblematic of Catholicism. This 13th-century Italian painted cross was an object of devotion.

him over to the Roman governor Pontius Pilate, claiming that he had been scheming against the state. Pilate was unconvinced, but the clamour of the Sanhedrin and their supporters was so great that in the end he called for water and literally "washed his hands" of the problem. Christ's accusers could have their way, he said.

THE EXECUTION

Jesus was scourged at a pillar before being made to carry a heavy timber cross to his place of execution. He was mocked and spat upon as he made his slow, painful way through the streets of Jerusalem. Outside the city, on Mount Calvary, he was placed on the Cross, attached to it by nails through his hands and feet, and set up on the hilltop between two condemned thieves. "Father forgive them; they do not know what they are doing," he said of those who tormented him. Only after hours of agony did he die. On that day, a Friday, darkness fell upon the earth, which was convulsed by tremors; the curtain that screened the holiest part of the Temple ripped down the middle.

Below Jesus staggering under the weight of his heavy Cross is depicted in this sumptuously carved, c.1460 wooden altarpiece from Antwerp.

Above Judas betrayed Jesus with the sign of love, a kiss, as captured in this 14th-century Spanish painting by the Master of Rubio.

PASCHAL PAST

The feast of Passover dates back to the deliverance of the Jews from Egyptian enslavement, as told in the Old Testament's Book of Exodus. God had sent nine plagues to afflict the Egyptians, but they still refused to let Moses and his people go. At last God sent an angel down to kill the firstborn of every family. So no Jews should be punished, Moses was instructed that each Israelite household should kill a lamb and mark their doorpost with its blood.

Christ was going to his own death, sacrificing himself to atone for all of humanity's sins. Where the Jehovah of the Old Testament had meted out punishment to the Egyptians for their wickedness, now the "lamb of God" was going to take on the sins of all the world. His death and Resurrection marked the beginning of a "new covenant" in which justice would be tempered with mercy and in which sins might be forgiven.

HE HAS RISEN

CHRIST'S DEATH WAS THE ULTIMATE EXPRESSION OF LOVE, BUT IT WAS HIS RESURRECTION THAT GAVE IT MEANING. STRIVING HUMANITY HAD A WAY BACK TO GOD, A CHANCE AT LIFE IN HEAVEN.

Numbed by shock and stunned by disbelief, Jesus' friends took him down from the Cross, and his mother cradled him in her arms for the last time. One of his followers, Joseph of Arimathea, had a burial chamber already prepared for himself in a cave nearby. He got Pontius Pilate's permission to lay Christ to rest inside.

With that done, fear for their own physical safety being the least of their problems, Jesus' followers

Below Christ appears to two travellers on the road to Emmaus in this 15th-century fresco from the Church of the Trinity, Piedmont, Italy.

turned to despair. What were they to do? Where were they to go? They had been left emotionally and spiritually bereft by the death of their saviour, the one who had promised them eternal life. The darkness that still enveloped the earth matched their complete disorientation and their utter gloom.

AN EMPTY TOMB

But life had to go on, and part of life is the ritual responsibility of the living to the dead. So on Sunday morning, Mary Magdalene and "the other Mary", mother of the apostle James the Less, made their way to the tomb. (The gospels

Above Christ cuts an awe-inspiring figure as he floats triumphantly above his open tomb in The Resurrection of Christ, *painted c.1502 by Raphael.*

differ, but Mark's Gospel mentions a third woman, another friend and follower, Salome.) There, they found that the stone protecting the entrance had been rolled aside. In the doorway, an angel greeted them, informing them that they had made a wasted journey: "He is not here, for he has risen, as he said he would."

In Matthew's account, as the astonished women ran to tell their friends the news, they met Jesus himself nearby. He asked them to tell the disciples to meet him in Galilee. Just hours later, two disciples walking along the road to Emmaus joined a stranger and went to an inn to eat with him. Only when this "stranger" blessed the bread before handing it to them did they realize who he was.

THE ASCENSION

The risen Christ then revealed himself to a number of disciples at various points, although these tended to be fleeting encounters. The apostles themselves were frightened and demoralized, and

Above The apostles gaze up as Jesus is borne aloft on a cloud by angels in this 12th-century Spanish stone relief.

Thomas was at first reluctant to believe that the sightings had even taken place. Finally, 40 days after the Resurrection, Jesus appeared before them in a room where they were all gathered. He urged them to carry his message to all the nations of the world. He told them not to fear: the Holy Spirit would protect them. He also said they would be able to pick up serpents and not be harmed, and they would have the power to cast out demons and heal the sick.

What happened next is unclear because the gospels differ on the details. However, there is agreement among the gospel writers that Jesus ascended to heaven: "a cloud took him from their sight", says the Acts of the Apostles (1:9).

PENTECOST

Left behind again, the apostles withdrew with Mary, the mother of Jesus, and other supporters to an "upper room" – the same one in which the Last Supper was celebrated. For the next few days they prayed together until, on the Jewish feast of Pentecost, the house was suddenly filled with a roaring noise, "as of a violent wind". Tongues of fire came to rest above their heads as the Holy Spirit descended upon them. With this inspiration, they ventured out into the streets to start spreading the word. Miraculously, those who listened, no matter what country they came from, could hear them speaking in their own native language.

THE GOSPELS AND THE GRAIL

Joseph of Arimathea is referred to in the gospels for the part he played in the burial of Christ, where he had a limited role in the event. However, he was given a more important role in a later legend. The tradition, most recently popularized by Dan Brown's novel *The Da Vinci Code,* has him carrying Christianity to Britain, along with the Holy Grail. This sacred vessel (widely assumed to be a chalice, although some sources see it as a serving dish) is said to have been used by Christ at the Last Supper. It is a colourful story, but no more than that. The earliest accounts of Christianity in Britain make no mention of Joseph of Arimathea, and it is not until the 9th century that we hear of his involvement. As for the Holy Grail narrative, that is even later in its origins, first appearing in French romances of the 12th century.

Below Mary takes pride of place among the apostles in this representation of Pentecost, painted in Florence by Jacopo Orcagna (active 1368–98).

THE DISCIPLES

"COME AFTER ME," CHRIST HAD TOLD THE FISHERMEN BESIDE THE
SEA OF GALILEE, "AND I WILL MAKE YOU IN TO FISHERS OF MEN."
HIS WORDS CAME TO PASS IN THE EARLY DAYS OF THE CHURCH.

*Above The apostles were soon finding
many ordinary people willing to
convert to Christianity, as shown in
this late 15th-century illumination
by Jean Poyet.*

Pentecost is a day of inspiration, marking the day of the descent of the Holy Spirit on the apostles. The disciples' joy was all but intoxicating – although cynics claim that they had, indeed, been drinking. Yet their euphoria, born of the Holy Spirit, is only heightened when they find ordinary people in the streets receptive to the message of Christ. As predicted by Jesus, these disciples became the "fishers of men". On that first day alone, the Acts of the Apostles assures us (2:41) some 3,000 converts were made, and more were recruited daily in the weeks that

*Below Jesus sends his followers to
"make disciples of all nations" in a
20th-century stained-glass window
by Gabriel Loire.*

followed. Christianity, it seems, was gathering momentum. This was a mass movement, no longer a community – but a Church.

A NEW WAY OF LIFE

At the time, the disciples' religion was more fervent than thoughtful; Christian doctrine and ritual were works in progress. However, one thing is clear: at this stage the Christians were still emphatically Jewish. At the heart of their ritual, we are told (Acts 2:46), were their daily visits to the Temple together; afterwards, they adjourned to the homes of the community members for the "breaking of bread". This appeared to be both a eucharistic ritual and an act of sharing. The same verse tells us that they "shared their food gladly

and generously". We are told, too, that they sold their possessions and divided up the proceeds so that everybody had what they needed. It is said that they were "looked up to by everyone", and were joined by a steady stream of new recruits.

Like Jesus before them, the apostles worked miracles, but they were careful that the glory went to God, not themselves. They fell foul of the Sanhedrin (the sacred judges of the Jews, who did not believe in resurrection), but they had no grounds on which to condemn them – nor could they explain how the Christians cured the sick and lame.

A FAITH FOR ALL

These Christians were indeed still scrupulous in their Jewish observance, worshipping regularly and that gentiles (non-Jews) could be baptized without circumcision. This was the start of the divergence of Christianity and Judaism. So, too, was St Peter's transfer of his ministry from Jerusalem to Antioch in Syria (modern-day Turkey), and later to Rome, where he was to take his message to the centre of the ancient world.

maintaining all the dietary laws. However, that was soon to change. St Peter had a dream in which God instructed him that from now on no animal or bird should be deemed "unclean" (Acts 10:10–15). Additionally, there was news that an angel had appeared to a Roman centurion, Cornelius, and this persuaded Peter that God wanted Christianity to be open to all, regardless of nationality.

For hundreds of years, the Jews had prided themselves on being God's "chosen people", so what Peter was saying was a complete departure. As he was addressing Cornelius and his Roman friends

Above St Peter continued the ministry of his departed Lord. In this Italian fresco, by Masolino da Panicale, he raises Tabitha from the dead.

and relatives, the Holy Spirit descended upon them – just as it had earlier on the disciples at Pentecost. Peter's Jewish companions were shocked, but their leader, unruffled, explained that this was a sign that "God has no favourites" (Acts 10:34).

The historical record shows that this principle was ratified at the Council of Jerusalem, held around AD 50 under Peter's guidance. The Council also agreed

A CHRISTIAN CAPITAL

Antioch, or Antakya, now in modern-day Turkey, is not an attractive place to visit. It is a noisy, congested city. However, behind this façade hides a historic and spiritual centre of extraordinary importance. The beautiful buildings may have been swept away, but the legacy of this past has endured in the people, in its small but active Christian community. Today, Antakya's Christians are in an often uncomfortable position: they are caught between the aggressive secularism of the Turkish state and the Islamic devotion of the majority of the population. Yet, they feel strengthened by their sense of 2,000 years of continuous Christian worship here. Under its old name, Antioch, this was a major metropolis. More than that, for a crucial period in the 1st and 2nd centuries, it was the capital of Christianity. St Peter himself is said to have made it his headquarters, and by the 3rd century, according to St John Chrysostom, there were 100,000 Christians in the city.

Left St Peter preaches in a street that has the distinct look of 15th-century Florence. The painting is from the Linaiuoli Triptych *by Fra Angelico (c. 1387–1455).*

ST PAUL THE CONVERT

SAUL STARTED OUT AS AN IMPLACABLE PERSECUTOR OF THE NEW RELIGION, BUT REBORN AS PAUL HE BECAME A TIRELESS EVANGELIST. HE PLAYED AN IMPORTANT ROLE IN BUILDING THE EARLY CHURCH.

Above Saul was stopped on the road to Damascus, as seen in this 19th-century stained-glass window from Lincoln Cathedral, England. His conversion greatly influenced the course of Christianity.

Saul was born in Tarsus, in what is now the south of Turkey. In the 2nd century BC, this country had been conquered by the Romans. Tarsus had been given an unusual amount of say over its own affairs, and Saul's well-born Jewish family had been granted citizenship. This set Saul apart from the Jews of his time and made him doubly suspicious of Christ's followers, who were a potential threat to Judaism and the Roman Empire.

According to the Acts of the Apostles (Chapters 7–8), Saul first came into contact with Christianity as a witness to the martyrdom of St Stephen, who was stoned in Jerusalem around AD 35. Saul appeared as a mere bystander: those about to kill the young man placed their cloaks at his feet for safe keeping. The man from Tarsus did not remain detached for long. Oddly enough, it does not seem to have been either Stephen's proclamations of Christian faith or his criticisms of the Jews that upset Saul. What got his attention was the serenity with which the first martyr met his death and the magnanimity with which he asked God to forgive his killers.

Saul, in anything but magnanimous mood, hurled himself into the task of hunting down and destroying the rest of Stephen's fellow Christians. It was with the aim of rounding up the Christian community in the Syrian city that Saul was on the road to Damascus.

THE LIGHT OF GOD

As he travelled, a dazzling light appeared. Felled by its force, Saul pitched forward, falling on the stony road. "Saul, Saul, why are you persecuting me?" thundered God from the sky. Saul, in his shock, lay cowering and helpless. "Who are you, Lord?" he said. "I am Jesus, whom you are persecuting," came the reply. This was a revelation for Saul, and his conversion on the road to Damascus was to be a defining moment for Christianity. Saul had never set eyes on the living Christ, yet, as Paul, he did much to shape the development of Christ's Church.

SIGHT RESTORED

Having been blinded by the light, Saul was taken on to Damascus by his companions. A disciple named Ananias was told in a dream to go to the house where Saul was staying and restore his sight. Having heard what type of man Saul was, Ananias questioned this instruction. To his amazement, the Lord told him that Saul had to be cured because he was central for his plans for his Christian Church.

The restoration of Saul's sight was of course a symbolic as well as a physical cure: he had been morally blind before but was now enlightened. He became as eager a proselytizer as he had been a persecutor, dedicating his life to the spreading of the gospels.

Below Paul preaches Christ's message in Luca di Tommè's 14th-century representation. The disciple believed the gospels should be spread to all people.

THE LETTERS OF THE LAW

Paul covered thousands of miles in the course of his ministry. He took his duty to the gentiles very seriously. Never satisfied with simply making converts, he kept in touch with the communities he had come to know in a series of letters. Part personal greetings, part sermons, part theological arguments with himself, the Epistles were to be incorporated into the Christian Scriptures. Paul's opinions, as set down in his Epistles, had an incalculable influence not only on his various congregations around the ancient world but on the way Christianity was to develop in modern times.

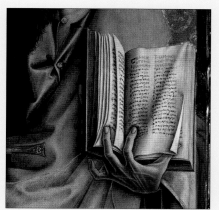

Right A page of Paul's Epistles can be seen in this detail from a 1473 polyptych (a many-panelled altarpiece) in Ascoli Piceno's Sant' Emidio Cathedral, Italy.

APOSTLE TO THE GENTILES

The Holy Spirit, we are told (Acts:13), specifically chose Saul for the task of taking the divine word to the gentiles, or non-Jews. It is no surprise, then, that he changed his name to the Roman "Paul" during his first mission to Cyprus, Greece and Asia Minor – or that he took sides with Peter in discussions at the Council of Jerusalem, which were to open the new religion to non-Jews. In subsequent missions, Paul criss-crossed the eastern Mediterranean and Middle East regions, making new converts and revisiting existing Christian communities.

Arrested in Jerusalem, allegedly for bringing gentiles into the Temple in defiance of Jewish law, Paul was accused of blasphemy – just like Christ had been before him. However, because of his background, Paul could appeal to his rights as a Roman citizen, which meant that he was eventually transported to Rome for trial there. His arrival coincided with the first major persecution of the Christians in AD 64. He died a martyr, though the exact date and circumstances are unknown.

Right Masaccio's 15th-century painting of St Paul shows the disciple armed with the sword of the fighter (and the martyr) and the Bible.

A FAITH IN FEAR

"BLESSED ARE YOU WHEN PEOPLE ABUSE YOU AND PERSECUTE YOU," CHRIST SAID. HIS FOLLOWERS WERE TO FIND OUT WHAT THAT FELT LIKE AS THEY BRAVED TORTURE FOR THE SAKE OF THEIR BELIEFS.

Toward the end of AD 64, Nero, Emperor of Rome, launched the first "Great Persecution". In these early days of Christianity, its disciples could pose no conceivable threat. By this time, the numbers in their community in the capital could have been only in the low hundreds at the most.

However, Nero had an agenda. He was widely blamed for the Great Fire of Rome, which had swept through the city that year.

There were reports that the emperor's own household slaves had been seen intentionally setting the fire so that Nero could advance his redevelopment plans for parts of the city centre. As things turned out, the conflagration gutted 10 of the capital's 14 districts. Under the circumstances, Nero was only too eager to have someone else to blame, and the Christian community made the perfect scapegoat.

Above A man is attacked by wild beasts in the arena in this 2nd-century mosaic from North Africa.

CRUEL DEATHS

On his orders, Christians were taken prisoner by the score. Some were tossed on to fires – alive – thrown to savage dogs to be torn apart or, notoriously, cast into the arena to be killed by wild animals as a public spectacle. Others were crucified, a common form of execution at the time, but also a sneer at the way the Christians' Messiah had been killed. Peter, who had arrived in Rome at the start of Nero's Great Persecution, was one of those crucified in Rome during this period. One tradition has it that he was hung upside down, at his own request, presumably because it would be presumptuous to be executed in the same manner as his saviour.

PROLONGED REPRESSION

In many places and for long periods, Christians were tolerated. Yet, sometimes, persecution came not

Left St Peter is often depicted being crucified upside down, such as in this 16th-century French manuscript.

from the state but from the general public. Christians were harassed – even physically attacked – by their pagan neighbours. Sometimes there were also more serious and sustained outbreaks of mob violence against Christians, with or without the connivance of the authorities.

As is generally the way with such things, hostility increased at times of political uncertainty or economic crisis. There were significant crackdowns during the reigns of Domitian, Trajan, Septimius Severus and Decius. Many priests and bishops were martyred in the reign of Valerian (253–60), including St Laurence, reputedly burnt on an iron grill.

In fairness, part of the problem was the Romans' incomprehension of what was motivating the Christians to resist. As far as they were concerned, they had given the Christians every chance to

Left St Sebastian, who was martyred in 287, is shown gazing stoically heavenward as arrows pierce his body in this 1480 painting by Mantegna.

Many others were killed during the eight years of the Great Persecution, but some modern scholars are sceptical about claims by contemporary sources that 10,000 martyrs were crucified on the first day of Diocletian's crackdown. Yet even the conservative estimates are in agreement that thousands were martyred and many thousands more had suffered harassment and torture. Again, the persecution appears to have been prompted by an economic crisis brought on by Diocletian's financial mismanagement. The emperor was also a religious conservative, concerned at what he saw as the abandonment of the traditional Roman gods in favour of new faiths, such as Christianity.

THE EMPEROR AND THE ANTICHRIST

After being driven underground by Nero's persecution, the Christians communicated using a code based on what was known as "gematria". This was a type of numerological theory that attributed mystical properties to different numbers and saw significance in their relations to the letters of the Hebrew alphabet. Some scholars have studied all the infinite subtleties of gematria for many years, but at its crudest level it can be used to make a straightforward cipher. For Nero, the figures came to 666: the "Number of the Beast" in the Book of Revelation. Many early Christians did, indeed, see this Roman ruler as the model for the "Antichrist".

save themselves by abjuring their religion. They simply could not understand that this new creed could be worth dying for.

ANOTHER PERSECUTION

In 303, Emperor Diocletian issued his "Edict Against the Christians", ordering that churches should be demolished and Christians enslaved. This would have been bad enough even if it had not been the signal for the start of another Great Persecution. Again, Christians were given a chance to save themselves by offering sacrifices to the pagan gods. Some were intimidated into compliance. Some sources say (though others deny this) that even the pope of the day, Marcellinus, had been persuaded to burn incense before Roman idols. However the pope repented his weakness, reasserted his Christian faith and died a martyr some time in 304.

Above The grisly manner of St Catherine's execution in Alexandria around 305 has clearly caught the imagination of this late medieval painter, whose work appeared in the 1280 History of Four Saints.

New Life among the Dead: The Catacombs

Beneath Rome, men, women and children came together in secret worship. They found a sanctuary in the domain of the dead, where they had buried their loved ones.

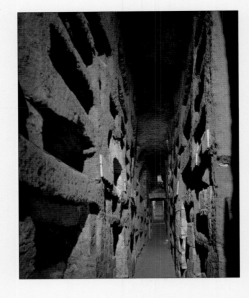

In the face of persecution in the world above for their adherence to the creed of Christ, early Roman Christians ventured deep into the earth to the homes of the dead to give their thanks and praise to the living God.

A PRACTICAL SOLUTION

The catacombs were first and foremost a place to bury the dead, but for the Christians, and perhaps others, they became a place of refuge in times of persecution. As many as 40 of these underground burial complexes existed around the periphery of Rome; construction had begun in pre-Christian times. The pagan Romans, while

Below Ancient skulls seem to survey the scene in a chamber at the heart of Rome's San Callisto catacombs.

revering the dead and making offerings at their graves, had also viewed them with fear and banished them beyond the city limits. Burial grounds had sprung up along the main routes out of town. Many people were cremated and their ashes stored in special columbaria ("dovecots"), so-called because the regular niches in which the urns were placed in their hundreds resembled the pigeonholes in which the birds nested in the dovecots of the day.

With pressure growing on space around the city, these facilities were tucked discreetly away underground. More subterranean complexes were built in Christian times, and these had to be more spacious. Burial had replaced cremation for the Christian faithful, who looked forward to

Above The catacombs were primarily a way of warehousing the dead: floor-to-ceiling niches line this passage.

the resurrection of the body. Fortunately, the soft and porous "tuff" (volcanic ash) on which much of Rome is founded made excavation easy, and these underground cemeteries quickly grew.

SAN CALLISTO

Rome's biggest catacombs, the San Callisto, are named after an early pope, St Callistus (although

Above Inside the Roman church of San Callisto, the "Crypt of the Popes" houses the relics of Church leaders from the 3rd and 4th centuries.

he was actually one of the few 3rd-century pontiffs not to have been buried in its rectangular "Crypt of the Popes"). They were rediscovered in 1849 by the Italian Giovanni Battista de Rossi, and while more than 20km (12½ miles) of tunnels and chambers have been mapped, there are large areas of labyrinthine passages that have yet to be explored. Tunnels were often created one on top of another, in up to four separate layers.

SACRED AND SECRET

For decades at a time the Christians had been left alone, and during these settled periods the catacombs appear to have been nothing more than burial places. It was only natural, though, that during periods of official crackdowns, when worshipping in public basilicas or homes was too hazardous, families that had grown used to visiting these underground passages to honour and pray for their dead thought of seeking a sanctuary here. The tombs of martyrs put to death in the persecutions became sacred sites in themselves, and their fellow Christians would visit them later to gather for worship and prayers.

Even in times of toleration, then, the catacombs were a powerful focus for Christian faith. And then, of course, there was the symbolic resonance: the sense of life and affirmation flourishing in the midst of death. It is inconceivable that this could have been lost on the men and women of the early Church.

MODERN INSPIRATION

Today we can marvel at the courage of these early Christians and see their story as exemplifying hope. The vanquishing of death, the triumph of new life – even in the grave itself – Christianity can hold out no greater promise to the believer. Hence, perhaps, the continuing hold the catacombs exercise over the imagination of the faithful.

UNDERGROUND ART

Areas in the catacombs were crudely customized as churches, and frescoes were painted showing what appear to be eucharistic scenes. The fish often crops up as a symbol – not just because Christ and his apostles had been fishermen but because the letters of the Greek word *Ichthus* ("fish") spelled out the secret slogan *Iesu Christos Theou* (or "Jesus Christ Saviour"). Old Testament scenes are represented as well, such as Moses striking the rock and sending water gushing forth and Jonah being swallowed by the whale.

San Callisto's "Gallery of the Sacraments" has some fascinating paintings. There are more in the San Domitilla catacombs, where key saints of the 4th century were laid to rest in an underground basilica. One side room has a ceiling adorned with a 3rd-century fresco of the Good Shepherd; in nearby niches and passages are paintings of Jesus, his apostles and the Magi.

Above Abraham prepares to sacrifice Isaac, his son, in this fresco. The catacombs hold some of the earliest Christian art.

THE CHURCH OF ROME

INCREASINGLY, CHRISTIANITY WAS EASING AWAY FROM ITS JEWISH ROOTS. ROME, THE CENTRE OF THE 1ST-CENTURY WORLD, WAS THE NATURAL HEADQUARTERS FOR THIS NEW RELIGION.

Why, despite its Middle Eastern origins, did this new religion become known as the "Roman" Catholic Church? To some extent, the development might seem accidental. The scene of so many martyrdoms had acquired strong emotional and spiritual associations for the early Christians. As early as the 2nd century – long before the age of persecutions had run its course – men and women were making pilgrimages to the tombs of St Peter and St Paul.

WORLD CAPITAL

There were other reasons that were also important. Rome was the capital of a vast empire: to all intents and purposes the centre of the world. Important decisions were all made there, and Rome ruled in many subject nations. The city was the centre of a web of well-made roads and busy shipping lanes.

Below Tertullian was a pagan who converted to Christianity c.AD 197. His writings covered many issues in the theological field, providing a picture of religious life and beliefs in his time.

These advantages would not always have been of interest to the Church, of course. To begin with, Christianity had been influenced by Judaism. In fact, debate had raged over whether gentiles should be baptized at all, and many had been resistant to this change. However, Peter and Paul had prevailed with their literal interpretation of Christ's words, "Go…and make disciples of all nations" (Matthew 28:19).

LATIN TAKES OVER

Significant, too, was the decision of Tertullian, the Church's leading thinker, to write his works in Latin, the Roman language. Until now, there had been two languages of Christianity: Hebrew, the tongue of the Jews, and Greek, the language of the Seleucid kingdom and the Middle East. The word "Christ" came from the Greek *Christos* ("the Anointed"). Tertullian's decision in *c.*AD 200 made clear the ambition of the Church to reach out beyond its territories of origin to the rest of the known world.

CONSTANTINE'S CROSS

In 312, the Church found an unexpected supporter in Emperor Constantine I. At noon, in the hours before an important battle with a rival for imperial power, Constantine the Great had been praying to the sun – as Sol Invictus, the supreme deity of his religion. Suddenly, he and his army were astonished to see the blazing face of the sun overlain by the figure of the cross. The unmistakable symbolism was spelled out by an

Above Rome is revealed to St Augustine as the "City of God", as shown here in a 15th-century French manuscript.

inscription written across the face of the heavens: *in hoc signo vinces* ("in this sign prevail").

Constantine's conversion at the Battle of Milvian Bridge and his patronage gave the Church a welcome boost. With the threat of persecution lifted, its members could meet and worship openly; its clergy could conduct its affairs in public. What had been – necessarily – a low-profile faith, with its adherents meeting quietly, was able to establish a presence in the world. Constantine advanced this process, endowing the Church with resources and working hard to build up its institutions. It was he who called the Council of Nicaea in 325, where important doctrinal questions were debated and resolved. While some felt that Constantine's patronage made Catholicism too "official", it allowed access to the structures of the imperial establishment that helped the Church to grow.

Constantine's Christianity was what the Church had needed at a tricky time. Even if the emperor himself was at times less than wholehearted in his commitment to his new faith, his mother St Helena ensured that he stayed loyal to its cause. Having converted following her son's example, she became his religious guide.

THE NEW CAPITAL

At the same time, Constantine took steps that were to lead to one of the saddest developments in the Church's history: he transferred the empire's capital to Byzantium, or Constantinople as he called it. In the centuries that followed, the city on the Bosporus became the real centre of the "Roman" world, while Rome itself sank into stagnation and decline. In time it was to recover, but by then the Eastern Church had broken away and Christ's followers were divided.

Above *Constantine I is depicted in this 16th-century fresco with his mother, St Helena, the traditional finder of the relics of the "True Cross". She ensured her son never wavered in his beliefs.*

Below *In this 13th-century fresco, Pope Sylvester I baptizes Constantine – a breakthrough for the Church. In fact, the emperor postponed this sacrament until his deathbed.*

A DOUBTFUL DONATION

Constantine gave Christianity his generous backing, building (among numerous other things) the original Basilica of St Peter's in Rome. However, the one thing the Roman does not appear to have given the Church is the rumoured "Donation of Constantine", in which he supposedly gave Pope Sylvester I and his successors temporal authority over Rome and many of its possessions in Europe and North Africa. Most of these realms fell to a variety of invaders and other rulers, but the popes held on to power in parts of central Italy into modern times. Even today, the Vatican remains a sovereign nation, its status sanctioned by custom, if not by legal title. In fact, the "Donation of Constantine" was revealed as a forgery in the 15th century. It is believed to have been created in the 8th century.

Below *A colossal head of Emperor Constantine from the Roman Forum. It was once the topmost part of a 4th-century full-length statue.*

THE FIRST POPES

THE INSTITUTION OF THE PAPACY BEGAN WITH CHRIST'S COMMISSION TO PETER, "I WILL GIVE YOU THE KEYS OF THE KINGDOM OF HEAVEN: WHATEVER YOU BIND ON EARTH WILL BE BOUND IN HEAVEN..."

The papacy started to take shape as an institution over time, but the first pope was Peter. His name had been Simon, but Christ gave him a new name to go with his new and crucial role. "You are Peter," he says (Matthew 16:18), punning on the Greek word *petros*, or "stone", "and on this rock I will build my community." The Church over which he presided would be proof against the powers of Satan, Jesus promised, and its leader would have complete spiritual authority on Earth.

CHRIST'S SUCCESSORS

The "apostolic succession" is key to Catholicism's claims to be the one true Church of God. According to this theory, authority has been transmitted via an unbroken line of pontiffs from Christ and Peter down to the present day.

Below Christ hands the keys of heaven to Peter, who becomes the first pope, as depicted by Pietro Perugino in this 15th-century fresco.

That authority is embodied in the office of the pope, who has as his emblem the crossed keys that recall the "keys of heaven" that Christ promised to Peter.

In its early days, of course, the Church was small and less structured, so to be its bishop would not have been a great honour in worldly terms. Christianity was often – due to Roman persecution – a furtive faith, forced to operate underground or on the run. There was no point in its bishops attracting attention to themselves, and they did not need to. Peter had no palace, no Vatican. Even so, his pre-eminence as "Prince of the Apostles" was acknowledged by Christ's followers. He was the Saviour's anointed successor here on earth, and no Christian would have dreamt of questioning his command.

A CHANGING CHURCH

In the Edict of Milan (313), the Roman state recognized the legitimacy of the Church. Larger and

Above The keys of heaven have been incorporated in Pope Leo X's coat-of-arms, which were carved in this Roman stone relief of 1513–20.

no longer persecuted, the Church had become a very different kind of institution. Leadership in what was now a big and international organization became not just a spiritual challenge but also an administrative one. Maintaining doctrinal discipline was proving to be more difficult as well. Individual teachers started striking out in their own directions and, by the end of the 4th century, theological anarchy was threatening the integrity of the Church.

This, moreover, occurred at a time when Rome was in steep decline, beset by both barbarian invasions and by instability that came from within. The centre of political power had shifted to the East, where Constantinople was booming as the capital of a more Asian-orientated "Roman" state. Rome had become a backwater in its own empire. All the indications were that, as the Western Empire declined, the Church was going to go down with it. It seemed that its brief history was going to end in oblivion.

A POWERFUL PAPACY

Pope Leo I, the Great, was influential in the development of the Church. His approach was far from subtle. He was unashamedly tough in his response to opposition. Democracy was a luxury he felt the Church could not afford. He was confronted with an organization that was in disarray, so he exercised dictatorial powers and centralized all power and doctrinal authority in himself. He formulated the view that the pope was heir to the powers of Peter, as stated in Matthew 16:18. Earlier generations of Christians had looked up to their popes, had valued the apostolic succession and had read and been inspired by Jesus' words to Peter, but they had not necessarily thought of the popes as heirs to Peter. Through these actions Leo the Great helped to strengthen the Church.

Below When Pope Fabian was elected in 236, the Church was a large organization. In this depiction of his coronation by an artist of the 15th-century Spanish School, a dove (symbolic of the Holy Spirit) is perched on his head.

A PERSUASIVE POPE

Leo the Great may have been a masterful pontiff, however he was not a tyrant. He could compel people by his kindness, and won people over with his warmth. That he had a gift for getting his own way could hardly be denied: however, this was, after all, the man who managed to talk Attila the Hun out of attacking Rome. Their meeting, in 452, came after the Asiatic warlord and his army had invaded Italy and were poised to sweep down and sack the capital. Despairing of defending their city against such a ferocious enemy, the military and civic leaders of Rome approached the Pope to ask for his help. Taking two officials with him, Leo went to meet Attila and ask for peace. The latter "was so impressed with the presence of the high priest," wrote one chronicler of the day, "that he ordered his army to give up warfare and, after he had promised peace, he disappeared beyond the Danube".

Below Leo the Great saved Rome from attack by Attila's forces when he met the Hunnish leader in 452. This c.1860 woodcut was inspired by a fresco in Munich.

THE CHURCH FATHERS

MANY SCHOLARS HAVE HELPED IN DEVELOPING THE DOCTRINAL
DETAILS OF CATHOLICISM — BUT FOUR IN PARTICULAR STAND OUT
AS THE "DOCTORS" OF THE EARLY CHURCH.

The Church owes an immeasurable debt to the great "doctors", or teachers, of the early Middle Ages, who helped shape not just its rituals but its faith. Clear though they were in essence, Christ's teachings had implications that had to be explored and examined, principles to be drawn out and systematized. The Church existed in the real world: Christians looked to it not just for inspiration but also for explanations, for moral guidance and for help in dealing with their doubts and fears. At first, it was ill equipped for this task. Its theology was undeveloped, and its institutional structures were limited.

AN UNBAPTIZED BISHOP

Just how disorganized it was is clear from the fact that, when the Bishop of Milan died in 374, his successor, Ambrose, had not been baptized or ordained as a priest, and he had not received any serious schooling in theology. Yet Ambrose understood the need for

Above St Jerome had reputedly taken
the thorn from a lame lion's paw,
hence the cat with which he is
traditionally shown, as here in this
15-century painting by an unknown
Swiss artist.

Below Gregory, Ambrose, Jerome and
Augustine: the four Church Fathers
attend the Virgin and Child in this
15th-century altarpiece.

THE CONFESSOR

Today, St Augustine is best known for his autobiography, *The Confessions* (397) and for his youthful cry, "Lord make me chaste, but not yet!" However, in his eagerness to underline the fact that humanity was, from the beginning of existence, in a "fallen" state, he belaboured himself about offences that far predated this. As a boy, he lamented he had stolen fruit that he did not need; even as a baby, he believed that he had cried deliberately to unsettle the adults around him. This is a strange book in some ways, yet Augustine's self-examination is today admired far beyond the Church for its striking insights into what we would call psychology.

Right The Devil holding up the Book of Vices to St Augustine *is the title of this work by Michael Pacher (c.1435–98). St Augustine saw evil and its temptations as a constant threat.*

theological rigour. His first move on his appointment was to give his possessions to the poor; his second was to embark on a programme of self-education. It was a spiritual and intellectual journey in which – thanks to the books he wrote – his fellow Christians were able to accompany him. Ambrose's courage was exemplary (his refusal to be bullied by Emperor Theodosius set the standard for subsequent pontiffs); so too was his piety. He was influential in his emphasis on the role of Mary, the Blessed Virgin.

LATIN WORDSMITHS

Ambrose benefited from his ease with the Greek sources in which much theological writing until that time had been set down. Writing in Latin, Ambrose can be seen as part of that same process of westernization that Tertullian had begun two centuries before. Jerome continued the process with his translation of the Bible into Latin, which he began in 382. Jerome was a Dalmatian-born

Right At "St Gregory's Mass", the Saviour appeared with his wounds bleeding and poured his blood into the chalice of the pope, as depicted in this c.1490 illumination.

scholar who worked from Greek editions because it was recognized that the finest scholarship was to be found in that language. At the same time, the Church was starting to define itself as Western. Greek, since Alexander's day, had been the language not just of Greece itself but of Asia, the home – in the Church's eyes – of heresy.

FIGHTER FOR ORTHODOXY

St Augustine of Hippo refuted two powerful heresies. As a young man, he held Manichaean views. These views were a product of Persian tradition that pitted the powers of light and virtue against darkness and sin. Manichaeism had exerted a strong influence over Christianity in the East. Augustine rejected this phase of his development, just as he did the dissolute lifestyle of his youth, and became a staunch defender of Western orthodoxy.

Augustine also defended the Roman Christians against the comforting creed of the Pelagians. Pelagius, a 4th-century monk, had argued that humanity had not irrevocably fallen in the Garden of Eden, so had no need of Christ's redemption. Individuals could choose to be good themselves, unaided. It was Augustine who helped to formulate the doctrine of original sin.

A GREAT REFORMER

Gregory I, the Great, was elected pontiff in 590. His reforms were tireless and far-reaching. From the celibacy of the clergy to the idea of the remission of time in Purgatory for acts of public and private penance, they touched just about every area of religious life. The clamour for his canonization had begun in his own lifetime, though critics claimed he had practically bankrupted the Church with his charitable giving.

A CHURCH DIVIDED

"ROME HAS SPOKEN, THE CASE IS CLOSED" ARE STRONG WORDS ATTRIBUTED TO ST AUGUSTINE. THE CHURCH'S INSISTENCE ON ORTHODOXY CAME ABOUT AFTER A LACK OF DOCTRINAL DISCIPLINE.

Rome was the centre of the world in the 1st century AD, but the power and control of this empire didn't last. The Dark Ages, from *c.*500 to the 11th century, were not as black as some popular histories claim, but it was an era in which the Church struggled. The Roman Empire was under relentless attack from invaders, and Rome itself was imploding politically, so the survival not just of the state but also of a civilization was at stake – as was the Church. Yet, at a time when Christian unity was all-important, rivalry threatened to tear the faith apart.

A CITY UNDER SIEGE

Augustine saw the danger. Rome had just been sacked by the Visigoths when, in the latter part of 410, he started writing *The City of God.* Many Romans believed the fall of their capital had been a judgement of the gods on its

Above The Church, a fortress, is defended against heresy and sin in this illumination from a 15th-century French manuscript.

toleration of the Christian religion. However, Augustine's vision was of the city of Rome and the Church as parallel states, beset by barbarism and paganism respectively. Hence the impassioned urgency with which he strove to secure the spiritual integrity of his Church.

DIFFERENCES OF OPINION

Augustine thought the heretics were the enemies within. There was no shortage of them at this time, and they were often powerful. The adherents of Arianism followed the teaching of Arius, an Egyptian monk who had claimed that Christ, though saintly, was not divine. St Ambrose had led the fight against this heresy as Bishop of Milan in the 4th century, but it flourished and was believed in by many within Europe's ruling class. This heresy was halted when Emperor Theodosius I spoke out against it at the Constantinople Conference of 381. That year's

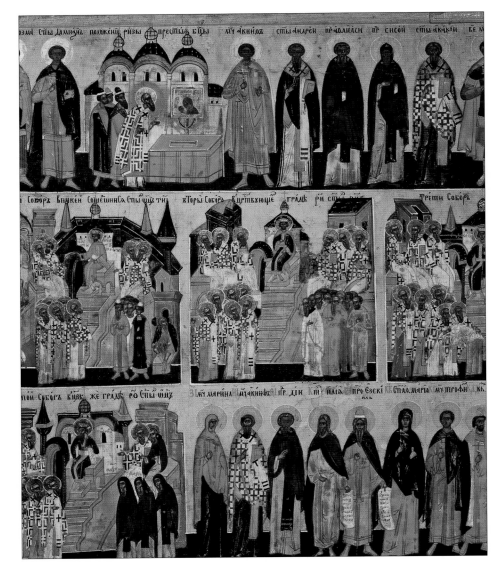

Left A series of Nicaean Councils in the 1st millennium allowed important doctrinal issues to be thrashed out. It is represented in this Russian calendar dating from the mid-18th century.

revised Nicene Creed (*see below*) clearly rejected Arianism's claims. Yet its influence persisted in outlying regions of the West.

The 5th century brought the Nestorian Schism. An Archbishop of Constantinople, Nestorius asserted that Christ as God and Christ as man were not two different aspects of the same being but two distinct persons. This heresy was taken up in the East, leading to the breaking away of what became known as the Assyrian Church. Monophysitism, by contrast, held that Christ had only one aspect, the divine. Its supporters were fiercely at odds with the Nestorians in the East.

OUT OF IRELAND

Augustine's fears for the Church under barbarian attack were by no means exaggerated. Within a century of the Sack of Rome, Christianity had been almost wiped out throughout western Europe. Only in the remotest reaches of Ireland's Atlantic coast were Christianity and its culture holding out. However, in the 6th and 7th centuries, missionaries from these far-flung monasteries fanned out across western and central Europe (even Italy), reintroducing the Church of Christ.

THE EAST–WEST SCHISM

With its own bustling capital at Constantinople, the centre of a thriving empire, the Church in the East was flourishing, and it was increasingly going its own way. Cultural and linguistic differences caused the two halves of the old Roman Empire to diverge: the West was European and Latin; the East Asiatic and Greek. The West was in apparently terminal crisis, while the fortunes of the East were buoyant, so the eastern patriarchs saw no reason to bow before the popes. They owed allegiance to

Left Heretical books are consigned to the fire in this illustration from a manuscript of the 9th century.

the Byzantine emperors, who had the right of appointing them. Their loyalty to the pontiff took second place. The authority of Rome was recognized formally, but deference was offered more grudgingly as time went on.

In 1054, Rome placed a papal bull denouncing the patriarch, Michael Kerullarios, upon the altar of Constantinople's great basilica, Hagia Sophia. Kerullarios responded in kind. Pope and patriarch had excommunicated one another – expelled each other from their Church community. The East–West Schism was under way, and the "Orthodox" Church of the East often existed separately from the Catholic Church.

THE NICENE CREED

We believe in one God,
the Father, the Almighty,
maker of heaven and earth,
of all that is, seen and unseen.

We believe in one Lord,
 Jesus Christ,
the only Son of God,
eternally begotten of the Father,
God from God, Light from Light,
true God from true God,
begotten, not made,
of one Being with the Father.
Through him all things were
 made.
For us men and for our salvation,
he came down from heaven:
by the power of the Holy Spirit
he became incarnate of the Virgin
 Mary,
and became man.
For our sake he was crucified
 under Pontius Pilate;
he suffered death and was buried.
On the third day he rose again

in accordance with the Scriptures;
he ascended into heaven
and is seated at the right hand of
 the Father.
He will come again in glory
to judge the living and the dead,
and his kingdom will have no end.

We believe in the Holy Spirit,
the Lord, the giver of life,
who proceeds from the Father and
 the Son.
With the Father and the Son he
 is worshipped and glorified.
He has spoken through the
 Prophets.
We believe in one holy Catholic
 and apostolic Church.
We acknowledge one baptism for
the forgiveness of sins.
We look for the resurrection of
 the dead,
and the life of the world to come.

Amen.

AVD·ITE· CÓDITIO
MAGNI·ET NIS·-ET·
PARVI·CV GRADVS
IVS·CVNQ ESTIS·

ORDO·ISTE
FVIT·A·DEO
REVELATVS
SCE·BRIGI
DE·AD·
HONOREM
VIRGI
NIS·
MARI
E·PRICI
PIV·HVI
VS·RELIGIO
NIS·ET·SALV
TIS·E·VERA
VMILITAS·ET
PVRA·CAS
TITAS·AIQ
VOLVTARIA
PAVPERTIS

·ORATE·
·PROPICTORE·
·1522·

THE MIDDLE AGES

The Church's second millennium could hardly have begun with a less auspicious start, split by the East–West Schism. What was really striking, though, was the easy assurance with which Catholicism shook off what should have been a catastrophic blow.

So-called in retrospect because it came between the classical period (Greece and Rome) and the Renaissance, the *medium aevum*, or Middle Ages, marked a breakthrough for the Church. Quite simply, in the West at least, there was no higher human institution: its teachings shaped the way men and women thought. The Church led the reconstruction of the West in the chaotic centuries that followed the fall of the Roman Empire in the 5th century, forming its institutions and culture and influencing architecture, music, literature and every area of learning. Catholicism had left its mark on all of these. The people saw the Church as the source of all their spiritual and moral laws, and rulers looked to it for their legitimacy.

Even so, there would be challenges. As early as the 7th century, Islam had emerged from Arabia. By the 11th century, the rapid expansion of its empire was seen as so great a threat to the West that a series of Crusades were mounted against the Muslims. Yet the existence of such a threat also gave Christendom an enemy against which it could define itself, and the Church continued to go from strength to strength.

Above Christ looks down from heaven as a choir of monks sings a hymn in this illumination from a c.1300 manuscript of an English psalter.

Left St Bridget of Sweden issues the rule for the Brigettine Order (Giovannantonio di Francesco Sogliani, 1522). Monasticism flourished in Europe during the Middle Ages.

MEDIEVAL CATHOLICISM

THE MIDDLE AGES IN EUROPE WAS A HIGH POINT FOR THE CHURCH:
EVERY ASPECT OF LIFE – FROM HOW PEOPLE FELT TO HOW THEY WERE
GOVERNED – WAS SHAPED BY CATHOLICISM.

As the main religion throughout Europe, the sect that had hidden itself away in the catacombs was no more. No monarchy could match its pervasive power. Kings consulted closely with its prelates and its pope, and ordinary men and women looked to their priests with all the deference due to God's representatives on Earth. Its teaching set the tone – morally, intellectually and culturally. Its monasteries were repositories of learning, driving forces in literature and science, and its cathedrals displayed the latest and the best in art and architecture.

FEUDALISM AND FAITH
The Church's power and authority were not just awesome, they were integral to the way in which medieval Europe viewed the world. In the Middle Ages, along with the idea of "faith" went that of "fealty" (from the Latin *fidelitas*, or "faithfulness"). It defined the bond of obedience and loyalty the man had to his overlord. Just as the serf owed fealty to his lord, who in turn acknowledged the overlordship of his king, so the Christian obeyed his or her priest, who was directed by the religious hierarchy.

Medieval Europeans implicitly believed that God had created an orderly cosmos and everything in the universe had its place. It was the responsibility of those entrusted with power, both spiritual and temporal, to ensure that order prevailed here on Earth. The power of the Church and State were thus regarded as two sides of the same coin. Despite their differences – there were disputes between popes and kings – it would

Above This 12th-century golden orb, emblematic of the world, surmounted by a jewelled cross, was part of the crown jewels of imperial Germany.

never have occurred to a king to question the divine authority of the pope or his hierarchy any more than it would have occurred to the Church to undermine the power of the king. It was in neither's interest to jeopardize that principle of order on which the entire worldview of the Middle Ages rested.

POWER AND WEALTH
In truth, the Church wielded a great deal of power over secular affairs as well, and few temporal rulers dared defy its will. None would have dreamt of taxing its wealthy monasteries. Whether in a spirit of piety or in fear for their fate in the afterlife, wealthy magnates bequeathed lavish gifts in land and treasures to their local religious foundations.

Left Serfs who worked the land used the crop to pay their tithe to the aristocracy and the Church, as seen in this late 15th-century French illustration from The Playfair Book of Hours.

Meanwhile, year in and year out, poor peasants and craftsmen had to pay a "tithe" (one-tenth) of their income to the Church. Although priests at village level lived pretty much as modestly as their parishioners, things were different further up the hierarchy. In time, the ethics of this would come to be questioned, but, in the meantime, senior churchmen often lived like lords.

THE ARTS AND LEARNING

At the same time that these senior church members wined and dined stupendously, they also bestowed their patronage freely. As a result of their conspicuous consumption,

art lovers today can appreciate what are considered the greatest masterpieces of Western art. Giotto, Cimabué and countless anonymous artists worked under the auspices of the Church. Church buildings were often also filled with the exquisite work of master woodcarvers and sculptors, whose works brought the stories of the Bible to the illiterate.

Education and learning were to all intents and purposes the monopoly of the Church – and this, too, would eventually become a source of friction. For the moment, though, intellectual discussion and debate all took place within the terms of reference established by

the great Catholic teachers of the day. Pre-eminent among these was Thomas Aquinas, born in Sicily c.1225. His *Summa Theologica* (1266–74) was literally a "theological summary", setting out in a single vast and coherent plan all the Church's teachings about God, the universe and the place of man within it. Aquinas' work is valued in its own right by philosophers today, but it was also an important conduit for earlier thought: the ideas of Aristotle, of Arabic thinkers such as Ibn Rushd (Averroës) and Ibn Sina (Avicenna), and of Jewish doctors such as Maimonides all found their way into Western tradition through his work.

Above *With Plato and Aristotle on either side, St Thomas Aquinas is shown with the Arab philosopher Averroës in the foreground in this 15th-century painting by Benozzo di Lese Gozzoli.*

DANTE

Born in Florence c.1265, Dante Alighieri has been revered in modern times as the poet who envisioned hell. His *Inferno* is indeed awe-inspiring, striking in its dreadful beauty but also in the sympathy it shows for the sufferings of the damned. Yet Dante would have been surprised to see it abstracted from his *Commedia* ("Comedy") as a whole.

Hell's torments could make no sense for him except as aspects of a universal order. His *Inferno*, like his *Purgatorio* and his *Paradiso*, is founded in the love of God. He can weep for the sinner while still giving thanks for the overall scheme.

Below *Dante enlightens the citizens of Florence with his vision of the universe in this 1465 painting.*

THE CRUSADES

SOON AFTER ISLAM AROSE IN THE EAST, VICTORIOUS ARAB ARMIES SPREAD THEIR FAITH TO THE VERY DOORS OF ROME. FOR NEARLY 500 YEARS, CHRISTIANS FOUGHT BACK IN A SERIES OF CRUSADES.

Roughly at about the same time that Catholicism had established itself as the dominant religion in Europe, Islam was on the rise in the East. This new expansionist religion posed a threat to Catholic authority, and the Church felt urgent pressure to try to stop its growth.

THE RISE OF ISLAM

The prophet Muhammad's mission to spread his Islamic religion began about 610. Arab armies carried his message to both the East and the West. By 638, less than three decades later, these armies were occupying Jerusalem.

Spilling across North Africa, the forces of Islam crossed the Straits of Gibraltar into Spain in the early 8th century. By 720 they were pushing into France, though they had

been turned back at Tours in 732. Christian rulers in northern Spain had embarked on a long-term Reconquista, or "reconquest", but the south of the peninsula seemed securely established as al-Andalus, a Muslim kingdom. With the borders of the Islamic world expanding at an incredible speed, Christendom was in fear for its survival.

A CALL TO ARMS

In November 1095, Pope Urban II gave an electrifying speech at the Council of Clermont. The armies of Islam stood on the very doorstep of Christian Europe, he warned. His words were recorded by the chronicler Fulcher of Chartres, and he finished his speech with a desperate appeal:

Above Pope Urban II proclaims the First Crusade during the Council of Clermont in 1095 in this illustration from Jean Fouquet's Les Grandes Chroniques de France, c. 1460.

For this reason I beg and urge you — no, not I, but God Himself begs and implores you, as the messengers of Christ, the poor and the wealthy, to rush and drive away this mob from your brothers' territories, and to bring swift assistance to those who also worship Christ.

Below The crusaders travelled to the Middle East by both land and sea.

Right Crusaders storm Constantinople – a Christian city – in this 16th-century painting of the Fourth Crusade by the Italian painter Jacopo Tintoretto.

In response to Pope Urban II's plea, a mass mobilization took place across Europe, involving not just knights and soldiers but also ordinary men and women – and children. Thousands were inspired by what they saw as their sacred duty. Others were drawn for secular reasons: the prospect of plunder or the promise of adventure.

TO JERUSALEM!

The Crusade had a difficult start. The army that arrived in Constantinople – ready to march through Anatolia (modern-day Turkey) and on to the Holy Land – was big, but it was poorly equipped. Of the 100,000 crusaders, only 40,000 survived the journey over the mountains to Antioch. It then took a seven-month siege to take the Syrian city. Afterward, the crusaders pushed on to Jerusalem. Amid ferocious fighting, the city fell on 13 July 1099, and thousands of its inhabitants were massacred.

CONTINUED CRUSADES

Jerusalem was soon under threat again from the resurgent "Saracens", as the Christians called the Arab forces. A Second Crusade occurred in 1147 but ended in an undignified rout. In 1187, the Kurdish leader Salah al-Din al-Ayyubi, or "Saladin", recaptured Jerusalem. The English king, Richard I, the Lionheart, and other Christian kings mounted a Third Crusade in 1189, but they fought in vain.

The Fourth Crusade (1202–4) was short of funds, so the crusaders sacked Constantinople, massacring thousands. This was followed by another tragedy: in 1212, thousands of young French and Germans enlisted in the Children's Crusade, but before they reached the Holy Land they starved or were sold into slavery in North Africa.

The Fifth Crusade (1217–21) approached Jerusalem from the south but proved no more successful than its predecessors. In 1228, Holy Roman Emperor Frederick II negotiated Jerusalem's return diplomatically, but it fell into Muslim hands again. Two further crusades were mounted in 1248 and 1270: both were catastrophic failures.

Retaking Jerusalem was out of the question after the Ottoman Turks took Byzantium in 1453, but the struggle against Islam went on. In Spain, the Reconquista was coming to a conclusion, which came with the capture of Granada in 1492. In 1529, the Ottomans besieged Vienna, but were finally repulsed. The West's decisive victory came at sea, at the Battle of Lepanto (1571). Christendom had been locked in conflict with Islam for five centuries. The struggle had been very costly in terms of lives and money, but it had done much to shape the Church.

Left Even now an intimidating sight, the 12th-century fortress of Krak des Chevaliers in Syria was built by crusaders.

MONASTICISM

THE MONASTERIES WERE IMPORTANT CULTURAL AND ECONOMIC CENTRES THAT HELPED SET THE TONE OF MEDIEVAL LIFE. THEY BROUGHT MEN TOGETHER IN COMMUNITIES OF WORK AND PRAYER.

From the beginning, Christians had met in informal communities, with sharing and co-operation being fundamental to their faith. For a beleaguered, sometimes persecuted, minority, the community provided comfort. However, as time went on, organized communities of Christians were established, often living far away from the distractions and temptations of society at large. St Benedict of Nursia (c.480–543) founded at least 12 such communities in the early 6th century.

THE RULE OF ST BENEDICT
One community in particular – the Benedictines, established about 430 at Monte Cassino, south of Rome – was to have enduring importance. This was where St Benedict first formulated his "Benedictine Rule", a regime prescribing set times for collective worship, private prayer and study. It also allowed time for daily stints of manual work, which Benedict saw as an important way of suppressing personal pride and of giving praise to God. The Rule also

Above The great pioneer of the monastic movement St Benedict of Nursia delivers the Rules of the Order to St Maurus in this 1129 illumination, produced at the Monastery of St Gilles, Nîmes.

put clear structures in place. One monk was to be elected "abbot" by his companions; he was to be in charge, though he had to consult with his community on key decisions and was not exempted from the general routines of work and prayer. With 73 points in all, the Rule gave detailed instructions about everything from forms of worship to food and clothing – it stipulated a lifestyle that was simple, but not punitively harsh.

MONASTIC LIFE
The Rule of St Benedict soon became the basis for an extensive network of monasteries across medieval Europe. Young men flocked to join these communities. They flung themselves into the monastic life in all its aspects, not just prayer and contemplation but also study and work. As beacons of learning, these monasteries soon commanded the respect of the wider communities in which they were based.

Run as they were by a well-motivated and educated workforce, their farms and market gardens thrived. So did their other economic ventures: some monks brewed beer

Left Monks work in the fields, as depicted by Breu the Elder (c.1475–1537) on this panel from an Austrian altarpiece.

St Benedict's, young men flocked to join the community. They were drawn by the possibility of a purer, more wholly dedicated religious life. Cluny subsequently became a major monastic centre.

Monasteries elsewhere begged the new community to send out teachers to instruct them in the new rule. The Cluniac Reform quickly spread throughout western Europe. Even where the Cluniac Rule was not explicitly adopted, its influence was felt. Its effects filtered beyond the monasteries and into the wider Church. Catholicism's conscience had been awakened, and individual believers, clergy and institutions all set about reforming themselves and the way they lived.

However, Cluny was a victim of its own success. It became so powerful and influential that some began to feel that it had become too worldly in its turn. In 1098, St Robert of Molesme and St Stephen Harding founded the Cistercian Order – so-called because it was established at the Abbey of Cîteaux. It too set out to restore the Benedictine Rule as originally ordained, and it did so with considerable success. From 1113, under the leadership of St Bernard of Clairvaux, it became an important force for monastic reform.

or other drinks while others prepared medicines from herbs they had grown themselves. The monasteries rapidly became important centres of industry and trade – and their abbots used their influence on local rulers.

MONASTICISM REINVENTED

But soon some people were asking whether this success had not come at too high a price. Were the monasteries losing their way, becoming too "worldly" in their concerns? In 910, William the Pious, the Duke of

Above The Cistercian Abbey of Sénanque, located in southern France, was founded in the mid-12th century.

Aquitaine, founded a new community at Cluny, in eastern France. His idea was that its members would return to the founding principles of monasticism, as originally set down in the Benedictine Rule. William had read the mood of the times and his call for a new kind of monasticism had struck a chord. Though, if anything, the code at Cluny was even stricter than

MONASTIC MYSTICISM

If the idea of community is as old as Christianity itself, so too is that of solitary contemplation. Christ's sojourn in the desert was emulated by a long tradition of hermits. Others wandered inward, deeper and deeper into their own minds, to find a peaceful place in which they could commune with God.

Some mystics, such as Julian of Norwich and Mechtilde of Magdebourg, can be seen as a kind of counterbalance to the monastic movement, pursuing the same aims as these religious communities but using contrary methods. The less these mystics attended to the world, they felt, the closer they could draw to God. In blindness to the world and its concerns, they could glimpse the truth that really mattered. Enlightenment, wrote one mystic, was to be found in a "Cloud of Unknowing".

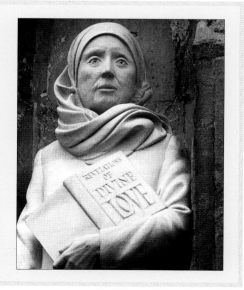

Right Mother Julian of Norwich was one of the great mystics of the Middle Ages. She is depicted in this 20th-century statue in Norwich Cathedral, England.

SHRINES AND RELICS

TANGIBLE TESTAMENTS TO HEROIC LOVE AND SACRIFICE, HOLY SHRINES AND SACRED RELICS HAVE REMINDED BELIEVERS THROUGHOUT HISTORY WHAT THEIR FAITH IS ALL ABOUT.

A shrine is considered a sacred place, usually one that has been specially blessed by the presence of a holy person, who carried out an important act, or who lived, died or was buried there. A relic is an item once associated with a saintly personage, anything from a fragment of bone to a scrap of shroud, or a possession of some sort. Catholics believe that shrines and relics have been sanctified by their associations to these holy people, so shrines have often become places of pilgrimage, while holy relics have become objects of veneration.

Even Catholics today find it hard to imagine the transporting spiritual excitement their medieval forebears experienced in the presence of holy shrines and sacred relics. Though the Catholic Church continues to encourage the veneration of genuine relics, this is often misunderstood outside the Church. There is discomfort with it among modern believers, and Catholics are still sensitive to any suggestion of superstition.

OPEN TO ABUSE

During the Middle Ages, there was undoubtedly an element of the grotesque in the cult of certain relics, and, indisputably, there was at times an air of opportunistic showmanship about their presentation. Much of their fascination for the faithful may well have been as much about vulgar curiosity as about faith.

At the time, businesses linked to the pilgrimages were thriving, and the possession of holy relics did not merely

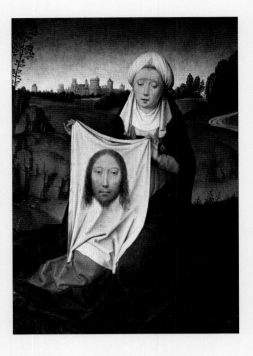

Above St Veronica wiped Christ's face as he carried his cross to Calvary. Miraculously, an imprint of Jesus' face was left on the cloth, as shown in this 15th-century painting by Hans Memling.

confer prestige, it could also bring (sometimes spectacular) earning potential. Pride of place in Venice's St Mark's Basilica was the tomb of the apostle – the Venetians had actually stolen St Mark's remains from their original resting place in Alexandria. In England, Canterbury was quick to cash in on the martyrdom of St Thomas, with entrepreneurially minded priests selling what was purported to be vials of his blood and scraps of his clothing.

A VALID TRADITION

So many churches had parts of the True Cross or the bones of various saints that not all of them could have been genuine. Yet even if not all relics were what they claimed to be, over the centuries millions of Catholics have derived great comfort and inspiration from them. Relics were of value not least as a subject for meditation. A visitor to St Thomas à Becket's tomb in Canterbury could wonder at the courage of one who

Below The cloth said to have been worn by Our Lady at the birth of Christ has been kept at Chartres Cathedral, France, since AD 876. The cathedral is a popular site of pilgrimage.

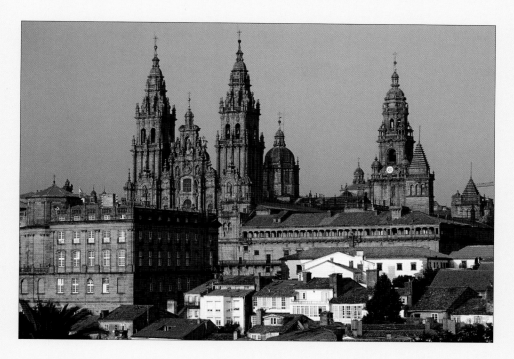

Above Reputed to be the last resting place of the apostle St James the Great, Santiago de Compostela is an important place of pilgrimage.

had stood up to his own king for what he knew was right. German visitors to the shrine of St Sebaldus in Nuremberg could reflect on what his early mission to Rome and preaching in Nuremburg had meant for their country. Several successive German emperors visited the shrine to pay him homage.

CONTACT WITH THE SAINTS

There is no doubt that the sense of being able to touch the saintly was part of the reason behind making a pilgrimage. Accordingly, a certain amount of tension arose between the instinct to present sacred relics in what would be appropriate magnificence and the pilgrims' desire for up-close contact. As monuments for these relics grew in size and splendour, they were built with open cavities, or "squeezing places", left in the tomb surround so the faithful could feel they were getting as close as possible to the source of grace.

DISTRUST FROM OTHERS

This need for contact would eventually be viewed by non-Catholics as somewhat grotesque. Protestant reformers, like many other modern intellectuals, distrusted Catholicism's instinct for the concrete – what can be seen and touched – an instinct revealed in everything from crucifixes and rosaries to statues and stained-glass windows. To them, the desire to touch a fragment of the "True Cross" or a visit to a saint's tomb could be compared to the time when Jesus told St Thomas to put his fingers in his wounds (John 20:25–9) before the doubting man would finally believe in his Resurrection.

In the 18th century, the philosophers of pre-revolutionary France had denounced Catholicism as a conspiracy to prop up corrupt institutions. Voltaire was one of these philosophers, and among his anti-religious comments was a sneer about the veneration of Christ's foreskin and the Virgin's milk, designed to humiliate Catholics.

For believers, though, the desire for contact with Christ and his saints was not rooted in weakness of faith. Contact was made for love, like that of the woman who touched the hem of Jesus' garment (Luke 8:40–8).

Below Sacred shrines, such as the one in this 15th-century painting by the Master of San Sebastian, have sometimes been linked to miraculous healings, making them popular pilgrimage sites for the lame and the sick in search of succour.

MIRRORS REFLECTING THE RELICS

In Aachen, Germany, in 1440, so many pilgrims flocked to see an exhibition of sacred relics that there was little prospect of anybody actually touching the reliquaries. The most the pilgrim could hope for was glimpses of these sacred treasures through the crush of the crowd. This situation led to the selling of metal-framed "pilgrim mirrors". These mirrors were designed to be clipped to the cap. They supposedly allowed the radiance emitted by the sacred relics to be captured, which the pilgrims could even take home to share with their family and friends.

PILGRIMAGE

EVERY YEAR, ALONG EUROPE'S HIGHWAYS, TRAVELLERS MADE THEIR WAY, SINGLY OR IN GROUPS, CRISS-CROSSING THE CONTINENT TO SEEK OUT THE MOST SACRED SHRINES OF THE CATHOLIC FAITH.

Above The Clerk of Oxenford, *one of Chaucer's fictional pilgrims, is shown in* The Canterbury Tales *(1400–10).*

The idea of the medieval pilgrimage is still well known today to students of literature, thanks to Geoffrey Chaucer's *The Canterbury Tales*. This 14th-century poem tells the story of a group of pilgrims from different walks of life, who travel from London to Canterbury in England. There they intend to offer their devotions at the tomb of St Thomas à Becket, who lies buried in the cathedral where he met his martyr's death. Like many Christians in the Middle Ages, Chaucer's pilgrims hoped to acquire grace in the eyes of God by the commitment they were showing in making a sacred journey.

AN OLD TRADITION

By this time, the tradition of pilgrimage, or spiritual journey, was already an old one. Since the 2nd century, believers had been travelling to Jerusalem to visit the scenes of their Saviour's ministry and sufferings and to think about what they meant in their own lives. The pilgrimage is by no means a uniquely Christian custom. By the 5th century BC, Buddhists had been trekking to the birthplace of their teacher, the Buddha, at Kapilavastu, Nepal.

Pilgrimage became embedded in the traditions of Catholicism. It was a gesture, a declaration of spiritual intent. Forsaking family, friends and everyday routines, the Catholic set out on what he or she hoped would be a new direction. The pilgrimage itself was just the start, but it could be a profoundly significant start. Removed from the rhythms of daily work and home life, the pilgrim could reflect on that life and how it might be led better. Arriving at the holy place itself, the pilgrim might meditate on the religious drama that had taken place there, or on the life of the saint whose mortal remains had sanctified the spot.

Some made their pilgrimages in hopes of saving a sick relative, or to help secure their salvation in the life beyond. Others were motivated by piety, a desire to perfect themselves; still others went as penitential pilgrims. They might have made their own decision to make a pilgrimage in expiation of some great wrong they had done. Or they might have been ordered by a court to make the journey, or else face a far harsher

HOUSES OF HOSPITALITY

With thousands of pilgrims on the move, often travelling long distances, a considerable infrastructure was needed to feed, accommodate and protect them. It had to cope with such normal activities as treating their ailments, shoeing their horses and even mending their clothes. Every bit as important in its own time as the tourist industry is to travellers today, the pilgrimage acted as a powerful economic engine. Rather than the desire for leisure, however, it was harnessing Christian piety and spreading prosperity far and wide.

In Jerusalem, and on the great pilgrimage routes such as the road to Santiago de Compostela, monasteries and other religious houses created special hospices, where the pilgrims could stay overnight in safety. These hospices were not like today's hospices, used as places for the sick. The original hospices took their name from the Latin word *hospes*, or "host", which is the root of our modern word "hospitality".

Right A hospice (hostel) for pilgrims, one of many established across medieval Europe, is shown in this 15th-century illustration from Antoine de la Sale's Les Cent Nouvelles Nouvelles.

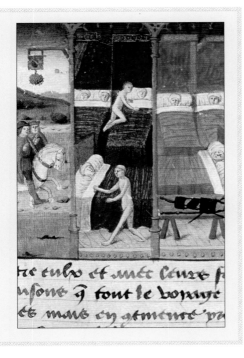

punishment. There were also those who were actuated by less pious motives: a yen for travel or adventure or simply a desire for change.

SACRED PLACES

The Holy Land, though the ultimate place of pilgrimage, was beyond most people's reach, geographically, financially, and often politically, given that Jerusalem was so long in Muslim hands. Even when it was not, Muslim pirates from Turkey and from North Africa's Barbary Coast preyed on Christian shipping, leaving no alternative to a long, costly and hazardous overland journey through the Balkans. Rome, as both the centre of the Church and with its shrine of St Peter, was another

Below A 17th-century French map shows the main pilgrimage routes to Santiago de Compostela in Spain.

popular place of pilgrimage. However, pilgrims from northern Europe had to find their way over the Alps on foot to get there, and many could not make their way across this treacherous mountain range.

There were less hazardous destinations, such as St Andrews in Scotland, reputedly the apostle's final resting place. In Galicia, Spain, the cathedral at Santiago de Compostela was supposed to house the remains of the apostle St James the Great. Another popular site in Spain was Zaragoza, where Our Lady had appeared atop a pillar before St James. Walsingham in Norfolk, England, had been the site of a different Marian apparition (appearance of Mary) in 1061, and it became an important place of pilgrimage.

Left A pilgrim badge was worn to show that a person had made a particular pilgrimage. This pewter badge of St Thomas à Becket was worn by a person who had travelled to Canterbury Cathedral.

SAFETY IN NUMBERS

Even short journeys could be hazardous, and pilgrims often felt obliged to travel in groups in order to avoid attack by brigands. According to an often-practised procedure, pilgrims gathered in their local town centre to receive a blessing from their priest before setting out on their journey together. On longer trips, these groups might join others, forming great congregations hundreds, sometimes thousands, strong.

GOTHIC GLORY

BUILT TO CELEBRATE THE GLORY OF GOD AND AS HOUSES OF WORSHIP, EUROPE'S IMPRESSIVE GOTHIC CATHEDRALS ARE SPECTACULAR MONUMENTS TO AN AGE OF FAITH.

Imagine how a medieval peasant might have felt on seeing a great cathedral such as Chartres for the first time. Dumbstruck with amazement as far across the fields on the horizon, shimmering slightly in the haze of the August heat, the gigantic structure appeared to be rising out of the ground. They had heard of Chartres' new cathedral, of course – how its spire seemed to soar to heaven, how the clear lines of its solid stone structure dissolved into a riot of statuary figures as you approached. As for its vast interior, its wood carvings and statues bathed in the otherworldly light of a hundred stained-glass windows: that was a promise of paradise on earth. Even so, nothing had prepared them for their first actual experience of one of the great Gothic architectural monuments of the medieval age.

THE GOTHIC STYLE

Similar to most artistic movements, Renaissance architecture sought to better its predecessors. The term "gothic" was employed pejoratively by the Italian architects of the Renaissance to describe the architecture of the Middle Ages, which they had mistakenly attributed to the Germanic tribes known as the Goths. These tribes had sacked Rome in the 5th century AD, and thus had earned a reputation for barbarism. They were seen as the destroyers of classical civilization, which the Renaissance had set out to reinstate. But although the term "Gothic Style" is still in use, it no longer has a negative connotation, and the medieval period is now generally seen as a golden age of European architecture. In fact, the Gothic style enjoyed a major revival in the 19th century.

REACHING FOR THE SKY

One striking feature of the Gothic style was its thrilling emphasis on verticality. However, for all its aesthetic and symbolic resonances, the style was reliant on advances in engineering. The old Romanesque churches had been held up by the massive masonry of their walls, their rounded arches suitable for only small windows. Now pointed arches distributed the weight, replacing a great deal of outward thrust with downward thrust. This allowed constructions to be taller, and walls and columns to be more slender. The liberal use of pointed pinnacles and spires underlined the accent on the vertical, which made even the grandest Romanesque monuments look squat and stubby.

Since the walls no longer had to bear such a load, they could afford to be less solid and could be fitted with huge, decorative windows filled with stained glass. Chartres Cathedral has more than a hundred of these. All kinds of biblical scenes were presented, creating a stunning pictorial scripture

Above *Built mainly in the 13th century, Chartres Cathedral in France is one of the great masterpieces of Gothic architecture (its second spire, on the left, was added on top of a previous tower in the 1500s).*

for the illiterate. No longer dark and gloomy, the inside of the Gothic church could be turned over to the best artists and craftsmen to express themselves in paint and metalwork, carved wood and stone: they created saints' statues and fonts, elaborately ornate wooden pulpits, pews and choir screens.

To go to church in such a setting was to be bombarded with sensory impressions. In many ways it was an experience of wonder and delight. Given the enthusiasm with which medieval artists represented devils and hell's torments, it might also be an experience of fear – but it would always be an experience to be remembered. Demons bedecked the outside, too, with waterspouts turned into hideously decorative gargoyles. Chartres' exterior offers a crash course in medieval culture. Along with religious scenes, the door surrounds are lined with figures of famous kings and queens, prophets and even philosophers.

Above *Stained glass, such as this one from a window in Chartres Cathedral showing Noah and his ark, gave the illiterate vivid access to the Bible stories.*

COLLECTIVE EFFORTS

The creators of these stunning works were content to remain anonymous, though at the same time it is clear that they were given an astonishingly free hand in determining the design of their works. Where in a modern building the sense of unified, overall design is all-important, Gothic churches seem somehow to have grown organically.

All things considered, this should not be surprising. Such vast and ambitious edifices were beyond the capacity of any one man to construct or even oversee. These churches took years, decades, to build – longer than an artisan's working life – so it was not realistic to expect any continuity of craftsmanship, and generations of workers were involved in their construction. Skilled builders, masons, joiners, woodcarvers and glaziers accordingly went from place to place through the cities of Europe. On any given project, within rough parameters, they would have free rein in producing their work.

It was haphazard, but it worked. The great Gothic churches were essentially communal projects. Apart from that of praising God, and impressing and educating the public, their main purpose was to announce the wealth and prestige of the communities that built them. In that, they were triumphantly successful.

Right Satan stokes the fire, while demons plunge the souls of the damned into a cauldron in this 12th-century relief from England's York Minster Cathedral.

Below The Last Supper is represented in beaten gold in this stunning 11th-century relief from Aachen, Germany.

RENAISSANCE AND REFORMATION

The Renaissance was the age of undisputed Catholic supremacy in Europe, but it ended in dissension and strife. Outside the Church, the conventional view of modern historians has been of a papacy growing in corruption as it grew in power, with its hierarchy becoming increasingly remote from the people – even from parish priests. Although there is truth in this narrative, it tells no more than half the story of a great institution struggling to negotiate a time of extraordinary upheaval. Social, political, economic and intellectual life – all these were being transformed during this period. Great epidemics had ravaged the communities of Europe; the printing press was democratizing learning; Columbus' voyage had opened the door to the New World.

Martin Luther's stand at Wittenberg in 1517 was one reaction and the creed of Calvin another. In England, King Henry VIII's refusal to obey the pope marked a severing of the old accord between Church and State. However, there were changes within the Church, too. These had been gathering momentum for centuries, but they gained new impetus in the growing ferment.

The Reformation was a period of trauma for the Church, and in several countries it found itself driven back underground. All of Europe suffered from the wars the crisis brought, with martyrs on both sides. At the same time, in forcing a far-reaching process of reappraisal and renewal upon the Church, the Reformation also became a moment of rebirth.

Above The prophet Daniel as depicted on the Sistine Chapel ceiling, painted by the Italian artist Michelangelo, 1508–12.

Left Religion was the inspiration for much of the greatest Renaissance art, as in this early 15th-century painting, The Resurrection of Christ, *by Mariotto di Cristofano.*

RIVAL POPES

DURING PART OF THE EARLY RENAISSANCE, THE ROMAN CATHOLIC CHURCH WAS BASED IN FRANCE. THERE WAS A SHORT-TERM PAPACY IN AVIGNON AND MUCH CONFLICT WITHIN THE CHURCH.

The Church was not only a religious institution but was also an extremely powerful and prominent social organization. Inevitably, it was involved in political affairs. As the Middle Ages concluded and the Renaissance began, the Church was finding its independence increasingly difficult to maintain, with secular rulers seeking to harness its influence to their own ends.

POPES AND POLITICS

The 13th century had already seen the supposedly transcendent authority of the papacy called into question by the growing interference of kings and aristocratic clans. Pope Nicholas IV had created added difficulties for the papacy when he

Below Built by Benedict XII and enlarged by Clement VI, the Palais des Papes in Avignon, France, was the home of a papacy in exile.

bought the support of the Colonnas – an important Roman family – by granting them favours, and when he agreed to crown the French Prince Charles of Anjou, making him King of Naples and Sicily in 1289. The family was in no mood to surrender its special status under Nicholas' successor, Celestine V. In deference to King Charles, he had established his papal court at Naples. However, Celestine was ignominiously out of his depth and abdicated just five months after his election in 1294, making way for the more formidable Boniface VIII, who moved the papacy back to Rome.

Boniface could not be frightened into submission by Charles – or by the French ascendancy he represented – but his confrontational manner served only to precipitate a crisis. From the first, Boniface had both the King of Naples and Sicily and the Colonna family against him.

Above Pope Boniface VIII is illustrated drafting canonical law in this 14th-century manuscript from the Decrees of Boniface VIII.

Years of harassment culminated in an assassination attempt in 1303. Although Boniface survived the attempt, he died of natural causes only a few weeks later.

THE AVIGNON PAPACY

Boniface's successor, Benedict XI, was pulled one way and then the other by Charles and the Colonnas. The French won after Benedict's death with the election of Clement V, who as Bertrand de Got had been the Archbishop of Bordeaux.

Clement had never visited Rome, and four years into his reign, in 1309, he transferred the seat of papal power to Avignon, in southern France. This was just one of the most obvious of Clement's concessions to King Philip IV. A host of new French cardinals were created in an intiative urged by Philip, and Clement outlawed the Order of the Knights Templar in 1307 throughout Europe. Their immense wealth in France was confiscated by the king.

POPE AND "ANTIPOPE"

It almost seemed the move to Avignon had done the papacy good: it was growing in institutional splendour and in wealth. However, behind the scenes, the French crown was wielding unprecedented power. After Clement's death in 1314, six successive popes reigned from Avignon. The arrangement worked – but at a considerable cost to the Church's autonomy.

The transfer to France had left the Church in Italy in a rebellious mood; Rome was bereft, its purpose of so many centuries gone. There was unease in the wider Catholic Church as well. Queen Bridget of Sweden joined St Catherine of Siena in lobbying for a return. In 1376, Pope Gregory XI removed his court from Avignon to Rome. But the rejoicing was cut short by his death just a few months later.

The French had not finished with the papacy – their possession, as they now saw it. When an Italian, Urban VI, was named as pope in Rome in 1378, the French created their own "pope", Clement VII. In the decades that followed, four "antipopes" were elected as French counters to the popes of Rome. Called to arbitrate in the dispute, the Council of Pisa (1408) made matters worse: for a time the Church boasted not two popes but three, because the French

cardinals could not agree among themselves. Finally, in 1417 Pope Martin V (a member of the Colonna family) received the recognition of the entire Catholic Church, with the papacy back in Rome.

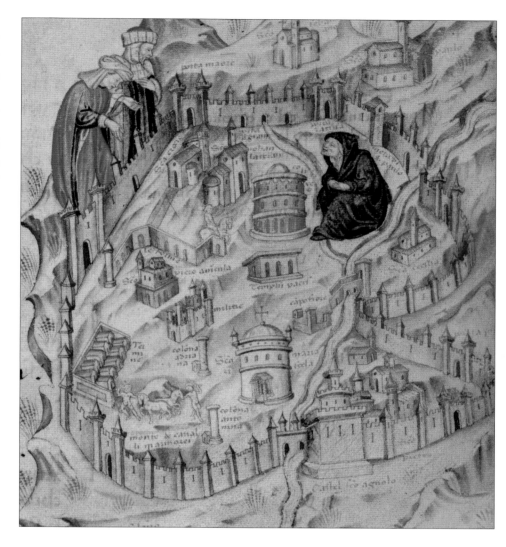

Above In Roma La Veuve, *an Italian manuscript produced in the Renaissance, the allegorical "Widow of Rome" is illustrated mourning her bereavement after the departure of the papacy, shown outside the city walls.*

THE WESTERN SCHISM

So-called to differentiate it from the earlier separation, which had seen the Orthodox Church established in 1054, the Western Schism had consequences far beyond the papal courts. Secular rulers had to decide which side to acknowledge: the Roman pontiff or the French-backed Avignon pope. Because both papal courts appointed their own bishops, the lower clergy and the people were left confused – and spiritually adrift. Each side had excommunicated the other's supporters, so ordinary people had no way of knowing whether the sacraments their priests were administering were valid; whether their marriages, or their loved ones' funerals, were acceptable to God.

Right Clement VII, the first "antipope" of the Western Schism, was enthroned at Avignon in 1378, shown here in the Chroniques de France ou de St Denis.

INDULGENCES

THE PAPACY HAD INITIALLY INTRODUCED INDULGENCES TO MEET A SPIRITUAL NEED. THESE REMISSIONS GAVE MILLIONS OF CATHOLICS THE HOPE TO STRIVE FOR THEIR SALVATION.

The Catholic Church is generally seen as being dogmatic in its teachings. It is easy to forget, then, that for much of the first millennium, its teachings in several areas were to some extent a work-in-progress in the development of doctrine. One issue that had from early on caused concern among Christians and their clergy was that they felt perilously poised between salvation and damnation. Surely, theologians reasoned, there must be a middle ground for those whose lives had been virtuous, though flawed?

PURIFYING THE SOUL

By the 5th century AD teachers were talking of a place of temporary chastisement, in which the soul would be purged or purified by the fire, but from which it would eventually be released into heaven, for eternity. The idea had been taken up and developed by Pope Gregory the Great in the 6th century. He had proposed that prayerful observance or good works in this life might lead to "indulgence".

An indulgence gives a period of remission to the sufferings of the soul in Purgatory after death, granted in return for some act of commitment – a pilgrimage, a programme of prayer, for example. It was a radical step, but it re-energized Christianity, giving ordinary men and women new grounds for hope. Few could hope to be saints in the hereafter, but anyone free of mortal sin could strive to do better in their daily lives, to throw themselves into their regimes of prayer and charitable works. The other great thing about the system was that, since people could earn "indulgence" not just for themselves but for their departed loved ones, it fostered a sense of solidarity between the living and the dead.

THE PLENARY INDULGENCE

As time went on, what had been an inspirational idea became a fully articulated system, with periods of indulgence established for certain observances or acts. In particularly special circumstances, a "plenary indulgence" might be granted, with a complete remission of temporal punishment for sin. If the receiver died in that moment, his or her soul could avoid going to Purgatory.

So far, this was nothing exceptional: the system may have seemed mechanistic, but it gave people a

Left The good are lofted heavenward by flights of angels, while the wicked are carried down into hell in a burning river in Jean Colombe's 14th-century painting.

Above Michael the archangel weighs souls, separating out the saved from the damned in this c.1450 Last Judgement, painted by Rogier van der Weyden.

spiritual incentive to which they could respond. However, at the same time, it was open to abuse: the temptation was always there for the Church to harness it to meet its worldly ends. When Pope Boniface VIII proclaimed a jubilee year for 1300, for example, he promised a plenary indulgence to those who made the pilgrimage to Jerusalem that year. Two million people heeded his call. The suspicion that he was putting on a show of strength for his political enemies in Rome must be set against the wider benefit his jubilee did in reinvigorating the whole Church.

A FINANCIAL TRANSACTION

More problematic was the financial note, which may have been innocent to start with but became corrupt over time. It began with the payment of fees for masses offered for the souls of the dead, another way of gaining them remission. The token sums paid were a welcome supplement to the incomes of poor parish priests. However, the practice spread as the Church first relied on the contributions it gained in this way and then exploited its people's piety. The poor were bullied into paying for prayers, the wealthy bribed with offers of an easy afterlife. Soon high prelates and great religious houses were growing rich on the proceeds.

The perception spread that indulgences existed not for the sake of fallen humanity but for the Church's monetary enrichment. However, this was not always the case. When Jesus gave Peter his papal power, he gave him the keys of heaven; he also promised him that the "powers of death" would not prevail against his Church. Purgatory wasn't mentioned, but by giving his pope authority to "bind" and "loose" the laws of earth and heaven, he gave him, and the popes who followed him, the right to ordain these things as he decided through God's grace.

Above A bull of Julius II, issued in 1505, announces the indulgences that had been conferred on a group of wealthy benefactors.

SALVATION FOR SALE

In 1245, when England's King Henry III set out to rebuild Westminster Abbey, the venture won Pope Innocent IV's approval. More than this, it won his promise that any individual who made a contribution of money to this reconstruction would receive 20 days' indulgence from the sufferings of Purgatory. This was a clear cash transaction, even if it was for a good cause. By the 14th century, indulgences were being openly bought and sold. In Chaucer's *The Canterbury Tales*, the Pardoner carried a sheaf of printed "pardons" in his saddlebag. In 1344, Clement VIII issued 200 plenary indulgences in England alone, which were "earned" entirely by financial endowments to the papacy.

Below England's King Henry III is shown with Westminster Abbey, which he rebuilt, in this c.1253 illustration from History of the English.

THE FRANCISCAN REVOLUTION

ST FRANCIS IS AMONG THE MOST BELOVED OF SAINTS. TO HIS SPIRITUAL ARDOUR AND LOVE OF NATURE, HE ALLIED A TACTFUL RADICALISM THAT WAS TO HAVE A FAR-REACHING IMPACT ON THE CHURCH.

Francesco di Pietro di Bernardone (c.1181–1226) was one of Assisi's most fashionable young men, known for his love of all things French. He was devoted to music, poetry, fashion and flirtation. However, he also had a more serious side. In the 1200s, when he was a young man in his twenties, a series of spiritual crises caused him to question his worldly preoccupations. He left behind his old pursuits and his old friends to care for lepers. The romantic enthusiasm of old was evident in the way he hurled himself into this new life, though now the mistress of his heart, he said, was "Lady Poverty".

BEGGARS IN CHRIST

This was a huge transformation, but the change in Francis was by no means done. In 1209, he was in a church in Assisi when a priest gave a sermon on Matthew's Gospel, Chapter 10.

Take no gold, nor silver, nor copper in your belts, no bag for your journey, nor two tunics, nor sandals, nor staff; for the labourer deserves his food… Do not be anxious how you are to speak or what you are to say; for what you are to say will be given to you in that hour; for it is not you who speak, but the Spirit of your Father through you.

Above *Christ officiates as St Francis takes Lady Poverty as his bride, depicted in this 13th–14th century allegorical scene by Giotto.*

Francis would need no further encouragement to live the words of the gospels. He took to the roads as a beggar – with no money, no bag, no spare clothing, no sandals and no staff. However, he did soon have a companion: Bernard of Quintavalle, another wealthy young man from Assisi, and the first recruit to Francis' order of Friars Minor. Unlike the monks who lived in monasteries – and so, however hard they tried to avoid it, had worldly ties – the friars would have only the air they breathed and the food and water strangers gave them.

A NEW ORDER

This "mendicant" lifestyle could clearly be seen as an implicit criticism of the religious establishment at a time when its institutions had grown enormously in power and wealth. Already, there had been signs of restlessness, with certain heretics

Left *St Francis maintained good relations with the papacy. In this 13th–14th century painting by Giotto, he preaches before Innocent's successor, Honorius III.*

Above The Dominicans, shown in this 16th-century painting by the Spanish School, were writers and teachers.

THE POOR CLARES

The daughter of a noble house, destined by her parents for an aristocratic marriage, Clare of Assisi (1194–1253) dreamt of a more meaningful religious life. She was inspired by St Francis, who had come from a background similar to her own, and in 1212 she went to him for help. With Francis' assistance, she started her own order, the Poor Ladies (also called the Poor Clares). They could not realistically travel the roads as the friars did, but had their own small convents. Despite the efforts of the established orders to absorb them into the monastic system, the Poor Ladies worked hard to maintain their independence and uphold their guiding principle of poverty.

Below St Francis is shown with his disciple St Clare in this 14th-century painting by Memmo di Filipuccio. With his advice, she founded an order of her own.

attacking the Church for its close relations with wealthy, worldly interests. The hierarchy could be forgiven for feeling defensive in the face of Francis' apparent challenge.

For his own part, however, Francis showed no interest in taking the hierarchy to task. On the contrary, he defended the institutions of the Church against all detractors and sued humbly to Pope Innocent III for his support. The Pope appears to have found Francis a perplexing character. One story claims that the Pope initially ordered the ragged, dirty vagabond before him to be sent away to tend swine; however, he then relented when Francis agreed without demur.

Whatever reservations he might have had, Innocent came to the conclusion that Francis should be encouraged: that decision itself showed a certain vision on the pontiff's part. A movement that might have been profoundly destabilizing was accommodated by a Church already making conscious efforts to reform itself.

THE DOMINICANS

St Dominic was a teacher trying to hold back the rising tide of heresy in southern France. He founded his own order in 1214, which also took up mendicant proverty. Dominic saw that the poor were increasingly out of reach of the Church, not just in the scattered hamlets of the countryside but in the fast-growing cities. He wanted an order of young men to carry the Word to these lost sheep. Since Dominic had been placed in charge of a convent as early as 1206, these Dominican nuns actually predated the Dominican friars.

CHURCH MUSIC

FROM THE AUSTERE GRACE OF GREGORIAN CHANT TO THE GLORIOUS POLYPHONIES OF THE BAROQUE AND BEYOND, MUSIC HAS PLAYED ITS PART IN THE LITURGIES OF THE CHURCH.

Both solemn and spare, the sound of plainsong (also called "plainchant") as it echoes through the aisles and cloisters is for many people the quintessential sound associated with the Catholic Church. For others, however, it will be the thunderous chorus of the Lourdes pilgrims'"Ave Maria!", or the graceful harmonies of Haydn's *The Creation* or James MacMillan's *Mass*.

AN ORDERLY COSMOS

It seems likely that music formed part of the Christian liturgy from early on in its establishment, though in the absence of written notation from that time we have no real way of knowing for certain. Music had an almost theological significance for the people of the ancient and medieval worlds. The way in which the different notes could resonate harmoniously was seen as analogous to the relations between the earth and the planets and stars – all set in their own rotating spheres within the overall order of God's universe. Hence the phrase, "the music of the spheres", and therefore the importance attached to music – which went far beyond the aesthetic pleasure it provided.

SONG OF ST GREGORY

It was natural, then, that music would have its place in the monastic order, at the services offered by monks each day to mark the passage of the hours. The emphasis was on austerity: plainsong was indeed plain, involving no accompanying instruments and just a single sustained melodic line. Even so, its eerie beauty must have been an inspiration to the monks, reminding them each day of the mysterious majesty of God.

Pope Gregory the Great had encouraged the practice of singing plainsong, which, its inestimable beauties apart, helped foster the monastic virtues of co-operation and discipline. His support lent impetus to a musical genre that grew rapidly in scale and sophistication, and a rudimentary form of notation was developed during the 9th century.

Gradually, over the centuries that followed, moves were made toward simple two- and eventually more complex three- and four-part compositions – toward polyphony ("many voices"), in other words.

Left Whether a little pipe-and-bellows affair or an elaborate one such as this from the Chapel at Versailles, the organ is the standard instrument for church music.

Above Much early music was performed by voice alone, as shown in this 15th-century illumination from the Bible of Borso d'Este.

The organ added yet another voice: it is thought to have been in use since the time of Pope Vitalian in the 7th century. The organ's pure tones were the perfect complement to the human voice, and it has been the mainstay of church music ever since. As the Middle Ages gave way to the Renaissance, other instrumental sounds were introduced to church music.

INFLUENCES ON MUSIC

Secular music was nourished by the church tradition. Though Claudio Monteverdi is famous for having composed the first operas in the 17th century, he was also a priest, and in this role brought baroque complexity to sacred music.

In his footsteps came fellow Italians, such as Antonio Vivaldi (1678–1741), a priest who wrote many of his great works for the orchestra of the Ospedale della Pietà, a church-run orphanage for girls. The kapellmeisters (or "chapel masters"), who wrote liturgical music for services at Austria's and

Germany's courts, also found time to write secular concerti, keyboard music and orchestral suites.

By this time, of course, the Reformation had swept Europe, and several of the great Baroque composers were Protestants. However, music was an ecumenical art: Catholic creativity was stimulated by the works of Bach and Handel, while the great Protestant geniuses themselves drew on the traditions of the Catholic past.

CLASSICAL TRADITION
Religion remained an important influence into music's classical heyday of the 18th and 19th centuries. Joseph Haydn was a committed Catholic. While he wrote many explicitly sacred works – such as his wonderful oratorio, *The Creation* (1798) – he saw the whole process of composition as an act of prayer, writing "Praise be to God" at the end of every completed piece.

His younger contemporary, Wolfgang Amadeus Mozart, may have been famously flawed as an individual, but his profound faith came through in the great *Requiem* he was working on when his own life was cut short in 1791. Franz Liszt, the great piano virtuoso and romantic composer of the 19th century, was notorious for his scandalous private life. Yet this intensely emotional man was also passionate in his attachment to Catholicism. He even took minor orders in the Church in 1865.

SONGS OF PRAISE
What might be called the elite culture of sacred music has endured in 20th-century works by several noted composers, from France's Olivier Messiaen to Scotland's James

Right Many of Vivaldi's works were premiered by the girls of the orphanage he served, seen here in this 18th-century painting entitled The Orphans' Cantata, *by Gabriele Bella.*

MacMillan. For most modern Catholics, though, Church music has taken the less sophisticated form of hymn singing. This has been more about participation than polished performance, but regardless it has been profoundly important to its participants. Communal singing can be crucial in bringing a congregation closer together, instilling in its members a sense of common purpose and common faith.

Right With such inspiring works as the Requiem, *Mozart created some of the most sublimely spiritual harmonies ever heard, enjoyed by Catholics and non-Catholics alike.*

HERETICS

SINCERE BELIEVERS WERE QUESTIONING THE AUTHORITY OF THE CHURCH. THE HIERARCHY HAD TO DECIDE WHICH CRITICISMS TO ACCEPT, WHICH TO IGNORE AND WHICH TO BRAND AS "HERESY".

An institution as far-reaching as the Church – and one with so many deeply thoughtful, idealistic individuals – was inevitably bound to have differences of opinion, even disputes, among its followers. To some extent these disputes could be contained and passionate debates took place with the Church's tacit acceptance – even its encouragement. However, some ideas were so wildly at variance with normal Catholic teaching that they could not be accommodated

without the integrity of the Church being threatened. These contentious views became known as "heresies".

St Augustine had led the fight against heresy as early as the end of the 4th century, condemning the Pelagian view that humankind could earn salvation by its own efforts, without God's intervention. His view that humankind was dragged down so drastically by original sin that salvation came only and exclusively from the intervention of God

Above Although members of a Christian faith, Waldensian followers were linked to witchcraft in this 15th-century illustration from the Book of Occult Sciences.

was to be taken to heretical extremes in the 16th century, when it was known as Jansenism. However, the late Middle Ages turned out to be a period of particular ferment, and in hindsight we can see this as the beginnings of the Reformation.

THE WALDENSIANS

In 1177, Peter Waldo, a prosperous merchant from Lyon, France, had undergone a spiritual crisis. Like St Francis, he had given away all his possessions and become a mendicant preacher. However, unlike the Franciscans, the "Waldensians" confronted the Church, denouncing it as representing only the richest and most powerful in society. Ultimately, they rejected the authority of its priests when Pope Lucius III banned Waldo from preaching in 1184. He and his followers set up their own Church, which survived prosecution

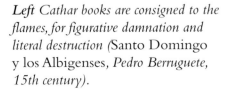

*Left Cathar books are consigned to the flames, for figurative damnation and literal destruction (*Santo Domingo y los Albigenses, *Pedro Berruguete, 15th century).*

during the following years. In 1848 the Catholic Church granted the Waldensians religious freedom.

THE CATHARS

Southern France had by this time become the centre of another great heresy: that of Catharism. This had its roots in the Manichaeism of earlier centuries, which preached a form of duelism that combined elements from several religions. A version of the heresy had been brought West through the Balkans by Pop Bogomil and his adherents, probably dispersed along the Mediterranean trade routes. Catharism carried to extremes the Manichaean opposition between good and evil, light and darkness, the spiritual and material. For its followers, the entire earthly Creation – the material world, the body and its desires – were evil. The aim of the godly was to transcend these things.

If the Word had been "made flesh" in Christ, that could only go to show that it, too, was evil – a fact the Cathars felt was confirmed by the wealth and power of the Church. Thousands flocked to the Cathar cause, despite the arguments of the Dominicans – newly formed to

defend the faith. The violence of the official crackdown that followed (*see The Albigensian Crusade, below right*) has been condemned, but it is hard to imagine a more potent threat to the medieval order.

THE LOLLARDS

The teachings of John Wycliffe, an English priest and scholar of the 14th century, struck a chord with many of his country's less educated people. Like Waldo, Wycliffe thought the Church had no business being rich or involving itself with the concerns of temporal government. Even in religious affairs, he argued, the Church had made too much of its own role. He wanted a scaled-down hierarchy and translations of the Bible from Latin so that people could read the Word of God themselves. He denied the doctrine of "transubstantiation". The bread and wine, he said, remained bread and wine even as they took on the nature of Christ's body and blood.

Below An extravagant depiction of the persecution of the Lollards was illustrated in the fiercely Protestant John Foxe's Acts and Monuments, *16th century.*

Wycliffe's followers, known as "Lollards", were seen as a threat to both secular and religious authority. Their ideas were spread into Europe by Jan Hus (or John Huss), the Czech reformer who campaigned against the sale of indulgences in the 15th century. The Lollards were a short-lived group, but their ideas were taken up by the Protestants.

THE ALBIGENSIAN CRUSADE

Named after Albi, a town in the Languedoc, a region in southern France, where Catharism was officially denounced in 1178, the "Albigensian Crusade" was proclaimed by Pope Innocent III in 1208. By calling it a crusade, he equated the challenge of heresy within the Church with the threat of Islam in the Middle East and Spain. In the years that followed, the forces of the French Crown and powerful northern nobles attacked the southern peasantry and the local lords who supported them. As many as a million people may have been killed.

Above Many atrocities were committed in the Albigensian Crusade. Here, Cathars are expelled from the city of Carcassonne (Chronicle of France, 15th century).

THE INQUISITION

FEW INSTITUTIONS OF CATHOLICISM HAVE BEEN MORE FEARED THAN THE "INQUISITION", OR SO WIDELY MISUNDERSTOOD. YET THE EXCESSES OF THE "HOLY OFFICE", AS IT WAS KNOWN, CANNOT BE DENIED.

Above Jan Hus is burnt at the stake for his heretical beliefs in this illustration from Ulrich von Reichenthal's Council Chronicle, *15th century.*

Throughout its history, the Catholic Church has fought against heresy, but it was not until the Renaissance that it formed an official institution against such preaching. The Albigensian Crusade, set up in France in 1208 in the hope of stemming the rising tide of Catharism, could be seen as a precursor to the official Inquisitions that followed. First ordered by Pope Gregory IX in 1232, an Inquisition was a tribunal ordered by the Catholic Church to suppress and punish heresy. The first inquisitors were chosen from the Dominicans and Franciscans, who were living mendicant lifestyles and therefore not influenced by worldly gains, and who were well educated in theology.

At about the same time an anti-Waldensian Inquisition followed in Italy, but then the Inquisition waned,

Below The Inquisition was especially active in the Netherlands and Ghent, where it was an arm of the Spanish occupation, as shown in this 16th-century engraving of the Flemish School.

to be revived in Spain and Portugal (and their overseas colonies) from the late 15th century. More of these ecclesiastical courts for suppressing heresy were constituted in France and Italy during the Reformation. The Congregation of the Holy Office, which is often shortened to the Holy Office, was formed to oversee the Inquisitions in 1542.

Although administered by the Church, the Inquisition worked with the temporal authorities. Generally, the state took the lead. Monarchs always had an interest in enforcing conformity and were happy enough to claim divine sanction for doing so. After the Reformation, religion took on a political aspect. A Protestant was no longer just a heretic but a dangerous subversive – potentially, an agent from another state in Europe.

SPANISH ACTS OF FAITH

It was in this febrile political context that the *Leyenda Negra* (or "Black Legend") was born. Spain, the Catholic superpower at the time, was

demonized by the propagandists of northern Europe's Protestant powers. Books and pamphlets were printed, describing in lurid detail the supposed excesses of the Spanish, from their American colonies to the torture chambers of the Inquisition. However, modern scholarship has shown that many of these accounts were mere fabrications, created by over-excited pamphleteers.

However, some of the accounts, though sensationalized, cannot be dismissed. Recent research has shown the scrupulous thoroughness with which the Holy Office sought to document its cases, avoiding prosecutions based on malicious denunciations. At the same time it

Above Spain's Grand Inquisitor, Tomás de Torquemada, was widely feared (Spanish School, 19th century).

THE SPANISH INQUISITION

The Inquisition in Spain had first been established in Aragon in the 13th century, but it came into its own in the 15th century under Ferdinand and Isabella, the "Catholic Monarchs". They bore that title, not because they staunchly defended Catholicism (though they did), but because by their marriage they had brought together the realms of Navarra, Aragon and Castile to form a single Spain. (The word "Catholic" originally meant "universal", "all-embracing" – hence its use for the Church of Rome.)

Ferdinand and Isabella saw the Holy Office as a way of using ecclesiastical structures as the basis for what we would now call a police state. Since the Reconquista was only recently completed, and many of the kingdom's Jews and Muslims had been converted by force, there was considerable fear that these alien groups were secretly upholding their old beliefs and practices in private meetings. Hence the drawing up of laws of *limpieza* ("cleanliness", "purity"), which anticipated the race laws of Nazi Germany. They were

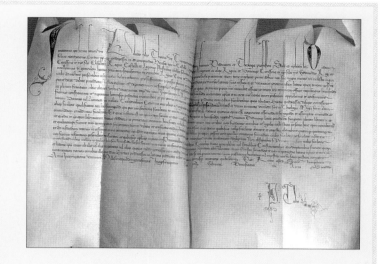

Above Torquemada received a bull of 1487 from Pope Innocent VIII, appointing him Inquisitor General of Spain.

imposed with terrifying thoroughness by the infamous Grand Inquisitor, Tomás de Torquemada, who was appointed to the position by the pope.

confirms the integral role of torture in the proceedings (after its explicit authorization by Pope Innocent IV in 1252). Although their frequency has been exaggerated, *autos-da-fé* ("acts of faith") assuredly took place. These rituals, in which there was a public penance for the guilty, were symbolic representations of the Last Judgement acted out before large crowds. An *auto-da-fé* ended with the accused being burnt at the stake.

OUTRAGEOUS ACTIONS

The readiness of the Church to consign its critics to the flames is easily exaggerated: the wilder claims of Reformation propaganda have proved obdurately persistent. The armies of the Albigensian Crusade did embark on a spree of slaughter, but the extent of the Church's blessing is unclear. Outraged though

Right St Dominic was committed to teaching – but when all else failed, the fear of death was used to persuade the people. Here, St Dominic presides over an auto-da-fé *(Pedro Berruguete, c.1495).*

it was by Wycliffe's teachings, the Church spent so long debating them that he had died of natural causes before he was denounced as a heretic.

However, Jan Hus, the Czech preacher who campaigned against the sale of indulgences, was burnt at the stake in 1415 (an act for which Pope John Paul II apologized in 1999). Nor was he alone in suffering this fate at the hands of the Church, which, with criticism mounting, was increasingly on the defensive – and all too ready to attack.

THE CHURCH IN TRANSITION

THE HISTORICAL HEADLINES MAY HAVE BEEN ABOUT THE STIFLING OF DISSENT, BUT QUIETER DEVELOPMENTS WERE TAKING PLACE BEHIND THE SCENES AS CATHOLICISM REFORMED ITSELF.

The Church in the Middle Ages had been very much the establishment. Secure in its position, it had no real interest in changing. However, this does not mean that the spiritual status quo had gone unquestioned. The heresies of the time had only been the most extreme manifestation of a ferment of debate. This concerned not just the finer points of Christian doctrine but also the place that Catholicism occupied within society, and the developing relationship between Church and State.

COUNCILS FOR CHANGE

These issues were explored by the Church hierarchy at such gatherings as the Third Lateran Council of 1179 and the Fourth, which followed

Below Figures representing the Seven Liberal Arts – Arithmetic, Music, Geometry, Astronomy, Logic, Rhetoric and Grammar – are shown in a 1503 publication on humanism from Gregor Reisch, Margarita Philosophica Nova.

in 1215. These conclaves were held in the vast council chamber of the Lateran Palace, which was the pope's official residence in Rome. Leading clerics came together to discuss the changes the Church would have to make to adapt to a changing world while at the same time staying true to its original principles.

The great emphasis of the communiqués agreed by the Third Lateran Council was on the maintenance of orthodoxy, while the Fourth is today known chiefly for its decree that Jews and Muslims should have to wear distinctive garb to set themselves apart from Christians.

Yet the small print tells a slightly different story. Most of the Council's energies had gone into the attempt to get the Church's house in order. New measures were introduced to make the clergy more accountable for its actions and to control the activities of religious foundations.

THE RISE OF HUMANISM

At the end of the 15th century, the Italian scholar Giovanni Pico Della Mirandola advanced the views that became known as "humanism". God's greatest gift to us as humans, he argued, was the capacity to reason for ourselves. It was not just our right but our duty to use that gift. Traditional Catholic scholarship, he suggested, had seen its role as essentially a passive one of interpreting and implementing the will of God. Scholars had seen that will represented in the doctrinal judgements handed down over generations within the Church, which had come to have the force of legal precedent in Catholic thought.

Above Convened in 1215, the Fourth Lateran Council, shown in this 19th-century engraving, introduced far-reaching reforms in the running of the Church.

Instead, Pico Della Mirandola claimed, people should be thinking for themselves and bypassing tradition to consult the ancient sources. In this view, he was reflecting the contemporary attitudes of the artists and writers of the wider Renaissance (rebirth), which was taking place in Italy at the time.

Inspired by the artwork of classical Greece and Rome, men such as Leonardo da Vinci saw the human form as the highest achievement of God's Creation. Scientists, too, were finding inspiration in the writings of the Greeks and Romans, gaining the confidence to set aside the perceived assumptions of centuries and to try out new theories and experiment with new ideas.

COUNCIL OF TRENT

Humanism, as then understood, did not dispute the greatness of God – still less his existence – but it did raise radical questions as to how he should be served. Church leaders were unsettled – not surprisingly, since humanist thinking did tempt some scholars toward the new Protestant theologies then emerging. However, in the works of writers such as St Thomas More and Erasmus, humanism offered a reinvigoration of a Catholic tradition, which had, to some extent, become fossilized over the passing years.

That the Church was capable of flexibility was to be demonstrated at the Council of Trent. Opening in 1545, when Europe was at the height of the Reformation, its sessions continued for several years until 1563. Its main conclusions were uncompromising, with the Church rejecting the theological heresies proposed by the Protestant rebels. At the same time, it tacitly acknowledged the justice of many of the criticisms of its own institution. It was these criticisms that caused the Church to institute root-and-branch reform. Measures were introduced to combat corruption, including regulation of the issuing of indulgences to prevent their sale. Diocesan seminaries were created to provide better training for priests, and disciplinary structures were formed to handle wrongdoers.

A CHRISTIAN JOKER
Desiderius Erasmus ("Erasmus of Rotterdam") was one of the most serious thinkers of the Renaissance, but it was with a joke that he caught the mood of an amazing time. His treatise, *Praise of Folly* (1511), was a masterly exercise in irony; among the absurdities it satirized were those of the Church. Its scholars' slavish reverence for tradition, its superstitions and its corruption: all these are ridiculed in its pages. However, this only makes the more moving the book's final reaffirmation of a Catholic faith whose truth transcends the earthly limitations of the Church.

Above Erasmus of Rotterdam, painted in 1523 by Hans Holbein the Younger, was a brilliant scholar and thinker. He published many works and led the humanist movement within the Church.

Left The Island of Utopia, as imagined by the great English humanist St Thomas More, was illustrated by Ambrosius Holbein and published in 1518 in the book of the same title.

POWERFUL POPES

THE RENAISSANCE SAW THE PAPACY AT ITS HEIGHT AS A POLITICAL FORCE — AND ITS MORAL REPUTATION AT ITS LOWEST EBB, RESPONSIBLE FOR SOME DISREPUTABLE CHAPTERS IN THE CHURCH'S HISTORY.

Above Pope Sixtus IV appoints a new prefect to preside over his library, another monument to the majesty of his reign, in Melozzo da Forli's painting (1477).

Today the idea of a "Renaissance Pope" suggests magnificence and political power. However, it also implies corruption on a huge scale. This is a stereotype, of course, but one that many pontiffs of the 15th and 16th centuries appear to have lived up to. To expect otherwise would perhaps have been unrealistic. The Church was the greatest institution of the day, and its leader commanded untold wealth and incalculable influence. At the same time it was very much a human institution. The meek and innocent might be blessed in heaven, but here on earth they were pushed aside by the ambitious, the unscrupulous and the ruthless.

A FAMILY BUSINESS

Among the Church's hierarchy, favours were exchanged, inducements were offered and friends and

Below Building the new St Peter's took many years. Antoine Lafréry's engraving (1575) shows a papal blessing being given beneath its uncompleted dome.

relations were taken care of. It was no surprise when the nephew of Pope Eugene IV followed him on to St Peter's throne as Pope Paul II in 1464.

Pope Sixtus IV followed in 1471. He made no fewer than six of his nephews cardinals during his papacy, on top of which he gave them benefices that brought in colossal wealth. (The Church had a vast income from a range of sources, including rents, donations, bequests and burial fees, all of which were a temptation to the corrupt.) Sixtus IV also married his nieces into Italy's leading aristocratic houses, building up a powerful network of familial connections, which he was ruthless in defending. He is believed to have been complicit in a plot carried out in 1478 in which two Medici brothers were attacked with daggers while attending Mass in the cathedral in Florence. One of them, Giuliano de' Medici, died of his wounds.

A strong sense of "family" was creeping in — of dynastic continuity and of bitter feuding — alien as this

should have been to a Church with a celibate clergy. Some popes were far from chaste. Pope Alexander VI (1492–1503) fathered nine children by an unknown number of different women. His most notorious son, Cesare Borgia, was a murderous wheeler-dealer; he became a cardinal before leaving the clergy to make an advantageous marriage.

PAPACY AND PATRONAGE

However far they may have fallen short of the principles they were supposed to serve, the Renaissance popes undoubtedly left us in their debt as the patrons of some of the most impressive Western art. It may have been extravagance, driven too much by human vanity, but their patronage had an impact on the whole history of Western culture.

Pope Sixtus IV spent a fortune beautifying the centre of Rome, which involved widening streets and constructing new churches and other buildings. His bridge, the Ponte Sisto, still spans the River Tiber.

Pope Julius II was also a great patron of the arts. It was this pope who asked Donato Bramante to design a replacement for the old

POPE IMPRISONED

In modern times, we have tended to think of the papacy as "above" politics, to some extent protected by their holy status. However, given the political power they wielded, the popes of the Renaissance could hardly claim to be simply men of God. Clement VII paid the price for this: though a member of the Medici family, ironically, he was innocent and unworldly by the standards of the times. His attempts to steer a safe diplomatic course between the great powers ruling Europe led to a dispute between him and Charles V, King of Spain and Emperor of Germany. In 1527, Charles' forces invaded Italy and sacked Rome. Pope Clement was held prisoner at Castel Sant' Angelo, from which he escaped.

Above The massive walls surrounding Rome offered the city some protection, but it lacked defensive troops, as shown in The Sack of Rome, *a 1527 painting by Johannes Lingelbach.*

St Peter's Basilica, and work on the greatest church built for Christendom began only two years into his papacy, in 1505. (That the astronomical costs were to be met by the greatest granting of indulgences yet seen was a fact that would not be lost on the Church's critics.) Julius was also responsible for commissioning Michelangelo to paint the ceiling of the Sistine Chapel.

The Medici family were already famous for their artistic patronage when the son of Lorenzo (the Magnificent) de' Medici became Pope Leo X in 1513. "God has given us the papacy," Leo X is said to have commented to a friend. "Now let us enjoy it." Fortunately for posterity, his greatest indulgence was art, including history-making works by the Italian artists Michelangelo and Raphael. He encouraged music, too, and writers such as Erasmus.

Right Raphael's c.1517 portrait of his patron, Pope Leo X, captures the power and authority of the man.

THE POPE AND THE PAINTER

THE CEILING OF THE SISTINE CHAPEL IS UNIVERSALLY ACCLAIMED AS A MASTERPIECE. IT HAS ALSO BECOME THE ARCHETYPE FOR THE DIFFICULT RELATIONSHIP BETWEEN THE ARTIST AND HIS PATRON.

If its ceiling had never been painted by Michelangelo, art lovers would still flock to see the Sistine Chapel for its frescoes by other great artists, which include Raphael, Botticelli, Perugino and Ghirlandaio. (The chapel is in the Apostolic Palace in the Vatican City, the official residence of the pope.) Some splendid tapestries, designed by Raphael, formed part of the plunder during Charles V's sack of Rome in 1527, but they were later restored and replaced. Although named after Pope Sixtus IV, who had built the structure, the chapel really found its role under Pope Julius II, who made it a magnificent showcase for the creativity of Renaissance art.

MICHELANGELO'S TASK
Today too many tourists look past the myriad wonders that line the walls, with eyes only for the ceiling, 20m (65ft) above. Admittedly, it is an astonishing sight: the whole sweep of human existence, from Creation to Last Judgement, in crowded scenes that seem to boil over in their energy. Yet if the artist had his own way, this masterpiece would not have existed.

Above The Deluge and the Drunkenness of Noah *illustrates transgression and punishment, important themes for the ceiling as a whole.*

Born outside Arezzo in Tuscany in 1475, Michelangelo had never doubted his artistic genius, but he saw himself as a sculptor first and foremost. When, in 1505, Julius II asked him to design his tomb, it seemed to Michelangelo to be the dream commission. He dedicated himself to the creation of his life's masterpiece. However, he was not to be left to his work for long. To his growing annoyance, Julius enlisted his help for various odd artistic jobs – and began to talk to him about a commission for painting frescoes on the ceiling of the Sistine Chapel.

A CONTEMPORARY REPORT
Giorgio Vasari, gossipy chronicler of the ins and outs of the Italian Renaissance art scene, says that this idea was not Julius' own. Raphael and Bramante talked him into it

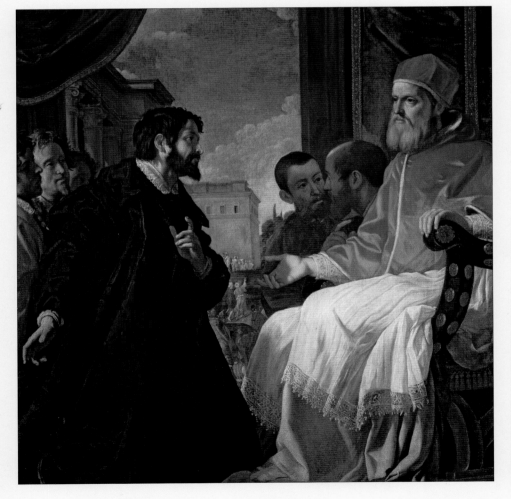

Left Michelangelo and Julius II had a fractious – but finally fruitful – working relationship. The artist and patron are shown together in this 16th-century painting by Anastasio Fontebuoni.

mischievously, he maintained. The former was the leading painter of the time, the latter, the star architect – and both were feeling threatened by Michelangelo's prodigious talents. The pope's preference for sculpture was well known to his contemporaries, and Michelangelo's supremacy in that arena was undisputed. By getting the artist weighed down in what appeared an impossibly ambitious task for such a comparatively inexperienced and reluctant painter, his rivals saw an opportunity to level the playing field. There was even the chance that Michelangelo would blunder the job so severely that his artistic credibility would become fatally compromised.

In truth, this version of events is unlikely, but Vasari was possibly briefed by Michelangelo himself, and his account may well reflect the workings of the artist's extravagantly suspicious mind.

A GRUDGING LABOUR

Suffice it to say that Michelangelo tried every means to avoid taking on the project. In the end, when it became clear that he was not going to be able to do so, he decided to get it over and done with as quickly as he could. It took him four years in all, which is an astonishingly short time considering the enormous scale of the work – and the fact that Michelangelo seems to have worked largely alone, apart from an assistant who mixed his colours. Even so, the pope apparently asked him constantly about his progress. *The Agony and the Ecstasy* was the name given to the famous film about this episode in the artist's life – *The Irritability and the Impatience* might have been a more accurate title.

However, if these frescoes were not a labour of love, this hardly shows in a spectacular work that takes the continuity of Christian faith and worship as its theme. Seen in the artist's all-encompassing view, the

Above An uncompromising Christ makes his appearance as Judge of the World: *the climactic, culminating scene of the Sistine Chapel ceiling.*

Old Testament is the prefiguring of Christ's New Covenant; Christ and his Church the fulfilment of what the prophets promised. However, Michelangelo is undoubtedly a man of the Renaissance in the way he places humanity at the centre of God's Creation and in his depiction of the beauty of the human form as the ultimate expression of God's greatness. These values are summed up in the outstretched hands in *The Creation of Adam*, where we see the moment in which God transmits life to man.

A RICH LEGACY

Michelangelo never did get the opportunity to finish Julius' tomb – a mausoleum was built when the pope died in 1513, but it was placed in the Church of San Pietro in Vincoli, rather than St Peter's Basilica. Little of it is Michelangelo's work – although the one piece that is, an awe-inspiring Moses, confirms that this would indeed have been a special work. It is hard, though, to feel that humanity has been the loser, as the Sistine Chapel ceiling is one of the most famous and most visited artworks in the world.

Below The ceiling's most celebrated scene is The Creation of Adam, *where God reaches out to Adam, giving him life.*

NEW HORIZONS

WITH OVERSEAS EXPLORATIONS AND SCIENTIFIC DISCOVERIES BEING MADE IN SUCH QUICK SUCCESSION, RENAISSANCE EUROPE WAS AN EXCITING – BUT ALSO CONFUSING – PLACE TO BE.

Above Despite hurricanes and mutiny, the Portuguese navigator Vasco da Gama was the first European to reach Asia by going around Africa's Cape of Good Hope in 1497/8.

As the ideological certainties of the preceeding centuries were dissolving, the Church was facing an uphill struggle to maintain its old intellectual authority. The medieval period was the "Age of Faith", when men and women never questioned their duty of subservience in God's order; but then neither did they doubt their centrality in his cosmos. Paradoxically, even as Renaissance humanism proclaimed the pre-eminence of humanity, that centrality was coming under threat.

As the voyages of the great navigators pushed back the boundaries of the world known to the Europeans, astronomers explored an expanding universe – which might not actually be revolving around the earth as had been thought.

THE AGE OF DISCOVERY

Europeans were aware that their continent did not encompass the entirety of the world: Africa lay just beyond the Mediterranean, after all. Spices and other luxuries were brought along the Silk Route from the East: moreover, Marco Polo had brought back tidings from China in the late 13th century. However, few Europeans had followed him. The Crusades had left the Middle East a hostile environment, and the trade that continued in this region was conducted mostly by middlemen.

The soaring costs of luxuries imported overland helped motivate the search for a sea route, which receieved a boost when Prince Henry the Navigator of Portugal established a naval academy *c.*1450. Portuguese navigators made great progress with Bartolomeu Diaz finding his way down the coast of Africa to the Cape of Good Hope in 1487, while Vasco da Gama pushed on to India a decade later.

Christopher Columbus, sailing for Spain's "Catholic Monarchs", had reached the Americas, making landfall on 12 October 1492. However, he remained convinced until he died that he had found the westerly route to East Asia. The Europeans came to realize that he had instead stumbled on a "New World" – and the Old World would never be the same.

"Who is my neighbour?" Jesus had been asked by the lawyer in Luke 10:29. That question was looking harder to answer now. Difficult as it had always been to live up to Christ's injunction to love one's neighbour as oneself, now it was a conceptual challenge, too. As Gomes Eanes de Zurara, the Portuguese chronicler, put it, how could those naked "savages", of whom navigators were now bringing home reports, really

Below Columbus' discoveries opened up a New World – and its peoples – to the Europeans, such as these Native Americans from Virginia, in this late 16th-century engraving by Theodore de Bry.

Above Christopher Columbus prepares to set out from the port of Palos, Spain, in August 1492, in this 19th-century fresco by Antonio Cabral y Aguado Bejarano.

be "of the generation of Adam"? Yet, shaped as they were, how could they not be? Were these strangers to be our neighbours? The European idea of the world was being challenged.

REVOLUTIONS

Things got worse. In 1543, Nicolaus Copernicus died. Only then was his great work *De revolutionibus orbium coelestium* (On the Revolution of the Heavenly Spheres) published. Copernicus, a priest himself and one of a family of priests and nuns, had received encouragement in his astronomical researches from fellow churchmen. However, he had been nervous about releasing his conclusions and no wonder: the Church had always followed the view of Aristotle and Ptolemy that the Sun and planets revolved around a stationary Earth. Copernicus believed the Earth and planets went around the Sun in what is called a heliocentric system.

The Church has since accepted this view, but at the time there were fears that it overturned scriptural accounts of the Creation and the cosmos – or that, if it did not, it would appear to do so. When, later in the century, another priest showed support for the Copernican theory, he was tried by the Roman Inquisition. Giordano Bruno faced a range of charges, from blasphemy to heresy: he was burnt at the stake in 1600.

Below Copernicus revealed that the true "harmony of the spheres" was produced by planets' concentric orbit around the Sun, shown in an illustration from Andreas Cellarius' Scenographia, c.1660.

GALILEO'S HERESY

In the early 17th century, another Catholic astronomer, Galileo Galilei, found his own observations lending fresh support to the Copernican case. For this backing he was tried by the Church for heresy in 1633 and was forced to recant his claims. In fairness, Galileo had found discreet support among leading clergy. Several members of the Church hierarchy had acknowledged their support for both the strength of Galileo's observational evidence and the force of his argument that Old Testament cosmology should be regarded more as poetry than as science. Cardinal Caesar Baronius spoke up for Galileo's ideas, joking that "The Bible teaches the way to go to heaven, not the way the heavens go." Officially, though, the Catholic Church had condemned such views.

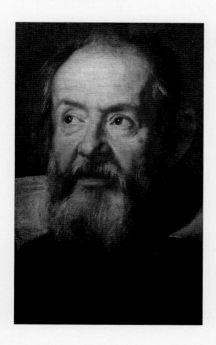

Above Galileo, shown in a 17th-century painting by the Flemish Justus Sustermans, fell foul of the Roman Inquisition with his public espousal of Copernican astronomy.

THE REFORMATION

IN THE EARLY 16TH CENTURY, MANY BELIEVERS TOOK THEIR STAND WITH THE REFORMER MARTIN LUTHER. IN ENGLAND, KING HENRY VIII PROCLAIMED HIMSELF HEAD OF THE CHURCH OF ENGLAND.

The great indulgence sale in which Pope Julius II set out to fund the rebuilding of St Peter's Basilica in 1505 caused outrage among many people across Europe. Indulgences had been around for centuries, of course, and, so too, had abuses of the system, which was widely satirized throughout the Middle Ages. It would be hard to claim that Julius' behaviour was much worse than anything that had occurred beforehand, yet it came after centuries of supposed reform – and at a time when the Church's overall authority

Below Martin Luther's famous protest is seen as the start of Protestantism. Ferdinand Pauwels' 19th-century painting shows the reformer nailing his "95 Theses" to the cathedral door.

was being questioned. In this climate, cleaning up such abuses within the Church's hierarchy was not going to be enough for the dissenters.

AUTHORITY IN QUESTION

In 1517, Martin Luther, priest and university professor, nailed his "95 Theses" to the door of the cathedral in Wittenberg, Germany, as a protest against the sale of indulgences. His arguments addressed the theology that allowed such indulgences to be awarded. The Church soon found itself under sustained attack from several sides. The scientific and intellectual tumults of the age had not left the Church unscathed. Moreover, the advent of the printing press had for the first time created what might be described as a reading

Above The pope acts as a moneychanger in the sale of indulgences and religious dispensations, as shown in this 1521 German woodcut by Lucas Cranach.

public – before the press, few books were available, and they could often be read only by the clerical elite, educated in Latin.

There was a growing sense that men and women might want to judge things for themselves. So Luther found a receptive ear when, questioning whether or not the Church hierarchy should even exist, he argued that every Christian believer should be his or her own priest. To further that end, he took an interest in making the Scriptures more accessible to the common people. The Church released a bull in 1520, proclaiming Luther's teachings as heretical, and only a few months later he was ex-communicated by the Church.

In 1522, Luther published his German translation of the New Testament, and William Tyndale's English Bible came out in 1525. The Church condemned both of these works: its fear was that the uneducated would be led astray without the interpretative assistance of their priests. However, to an increasing number of the educated middle class now emerging, especially in northern Europe, such thinking simply reeked of condescension.

KING HENRY VIII BREAKS AWAY

British coins still carry the abbreviation "F.D." after the name of the monarch: it means *Fidei Defensor*, or "Defender of the Faith". Ironically, this title was awarded by Pope Leo X to England's King Henry VIII in gratitude for his pamphlet, "A Defence of the Seven Sacraments" (1521), an eloquent response to Luther's criticisms. However, the failure of Henry's queen, Catherine of Aragon, to bear him a male heir led to a conflict between the king and Rome. Henry requested the annulment of their marriage, so he could wed Anne Boleyn, but it was rejected by Pope Clement VII. The king responded in 1532 by announcing that the monarch of England would also be head of the Church of England. He also confiscated the wealth in England's Catholic churches.

Right King Henry VIII puts Pope Clement VII in his place in an approving English satirical engraving of the 16th century.

A SPLIT FROM THE CHURCH

These Christians became known as "Protestants", which is from the Latin word *protestari*, or "to protest". Another meaning for *protestari* is "to affirm" or "to avow", which can also be seen as appropriate for a group whose members sought to seek guidance from the Scriptures, not from the Church's teachings. They believed that the individual person should have his or her own relationship with God. Catholicism never had the right to claim proprietorship over the "keys of heaven". What mattered was the divine Word, as revealed in the Scriptures, which it was the duty of every man and woman to read.

It could be argued that they took more moral responsibility for themselves, and there was no prospect of buying indulgences, or of pattering mechanically through a set of prayers. However, there was a tendency for a self-selecting community to feel that simply by proclaiming their belief they showed themselves to be "saved" and that there could be justification by faith instead of by works.

CALVINISM

In Geneva, John Calvin drew a distinction between the "Elect", marked out for salvation, and the rest, "pre-destined" for damnation by God himself even before they were created. That Calvin rejected Rome and all its works was just the start of his offence, as far as the Catholic hierarchy was concerned. His doctrines affronted their sense of Christian mercy and forgiveness. The way in which Calvin and his followers accepted the consignment of so many to eternal suffering seemed not just ungodly to them but inhuman.

Catholics believed that God, though indeed all-knowing, did not actually pre-ordain the sins of the souls he created, compromising their free will. This meant that the door to salvation would always be left open.

Below The Calvinist chapel contrasted starkly with the ornate Catholic churches of old. Such a chapel is shown in this c. 1565 painting by Jean Perrissin.

THE COUNTER-REFORMATION

IF THE REFORMATION THREW DOWN A CHALLENGE TO CATHOLICISM, IT WAS ONE TO WHICH THE CHURCH WAS ABLE TO RESPOND. AN URGENT EXAMINATION OF CONSCIENCE RESULTED IN FAR-REACHING CHANGES.

Above Convened in 1545, the Council of Trent instituted wide-ranging reforms within the Church. The members of the council are depicted in this 18th-century copy of a contemporary painting.

While the leaders of the Church were debating its institutional reform at the Council of Trent, a book was causing a stir in Italy. The story of *The Miraculous Life and Doctrine of St Catherine of Genoa* seemed somehow to speak to Catholicism in its crisis. It was hard to see why this should be so. Catherine had died half a century before, and she had barely registered on the consciousness of the Church in her own lifetime. Although nobly born, she had lost any status she had once enjoyed in a loveless, violent marriage; she had never taken orders as a nun. However, she had given her life to God, tending the sick and helping the poor. She had bravely faced the agonies of her last illness.

While Catherine's biography was being read in many hundreds of European homes, a very different life

was unfolding far away in a Spanish convent. There, Teresa of Ávila was experiencing visions of Christ that seemed to take possession of her whole being, body and soul. She described these visions in an autobiography in the 1560s.

PIETY AND PASSION

The experiences of Catherine and Teresa were their own, but they can still be seen as the products of their time. The Church had been ready for two such figures. Both were comparative outsiders and women, and were remarkable not for their services to the Church establishment but for the intensity – the drama, even – of their spiritual lives. Although Catherine's path to God had been arduous and difficult, it was one that many ordinary Catholics could imagine themselves following. Moreover, the passion shown in Teresa's faith proved to be deeply moving to the many people who had been finding themselves increasingly unmoved by a religious life that had become routine.

The Catholics who embraced these women might never have dreamt of turning to Protestantism – any more than Catherine or Teresa would have done – but they were responding to some of the same underlying discontents. Luther's call to Christians was based on rejecting a Catholicism of empty forms for

Left St Teresa of Ávila came to represent a new kind of spirituality – impassioned and intense – as shown in the Ecstasy of St Teresa, *sculpted by Gian Lorenzo Bernini in 1645–52.*

a deep and authentic spirituality, which was founded in the faith of the individual.

THE JESUITS

Among St Teresa's inspirations had been the Spiritual Exercises, written in the 1520s by Ignatius Loyola. This Spanish thinker is now famous as the founder of a great religious order, the Society of Jesus (*see* The Society of Jesus, *opposite page*), but he always saw faith as being rooted in the individual. His Spiritual Exercises could be seen as a sort of self-help course in Christian devotion, a regime of daily meditations and guided prayer. However, for Loyola, faith had to exist within the framework of the Church: his Exercises had to be followed under the guidance of a spiritual director.

The interconnection between the Church and its followers was perhaps the crucial insight that fuelled the Counter-Reformation. Personal faith, for all its passion, was ultimately

THE SOCIETY OF JESUS

Ignatius Loyola had been born into a noble family in the Basque country and grew up with an exaggerated sense of what that meant. Like the Spanish writer Cervantes' comic hero Don Quixote, he had been addicted to the chivalric romances of the Middle Ages, with their stirring stories of gallantry. On growing up, Loyola enlisted in the army, resolved to win renown in battle, but he found soldiering had changed over the centuries. Instead of exchanging courtesies with fellow aristocrats whom he fought with sword and lance, he lost a leg to a cannonball at the siege of Pamplona. However, even then, Loyola was not disillusioned: recuperating in hospital, he asked for romances to read. Since none were available, he had to make do with reading about the lives of the saints. They inspired him to fight spiritually for Christ instead – but, a true romantic to the last, Loyola conceived of his Society of Jesus, known as the Jesuits, as a chivalric company.

Above Ignatius Loyola thought of himself as a knight in the cause of Christ. This 1556 portrait of him is by Jacopino del Conte.

directionless; at the same time, a large institution could have no soul without developing a fruitful relationship with the individual. What was called for, and what Loyola's Jesuits were able to provide, was a Catholicism in which these two components went together hand in hand.

The same impulse can be seen in the life and work of St Francis of Sales who, in the early 17th century,

Above Pope Urban VIII takes part in celebrations marking the Jesuits' centenary, shown in this c.1640 painting by Andrea Sacchi, Filippo Gagliardi and Jan Miel.

decided to tackle the Reformation head on. As Bishop of Geneva, St Francis had his seat in the very headquarters of Calvinism, but he made it his mission to convert Protestants back to the Catholic Church.

ECSTATIC ART

THE COUNTER-REFORMATION GAVE RISE TO A NEW – AND INTENSELY
EMOTIONAL – AESTHETIC. ARTISTS AND ARCHITECTS LOOKED FOR WAYS
TO DRAMATIZE THE PASSION AND FERVOUR OF RELIGIOUS FAITH.

Art had been one of the issues at the heart of the Reformation controversy. Protestants tended to regard the Church's display of wealth with suspicion. While secular art was one of the vanities that the Christian should be forsaking, "religious art" was really a contradiction in terms. What mattered was the Word of God: sacred pictures and statues were seen as "graven images" that had been prohibited by the Bible, evidence of a heathen adoration of Our Lady and the saints. The Church's collection of artistic treasures was considered one of the trappings of the "Whore of Babylon", their worldly beauties temptations to the struggling soul.

So strongly did Protestants feel about this that some extremists went on sprees of iconoclasm (literally, "breaking images"), smashing statues and stained-glass windows and whitewashing over frescoes. Many English churches still bear the scars – the disfigured statues and blank replacement glass of Ely Cathedral's Lady Chapel are just one example.

Above *Flamboyant expressiveness was key to the Counter-Reformation aesthetic, as seen in this 17th-century painting,* The Virgin Appearing to St Peter Damian, *attributed to Pietro da Cortona.*

ON THE OFFENSIVE

The Catholic Church responded by redoubling its efforts and launched what amounted to a major artistic offensive. At the same time, religious art took on an altogether different emphasis. Where once the architect had been content to suggest the grandeur of God and the splendour of his Church, the feelings involved in religious faith were now incorporated into the designs. While the artist had previously been content to commemorate worthy piety and honest service, the new spirituality was passionate and intense. Agony, ecstasy, tragedy, triumph: all of these dramatic human sensations were harnessed by artists, designed to both arrest the attention and engage the emotions.

Left *Bernini's assistant, Giovanni Battista Gaulli, nicknamed "Baciccia", painted the Il Gesù ceiling, with much of his master's flair, in 1672–85. His work can be seen continuing past the boundaries normally created by barrel vaulting.*

The element of surprise was exploited: artists and architects of this period showed an unabashed instinct for showmanship. Rome's Church of the Gesù is a case in point. Its dazzling white façade is elegant in its symmetries, but the overall effect is simple, even chaste. This only heightens the shock (no other word would be appropriate) when the visitor pushes through the doors to be assaulted by the ravishing beauty – and riotous exuberance – that can be found within.

There are frescoes, columns, statues, pilasters and so much ornamentation in marble and gilt that the scene seems to dissolve into a single disorientating vision, with every line and plane being thrown into doubt. The previously used boundaries disappear, with artwork spilling spectacularly across the demarcations made by the barrel vaulting in the ceiling overhead. Christ and his angels appear to waft heavenward through the ceiling itself.

The overall effect is staggering. Whereas the statues and stained glass of the Gothic churches had been visual "books" for instructing the unlettered, this interior was intended to take the senses – and hence the soul – by storm.

HIGH DRAMA

Built toward the end of the 16th century, the Church of the Gesù is the spiritual headquarters of the Society of Jesus, whose founder St Ignatius has his tomb in a side chapel. Beside the altar there is an allegorical sculpture that stands almost 3m (10ft) in height, representing *Religion Overthrowing Heresy and Hatred*. This is the work of Pierre Le Gros the Younger, a French sculptor based in Rome. With the cross of Christianity in one hand and thunderbolts of heavenly anger in the other, Lady Religion stands slightly off balance as she kicks out at Heresy, represented as an ugly old man. Sent

Above *What might have been a stagey and schematic scene becomes a powerful human drama in the c.1696 statue* Religion Overthrowing Heresy and Hatred *by Pierre Le Gros the Younger.*

sprawling, he appears to be falling over the edge of the sculpture's pedestal: the rules of gravity do not seem to apply. Hatred, a withered old woman, flinches away in fear before Religion's righteous anger. At bottom left, a little angel busily tears up books by the Protestant writers Ulrich Zwingli and Martin Luther.

TOO SENSATIONALIST?

Le Gros' impressive creation is all but overwhelming in its impact. The technical accomplishment involved is also awe-inspiring. It is hard to believe that so obviously schematic a work could be so powerful or that such dynamism could be captured in a lump of cold stone. Yet the miraculous transformation of marble to moving drapery, warm flesh and breathing life seen in this statue was achieved even more astonishingly in Gian Lorenzo Bernini's famous *Ecstasy of St Teresa* (1645–52), another great sculpture of the period.

Inevitably, there have been some criticisms that such sculptures are shallow and sensationalist, being no more than exhibitionistic tours de force by artistic virtuosos. However, these objections miss the real point of the works. They were created by an avowedly evangelizing aesthetic that used sheer emotional force to compel an intensely personal engagement between God and the followers of the faith.

Below *Talented Renaissance sculptors could coax strong emotion out of cold stone. The 1674* Beatified Lodovica Albertoni, *by Gian Lorenzo Bernini, is a stunning example of the artist's work.*

TEMPORAL AUTHORITY

ALTHOUGH THE CATHOLIC CHURCH WAS GROWING IN POWER AND MAJESTY AT ITS CENTRE IN ITALY, ELSEWHERE IN EUROPE ANARCHY AND WAR MADE IT HARDER FOR THE CHURCH TO GAIN PRIMACY.

Above Posing with a miniature Aachen Cathedral in an 1825 painting by J.P. Scheuren, Emperor Charlemagne did much to build the bond between sacred and secular power in Europe.

The Church was a powerful force in Rome partly due to two donations. Although it was exposed as a forgery in the 15th century, for several centuries it was thought that the Donation of Constantine had given temporal authority over Rome and its possessions to the papacy. This misconception enabled the Catholic Church to wield an impressive political authority in Rome.

A different donation, made by the Merovingian king Pepin I, was genuine. He reigned over most of France and also over the western part of Germany and northern Italy. In 754, he had given the Church

Below Fought in 1634, the Second Battle of Nördlingen was one of many such encounters in the Thirty Years' War. The battle is depicted in a mid-17th-century painting by Pieter Meulener.

temporal authority over the Duchy of Rome and adjacent regions. Under the Holy Roman Empire, which was established by Pepin's son Charlemagne, these privileges had been upheld and even increased. By the time of Pope Innocent III in the 13th century, the Papal States embraced the whole of central Italy and much of the north-east.

These possessions brought the papacy not just great wealth but also considerable political power: great Renaissance popes such as Alexander VI and Julius II stood on an equal diplomatic footing with Europe's greatest monarchs. However, this was not always such a comfortable place to be, as Clement VII was to discover in 1527, when he was imprisoned during the sacking of Rome. Any idea that the Church was somehow spiritually removed, above politics

and the grubby machinations of international diplomacy, could not credibly be maintained when the pope was practically a king.

CONFLICTS OF INTEREST

Tensions between these secular and religious roles were inevitable. In the early 17th century, for instance, the papacy found itself in dispute with Venice. The city-state had remained Catholic in its allegiances; but, because its economy was based on trade, it was important it kept open its commerce with the Protestant states of central Europe. Also, as a republic, it did not see why it had to be in the control of an external authority.

In 1606, Pope Paul V placed the city under an "interdict" – this effectively excommunicated all its people, denying them the sacraments. This inflicting of a spiritual punishment for what amounted to a rejection of temporal authority was extremely unpopular, not just in Venice but elsewhere, too. While the modern opposition of Church and State had yet to be formulated explicitly, it is clear that, at some level, the pope was seen to be abusing his power.

THE THIRTY YEARS' WAR

Such goings on in southern Europe soon became parochial when the centre of economic power shifed to the north. Since Charlemagne had founded the Holy Roman Empire, Germany and Italy had been associated, but Germany was now emerging as the greater force. However, as far as the Church was concerned, it was a country that could no longer be relied on, because many of its rulers had embraced the Lutheran cause. The Peace of Augsburg in 1555 had only delayed the showdown struggle between the Catholic and Protestant principalities of what had been the Holy Roman Empire. By the time Pope Gregory XV was enthroned in 1621, war was under way in Germany. Emboldened by the spirit of the Counter-Reformation, the Catholic princes, supported by the Church, had seen their chance to sweep away the Protestant presence in their midst. However, power politics is never so simple: individual rulers pursued their own agendas, and peripheral states were drawn into a rapidly escalating conflict.

The war continued for 30 years, turning the heart of Europe into an inferno. Civilians bore the brunt as mercenary armies embarked on sprees of rape and pillage. One-fifth or more of Germany's people were killed, some slaughtered in the carnage, others caught up in the famines and plagues precipitated by the war and the large-scale population movements it brought with it.

A HOLLOW TRIUMPH

The Catholic powers won, having made significant territorial gains, especially in France. Humanity had, of course, been the loser. Paradoxically, so too had the Church. Under

the terms of the Treaty of Westphalia (1648), the principle of *cuius regio, eius religio*, or "whose region, his religion", was set in stone. Protestantism became embedded in several states and even Calvinism was protected.

The Catholic rulers, meanwhile, were ceasing to side automatically with Rome. They had their own strategic aims: France, for instance, had seen the war less as a religious crusade than as a way of containing the expansion of (Catholic) Spain. To thwart the Habsburgs, it had chosen to form an alliance with Protestant Sweden, ignoring the outrage of the pope. This, it seemed, was the shape of things to come: Catholic kings would support their Church when it suited them – and only then.

Above Urban VIII was pope through the most difficult period of the Thirty Years' War. A sculpture of the pope by Gian Lorenzo Bernini sits by his tomb in St Peter's Basilica, Rome.

Below Signed at Münster on 24 October 1648, the Treaty of Westphalia finally brought the hostilities of the Thirty Years' War to a close.

POLITICAL RAMIFICATIONS

THE REFORMATION REPRESENTED A SEISMIC SHOCK FOR THE
CATHOLIC CHURCH, BUT ITS REPERCUSSIONS CERTAINLY DID NOT
STOP THERE. ITS POLITICAL CONSEQUENCES WERE ALSO PROFOUND.

There was no separating the religious sphere from the political world in Renaissance Europe. The stability of the social order rested on the unquestioning respect for authority that the Catholic Church had previously enshrined. With division between the European states, the Church was losing ground.

SECULAR REACTION

Such a blow to the Church's standing compromised the security of the state as far as the Spanish establishment saw it. The Crown in Spain linked its authority explicitly with that of the Church: to be a Protestant was not just to be ungodly but also to

Below Half a millennium's Catholic culture came to an end with the Dissolution of the Monasteries. These ruins are all that is left of Fountains Abbey in Yorkshire, England.

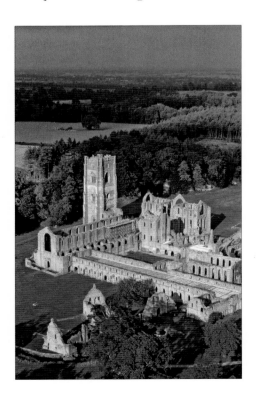

be un-Spanish. Given the extent of the country's empire in the Americas and the Pacific, the sponsorship of Spain was not to be dismissed lightly. Meanwhile, demands from French Protestants, known as Huguenots, for religious toleration were met with blunt refusal. In 1572, with an explosion of ferocity, thousands were murdered in the St Bartholomew's Day Massacre. While Henri IV had allowed the Protestants to practise their faith in peace, announcing the Edict of Nantes in 1598, that measure was rescinded by Louis XIV in 1685. The Huguenots saw their property confiscated and their churches closed down; more than 200,000 left the country to live in exile.

Northern Europe, which was the Reformation's heartland, was also a place of political division. In the Netherlands, which was a Spanish territory at the time, the people embraced Protestantism partly in a spirit of nationalist resistance.

REACHING A COMPROMISE

Germany, Luther's homeland, was in theory a single entity under the Holy Roman Empire, but it was actually a patchwork of smaller states. Protestantism had been embraced with genuine enthusiasm in many of these areas. Several local rulers aligned themselves with the new religion to build up their own political power. A compromise was reached in 1555, when the Peace of Augsburg originally agreed the principle *cuius regio, eius religio* ("whose region, his religion"). Where a ruler was Catholic, in other words, Catholicism should hold sway; but where the king was a Lutheran, that religion would prevail in his country.

Above Huguenots are being killed in the St Bartholomew's Day Massacre in this 19th-century painting by François Dubois.

Instead of a recipe for tolerance it was one for systematic persecution, as rulers cleansed their countries along sectarian lines. Catholic kings were by no means innocent, but in the Protestant states of Germany and in Switzerland, home of Calvinism, priests were burnt at the stake and Catholicism was suppressed.

DISSOLVED IN ENGLAND

The English Reformation had been opportunistic in its origins. King Henry VIII had not disagreed doctrinally with the Church; his conflict was based on his marriage status. Yet Catholicism quickly became identified as a threat to the country and its Crown, and its adherents punished its followers without mercy. Under the Act of Supremacy (1534), Henry became official head of the Church of England, and this allowed him to close Catholic foundations and confiscate their wealth. The Dissolution of the Monasteries shattered an ecclesiastical infrastructure that had been built up over centuries.

The Dissolution had opposition: 1536 saw the Pilgrimage of Grace – an uprising in Yorkshire (where there was to be a second rebellion, the Rising in the North, in 1569). Catholicism was reprieved in 1553, when Henry's daughter, Mary I, succeeded him and sought to turn the clock back. In the event, the wave of counter-repression she ordered against Protestantism succeeded only in seeing her branded with the nickname "Bloody Mary".

In 1593, Queen Elizabeth I, a non-Catholic, introduced legislation against "recusants" who refused to accept the authority of the Church of England. Those who remained Catholic included many of the country's leading families, especially in the north and the West Country. The father of William Shakespeare is believed to have been a recusant, and there has been speculation that England's greatest playwright was one as well.

King Philip II of Spain, Mary's widower, had supported his wife's mission to re-convert England. It was

Above *Protestant Elizabeth I sits in splendour before her Parliament. To her left stands Sir Francis Walsingham, a ruthless hunter of "recusants".*

with the intention of restoring Catholicism to England that, in 1588, he dispatched the Spanish Armada, hoping to invade the country. In the event, the *Armada Invencible* ("Invincible Fleet") was stopped by the English navy and dispersed by a "Protestant wind".

UNDERCOVER CLERICS

English priests were trained in continental seminaries and then smuggled back into the country. They slipped in disguise from one private house to another around the country to give Mass. It had to be held in secret because participants never knew when they might be denounced by a suspicious neighbour or a servant with a grudge.

Although a number of these houses had hiding holes for visiting priests, many were caught and executed. Typically, they were hanged, drawn and quartered. Ordinary Catholics were killed, too, but they were often tortured first in hopes that they would give up the whereabouts of other Catholics, particularly their priests. The missionaries were feared by the authorities, not just as religious dissidents but as enemy agents. It hardly helped that the headquarters of English Catholicism were abroad, at Douai in France, and Valladolid in Spain.

Above *A number of English houses had hiding holes, so priests could quickly be concealed from the authorities. This hiding hole is in the King's Room in Moseley Old Hall, Staffordshire.*

Below *The Michelade was a massacre of Catholics in Nîmes, after St Michel's Fair in September 1567. Franz Hogenberg captured it in this 16th-century painting.*

S.Catherina Ins

A WORLD RELIGION

The Catholic religion underwent a major cultural and geographical shift when a Middle Eastern sect became the European Church of Rome. As horizons widened, missionaries ventured out into the farthest reaches of Asia, the Americas and Africa, bringing the Word of God to some of the millions who had not yet heard it.

For a long time in Europe the idea of a godless universe had been – quite literally – unthinkable. In the 17th, 18th and 19th centuries, intellectuals, scientists and politicians began to place their faith in "reason". Christianity was so much superstition, said the rationalists, an instrument of oppression; the Church was a reactionary force. When two secularist ideologies – fascism and communism – plunged the world into chaos in the 20th century, the Church was caught up in the accompanying conflicts. Peace did return, at least for Western Europe and North America, where a new generation grew up in affluent societies. In the consumerist society, everything was a matter of choice – including religious belief and personal morality. Yet most of the world still lived in poverty and the Church had a duty to those people, too.

In the new millennium, Catholicism finds itself facing huge challenges, as it has throughout its history. Time and again, it has shown its capacity to recover from its setbacks and learn from its mistakes while holding firmly to its founding principles to be a guiding light of faith for a struggling world.

Above When the Europeans became established in the Americas, Catholicism quickly spread throughout Latin America. Sister Juana Inés de la Cruz, a Mexican poet, scholar and nun, was painted in the 17th century by an unknown Mexican artist.

Left European explorers introduce the Cross – and Christianity – as they come into contact with previously unknown civilizations in the New World. Théodor de Bry illustrated scenes of these meetings in his 1592 Americae Tertia Pars....

MISSIONS TO THE EAST

THE APOSTLES WERE THE FIRST CHRISTIANS TO SPREAD THE GOSPELS. FROM THE 15TH TO 17TH CENTURY, EUROPEANS BEGAN TO TRAVEL FARTHER EAST, WHERE THEY SPREAD THE MESSAGE OF THE CHURCH.

"Go therefore and make disciples of all nations…" was Christ's command (Matthew 28:19). To the apostles the missionary impulse was part of Christianity. They spread Christ's message through Syria and Asia Minor, and westward to Rome, the centre of an extensive empire. There was even a tradition that St Thomas carried the gospels to India. Christian communities thrived in Iraq and Iran, too, but in the 5th century their Church no longer recognized the authority of Rome when it embraced Nestorianism, a heresy that believes Christ is divided into two: the divine and the human. It was now time for missionaries to carry the gospels to the farthest corners of Asia.

CENTRAL ASIA

The willingness of the Mongols to adopt Nestorianism may have contributed to the rise of the legend of Prester John *(see right)*. In 1289, Pope Nicholas IV dispatched John of Montecorvino to take messages to Kublai Khan of China and other Mongol leaders. He was the first Roman Catholic missionary in China and translated the New Testament and Psalms into the Mongol language. Missionary work appealed to the enterprising spirit of the new Franciscan and Dominican orders, who sent missions to western and central Asia from the 13th century.

Above St Francis Xavier (1506–52) did more than anyone else to carry the Christian message to the East. This 17th-century portrait is by an unknown painter.

(see right)

PRESTER JOHN

By the 12th century, the failure of the Crusades and the growing strength of the Islamic world had left western Christendom in a state of demoralization. People were prepared to clutch at straws – even the legend that, somewhere in the East, there was a powerful empire ruled by a Christian king. Prester John had even written a letter, it was said, promising to come to Europe's rescue, attacking the Muslim enemy from the rear. So vague were the stories, and so inexact the geographical knowledge of Europe at this time, that Prester John's realms were variously reported as lying in Ethiopia and Central Asia. In 1177, Pope Alexander III went as far as writing a letter to Prester John seeking his assistance, but his messenger appears to have been lost somewhere in the vastness of Asia.

Below China's Mongol emperor Kublai Khan greets the Polo brothers on their visit to China. In this c.1412 illustration from the Book of the World's Marvels, *they receive a letter to deliver to the newly elected Pope Gregory X.*

SPREADING OUT

The missions into Asia were bold but small-scale ventures. Anything more was unrealistic, given Christendom's political and geographical situation. Europe was effectively "boxed in": by Islam on its eastern frontier, by Africa's Sahara to the south and by an apparently infinite Atlantic Ocean to the west. However, the Age of Discovery changed all that, opening a door upon a much wider world. This was a period between the early 15th century and the 17th century in which Europeans explored the oceans, seeking new trading routes. As these great voyages broadened horizons, they brought Christians into contact with nations which had never heard the Gospel Word.

The evangelizing impulse was never lost and found fresh impetus in the 16th century. The Counter-Reformation brought a new spiritual energy, with the Jesuits leading the way. St Francis Xavier founded a mission in Goa, on the coast of India, in 1542. The "Apostle of the Indies" went on to preach Christianity in Indonesia and, from 1549, Japan. The other orders were not idle: the Franciscans were by now well-established in Malacca and Malaysia, and Augustinian friars had a mission in the Philippines from 1565.

THE CHINESE ENDEAVOUR

The greatest challenge for the missionaries at the time was China, a vast and complex country that had an ancient history and strong religious traditions of its own. In 1552, St Francis Xavier was preparing to embark on another mission, this time to China, when he died on an island off Guangdong, on its southern coast. However, 30 years later, his fellow-Jesuits, Michele Ruggieri and Matteo Ricci, established their own mission in Beijing.

The Jesuits were under no illusions about the huge scale of the task that awaited them, and not merely

Above Many missionaries paid the ultimate price for their devotion to their religion. An unknown 17th-century Japanese artist illustrated Jesuits being martyred in Japan in 1622.

Below Jesuit missionary Matteo Ricci and scholar Li Paul Xu Guangqi became friends, shown together in this 17th-century engraving. They translated key works of Western science into Chinese.

because of the enormous population of the country. Chinese society was sophisticated and its sense of cultural identity secure. There could be no pretence that these were "savages" in need of civilization.

A CULTURAL EXCHANGE

The Westerners sought out the Chinese scholarly elite and, addressing them as equals, opened up a dialogue on just about every aspect of life and thought. In the process, they introduced the Chinese to the whole range of Western culture, from art and literature to mathematics and science. They earned the respect and trust of China's rulers — and several Jesuits were even given posts in the imperial administration. Many Chinese intellectuals willingly converted to Christianity.

Sadly, as time went on, dissension between the Jesuits and Franciscans ended up hampering the effectiveness of both. In 1644, moreover, Manchu invaders swept away the old Qing dynasty in China and inaugurated a new order that was far less tolerant toward foreign faiths.

MISSIONS IN THE AMERICAS

THE DISCOVERY AND EXPLORATION OF THE NEW WORLD DURING THE 16TH TO 18TH CENTURIES BROUGHT WITH IT THE DISCOVERY OF NEW NATIONS AND CULTURES — AND ANOTHER WAVE OF MISSIONS.

Above Fray Bartolomé de Las Casas (1484–1566) became Catholicism's conscience in the Americas, with his impassioned pleas for humanity toward the native peoples (artist unknown).

The newly discovered peoples of the Americas were the subject of an important debate held in Valladolid, at that time the capital of Spain, in 1550–1. Two Dominicans, Juan Ginés de Sepúlveda and Bartolomé de Las Casas, argued the burning question of the day. Were the native peoples of "New Spain" really men and women, like Europeans? They looked like humans, but they apparently went unclothed, like animals,

Below After Columbus' first landfall in the Caribbean, Christianity soon spread down through South America.

and their customs were alien to Europeans. Should they be treated as equals, or put under subjection?

There were good grounds for taking the latter view, Sepúlveda said. Had not Aristotle himself written that some peoples were by their very nature slaves, and needed to be subjected for their own good? On the contrary, Las Casas maintained. He believed that the "Indians" were entitled to exactly the same treatment as Europeans, but these rights were being scandalously ignored. Both in his Valladolid address and in a series of polemical writings on

the subject, Las Casas catalogued every kind of exploitation and abuse that the native peoples were being subjected to. From Columbus' voyages to the Caribbean islands to the conquests of Mexico and Peru, by Cortès and Pizarro respectively, the native peoples, including the Taino, Aztec, Maya and Inca, were harshly treated by the Spaniards.

NEW WORLD, NEW WAYS

Both sides of the debate claimed victory, but the controversy went on for years. The Church was divided:

Below Spanish conquistadors massacre the Inca after capturing their capital, Cuzco, in 1532. The event is captured in this 1602 engraving by Théodor de Bry from the Historia Americae.

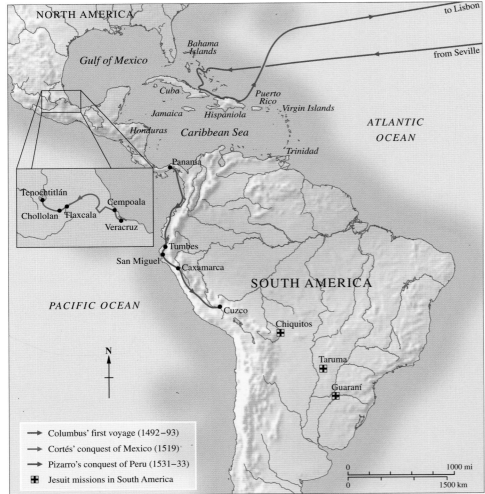

NORTH AMERICA

to Lisbon

Gulf of Mexico

Bahama Islands

from Seville

Cuba

Puerto Rico

Jamaica   Hispaniola   Virgin Islands

Honduras   Caribbean Sea

ATLANTIC OCEAN

Trinidad

Panama

Tenochtitlán

Cempoala

Chollolan   Tlaxcala

Veracruz

Tumbes

San Miguel   Caxamarca

SOUTH AMERICA

PACIFIC OCEAN

Cuzco

Chiquitos

N

Taruma

Guaraní

→ Columbus' first voyage (1492–93)
→ Cortés' conquest of Mexico (1519)
→ Pizarro's conquest of Peru (1531–33)
✠ Jesuit missions in South America

0   1000 mi
0   1500 km

in some places it had become an arm of oppression, while elsewhere it had become a fighter for the indigenous peoples and their rights. An encomienda system was established, in which Europeans took land for themselves, in effect enslaving its indigenous occupiers.

In theory expropriation came with a duty of guardianship. Some took this obligation seriously: the Society of Jesus led the way in trying to make the New World a better one. The Jesuits reigned over *reducciones* ("reductions") that covered most of what is now Paraguay, along with vast tracts in Uruguay, Brazil, Bolivia and Argentina. There they had the rights of the representatives of the colonial power. However, instead of enslaving the indigenous peoples, they settled them around their mission stations, giving them schools and establishing farms to teach skills in agriculture.

The Jesuits' approach could be accused of high-handedness, but their paternalism was preferable to the outrageous exploitation going on elsewhere. The indigenous peoples made it clear where their preferences lay, flocking to the *reducciones* in large numbers. Neighbouring colonists had no alternative but to improve conditions radically if they were to have any hope of hanging on to their subject Indians. As Bishop

Above Made for Aztec offerings, this casket cover found a new role in the Christian liturgy. It is now kept in the Templo Mayor Museum, Mexico City.

of Michoacán, Mexico, from 1537, Bishop Vasco de Quiroga introduced a system of his own. Along with a foundation in Christian education, he had "his" indigenous people taught craft skills, each village being given a different speciality, from weaving and metalwork to pottery. His subjects even had a degree of political autonomy.

Not surprisingly, such utopias sparked controversy and other Europeans lobbied against them. There, lobbying was so successful that in the middle of the 18th century the Jesuits were formally expelled from Spanish and Portuguese America.

NORTHERN MISSIONS

Along North America's eastern sea coast, the main colonial power was Protestant England – with the exception of the colony of Maryland, which was founded by Catholic refugees from the same country in 1633. Farther north, in Canada, the French were in charge. Their intrepid priests played a major part in exploring the interior, venturing up the St Lawrence River to the Great Lakes.

The west coast, though nominally Spanish-ruled, saw little sign of European settlement at first. It was not until the 18th century that encroachments were made down the coast by Russian traders, which created nervousness at home.

In 1769, Father Junípero Serra set out from San Diego with the Spanish soldier and official Gaspar de Portola to build a chain of missions. They founded 21 missions in total, up and down what became known as the *Camino Real*, or "Royal Road". Junípero Serra set up nine of them personally, travelling an estimated 38,000 km (23,600 miles) in the 15 years before he died.

Below A figure of founder Junípero Serra stands before the Mission Church of San Diego de Alcalá, San Diego – California's first church, established in 1769.

THE HURON CAROL

In 1643, the Jesuit priest and explorer Jean de Brébeuf wrote his "Huron Carol", referring to God as Gitchi Manitou – the great deity of the Algonquin people – and giving the Christmas story a new setting in Canada.

Twas in the moon of wintertime when all the birds had fled
That mighty Gitchi Manitou sent angel choirs instead;
Before their light the stars grew dim, and wondering hunters heard the hymn:
Jesus your King is born, Jesus is born, in excelsis gloria…

Within a lodge of broken bark the tender babe was found;
A ragged robe of rabbit skin enwrapped his beauty round
But as the hunter braves drew nigh, the angel song rang loud and high:
Jesus your King is born, Jesus is born, in excelsis gloria.

THE GOSPEL IN AFRICA

THE STORY OF CATHOLICISM IN AFRICA IS TIED UP INEXTRICABLY WITH THAT OF COLONIALISM IN THE 16TH TO 19TH CENTURIES. TODAY'S CHURCH MUST LOOK BACK ON A RECORD THAT IS DECIDEDLY MIXED.

Exploration of sub-Saharan Africa by Europeans came late. Prior to the 19th century, Africa was for the most part considered only as a place for buying slaves. Sea captains of different nations sailed down the hazardous coast, but generally stopped for only as long as it took to load up with their helpless human cargo. Then the ships set off again – some sailing to the plantations of British North America, but many to the New World colonies founded by Catholic Portugal, Spain and France.

Although this slave trade was a monstrous business, at the same time it was immensely profitable, and the American venture was central to the strategic aims of these great powers. So closely were the clergies

Above To many Africans, such as these slaves photographed in Zanzibar in the 1880s, the Christian message could give meaning to a downtrodden life.

of these conquering countries involved in this project that few seem to have questioned its moral implications for Christians. Although a succession of popes did condemn the trade – such as Gregory XIV in 1591, Urban VIII in 1639 and Benedict XIV in 1741 – with so much at stake they failed to make their message heard.

AFRICAN CATHOLICISM?

Some efforts were made to preach the gospel: indeed, Portuguese priests made great strides in the Kingdom of Kongo (which included much of what is now Angola, as well as parts of the modern Republic of the Congo and Democratic Republic of the Congo). However, in a spirit of tolerance, the Church allowed the incorporation of elements of African religion, and soon Kongolese Catholicism was barely recognizable as Catholicism at all. At the start of the 18th century, for example, a woman named Kimpa Vita mobilized the masses, claiming to be the reincarnation of St Anthony of Padua. She insisted that Christ had been Kongolese, and that St Anthony was a deity alongside him.

Left A contemporary cartoonist addressed the imperial ambitions of the wealthy businessman Cecil Rhodes: Europeans were tripping over one another in their "Scramble for Africa".

A SPIRITUAL SCRAMBLE

The exploration of Africa's vast interior began in real earnest in the 19th century, when it was still seen as a "dark continent" by many Catholics. Nevertheless, the Church was equipped: a wealth of missionary experience had been acquired in the Americas and Asia, and in 1622 a co-ordinating Congregation for Propagation of the Faith had been founded. (In the 20th century this was renamed the Congregation for the Evangelization of Peoples.)

The Catholic Church had competition. The most famous British traveller in Africa, David Livingstone, though today generally thought of simply as an explorer, was just one of many highly motivated Protestant missionaries. Livingstone's explorations, moreover, are difficult to disentangle from the wider British effort to colonize the African interior. Cecil Rhodes' boastful ambition to build a railway "from the Cape to Cairo" typified the colonialists' view of Africa as a blank canvas on which to capture their grand designs. Catholic and Protestant missionaries had brought with them, along with the gospels, an unmistakable message of European supremacy.

ABUSIVE RULERS

The presence of the French Archbishop Charles Lavigerie in Tunisia, a French statesman once remarked, "is worth an army to France". Lavigerie had once said, "as missionaries we also work for France". Where Catholic powers prevailed, the Church often acted as an arm of the colonial administration. Terrible atrocities were committed when the French ruled in what is now the Republic of the Congo.

Still worse was the holocaust committed by Belgium's King Leopold II in the south in his so-called Congo Free State, now the Democratic Republic of the Congo. Mass rape and mutilations were carried out by troops to discourage dissent and boost productivity on the plantations and in the mines. By 1908, up to ten million citizens had been killed by the troops.

These missionaries were fighting a (sometimes unseemly) turf war, analogous to the great colonial "Scramble for Africa" itself, where Europeans competed to claim African territories as their own in the late 19th century until World War I. In some places this had tragic consequences. In Buganda, the main kingdom of what is now Uganda, the local king – a despot of hideous cruelty – kept himself in power by playing Protestant and Catholic missionaries off against one another.

The Catholic missionaries at work in Africa belonged to the Society of the Missionaries of Africa, which was better known as the "White Fathers". The society was founded in 1868 by the Archbishop of Algeria, Charles Lavigerie, who was originally sent to work in French North Africa. The distinctive white garb for which its members were named was modelled on the robes of the desert nomads. Also in the vanguard were the priests of the Society of African Missions, which was founded in 1850 by Bishop Melchior de Marion-Brésillac.

Below French White Fathers pose amid a congregation of local converts outside their traditionally built mission in Urundi (now Burundi) in the years before World War I.

Above A French missionary bulletin of 1878 sends an uplifting message to encourage generosity from back home.

THE ENLIGHTENMENT ASSAULT

FROM THE SCIENTIFIC, INTELLECTUAL AND POLITICAL COMMUNITIES CAME TRENCHANT CRITICISMS OF CATHOLICISM: SOON THE CHURCH WAS STRUGGLING TO HOLD ITS OWN.

The Copernican revolution, in which the 16th-century astronomer claimed that the Earth revolved around the Sun – which meant that the Earth was not, as the Church believed, the centre of the universe – had been only a foretaste of the formidable challenges to come. In 1687, the English scientist Sir Isaac Newton published his *Philosophiae Naturalis Principia Mathematica* ("Mathematical Principles of Natural Philosophy"). While Newton was not an atheist, it was hard to resist a feeling that his far-reaching theories could be suggesting a universe that was governed not by God but instead by mathematics and science.

Below Sir Isaac Newton's theories transformed perceptions of the universe – and, inevitably, of God. This 1687 frontispiece is from the Philosophiae Naturalis Principia Mathematica.

The English poet Alexander Pope, a Catholic, had no difficulty in reconciling his fellow countryman's new science with his deeply felt religious views on the Creation:

Nature and Nature's laws lay hid
* in night,*
God said "Let Newton Be!" and
* all was light.*

In a perverse sort of way, it probably helped that the poet was living in a Protestant country in which anti-Catholic feeling was rife. Catholics had even been blamed for the Great Fire of London of 1666. Under the Penal Laws then prevailing, the poet was not allowed to live in London, but had been forced to take a house outside the city, at Twickenham. Pope's faith was almost certainly steeled by the humiliations he had to undergo.

Above Brilliant in his thinking, vicious in his satire, Voltaire became the scourge of the Catholic Church. This 1811 portrait is by Jacques Augustin Pajou.

THE FRENCH "INFAMY"

In Catholic France, the situation was different: there the Church was closely identified with a monarchical establishment that oppressed the poor and repressed all freedoms. In such circumstances, young intellectuals were more predisposed to regard religion as superstition and to dismiss the liturgy and sacraments as mumbo-jumbo. These intellectuals, and soon the general French public, were quick to adopt anything that seemed to offer a rational explanation for the wonders of creation. *Écrasez l'Infâme* ("Crush the Infamy") became the war cry of François-Marie Arouet, who is much better known today by his pseudonym Voltaire. The infamy he was referring to was the alliance of the Church and Crown against freedom, justice and the rule of reason.

Voltaire was the most famous of the 18th-century *philosophes*, whose work extended far beyond the realm of philosophy as normally understood into just about every area of

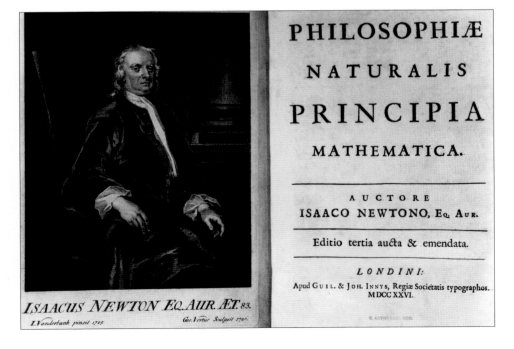

ISAACUS NEWTON EQ.AUR. ÆT. 83.

I. Vanderbank pinxit 1725.   Geo. Vertue Sculpsit 1740.

PHILOSOPHIÆ

NATURALIS

PRINCIPIA

MATHEMATICA.

AUCTORE
ISAACO NEWTONO, Eq. Aur.

Editio tertia aucta & emendata.

LONDINI:
Apud GUIL. & JOH. INNYS, Regiæ Societatis typographos.
MDCCXXVI.

life and politics. Other prominent *philosophes* included Jean Jacques Rousseau, who said "Man was born free, but he is everywhere in chains". These metaphorical chains were not just those of tyranny but of public institutions, even of morality: children were born innocent, he said, then corrupted by their education. He also claimed that no institution did more to blight the pure soul than the Catholic Church, which was steward of a morality that destroyed the very virtue it claimed to save.

COMPREHENSIVE CRITIQUE

By 1750, under the leadership of Denis Diderot, a group of scholars worked on a great, multi-volume *Encyclopédie*. This was to be a "systematic dictionary of the sciences, arts and crafts", and it was to be drawn up, said Diderot, "without regard to anybody's feelings". They wanted to include every branch of human knowledge.

The Encyclopedists questioned Christianity's most fundamental tenets, arguing that theology was just another branch of philosophical investigation, and that religious doctrine should be submitted to the same sort of scientific testing as anything else.

Above An intimidating late 18th-century French illustration shows an army sapper and a revolutionary exhorting "Liberty, Equality and Fraternity…Or Death".

REVOLUTION

The *Ancien Régime* was finally swept away in 1789. Although the French Revolution did bring a sort of freedom, it also brought its own infamy, too, in the Reign of Terror. The new Republic was defiantly secular in its approach. The idea of *laïcité* was established: France was to be run by and for lay people, not the clergy. Christian values were to be replaced by those of *Liberté*, *Egalité* and *Fraternité* ("Liberty", "Equality" and "Fraternity").

Religion was not actually outlawed (as it would be later in some communist countries), but it was restrained and no longer enjoyed special favours from the state, and it was certainly not allowed to set the tone for ruling the country. Catholicism was given the same slightly grudging tolerance as the Protestants: gone were the days when its cardinals and bishops were active participants in the government of the state.

In the absence of any real understanding developing between the state authorities and the Church hierarchy, the concept of "Ultramontanism" soon grew among the Catholics in opposition to *laïcité*. *Ultramontane* literally means "beyond the mountains": the range in question was the Alps, on the other side of which lay Italy and Rome. French Catholics were told by their clergy that, whatever their state might try to tell them, its authority was trumped by that of their Church.

THE IMPERIAL CATECHISM

In 1804, Napoleon Bonaparte overthrew the revolutionary state, installing himself as Emperor Napoleon I. However, any hopes that the Church might find its old authority restored were cruelly dashed. On the contrary, the ultimate ignominy came in 1806 with the "Imperial Catechism", rewritten by the emperor himself and imposed on France's Catholic educators:

What are the duties of Christians toward those who govern them, and in particular toward Napoleon I, our emperor?

Christians owe the princes who govern them – and we in particular owe Napoleon I, our emperor – love, respect, obedience, fidelity, military service, and the taxes levied for the preservation and defence of the empire and of his throne…

Right *Pope Pius VII and his legates suffered the indignity of being obliged to be present during Napoleon's Coronation in 1804. The pope is the subject of this 1807 painting by Jacques Louis David.*

HOLDING BACK THE TIDE

THE 19TH AND 20TH CENTURIES SAW THE CHURCH ENGAGED IN AN INCREASINGLY FRANTIC REARGUARD ACTION TO DEFEND ITSELF AGAINST FREE-THINKING LIBERALISM AND REFORM.

The Church's identification with its conservative causes was to leave a lasting legacy that would be difficult for Catholicism to live down. It has always insisted that it was no enemy of science or reason – only to the "rationalism" that makes an idol out of human thought. Although Catholicism would come to terms with the discoveries of Newton and his successors, during the 19th and early 20th centuries the clergy often found itself acting as apologists for scientific backwardness, which only seemed to confirm the charge that the Church stood for superstition.

CONSERVATIVE VIEWS

It hardly helped that the most obvious product of the "Enlightenment" had been bloody revolution in Catholic France. The ferment there

Above Giuseppe Garibaldi led the Italians in their 19th-century struggle for nationhood. Most could not understand why the Church opposed this movement.

was viewed with consternation in other countries, whose rulers saw their own authority under threat. Rome's unease at the rise of *laïcité* may have been understandable, but it also placed the Church firmly in the camp of the conservatives.

Under the guise of resisting revolution, the Habsburg rulers of Austria, for instance, set themselves against every kind of social change. Backed by the state chancellor and Emperors Francis I and Ferdinand I, they refused the ambitions expressed by subject populations for national sovereignty – not just in Hungary and the Balkans but also in Italy.

THE *RISORGIMENTO*

In 19th-century Italy, a resurgence of national feeling, known as the *Risorgimento*, arose among a people who had for too long lived under Austrian domination. The movement received no encouragement from the Church, which saw any attack on authority as corrosive of its own. Conservatives in Italy shared

Left By the 1860s, Pope Pius IX was completely dependent on French backing. He blesses Bourbon troops outside the Royal Palace in Naples in this 19th-century painting by Achille Vespa.

this view, but as time went on and the ferment rose, theirs became an increasingly unpopular position. Because the Vatican identified itself more closely with despotic rulers in Vienna than with the overwhelming will of the Italian people, it severely damaged the Church's reputation.

Pope Pius IX still insisted that, as pope, he was temporal ruler of the Papal States, the central Italian territories traditionally under the rule of the Vatican. Increasingly, the Italians disagreed and, in 1849, Pius IX needed military intervention by France's Emperor Napoleon III to secure his position. Repeatedly, he had to rely on the support of foreign imperialists – sometimes the French, sometimes the Austrians – against the Italian freedom fighter Giuseppe Garibaldi and his patriotic Red Shirt army. Finally, in 1871, papal rule in the city of Rome came to an end. The tiny enclave of the Vatican apart, the former territories were annexed by the state. Rome was now the capital of a unified Italy.

SET AGAINST CHANGE

The episode left a bad feeling behind. Liberals saw the Catholic Church not as a champion but as the foe of freedom; workers saw it as the enemy of change. The Church itself

had been wounded and it lashed out, responding to threats to its authority with a flurry of authoritarian pronouncements. Already, in 1864, Pius IX had issued his Syllabus of Errors, a catalogue of new liberal ideas that he felt were damaging. He summed up by rejecting any notion that the Church should take steps to accommodate "progress…liberalism, or recent civilization". (Called in 1869 to ratify the Syllabus, the First Vatican Council sprang another surprise when, in a statement of 1870, Pius IX proclaimed the dogma of papal infallibility, claiming that popes are divinely guided, so infallible.)

In Protestant-dominated countries, the Church's political position might be more subtly nuanced. For the most part, though, it was identified with conservatism. In Spain, the poor knew better than to look to the Church for support in bettering their situation. They had learned to see the black-garbed priests as scavenging, flesh-eating *corvos* ("crows"). When Civil War broke out in the country in 1936, priests and nuns were massacred in their hundreds.

Below General Franco greets some of his clerical supporters with studied courtesy: relations were not quite so warm between Spain's working people and the Church.

THE WORKERS' POPE

Despite the conservative stand taken by the Church, there was one pope who held a different view. Pope Leo XIII's proclamations on behalf of the world's workers would put many a socialist to shame. He himself was anything but a democrat, putting down one dissenting adviser with an unceremonious *Ego sum Petrus* ("I am Peter") but he saw the need for radical change, if only to rescue the status quo.

In his 1891 encyclical *Rerum Novarum* ("Of New Things"), he addressed the condition of the working classes as one of the great issues of the age. Reasoning that failure to reform would lead to revolution, he called for far-reaching changes in the way modern economies were organized. Denouncing the glaring gulf between rich and poor, he spoke out in support of workers' rights and trade unions, expressing his sympathy for those who went on strike to ensure the welfare of their families.

Above Addressing the Church – and looking to the future – Pope Leo XIII is shown recording his blessing by phonograph in this 1903 print by Achille Beltrame.

DARK TIMES

WITH FASCISTS MARCHING ON ROME ITSELF, NAZISM ON THE RISE IN GERMANY AND COMMUNISTS IN EASTERN EUROPE, THE FIRST HALF OF THE 20TH CENTURY WAS A TUMULTUOUS TIME FOR THE CHURCH.

In 1922, cheering crowds turned out to welcome Benito Mussolini and his "Blackshirts" – the nickname given to members of his Fascist paramilitary – as they made their triumphal entrance into Rome. However, Italy's senior churchmen were rather more muted in their welcome: they had little in common with the young thugs who were following *Il Duce* ("The Leader").

Even so, there was something in Fascism to which these churchmen found themselves able to respond: its reverence for authority, its avowed respect for established tradition. Years of liberalism, with its vaunted freedoms, had brought the country only incessant labour unrest and public immorality – and a press that held the Church and all its values in clear contempt. Worse still, there was evidence everywhere in Europe of the

Below Cardinal Pacelli, the future Pope Pius XII, signs the infamous Concordat with Germany in 1933 on behalf of Pope Pius XI.

advances made by the Communists, who had already established an atheistic state in the Soviet Union.

SENT BY PROVIDENCE

The Holy See had refused to acknowledge Italy's annexation of Rome in 1871, spending the next six decades in denial – and in endless wrangling with successive governments. Under the terms of the Lateran Treaty of 1929, Mussolini agreed compensation for the loss of the old Papal States. Mussolini had discarded the Catholicism of his upbringing, and privately despised it, but he also recognized its importance to the conservative Italians he wanted on his side. He made Catholicism the state religion, made criticism of the Church a crime, outlawed divorce and made religious education mandatory in all schools. All state legislation would be reviewed to ensure that it conformed with canon law. Pope Pius XI declared that *Il Duce* was "a man sent by providence": there were some

Above At the height of his power, Benito Mussolini visits the Vatican in 1932 to meet Pope Pius XI and his officials.

who did not question the moral price the Church would have to pay for this arrangement.

Both Mussolini and Hitler were lapsed Catholics. Like Mussolini, Hitler saw Christianity as a weaklings' creed, but he recognized the value of good relations with the Church. Pius XI signed a Concordat – an agreement between pope and secular ruler on religious matters – with Hitler's government in 1933, eager to have another ally in resisting the Communist advance.

However, the Nazis made more uncomfortable bedfellows than the Italian Fascists, especially when the ugliness of their anti-semitism became evident to all. In 1937, the pope sent out a letter to be read in German churches. *Mit Brennender Sorge* ("With Burning Sorrow") contained a forthright condemnation of the Nazis' attacks on the Jewish population as well as their attempts to establish control over the Catholic Church within Germany.

STANDING BY?

The ensuing Holocaust was one of the darkest episodes of modern history, and the Church is one of many institutions that emerged with its reputation tarnished. Pope Pius XII, who succeeded Pius XI in 1939, has rightly been condemned. Broadly speaking, any good he did was done by stealth; he was guarded in his public denunciations. He had a love for Germany and its culture (earlier in his career he had been Papal Nuncio – akin to a Vatican ambassador – in the country) and held Hitler's populism in deep disdain. Yet the uncomfortable fact remains that what really excited his moral ardour was the threat represented by Communism in the East. Nazism appeared to him to be the lesser of two evils.

While acknowledging Pius XII's attempts to relieve the plight of World War II's victims, including Jews, some critics charge him and the Catholic Church with a failure of moral leadership. Although there were heroic efforts made by individual priests and nuns, these critics saw the institution as being weak during the war. There was general approval within the Church when, on a visit to Jerusalem in 2000, Pope John Paul II made a heartfelt apology to the Jewish community.

AFTER THE WAR

Fascism had been all but vanquished by the end of World War II, though authoritarian governments endured for a few decades in Spain and Portugal. The Communists gained a strong hold in Eastern Europe, putting the Church there in a weak position. After the lessons of the Nazi era, the Church became outspoken critics of Communist oppression. Yet the Church's earlier links with Fascism meant some Western liberals remained sceptical that the Church's opposition to Communism was truly rooted in principle.

CATHOLICS UNDER COMMUNISM

The Soviet Union had been among the victors of World War II in 1945. With Communism's avowedly materialist principles, there was no place in the Communist scheme for the religious institution. In Russia itself, the established Church had been Orthodox, and its more independent-minded clergy was quickly hounded out by the Soviet authorities. A collaborationist congregation was created in its place. In the Ukraine, Romania and Czechoslovakia, Catholics were forced to join this officially sanctioned pseudo-Church in the tens of thousands, though many of the faithful continued their accustomed worship underground. In Poland, too, a "silent Church" clung on precariously in a mutually uncomfortable co-existence with the Communist state.

Above Pope John Paul II visited the "Hill of Crosses" in 1993. On several previous occasions the Soviet authorities had attempted to remove this massive memorial to the Lithuanians' faith.

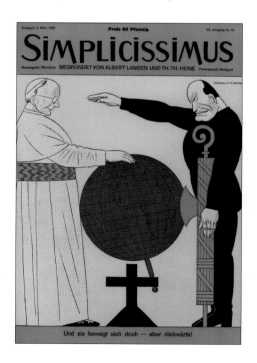

Above Pius XI and Mussolini agree upon the Lateran Treaty, as illustrated on the cover of the March 1929 edition of Simplicissimus, *a liberal satirical magazine published in Germany.*

THE MODERNIZERS

THE 20TH-CENTURY POPES BROUGHT ABOUT RELIGIOUS CHANGES, AND THEIR REFORMS TRANSFORMED BOTH THE PROFILE OF THE CHURCH AND THE EXPERIENCE OF BEING CATHOLIC.

Though Pope Pius XII's pontificate is considered controversial now, in the 1950s his authority seemed impregnable. The pope who had brought the Church through World War II was naturally regarded with gratitude – his own personal role, and that of his Church, were as yet unexamined. In the Cold War climate, moreover, his uncompromising stand against Communism had won him respect well beyond the boundaries of his Church. As the first "media Pope", he became known to the world through newspaper pictures, television appearances and radio broadcasts. Within the Church, his power was immense, even by papal standards, because he had surrounded himself with elderly and like-minded cardinals.

A CONVENTIONAL CHOICE

Pius XII's unabashedly conservative Church was a frustrating place for the young and the radical. When he died in 1958, some saw a chance to advance reforms. However the cardinals elected Angelo Roncalli, Patriarch of Venice, to serve as Pope John XXIII. The new pontiff was already 77 years of age, and in a long career he had shown himself a meek and unquestioning servant of his

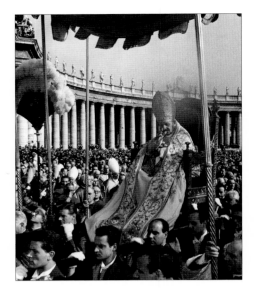

Above Pope John XXIII blesses the crowd as he is carried in to officiate at the opening of the Second Vatican Council in 1962.

superiors. He was not the breath of fresh air the progressives had been wanting. All the evidence indicated that this was what had recommended him as Pius' replacement: he could be relied upon not to rock the boat.

The only issue that appeared to stir up any passion in the new pope was that of Christian unity. John mourned the gradual disintegration of Jesus' Church down the centuries and longed to build bridges with Catholicism's "separated brethren". Hence, he arranged meetings with England's Archbishop of Canterbury and had talks with representatives of other churches. This, though clearly a worthy cause, was hardly an exciting one. There was no immediate prospect of real change.

SECOND VATICAN COUNCIL

John XXIII's dream of Christian unity has remained elusive to this day. However, it was to have one very real and immediate consequence.

Left The scene inside St Peter's Basilica at one of the climactic moments of the Vatican Council. Pope John is enthroned beneath the baldacchino in the distance.

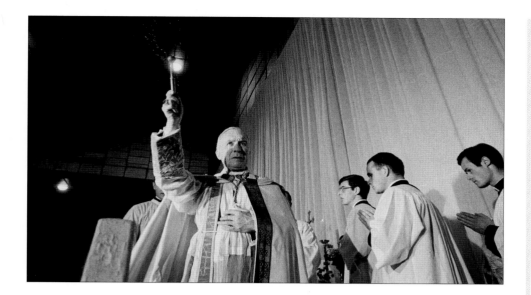

In 1962, the pope called together the Second Vatican Council, and from then onward the Catholic Church would never be the same.

Although some critics might see the changes as superficial, the Council re-emphasized (in some ways reinforced) the hierarchical nature of the Church. At the same time, it acknowledged the need for "top-down" directives to be supplemented by "bottom-up" reform. There was a new tone of openness, and a genuine receptiveness to criticism – lay observers, including women, were encouraged to be involved. Ordinary Catholics were to play a fuller part in the conduct of their faith, and there was to be a drive to make the Scriptures more widely available in the vernacular (people's own languages).

Measures were also taken to give lay Catholics a greater role in the Mass, and in the liturgy, too, there was to be a vernacular component. This process was completed under Pope Paul VI in 1969 when, along with a full transition to the vernacular, the practice of having the priest face the congregation when saying Mass was introduced. Previously, he had faced the altar, which was typically at the eastern end of the church, in the direction of Jerusalem (just as Muslims orientate themselves

Above In 1976 the reactionary Archbishop Marcel Lefebvre defiantly celebrated the traditional Tridentine Mass. This celebration has been encouraged by recent popes.

toward Mecca for daily prayers). Worshippers might feel a sense of wonder at being present for such a sacred ritual, but the new Catholicism wanted to draw parishoners in to make them feel involved.

THE BACKLASH
The Second Vatican Council was in many ways less far-reaching than has since been assumed. Issues that were already becoming controversial, such as contraception and divorce, were mostly unaddressed. Yet Catholicism now had a completely different feel, and Pope John XXIII's critics were in no doubt that there was substance in the changes.

The French Archbishop Marcel Lefebvre led a movement within the Church to return to the old ways and the Tridentine Mass, the Latin liturgy approved by the Council of Trent in the 16th century. Ultimately, he had to lead it from outside the Church. In 1988, he was excommunicated by Pope John Paul II (himself a conservative) after the archbishop consecrated four new bishops without official sanction.

POP RELIGION
The new-look Catholicism was taken up with great enthusiasm, its advent corresponding with that of the 1960s' pop culture. Guitars strummed, children acted out scriptural scenes and kisses of peace were freely exchanged at self-consciously informal "folk masses". This occurred nowhere more so than in Liverpool, England, home of the Beatles and, from 1967, of a thoroughly modern "Metropolitan Cathedral of Christ the King". Although shaped like a stylized crown with a spectacular stained-glass lantern, its circular ground plan was inclusive and democratic. Poet Roger McGough caught the mood with his poem of dedication: "O Lord on Thy New Liverpool Address". The poem has a reference to a priest wearing the cassock, concluding that if it is worn, "Then let's glimpse the jeans beneath".

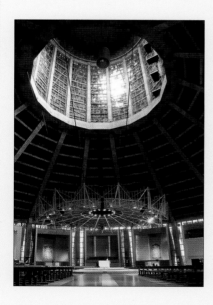

Above In the modern design of the Liverpool Metropolitan Cathedral, stained-glass windows in the roof complement the colourful lighting that highlights the altar.

THE CHURCH MILITANT

THE CHRISTIAN'S DUTY TO HELP THE POOR IS CLEAR, BUT JUST HOW FAR THE CATHOLIC CHURCH SHOULD BE PREPARED TO GO WAS A QUESTION RAISED BY LIBERATION THEOLOGY.

In the 20th century, many South Americans lived in deprivation and from this arose Liberation Theology. It challenged the Church to make the spirit of the Beatitudes prevail by helping to overthrow established political and economic systems.

> He has put down the mighty from their thrones and exalted those of low degree;
> He has filled the hungry with good things, and the rich he has sent empty away.

This is one of the most remarkable passages in the gospels, from Mary's "Magnificat" (Luke 1:46–55).

Below Óscar Romero, Archbishop of San Salvador, was an advocate for the poor and victims of the country's civil war. He was killed in 1980 while celebrating Mass.

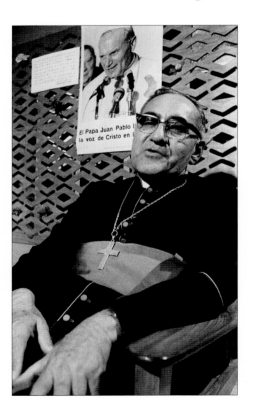

Our Lady's words celebrate the Christ who, for all his divine greatness, would keep company with prostitutes and lepers. He is the Christ who, for all his gentleness and his injunction to "turn the other cheek", was moved to violence by the sight of the moneychangers in the Temple. Further, he is the same Christ who, while summoning all to salvation, warned the rich young man that it is easier for a camel to pass through the eye of a needle than for a rich man to enter the kingdom of heaven.

MARX'S "GOSPEL"

Was Jesus not just a saviour but also a revolutionary? It is easy to see why many should have thought so, although it is harder to see what form a real-world Christian revolution would actually take. Especially given that, from the 18th century onward, the revolutionary orthodoxy has seen religion not as an aid to humanity but as a great part of the problem. Karl Marx, the renowned founder of Communism, notoriously saw religion as "the opium of the people" – though to put this into context, it should be noted that he was writing at a time that was lenient toward taking recreational drugs. His suggestion that religion was "the sigh of the oppressed creature", "the heart of a heartless world" showed at least a degree of sympathy for those who sought religious comfort. However, he saw that comfort as illusory.

Marx's later followers took a less nuanced view and settled into the conviction that religion was a cruel hoax designed to reconcile the people to their oppression. In the false hope of salvation hereafter, they

Above Russia's Bolsheviks expressed their antagonism to religion in no uncertain terms, shown in this 1930 print by Achille Beltrame, from the Italian newspaper La Domenica del Corriere.

would accept their lot on the earth: a dismal status quo was thus perpetuated. It was not difficult to find supporting evidence, not just in the sufferings of the world's poor but in the cosy relations between religious leaders and those who held great political power.

20TH-CENTURY RADICALS

That the Church might be letting down the poor had, of course, occurred to many in its history. Even in the 19th century, Pope Leo XIII had met the labour movement halfway with his *Rerum Novarum*, a letter that addressed the condition of the working classes. However, in the 1960s, radicalism was present around the world: this was a time of student sit-ins and anti-war demonstrations. African Americans (as well as Catholics in Protestant-dominated Northern Ireland) marched in the thousands to demand their civil rights; there were general strikes and student riots in France. The aims of the activists might have been vague, but the mood of rebellion was infectious, and many Catholics – the young in particular – felt they should be making their own contribution to the "struggle".

SOUTH AMERICAN LIBERALS

In Latin America, many millions were living in abject poverty while a helpless Church hierarchy looked on. By contrast, the leftists were able to report real achievements. In 1959, Fidel Castro, Che Guevara and their guerrilla army overthrew a repressive regime in Cuba. As proclaimed by Gustavo Gutiérrez, a priest from Peru, Liberation Theology called for a Catholicism that, not content with promising salvation in the next life, would do whatever it took to bring about revolutionary change in this one on earth.

There is no doubting the movement's sincerity in trying to improve the living conditions of the South

Below Pope John Paul II listened to a speech made by Daniel Ortega, leader of the Sandinistas, when the pontiff visited Nicaragua in 1983.

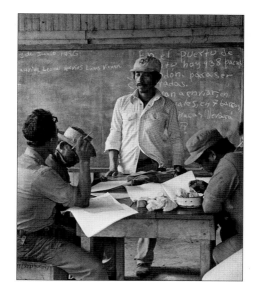

Above Many Catholics reasoned that Christ would have approved of the Nicaraguan Literacy Campaign run by the Sandinistas, but the Church took issue with the Sandinistas' wider aims.

American people – or, for a time, its real significance. Thousands of priests, nuns and lay Catholics were inspired by the Liberationist message, and several important Catholic figures died for their beliefs. Archbishop Óscar Romero, who had led the popular opposition to El Salvador's oppressive military regime, was gunned down at the altar as he was saying Mass on 24 March 1980. Catholic clerics were well represented among the Sandinistas, who came to power in Nicaragua in the 1980s, including the famous poet-priest Ernesto Cardenal.

However, it was inevitable that the hierarchy of the Church would look askance at such developments, and not only through ingrained conservatism. Liberation Theology failed, as the Marxists would say, because of its contradictions. Despite certain common aims, the marriage of Communism and Christianity was always going to be problematic given the former's refusal to acknowledge the existence of a spiritual dimension. No one could see this more clearly than Pope John Paul II, who had experienced the tyranny that resulted when Communism set out to establish heaven on earth.

CAMILO TORRES

"If Christ were alive today, he would be a guerrilla," claimed Camilo Torres. Born in 1929, and a priest since the early 1950s, he had become disillusioned with the Church's failure to relieve the sufferings of the poor. Deciding that radical action was needed – even violent action if need be – he went as far as enlisting with his country's Marxist guerrillas. The ELN (*Ejército de Liberación Nacional*, or National Liberation Army) was engaged in open war with the Colombian government. However, Torres was killed in 1966 during his first operation with the ELN, becoming the Liberation Army's most famous martyr.

THE PEOPLE'S POPE

TODAY'S PAPACY HAS BEEN INFLUENCED LARGELY BY ONE PARTICULAR POPE, JOHN PAUL II – THE CHARISMATIC HOLY FATHER WHO BECAME A FATHER FIGURE FOR THE WORLD.

Although the final decades of the 20th century posed new challenges for the papacy, the development of modern technology had presented unprecedented opportunities as well. Pope Pius XII was recognized around the world thanks to television and press images. Pope Paul VI, the first pope of the jet age, was able to embark upon important foreign tours. However, where these previous popes had more or less uncomfortably gone through the

Below A "rock-star" reputation was in many ways ill-suited to a deeply serious, spiritual man, but there was no denying John Paul II's popular appeal. Here he blesses the crowd at St Peter's in 1982.

motions as media performers, Pope John Paul II took to stardom with the utmost ease.

AN UNEXPECTED STAR

This was in some ways surprising. John Paul II was the first non-Italian pope in half a millennium and he was an intensely serious, scholarly man whose faith had a strongly private, even mystical aspect. The youngest of three children, he was born in Poland in 1920 and named Karol Wojtyla. He had been afflicted in childhood by the loss first of his mother and then of a much-loved elder brother. He'd lost all his family members before he became a priest. In youth, Wojtyla had been a brilliant student

Above At the time when Karol Wojtyla was a young seminarian in 1942, in Kraków, Poland, the city was under German occupation.

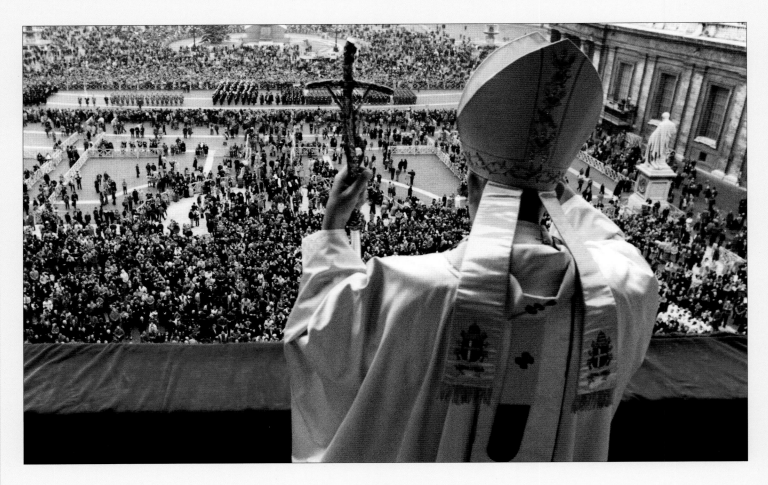

and, more broadly, an intellectual. He was fluent in a number of languages, was widely read, and wrote both poems and plays himself. Wojtyla loved sport, too (playing as a goalkeeper for a soccer team), and had a sociable side that he was able to draw on when making his public appearances as pope.

FREEDOM AND OBLIGATION
His early bereavements apart, the great formative experiences in Wojtyla's life were those of totalitarianism in two different forms. As a young seminarian he lived underground for months at the time of the Warsaw Uprising against the Nazis. He pursued his vocation under Communism and rose to the position of Archbishop of Kraków in a Church that had to keep silent if it was to continue to exist. Wojtyla emerged as an individualist – not an egotist, but a firm believer in the importance of the private voice of conscience. He could never accept that this should be subordinated either to the "collective will" of the Fascists or to the "dictatorship of the proletariat" of the Communists.

It might be expected that John Paul II had little time for Latin America's Liberation Theology. However, those who dismissed him as an old-fashioned reactionary were wide of the mark. He was generally more than ready to condemn the Western powers when the occasion demanded. He was forthright in denouncing the invasion of Iraq in 2003. He was also withering in his assessment of the capitalist system, which he considered was responsible for intolerable economic inequalities and which encouraged a consumer culture that exercised a tyranny all its own.

However, this prophet of freedom had managed to disappoint Western liberals by his refusal to give ground on such issues as contraception, divorce and same-sex marriage. He could never accept that human sexuality could diverge from Church norms. Likewise he resisted calls for married clergy and women priests, reforms that might seem commonsensical to others. He argued that the Church was not just an institution to be brought up to date like any other, but one that was bound by laws lain down by Christ himself.

WIDESPREAD POPULARITY
It was gall to his more progressive critics that John Paul II was so unrestrainedly loved, not just among Catholics but beyond the Church. This was attributable not only to his immense charisma but also to his instinctive gifts as a communicator. He visited 129 different countries, taking his papacy to ordinary people around the world. Wherever he went, he kissed airport runways, cuddled babies, showed himself to vast crowds in his "popemobile" and said Mass to millions at a time. Conservative as his attitudes may have been, his belief that ordinary Catholics should have access to his papacy was entirely in the spirit of the Second Vatican Council.

THE SAINT MAKER
John Paul II's enthusiasm for canonizing saints has been derided (it was said that he beatified more men and women than all his predecessors put together, but incomplete records make this hard to establish). This may speak of an old-fashioned view of Christian heroism, but at the same time it also suggests John Paul II had an utterly modern understanding of media culture. Not since the early Middle Ages had there been such an interest in icons – even if the new ones were singers, models and sports stars. In giving the peoples of the world new saints, the pope was giving them exemplars from their own cultures whose courage and commitment they could aspire to and emulate.

Most of all, his supporters looked up to John Paul II himself, beyond any doubt one of the most popular popes in modern history. This was the man who, as Ireland's young people chorused in their hundreds of thousands at the open-air Mass in Dublin's Phoenix Park in 1979, appeared to have "the whole world in his hands".

Above Pope John Paul II was identified with Solidarnosc *("Solidarity"), the free trade union that helped bring down Communism in Poland and beyond.*

Above John Paul II rides in his popemobile during a tour of the United States in 1995. Everywhere he went he drew enormous and ecstatic crowds.

REACHING OUT TO OTHER FAITHS

IN THE 20TH AND 21ST CENTURIES, THE CATHOLIC CHURCH HAS BEEN EXCHANGING VIEWS WITH OTHER CHRISTIAN COMMUNITIES – AS WELL AS WITH LEADERS OF THE DIFFERENT GREAT WORLD FAITHS.

With the exception of Poland, the Christians of Eastern Europe have historically looked to the Orthodox Church rather than to Rome. The Polish people have always defined themselves against their Russian neighbours (who were often also their oppressors). Their Catholicism was a matter not just of religious faith but of patriotic pride. Yet the Poles were Slavs as well, and Pope John Paul II, who always remembered his Polish origins, was mindful of that ethnic inheritance. The desire for reconciliation with the Eastern Church ran as deep in his heart as, so many years before, it had run in that of Pope John XXIII.

Above An ecumenical service at Paris' Notre-Dame Cathedral is celebrated by leading Catholic prelates alongside an Orthodox metropolitan bishop (centre) and a Protestant minister (right).

A DIVISIVE DIPLOMAT?

In more than a quarter of a century as pope, John Paul II accomplished much for the Catholic Church, but his particular dream of reconciliation had to be deferred. It has been suggested by his critics that the pope himself had created part of the problem: his own instinctive authoritarianism rendered impossible the soft approach that would have been required. It was the same, some critics believe, with his approach to the Church of England, whose doctrine was not so far removed from that of Rome's. Although the decision of the Anglican Church to ordain women priests caused dissension between the two communities, liberal critics have claimed it was a matter in which a less stubborn pope would have found some type of accordance.

On the other hand, John Paul II's charisma propelled Christianity back on to the front page of many of the big newspapers, reminding jaded Westerners that religion could still hold relevance in a modern society. Elsewhere, adherents of the other world religions could find evidence

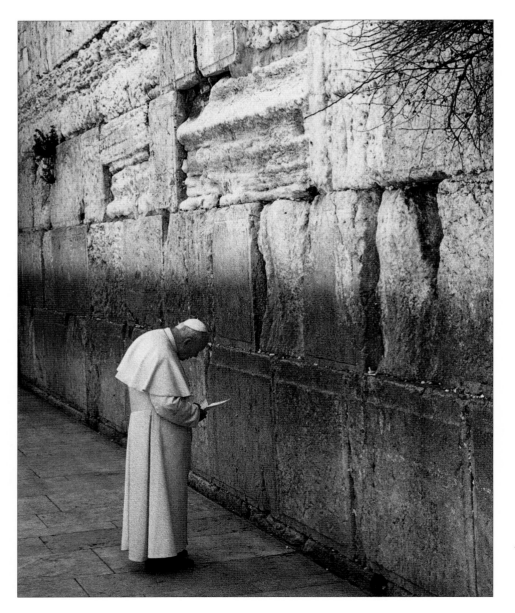

Left In 2000, Pope John Paul II visited Jerusalem and the Western ("Wailing") Wall, where he begged forgiveness on behalf of the Catholic Church for centuries of anti-semitic persecution.

in his energy and enthusiasm that the Christian West was not entirely sunk in cynicism and apathy.

Ultimately, his love of humanity – and the love that humanity felt for John Paul II – made him a more effective bridge-builder than anyone might have expected. His impetuous style certainly helped his cause. A more cautious man might never have dreamt of making his historic (and, at the time, controversial) visit to the Auschwitz concentration camp in 1979. The first-ever papal visit to Israel followed in 2000, where John Paul II's heartfelt apology for centuries of Christian persecution of Jews opened the way to a new era of discussion and co-operation.

COMMON CAUSE

There are, of course, limits to how much progress can be made between different communities. The Catholic creed professes that it is the "one" true Church. John Paul II's successor, Pope Benedict XVI, maintains that, while other Christian Churches and non-Christian religions may offer aspects of the truth and may thereby be instruments of salvation, the

Above In 2006, Pope Benedict XVI met the Orthodox Patriarch in Istanbul, Turkey. It was his first official visit to a Muslim country.

whole truth is to be found only in Catholicism. Although working hard to find points of contact, he has left no doubt that he sees the world's other faiths as fundamentally misdirected, for all their undoubted honesty and zeal.

If anything unifies the world's religions, as far as Benedict XVI is concerned, it is their rejection of modern secularism and the culture it has fostered. The consumerist irreligion, he argues, says that everyone should live as he or she chooses, without reference to any higher laws. Believers of every faith have not just the right but also a duty to make a common cause against this "dictatorship of relativism".

THE POPES AND THE IMAMS

When the Ayatollah Khomeini died in 1989, Pope John Paul II called for his achievements to be reflected upon "with great respect and deep thought". There have been more effusive eulogies, perhaps, but the pope's was still strikingly cordial in the circumstances. John Paul II had refused to lend his authority to other Christian leaders who earlier that year had expressed sympathy with the leader of Islam in Iran. The Ayatollah had issued a *fatwa* – a religious decree – calling for the killing of author Salman Rushdie for writing his novel, *The Satanic Verses*, which was said to be blasphemous. The years that followed would find John Paul II continuing his dialogue with Islam's leaders, and in 2000 he became the first pope to pray in a Muslim mosque.

Contact with the Muslim world has continued during the papacy of Benedict XVI, despite the offence caused by his quotation from an anti-Islamic text by a medieval writer in a talk at the University of Regensburg, Germany, in 2006. Relations soon recovered, and in 2008 Muslim scholars were invited to a joint seminar with Catholic thinkers held in Rome.

Right Pope Benedict XVI clasps hands with the head of Turkey's Religious Affairs Directorate after talks about Catholic–Islamic relations and terrorism.

NEW CHALLENGES

THE NUMBER OF CATHOLICS DECREASED IN MANY WESTERN SOCIETIES DURING THE LAST CENTURY. THE INFLUENCES OF CAPITALISM AND CONSUMERISM ARE PERHAPS PARTLY TO BLAME.

In recent years, the Church has seen its support ebb away in the advanced industrialized societies. In the mostly Protestant and Anglo-Saxon countries of Europe, Catholicism was long regarded as a peasant creed that was associated with "backward" regions: southern Italy, Spain, remote parts of France – and pre-eminently with Ireland. Yet Christ had always loved the poor, and the poor had always reciprocated, offering their sons and daughters into his service.

CHANGING SOCIETIES

When a previously poor region begins to thrive, no one mourns the passing of mass poverty – however, economic development often brings

Below Sardinians process through their village as they have done for so many centuries, but can Catholicism offer more than history and local colour?

problems as well as benefits. In some places, historical tendencies can be traced. For example, that most Spaniards say they no longer bother to go to Church may reflect resentments dating back to the Franco era and beyond. Italy is another country in which the Church's most visible adherents recall an authoritarian past. Although comparatively few Italians have rejected the Church outright, it is for many now no more than a part of their cultural rituals – baptisms, marriages and funerals – and is otherwise ignored.

Increased wealth has resulted in population shifts, which have created their own impact. The old over-crowded communities of the cities have been dispersed to suburbs, where more secular attitudes have prevailed. One example can be seen in St Anthony's parish in Jersey City in New Jersey, USA. In the 1950s, a

Above Falling levels of attendance and reduced collections have sent parochial incomes tumbling, a formidable challenge for the Church in the new century.

typical Sunday Mass was attended by around 10,000 Christians; today, less than 300 people turn out.

The problem has partly been that there is so much more to do at weekends for families with cars and money to spend – but who have precious little quality time together. Although Christ was clear in his insistence that material wealth was not spiritually enriching, Catholics are not immune to the attractions of material consumerism. Nor are they immune to the consumeristic attitude that encourages people toward the various spiritual options available these days, from yoga and meditation to New Age practices.

A DECLINE IN CLERGY

Something is clearly wrong with the Church when Ireland is running out of priests. In 2007, 166 priests died, while only 9 new ordinations were made. The priests constitute an ageing population: in the next generation, their numbers are bound to fall further. This is because as societies prosper, life expectancy increases and families feel more secure. With this security, families tend to have fewer children. This has happened in many industrialized countries, regardless of religious culture. It has certainly occurred in Ireland, which has enjoyed great economic success in recent decades. The youths who would once have gone into the Church no longer exist in such abundance, and they have other life choices and distractions. Ireland faces the kind of administrative adjustments with which Catholics in the United States and Great Britain have become familiar, with small groups of priests and lay helpers taking charge of sprawling parish clusters.

NEW OPPORTUNITIES

The difficulties can hardly be denied, yet given the age of the institution, talk of doom and gloom is misplaced. In 2,000 years, Catholicism has come through many more challenging times. Despite all its claims for apostolic continuity, the Church has shown the capacity to reinvent itself again and again down the centuries.

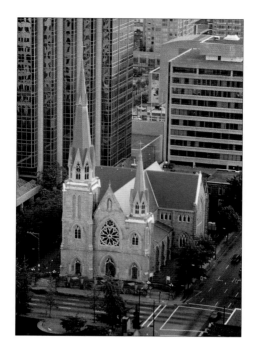

Above Once Vancouver's Holy Rosary Cathedral dominated the skyline. Today the Christian message risks being lost amid the pressures and distractions of modern life.

Below A businessman finds comfort confiding with his priest in the confessional, something that many middle-class Westerners have decided is not for them.

That it will have to do so again has become clear, with its great structures perhaps learning to accommodate a more administratively flexible, "small is beautiful" community-based system. There could be scope for lay Catholics to play a far greater role in their local communities, which has been an official goal ever since the time of the Second Vatican Council.

THE SINS OF THE FATHERS

The Church has admitted it has not always been worthy of its members' trust. Catholics have been rocked in recent years by a series of allegations of sexual impropriety on the part of members of its clergy. From the mid-1980s onward, a series of scandals in the United States, Ireland, Australia and other countries focused attention on alleged sexual abuse of young people by diocesan priests and members of the religious orders. In some cases the Church hierarchy was accused of attempting to cover up accusations, and even of moving sexual abusers away from one scandal and into a position where he or she could offend again.

In the United States, the Church made financial settlements of $2 billion to victims of sex abuse in the past 60 years. In the largest settlement, in 2007, the Archdiocese of Los Angeles paid $660 million (£324 million) to settle 508 cases of alleged sexual abuse.

Pope Benedict XVI has departed from this shameful stance. He has gone out of his way to meet members of victims' groups and to express his shame and sorrow on behalf of the Catholic Church.

FACING COMPETITION

IN TODAY'S SOUTH AMERICA AND AFRICA, THE CATHOLIC CHURCH IS BEING CHALLENGED BY OTHER CREEDS THAT MAY APPEAR MORE ENERGETIC, AND MORE IMMEDIATELY RELEVANT TO PEOPLE'S LIVES.

As recently as a generation or so ago, South America was one of the bastions of world Catholicism, a region consecrated to Christ and the Virgin Mary, utterly loyal to the pope. The idea of a Protestant Brazil or Chile was practically unthinkable. Catholicism was in the culture, in the air the people breathed.

Nevertheless, Pentecostalism has spread like wildfire throughout the region in recent decades. This new form of Christianity first appeared in the United States at the beginning of the 20th century. Rooted in a range of different Protestant churches, Pentecostalism is a faith of enthusiastic evangelism that demands that the believer be born again in the Holy Spirit – just like the disciples at the first Pentecost.

AN ALTERNATIVE CREED

The explanations given for such a quick expansion in South America vary. Pentecostalism is strongly emotional in its emphasis, which offers the individual Christian a spiritual (or, perhaps, merely psychological) high. Catholicism has always tended to distrust this type of extravagant emotionalism. Yet the importance of the ecstatic sense of self-worth it brings to the Pentecostalist convert can hardly be exaggerated. However, in some ways, it is the logical outcome of the attentions given by dedicated missionaries, hard at work for decades among poor people who may well feel that their traditional religious leaders have often taken them for granted.

Some South Americans have pointed to the remoteness of a conservative clergy, reluctant to involve itself with the problems of the masses. Others have seen the failure of ideologically driven Liberation Theology to see the poor as real people. Either way, the Protestant missionaries have made huge strides.

By 2005, an estimated 13 per cent of Latin America's huge population had embraced Pentecostalism; that is, 75 million out of 560 million people. This overall figure conceals the fact that there are areas in which Catholicism has been in headlong retreat. In some of Rio de Janeiro's poorest districts, Protestant chapels now outnumber Catholic churches in a ratio of seven to one.

Above A worshipper is energetically welcomed to a Pentecostal congregation in Rio de Janeiro. Latin Americans have been flocking to the new chapels in their thousands.

A PLACE OF SAFETY

In some areas, politics have certainly played a part. For example, through the many long years of vicious state repression in Guatemala, courageous priests and nuns made a stand against the military, which also made them targets. The conspicuously apolitical stand of (overwhelmingly American) Pentecostalist missionaries made their church a refuge from the violence and turmoil of the time. Middle-class Guatemalans, who were instinctively uneasy at the thought of any association with the leftists, have turned to Pentecostalism in large numbers. Today about 20 per cent of the population now considers itself Protestant; that figure rises to almost one-third among the urban middle class.

COMPETITION FROM ISLAM

In West and Central Africa, the main competition is not from Pentecostalism but from Islam. This is not surprising since Islam's history in the region is at least as long as Catholicism's. Muhammad's faith was first brought south across the Sahara by

Left Pentecostalism is not just for the poor. These bourgeois Brazilians have crossed the ocean to be baptized in the sacred waters of the River Jordan.

desert traders; nomadic tribes thereafter carried it farther to the south. A kind of frontier has long existed across this part of the continent, with – broadly speaking – Islam to the north, Christianity to the south. In reality, this border has been highly porous, with any number of communities to be found on the "wrong" side, and with close contacts, even family relations, between the two.

MODERN RADICALS

Peaceful co-existence has until recent history been maintained, but the emergence of Islamic fundamentalism has altered the dynamics. With its agenda being as much political as religious, radical Islamic groups have engaged in direct competition for converts with Catholicism, and their evangelization has to some extent paid off.

Conflict has flared as well, most famously in the Sudan, whose Islamic Khartoum government has for years been at war with the Catholic communities of the south. Elsewhere, too, there has been trouble, most notably perhaps, in parts of Nigeria, where attempts have been made to introduce the full rigour of Sharia law.

RESPONDING TO CHANGE

Ultimately, the only way for the Catholic Church to respond to such changes will be to change itself, while staying true to the central principals of so many centuries. Rome may remain its centre, but a Eurocentric Church will hardly be able to provide Catholicism with the worldwide guidance and support it needs. The ethnic mixture of the hierarchy has already been transformed by the addition of new African, Asian and

Right Followers of Islam gather to pray outside the main mosque in Asmara, Eritrea. Islam is on the rise across much of North and Central Africa.

South American faces, and more changes may occur in the years to come. It would seem strange indeed if the first great world religion were unable to meet the challenge of globalization. Despite its past difficulties, the Catholic Church appears well placed to face the future.

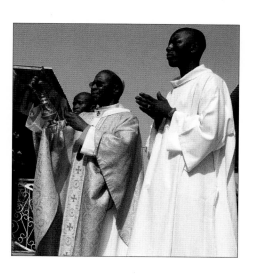

Right Théodore-Adrien Sarr celebrates Mass after being made a cardinal by Pope Benedict XVI in 2007. Senegalese Muslims also joined in acclaiming the new Cardinal.

CATHOLIC DOCTRINE

As the early Catholic Church grew in numbers, it struggled to express it teachings to its followers, many of whom were poorly educated. In a confusing time when there were conflicting ideas about God, the Catholic Church had to present an official source for its followers, and leading Church members formulated Catholic doctrine. This "deposit of faith" is at the core of the Church's teachings and provides Christians with an understanding of the mysteries of Catholicism, including the Trinity, original sin and salvation. Today's Catholics draw on this rich, religious tradition.

A sculpture on the south portal of the western façade of Chartres Cathedral in France depicts several accounts of Jesus' childhood, including the Presentation in the Temple and the Nativity.

THE MYSTERY OF FAITH

As the nascent Catholic Church began to develop its doctrines in the first centuries after Christ's death, it was faced with many challenges, including persecution, the difficulty of communicating abstruse concepts, such as the Trinity, to an uneducated and superstitious populace, and the constant threat of heretical beliefs and teachings. Such challenges forced early ecclesiastics and Catholic theologians to be vigilant and proactive as they formulated and disseminated Church doctrine.

The early Church councils acted as both the universities and the senates of the Church to standardize beliefs and promulgate them as law. The early Church was blessed with a number of brilliant early thinkers such as Sts Augustine, Athanasius, Jerome and Thomas Aquinas, whose devotion to understanding Christ and his teachings, as well as to the development of the Church, was absolute. As Catholic beliefs developed into officially disseminated teachings and practice, they became part of the "deposit of faith", the vast bulwark of accepted Church tradition that had its genesis in the earliest oral apostolic teachings, the canons of the New Testament and in the decisions and decrees of the Church councils.

At the core of Church doctrine are the Trinitarian nature of God, the Incarnation of Christ as God–Man, his real presence in the Eucharist, his suffering and death, and his resurrection for our salvation. All other Catholic beliefs and teaching are nourished from the deep wellspring of these particular articles of faith.

Above The Eastern European influence on the early Roman Church is evident in this Byzantine-style, mid-8th-century Russian illustration of the First Ecumenical Council of Nicaea, which convened in Turkey in AD 325.

Left The three persons of the Trinity – Christ, the Holy Spirit (in the form of a dove) and God – are the focus of this 17th-century painting by Pierre Mignard. Christ's bare chest alludes to his crucifixion, when he was stripped of his garments.

GOD IN THREE PERSONS

CATHOLICS BELIEVE IN THE TRINITY OF GOD, OFTEN TRADITIONALLY PORTRAYED WITH THE FATHER AS A REGAL OLDER MAN, THE SON AS A YOUNG, SORROWFUL MAN AND THE HOLY SPIRIT AS A DOVE OR FLAME.

Belief in the Trinity is an absolutely central tenet of the Roman Catholic faith, but it is also an item of doctrine that has a controversial past among Christians. It is a paradox that is difficult to understand rationally. The doctrine states that there is only one eternal, almighty God, who exists without beginning or end, and who is the creator of all that exists. However, there are three "persons" – the Father, the Son and the Holy Spirit – existing "one in being" as that God. The three are equal and eternal, each existing without beginning or end.

THE SAME BUT DIFFERENT

As stated in the Nicene Creed, which deals specifically with the nature of Christ, the Son is said to be "eternally begotten" of the Father, but "not made", emphasizing that there was never a time when he did not exist and that he partakes of the substance of the Father even while he is another person. The Holy Spirit "proceeds" from the Father and the Son – this is an active verb that emphasizes a continuous being, a kind of eternally advancing horizon of existence. The Greek word for

Above In this 13th-century French image, the "Creator of heaven and earth" takes the measure of his raw materials with a compass. This image may have influenced William Blake's 1794 Ancient of Days.

proceed emphasizes "movement out of". The Greek word *perichoresis,* meaning "permeation without confusion", is also used by theologians to express how the persons of the Trinity interpenetrate each other, yet remain distinct.

DIVINE BEINGS

The three persons of the Trinity are perceived by most Catholics as having particular, appropriate divine aspects. The Father is the Creator, the maker of all and the interlocutor with Adam and Eve. The Son's defining attribute is that he was made man. He demonstrated the infinite depth of divine love by becoming human, walking among us and acceding to an agonizing sacrifice of his simultaneously human and divine self as an

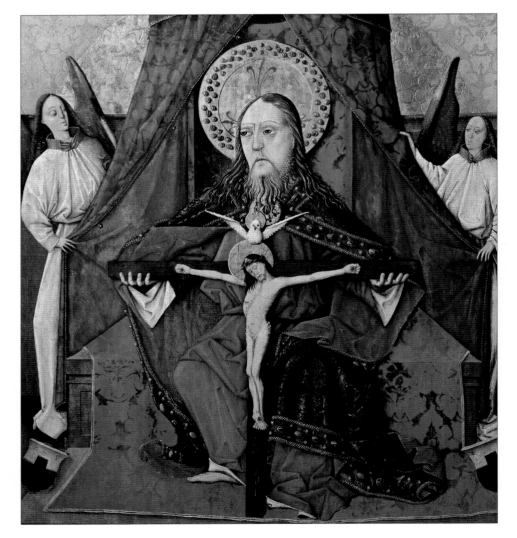

Left The Catholic mystery of the Trinity is shown in this 15th-century European painting. They are intimately connected yet distinct, with God the Father holding his crucified Son, while the Holy Spirit as a dove rests on Christ's halo.

offering to re-open the possibility of man's freedom from Adam and Eve's original sin.

The Holy Spirit, as implied by his name, is the only divine persona without a human form in traditional Catholic iconography. He is usually artistically represented as either a dove or a tongue of flame, the form in which, ten days after Christ's ascension to heaven, he descended to inspire the apostles as teachers of the Word of God (the day now known as Whitsunday, or more commonly in Catholic theology, Pentecost). Metaphorically, in his role as bringer of grace and an inspirer of wisdom, he is spoken of as a mighty wind or as the inspiration or breath of God. He is also known as the "Paraclete", or advocate, which refers to his role as a spiritual teacher or guide.

A CONTROVERSIAL TIME

The doctrine of the Trinity was fiercely debated by the bishops and Church fathers in the early days of Christianity. The 4th-century controversy surrounding Arianism — a heresy that claimed the Son of God

Above At Jesus' baptism, the heavens opened, the Holy Spirit descended and the Father spoke, "This is my beloved son…" Giovanni Guercino's 17th-century painting shows a powerful God the Father.

was not truly God but was created by God — in particular, served as a spur to bishops to set and define the immanent divinity of the three persons of the one God as a crucial and defining Catholic doctrine.

Arianism argued that Christ was inferior to the Father in that "there was a then when he was not" — in other words, there was a time when Christ did not exist. Christ was described as the first of the Father's created beings, not "eternally begotten", but simply "begotten", thus denigrating his divine nature as a being without beginning or end.

The Council of Nicaea was convened in AD 325 by Constantine, Emperor of Rome, in large part to counteract Arianism. The Nicene Creed that was formulated at the council, then finalized at the Council of Constantinople in AD 381, is still the familiar creed recited in Roman Catholic churches today.

Even more contentious was the relationship of the Holy Spirit to the Father and the Son. The Nicene Creed of AD 325 merely stated "we believe in the Holy Spirit". In AD 381, the "filioque" ("and the son") clause was added, stating that the Holy Spirit "proceeds from the Father and the Son". It was disagreement about this "dual procession" doctrine that caused the Eastern Christian Church to split from the Roman Church in the Great Schism of 1054.

Above The Holy Spirit is the only person of the Trinity who never speaks, but we can almost hear the whirr of his wings in this graceful French c.1490 illumination by Jean Colombe.

THE TRINITY

The term "Trinity", from the Latin noun *trinitas*, meaning "three at once", does not occur in the Bible, but the gospels do contain references to the divinity of the Father, Son and Holy Spirit. For example, after Christ rose from the dead, he bid the apostles to "go forth and teach all nations, baptizing them in the name of the Father, and of the Son and of the Holy Spirit" (Matthew 28:20). The term Trinity in relation to the Godhead was first used by Tertullian, the 3rd-century son of a Roman centurion and an early convert to Christianity, who was a prolific writer and contributor to evolving Christian theology in the early centuries after Christ's death.

CHRIST THE REDEEMER

IN CATHOLIC THEOLOGY, ORIGINAL SIN IS THE METAPHORICAL "STAIN"
ALL HUMAN BEINGS ARE BORN WITH — AND IT IS THE REASON WHY
CHRIST SACRIFICED HIMSELF TO REDEEM THE HUMAN RACE.

Original sin is inherited, like a genetic disease, from the first man – our ancestor Adam – and all humans have inherited it. The Catholic catechism says, "The whole human race is in Adam".This does not mean that original sin is a sinful action of Adam that we imitate or recreate. It is, rather, our tragic patrimony, meaning that we have been born deprived of the original grace that was God's initial endowment to our ancestral parents, Adam and Eve.The poet John Milton (although not a Catholic himself) expressed it well:

Of man's first disobedience,
  and the Fruit
Of that Forbidden Tree,
  whose mortal taste
Brought Death into the World,
  and all our woe…

FORBIDDEN FRUIT

The actual sin, described in Genesis, was eating the fruit of the Tree of Knowledge of Good and Evil, the only tree in paradise prohibited by God to Adam and Eve. Eve was tempted by Satan in the guise of a serpent, who told her she would be like a god and understand good and evil. Adam then took the fruit from Eve and ate as well.

As a result of Adam and Eve's wilfully disobedient act, Catholicism teaches that we are born fallen, with our souls deprived of sanctifying grace, not fully and freely open and receptive to God's love.The fall of the first man infused not just humanity but the entire world – the originally harmonious world made by God became discordant. Instead of every type of fruit tree, God prophesied that the earth would bring forth thorns and thistles. Instead of being blissfully unaware of their nakedness, Adam and Eve perceived it as shameful and hid. Original sin set man against himself and the earth – first intended to be our garden of delight – against man.

Catholics believe that death became part of life with original sin. As a direct response to Adam and Eve's disobedience, God pronounced, "In the sweat of thy face shalt thou eat bread till thou return to the earth out of which thou wast taken: for dust thou art, and into dust thou shalt return" (Genesis 3:19).

Left Eve, having already eaten from the forbidden fruit, colludes with the serpent, who places the apple in her waiting hand as she draws Adam close. This detail is from a 16th-century German triptych.

***Above** Because of original sin, death gained power over us and took us from the garden of paradise. In Evelyn de Morgan's 1890* The Angel of Death, *death has wings.*

BODY AND SOUL

Although the concept of original sin already existed, it was first defined as a doctrine in the 5th century AD by St Augustine of Hippo. Augustine had lived a dissolute life before his conversion from Manichaeism (a type of gnostic religion) to Catholicism, so he was particularly alert to man's sinful nature. The Second Council of Orange in AD 529 specified that while death of the body was the punishment for original sin, death of the soul was the sin itself.

Death of the soul is emphasized because original sin is responsible for destroying our first intimate union with God. Adam and Eve's action deprived them of the original grace that was their birthright, and this loss introduced the tendency toward corruption into the world, as though the previously perfect fabric of Creation was rent with a fatal flaw, weakening it so that it easily became tattered. Original sin is also responsible for allowing our

CHRIST'S CRUCIAL SACRIFICE

At both the Council of Orange in AD 529 and the Council of Trent in 1546, the Church fathers defined the doctrine of justification. This emphasized that our redemption was not possible without Christ's mediation, or the merit that he obtained for us by his obedient death, to make restitution for our disobedience. Redemption is not possible by human good works and good behaviour alone. The Church fathers pronounced anathema (a kind of doctrinal condemnation) on anyone who believed humans could save themselves without Christ – specifically, Pelagius, an Irish monk whose heretical beliefs triggered the Council of Orange's pronouncements.

Pelagius believed we could save ourselves by our good works and he de-emphasized the role of God's Grace. The Catholic Church teaches that we need the grace that Christ first obtained for us by his sacrifice. Additionally, we also require the sanctifying grace that fills our soul in baptism, the educating aid of the Holy Spirit that comes to us through participation in the sacraments, and continuous obedience to God's commandments in order to avoid damnation and find eternal life with God.

Above Pelagius (AD 355–425) believed that original sin was not every man's inheritance, and that man could save himself without Christ's sacrifice.

inferior worldly and carnal desires, known as "concupiscence", to prevail over our reason.

SEEKING REDEMPTION

The counterpoint to this tragic fall from grace is our ability to essentially re-enact our first parents' temptation and choice – but this time, individually, because we still retain the free will with which they were endowed by God, to choose to turn toward God, or *conversio ad deum*. The possible redemption of each individual is a direct result of the offering Christ made of himself to the Father: as man out of his own free will chose to turn away and reject God's love (*adversio ad deum*) and instead act to satisfy his own egotistical desire, Christ out of his own free will did not resist actual torture on the Cross to pay the price to redeem man. The Latin word *redemptio* is related to Hebrew and Greek words meaning "a ransom price".

Right Our first defence against original sin comes through the grace of baptism. In this late 16th-century painted stone, St Augustine, once a libertine, and his illegitimate son Adeodatus are baptized by St Ambrose.

THE EUCHARIST

LIKE THE HOLY TRINITY, THE DOCTRINE OF THE EUCHARIST, WHICH CELEBRATES JESUS' LAST SUPPER WITH HIS APOSTLES, IS ONE OF THE MOST IMPORTANT, CENTRAL BELIEFS OF THE CATHOLIC CHURCH.

The Roman Catholic catechism calls the Eucharist "the source and summit of the Christian life". Most Catholics would probably agree that the Eucharist is a particularly special doctrine. It is one that each practising Catholic is introduced to at an early age, and it continues through the years, becoming a customary thread of the faith drawing together generations of families.

Almost any person brought up in the Catholic faith will have specific memories of their first Holy Communion, because it is a joyful day that has delightful worldly celebrations

Above *The most sacred moment of the Mass is the consecration, when the bread and wine are transubstantiated into the body and blood of Christ, as seen in this 15th/16th-century image by Giovanni di Giuliano Boccardi.*

surrounding it. It is also the first time that a child is called to participate in one of the central mysteries of the faith, the Eucharist. This is a particularly special occasion, when the child is first asked to try to extend his or her perception to encompass a numinous dimension of the infinite by participation in a very specific individual act.

THE LORD'S SUPPER

The word "Eucharist" comes from the Greek *eucharistein*, or "grateful, thankful". It is the name given to the communion that has been repeated through the centuries at every Catholic Mass. Its origin lies in the Last Supper, the story of which is engraved on the consciousness of every Catholic. The Last Supper is described in almost the same words in Matthew 26:26–28, Mark 14:22–24 and Luke 22:17–20. Celebrating the paschal meal with his apostles, and well aware that he was about to be betrayed and put to death, Christ took bread, broke it and offered it to his apostles, saying, "Take

THE LAST SUPPER

Leonardo da Vinci's renowned mural painting, *The Last Supper* (1495–8), depicts the paschal supper at which Christ broke bread and offered wine. The painting dramatizes the moment described in the gospels when Jesus, "troubled in spirit", announces "Amen, amen, I say to you, one of you shall betray me." The disciples therefore looked upon one another, doubting of whom he spoke.

Despite the press of the apostles around the table and the apparent furor caused by Christ's words, there are two figures who remain alone with their thoughts. Judas' hand hovers slightly above a dish, illustrating Christ's words, "he that dippeth his hands with me in the dish, he shall betray me". All the other apostles lean toward Christ or toward each other, exchanging glances. Judas leans away from Christ without touching anyone else, and while the others look at Christ beseechingly, Judas simply stares. Christ's arms extend down with his palms turned upwards in a gesture that is one of submission, yet he also seems to be gathering power from the heavens toward which his hands open. Although Christ's gaze is directed away from Judas, the entire side of his face is angled toward him, almost as if he were offering a cheek to be kissed – and, of course, it is with a kiss on Jesus' cheek that Judas will betray him to his captors on the following day.

Above *Da Vinci's late 15th-century painting* The Last Supper *not ony recalls the last meal between Jesus and his apostles but is also full of symbolism, referring to the momentous event that will occur when Judas betrays Christ.*

ye, and eat. This is my body." Taking the chalice, he gave thanks, and gave it to them, saying, "Drink ye all of this. For this is my blood of the new testament, which shall be shed for many unto remission of sins." During this supper, Christ spoke the simple words, "Do this in memory of me." This quiet command is the genesis of the Eucharistic sacrifice around which a great world religion has been formed. In allusion to the Last Supper, communion is sometimes called the Lord's Supper.

Christ prefigured these actions before his death when he fed a crowd of people that had come to hear him preach and who were hungry, yet with little food. In the hands of Jesus, on that day the five loaves and two fishes available miraculously became enough to feed the multitude. When preaching in the synagogue at Capharnaum soon after performing this miracle, Jesus said, "I am the bread of Life…. He that eateth my flesh and drinketh my blood have everlasting life: and I will raise him up in the last day."

BREAD AND WINE

Through the centuries, the central act of Mass has been the priest's consecration of wheaten bread and grape wine into Christ. The Council of Trent in 1546 defined the Eucharist as "the Body and Blood, together with the Soul and Divinity of our Lord Jesus Christ, and therefore the whole Christ, is truly, really and substantially contained in the sacrament of the Holy Eucharist."

Various theologians over the years have attempted to define the Holy Eucharist as a symbol of the body and blood of Christ (16th-century Zwinglians), or as a dynamic trans-

Right A literal interpretation of the doctrine that the host is transubstantiated into the entirety of the body and blood of Christ can be seen in this 14th-century painting by Ugolino di Prete Ilario.

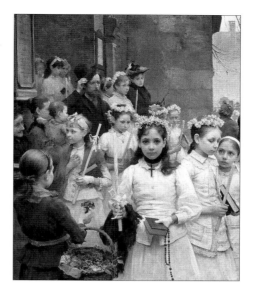

Left The first Holy Communion is an inspiring milestone in the lives of Catholic children. In this late 19th-century painting by Carl Frithjof Smith, a young girl proudly wears her new crucifix.

ferral of the efficacy of Christ's body and blood to the souls of the elect at the moment of reception of the host (Calvinists), but the Church declared all such limitations on the definition of the Eucharist to be heresies.

THE CONSECRATION

Catholic doctrine is specific regarding the holiest moment of Mass. This is known as the consecration, when the priest repeats the words of Christ at the Last Supper. "This is my body" is spoken when the priest raises the bread and "This is my blood" is uttered with the wine, and at each and every Mass a miracle occurs and the bread and wine are changed, or "transubstantiated", into the body and blood of Christ. How the change occurs when the priest speaks the words is a mystery known only to God. What is changed is the entire substance – the being – of the bread and wine into the entirety of the substance, or being, of Christ, with only the "species", or appearance, of bread and wine remaining.

The Church holds that, in essence and in actuality (not symbolically), Christ is present in the Eucharist. In order to skirt an association with cannibalism, the Church does not usually emphasize (but it would not deny) that Christ is physically present (like the person sitting next to you in Church, for example), but that he is substantially present, which is known as the "Real Presence".

THE CLASSIC CREEDS

THERE ARE THREE CLASSIC CREEDS OF THE CATHOLIC CHURCH: THE APOSTLES', NICENE AND ATHANASIAN CREEDS. EACH WAS DEVELOPED TO SHIELD THE CHURCH FROM A SPECIFIC HERESY.

Many modern Catholics can usually repeat by rote the Nicene Creed, imprinted on their memory since childhood. However, they may not realize that in the early centuries after Christ's death, when Christianity was still seeking to define and establish itself in the face of uncertainty, danger and opposition, creeds were developed and perceived as true badges of faith. They were developed to fight heresies, to establish, teach and promote right doctrine, and, in the words of the Catholic catechism, to be "the spiritual seal, our heart's meditation."

THE FIRST SYSTEM OF BELIEF

The Apostles' Creed is the oldest. It originated in the first century after Christ's death and sets forth the teachings of the Church under the leadership of St Peter, the first pope.

During the Middle Ages it was believed that the first 12 apostles had composed the Creed on Pentecost, the day that the Holy Spirit descended to inspire them; however, this is probably a legend.

About two-thirds of the Apostles' Creed sets forth in straightforward language beliefs about the identity of Jesus Christ. This is because, during the first five centuries of the Church's existence, when the Apostles' Creed was formulated, Gnosticism was an influential heresy. Followers of this faith believed that the material world was completely corrupt (beyond the "tendency to sin" of the doctrine of original sin) and, therefore, although they were willing to believe that Jesus was God, the Gnostics denied that he had ever been a true man, a flesh and blood corporeal man who had died, as well as being divine.

Above St Athanasius, shown in this 18th-century Greek icon, was an Egyptian theologian known as the Father of Orthodoxy. His fight against Arianism was influential in the development of the doctrine of the Trinity.

Below The ravaged body of Christ, showing he was flesh and mortal, stands out in a contemporary landscape, an attempt by a 16th-century French artist to help refute the Gnostic doctrine that Christ had never been truly mortal.

By denying Jesus' humanity, the followers of Gnosticism were also denying that he died for us, which was a blatant contradiction of a bedrock Catholic doctrine. The Apostles' Creed refutes this Gnostic heresy by dwelling on the corporeal history of Christ on earth, stating that he "suffered, died and was buried". This creed may have been used as a profession of faith for early Christians about to be baptized, and even today the Apostle's Creed is part of the baptismal rite.

ONE IN BEING

The second of the classic creeds, the Nicene Creed, which is also known as the Niceno-Constantinopolitan Creed, clarified Jesus' standing. It was developed in the 4th century and endures today in both the Roman and Eastern Catholic Churches. During the 4th century, Arianism – essentially the belief that Jesus, while divine, was an inferior divinity to the Father – became such a widespread and contentious issue that it threatened the stability of the Roman Empire itself. In the Edict of Milan (AD 313), Constantine declared that Christians were free to practise their religion, so the disputes over Catholic doctrine, freed from the earlier need for secrecy, became even more acrimonious than before.

Constantine ordered a council of bishops to be convened in Nicaea (in present-day Turkey) to make a ruling on the heated issue. The Nicene Creed, which was developed at that conference, declared in its

Above Simon Magus, shown in this 14th-century French manuscript, was a Gnostic teacher and magician known as the "first heretic". Legend says he fell to his death from the Roman Forum while trying to prove to St Peter that he could fly.

most significant line that Jesus was "one in being with the father". The most significant Greek term used in this phrase was *homoousios*, or "consubstantial", meaning of the same substance, not *homoiousios*, which means "similar" (but not the same) substance.

In AD 381, the creed was revised to expand its definition of the Holy Spirit. The earlier AD 325 version had only noted "We believe in the Holy Spirit", somewhat short-changing the third person.

THE STERNEST CREED

The newest of the three classic creeds, the Athanasian Creed, is a resolute profession of doctrines on the nature of the Trinity and of the Incarnation (particularly with regard to the divinity and humanity of Jesus). It also declares the absolute necessity of belief in these doctrines in order to achieve one's salvation.

The creed was written in a series of declarations that were clearly and inclusively formulated in an obvious attempt to stifle all the various heresies on the Trinity and the nature of Christ that plagued the Catholic Church, among them being Arianism, Modalism, Sabellianism, Apollinarianism and Eutychianism. To emphasize that this was a serious matter, the creed contains a series of clauses that outline two stark choices: belief, or the road to damnation. It concludes: "This is the Catholic faith, which except a man believe faithfully and firmly, he cannot be saved."

Below The large hands of the Madonna protectively enfold the Christ child in this 15th/16th-century painting by Giovanni Bellini. He grasps his mother's thumb, even as he asserts his divinity by offering a blessing.

OF UNKNOWN ORIGIN

The Athanasian Creed is also known as the Symbol Quicunque for its first Latin words, "*Quicunque vult salvus esse…*" ("Whosoever wishes to be saved…"). Tradition has ascribed the Athanasian Creed to Athanasius, the 4th-century Bishop of Alexandria, but this has been proved untrue. Although many plausible theories have been put forward as to its origin, none have been conclusive. However, scholars tend to agree that it was written in France *c.* mid-5th century.

THE CATECHISM

TO HELP THE FAITHFUL LEARN THE BELIEFS OF THE CATHOLIC CHURCH, ALL ITS GREAT THEOLOGICAL TEACHINGS HAVE BEEN SUMMARIZED IN WHAT IS POPULARLY KNOWN AS THE CATECHISM.

"Catechetics" comes from the Greek *katechesis*, meaning instruction by word of mouth. A "catechumen" is the person being instructed in religious doctrine. The New Testament portrays the 12-year-old Jesus as an exceptional catechumen:

And it came to pass, that, after three days, they found him in the temple, sitting in the midst of the doctors, hearing them and asking them questions. And all that heard him were astonished at his wisdom and his answers. (Luke 2:46)

THE WORDS IN WRITING
A catechism is doctrinal instruction provided in written form. It is in a question and answer format because the Church considers it the best method for ensuring that the doctrine being taught is correct and uniform – which is important in a religion where shades of meaning are crucial and confusion can unwittingly lead to heresy.

In Catholicism's early history, written doctrinal instruction was generally sparse, a deficiency that contributed to the Church's

Above A youthful Jesus turned the usual catechetical order inside out by teaching the rabbis. In this 15th/16th-century painting by Albrecht Dürer, Jesus amazed them with his preternatural wisdom.

vulnerability to the Reformation. Fifteenth-century parish priests, who were often poorly educated in abstruse Church doctrines themselves, were usually unable to help their confused parishioners. Poor instruction and misunderstanding of the complexities of the doctrines, including the plenary indulgence, enabled corrupt practices, such as selling indulgences for money. Martin Luther was one of the reformers who pounced on these practices, and many left the Church to join the reformers as a result.

The first-ever Catholic catechism was published in Vienna in 1555 by Peter Canisius, a Dutch Jesuit. Canisius compiled a single volume

Left Peter Canisius (1521–97), shown in this 17th-century Flemish painting, wrote three Latin and German catechisms and helped to found the University of Fribourg, Switzerland, still an influential school of Catholic theology.

that contained 222 questions and 2,000 scriptural quotations. This catechism is still a favourite of theologians and historians centuries later; however, at the time it was first published, it was too sophisticated to be of much help to the ordinary priest and parishioner.

EDUCATING THE CLERGY

The Church recognized the need for, in the words of the 16th-century Council of Trent, "...a formulary and method for teaching the rudiments of the faith, to be used by all legitimate pastors and teachers". This was to take the shape of a simpler catechism that would be helpful for ordinary priests as they cared for the souls of their flocks. The resulting Roman catechism was published in 1566 and translated into the vernacular languages used by all Catholic countries.

The Roman catechism was intended to educate the clergy, and parish priests were ordered by their bishops to memorize it and to pass on that rote knowledge to their parishioners. It was the work of a number of distinguished theologians and cardinals of the day, and the authority of the Roman catechism was considered unimpeachable.

THE DISCIPLINE OF THE SECRET

In the early centuries of the Church, during and just after the Roman persecutions, admission to the mysterious doctrines and rites of the new religion called Christianity was treated with great reserve. Scriptural support for a gradual revelation of the mysteries was provided by Matthew 7:6: "Give not that which is holy to dogs; neither cast ye your pearls before swine, lest they trample them under their feet, and turning upon you, they tear you."

The gradual revelation of the doctrines and rituals of the Church was known as the Discipline of the Secret. In particular, early Christians considered that the teachings of the Trinity and the Eucharist should be revealed to postulants only after careful preparation, because the doctrines imparted to the poorly prepared could easily be misconstrued as tritheism (the Trinity) or cannibalism (the Eucharist). As Christianity became more established, the practice of the Discipline of the Secret began to diminish and it was for the most part finished by the 5th century AD.

MODERN VERSIONS

New catechisms continue to be developed. The catechism familiar to Americans is the Baltimore Catechism. In 1829, American bishops asked for a catechism adapted to the needs of the diverse American Catholic audience. *A Catechism of Christian Doctrine, Prepared and Enjoined by Order of the Third Council of Baltimore*, was issued in 1855 and became the standard United States catechism. A modernized edition of the Baltimore Catechism is still available today.

Another new catechism, entitled *Compendium of the Catechism of the Catholic Church*, was started on the 20th anniversary of the Second Vatican Council, brought to completion by Pope John Paul II and published by Pope Benedict in 2005.

Below Founded in 1253 by the Chaplain of Louis V, the Sorbonne was an institution of education, famed for its influential, but conservative, school of theology.

Below A nun from the Missionaries of Charity, the order founded by Mother Teresa, is engaged in the traditional catechetical method of oral instruction.

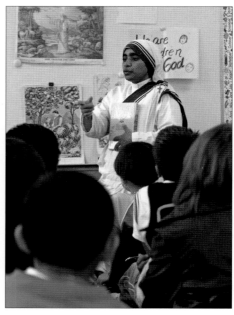

IN ACCORDANCE WITH THE SCRIPTURES

CATHOLICISM VIEWS THE SCRIPTURES AS THE WORD OF GOD, PASSED ON BY WRITERS INSPIRED BY THE HOLY SPIRIT. THEY ARE CONSIDERED DIVINE REVELATION IN WRITTEN FORM.

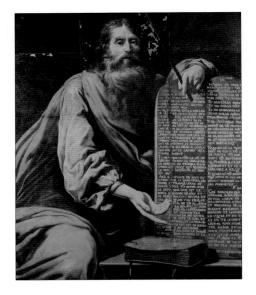

The Scriptures that form the sacred canon are the biblical books accepted by the Church as genuine. Catholicism sees the Old Testament, which existed years before the birth of Christ, as part of a divine plan, calling the Old Testament an "active and steady preparation" for the revelations of Christ in the New and credited with tilling the ground for the coming of the Messiah. According to the Catholic catechism, this is a covenant that is "strikingly fulfilled" in the New Testament. It says the Old Testament books:

> ...give expression to a lively sense of God, contain a store of sublime teachings about God, sound wisdom about human life, and a wonderful treasury of prayers, and in them the mystery of our salvation is present in a hidden way.

"Typology" is the term that describes seeing the revelations of the New Testament prefigured in the books and stories of the Old.

THE DEPOSIT OF FAITH

Unlike Protestant Christianity, the Catholic Church does not view Scripture as the sole source of divine revelation. This was a major issue during the Reformation, with the Protestant reformers claiming that all belief required specific evidence or *sola scriptura* ("scriptural proof"). The Catholic Church, in contrast, argued that scripture should be read from the perspective of a sacred tradition, and that it should include the non-scriptural compendium of teachings and traditional beliefs – referred to by the Church as the "deposit of faith". These teachings and beliefs were revealed by Jesus

Above Moses keeps a protective arm around the second tablets of law written by the hand of God in this 17th-century painting by Laurent de la Hyre. Moses had smashed the first tablets when he saw his people worshipping a golden calf.

to the apostles and passed down through the apostles and early Church fathers to become Catholic customary belief and practice through the centuries.

At the same time, the Church does not encourage individualistic interpretations of Scripture, especially when they are not supported by valid study and scholarship. Instead, the ultimate authority for scriptural interpretation is the magisterium, or the teaching authority of the Church comprised of the pope and the bishops of the Church. The magisterium's scriptural interpretations, according to Church doctrine, are infallible because they are inspired by the Holy Spirit. That said, the Catholic Church does encourage serious biblical study, so that readers will not react to the Bible only according to their own subjective emotional responses.

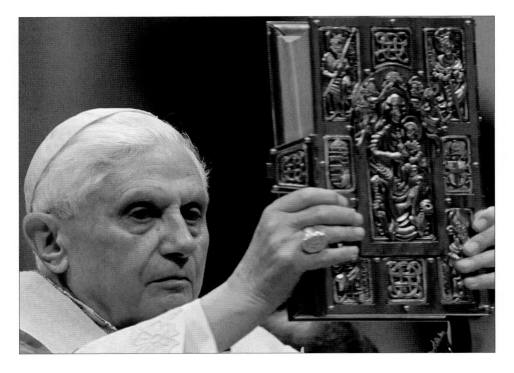

Left Pope Benedict XVI provided an extensive commentary on modern methods of Biblical exegesis in his 1988 Erasmus lecture, "Biblical Interpretation in Crisis".

THE BACKGROUND

In "The Interpretation of the Bible in the Church", a 1993 document written by Cardinal Joseph Ratzinger (who became Pope Benedict XVI in 2005), the cardinal freely asserted that the Bible would be more fully appreciated if its readers had a working knowledge of the society, history, languages and geography that influenced its writers. Of this "historical-critical" approach, Cardinal Ratzinger pointed out that the "eternal word" of God, the Bible, was brought into being during specific historical periods, and that readers of the Bible must necessarily be grounded in the cultural and social details of those eras for proper and accurate comprehension of the text.

However, an overemphasis on these methods could obscure what the Church refers to as the "spiritual sense", a dimension of the Scriptures that extends far beyond the reality of other human texts. Benedict warned that modern historical-grammatical methods of interpretation can lead to the distancing of God's original words if too much emphasis is put on the human dimension of the words.

Benedict went on to assert that while approaching biblical exegesis (or interpretation) with the proper respect for the texts, as God's Word requires, all the possible methods of interpretation – historical, philological, sociological – should also be given their due. It is essential for Catholics to keep in mind that the principal aim of their studies should be the deepening of their faith.

Above Biblical exegesis – the critical explanation of the text – takes many forms. This medieval French Bible Moralisée *from c.1230 features brief biblical passages interspersed with moral or allegorical lessons.*

DIFFERENT TESTAMENTS

The Protestant and Catholic Bibles differ in the number of canonical books contained in their respective Old Testaments. Catholic Bibles have 46 books, Protestant Bibles, 39. The reasons for the discrepancy go back to ancient political and religious history. Early Christians accepted as divinely inspired the *Septuagint* (Greek for 70, referring to the 70 translators from Hebrew into Greek) version of the Jewish Old Testament. When the *Septuagint* was translated from Hebrew into Greek, it contained seven newer Greek books that had never been in the Hebrew language, but they were still considered part of the divinely inspired canon by Jews at the time of Jesus.

In AD 100, Jews purged their canon of these non-Hebrew books, known as the Deuterocanonical (for second canon, because they were newer) books. Christians chose to keep the seven, because at the time of Christ, they had been considered inspired texts. However, in 1517 during the Reformation, Martin Luther advocated the old Hebrew canon, partly because he objected to references to Purgatory in some of the Deuterocanonical Books. Even today, many Protestant Bibles include the seven disputed books only at the back of the volume and refer to them as the Apocrypha (hidden) books. The Seven Books of the Apocrypha are Baruch, Maccabees I and II, Tobit, Judith, Ecclesiasticus (or Sirach) and Wisdom.

Below The English translation of the New Testament by William Tyndale (1494–1536) was the first based on Hebrew and Greek texts.

THE EVANGELISTS

THE "FOUR EVANGELISTS" — MARK, MATTHEW, LUKE AND JOHN — ARE CREDITED IN THE TRADITION OF THE CATHOLIC CHURCH AS THE AUTHORS OF THE GOSPELS IN THE NEW TESTAMENT.

"Evangelist" is from the Greek for "one who proclaims good news", so the title when referring to the gospel writers emphasizes they are spreading the word of Jesus' life to inspire others to believe in Jesus as God. The earliest Gospel, Mark, was written about 40 years after Jesus' Resurrection. In that intervening time, accounts of Jesus were passed on orally, and all the Evangelists used this oral tradition for the content of their gospels. The four gospels were composed from about AD 65 to 100.

Above A portrayal of the four Evangelists eschews symbology and shows the four as reverent scholars, each cradling his precious gospel (Greek school, 18th century).

AUTHOR UNKNOWN

Secular biblical scholars generally agree that the actual authorship of the gospels is anonymous; the titles "according to…" (not "by") Matthew, Mark, Luke or John, were added in the late 2nd century. Secular scholars also believe that the gospels were written according to the oral traditions of, rather than written by, the particular Evangelists. Yet the Church, while acknowledging the likely accuracy of the historians' position, has essentially declared that scholarly debate over the specific human authorship of the gospels is beside the point. In *Dei Verbum* (or "Word of God"), a "dogmatic constitution on divine revelation" issued by Pope Paul VI in 1965, the Church stated that as whoever "wrote" the gospels was inspired by the Holy Spirit, the real author of the gospels is God — and as such, the Church accepts them in their entirety as sacred and canonical. In other words, the authors, no matter who, were divinely inspired.

THE ORATORS

Tradition describes the Evangelists as four distinct people: Mark was a missionary with Paul, and Peter's follower. Matthew, one of the apostles, was a tax collector from Galilee. Luke, another missionary with Paul, was a Greek doctor, and is also believed to be the first Christian

Left Tradition says that St Luke painted some of the earliest icons of the Virgin Mary. This has become a popular subject in art, as in this 16th-century painting by Maerten van Heemskerck.

FOUR CREATURES BOUND TOGETHER IN SPIRIT

For centuries, the four Evangelists have been magnificently illustrated in Christian iconography and art as the "four living creatures" that flank God's throne in Revelation and Ezekiel. Described as six-winged and "full of eyes", the living creatures are fierce testaments to God's majesty and power. Traditionally, the first living creature, a lion, symbolizes Mark; the second, an ox, Luke; the third, a man, Matthew; and the fourth, an eagle, John. Each creature encompasses certain virtues: Mark's lion is royal and courageous; Luke's ox represents endurance and sacrifice; Matthew's man suggests the primacy of human intellect; and John's eagle, spirit and aspiration.

The Book of Kells, the superb 9th-century illuminated manuscript produced by Irish monks on the island of Iona, devotes a full page to the four living creatures. They frequently guard the portals of medieval cathedrals and glow in the light of ancient stained-glass windows. The symbols of the Evangelists are most often seen together, reflecting the beautiful words of St Irenaeus of Lyons (AD 120–202), "He who was manifested to men, has given us the gospel under four aspects, but bound together by one Spirit."

Right *The symbols of each of the four Evangelists are shown in this introductory page to the Gospel of St Matthew, from* The Book of Kells.

painter (he is often portrayed holding a brush and is said to have painted the Black Madonna of Czestochowa, now the centrepiece of a Polish shrine). John was the beloved youngest apostle of Jesus.

THE "SYNOPTIC GOSPELS"

The first three gospels, Mark, Matthew and Luke, which are similar in content, are known as the "Synoptic Gospels", meaning they "see with the same eyes". Scholars believe the Synoptics have a common, lost source document, which is referred to as "Q" (from the German *Quelle*, or "source"). The Gospel of John, which is notably different, is known as the "maverick" gospel.

Each gospel was developed with unique characteristics. Mark is referred to as the "action" gospel,

Right *Christ walking on water, as depicted in this 20th-century painting by Frederic Montenard, is described in the gospels of Matthew, Mark and John. The miracle is prefigured in the Old Testament when the River Jordan parts for Joshua. "Jesus" is Latin for the Hebrew name Joshua.*

because it contains the most miracles and has a quick narrative pace – in fact, the word "immediately" appears 39 times. Luke contains more parables, and, as befitting a doctor, has a somewhat scientific tone. Its opening words state that it is intended as an orderly account for attaining knowledge. Matthew opens with a genealogy of Jesus, with frequent references to the Old Testament, and it emphasizes that Jesus is the prophesied Messiah. His work appears to have been written for a Jewish audience.

John opens with the famous passage, "In the beginning was the Word: and the Word was with God: and the Word was God." John is the most spiritual of the four gospels and the only one to state an evangelical purpose, "that ye might believe that Jesus is the Christ, the son of God; and that believing ye might have life through his name". John is also the only Gospel not to describe Jesus offering bread and wine at the Last Supper (the acts that instituted the Eucharist). In its place is the account of Jesus washing the apostles' feet.

OUR LADY

MANY OF TODAY'S CATHOLICS GROW UP SURROUNDED BY IMAGES OF THE VIRGIN MARY, BUT IT WAS NOT UNTIL THE 5TH CENTURY AD THAT MARY'S UNIQUE STATUS AS GOD-BEARER WAS EVEN RECOGNIZED.

Mary's eminent position in the Catholic pantheon was slow to develop. St Paul does not mention Mary, mother of Jesus, in any of his epistles. The Bible does not mention Mary's ultimate fate after Christ's death on the Cross. The last mention of Mary is in Acts 1:14, when she was present with the apostles as they persevered in prayer after Jesus' Ascension and just before Pentecost. We do not know where, how or even if Mary actually died. The Scriptures are silent on all of these things.

THE GOD-BEARER
Mary's status in the Church began to develop after she was declared *Theotokos* (Greek for "God-bearer") by the Council of Ephesus in AD 431. As was their wont, the early Church

Below Mary spreads her cloak in a gesture of protection in this detail from a c.1422 painting by Jean Miralhet. The Sub Tuum Presidium, *a hymn dating from the 3rd century, begins, "Beneath thy compassion, we take refuge, O Theotokos".*

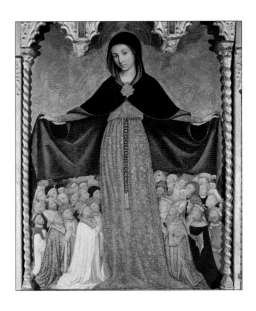

fathers debated for a long time before endowing Mary with this title. Its ultimate conferral was yet another means for the Church fathers to promulgate the concept of Christ as God-man, indivisibly true man and true God. By officially proclaiming Mary "God-bearer", it meant that she did not give birth to just the "man" aspect of God, as believed by Nestorius, the 3rd-century Bishop of Constantinople. Calling Mary *Theotokos* was just one more way to affirm the indivisible divine-human nature of Christ.

A PRAYER FOR MARY
It was only after the Council of Ephesus that liturgical feasts were held in Mary's honour, though the earliest known prayer to Mary, the *Sub Tuum Praesidium* ("Beneath Thy Compassion"), dates from *c.* AD 250. The prayer is a plea to Mary in her role as an intercessor for humanity with God. Pope John Paul II mentions this important mediatory role of Mary in *Redemptoris Mater*, his 1987 encyclical letter concerning Mary, noting that she intercedes "…not as an outsider, but in her position as mother". Mary, as both mortal woman and mother of the God-man, has a special attentiveness to the needs of mankind as well as a unique intimacy with her son. As a suffering mother, she has earned the right to be an adviser – even to God.

CONCEIVED WITHOUT SIN
There are three Catholic doctrines regarding Mary. The Immaculate Conception claims that alone among human beings, Mary was conceived without the inherited stain of original sin. It states "…the most

Above As he hung on the Cross, Christ placed Mary under the protection of the apostle John, shown in this painting by Rogier van der Weyden. Christ spoke words to each in turn, "Woman behold thy son…Behold thy mother."

Blessed Virgin Mary, from the first moment of her conception, by a singular grace and privilege from Almighty God and in view of the merits of Jesus Christ, was kept free of every stain of original sin."

This dogma sets forth the utter singularity of Mary. No other human being received this privilege from God. Besides the logic that the woman who was to bear and raise God would be free of a fallen nature, this doctrine also endows Mary with a special role, if not of our Redeemer, as is Christ, then as the one who made redemption possible through her obedience.

PERPETUAL VIRGINITY
Mary was a virgin at Christ's conception and remained so despite his gestation and birth and indeed for the rest of her life. Known as Perpetual Virginity, in the words of the Lateran Council (AD 649), Mary

conceived "without any detriment to her virginity, which remained inviolate even after his birth". Mary's lasting virginity was accepted by most of the early Church fathers, although Tertullian disagreed with it.

The doctrine provided a prototype for the monastic movement as it gained strength in the Church, starting *c.* the 4th century with St Anthony. Mary's celibacy is also representative of the metaphor of being "wedded to Christ", or so devoted to Christ that this relationship subsumes all others. The Church is known as the Bride or Spouse of the Lamb, nuns are brides of Christ and the Church continues to insist on the celibacy of priests, so that their devotion to God remains completely unchallenged by earthly vows.

THE ASSUMPTION

Celebrated by Catholics each year on 15 August, the Assumption is the doctrine that "…at the end of her

Below The Eastern Catholic tradition of the Dormition (falling asleep) of Mary teaches that she died a natural death, surrounded by all of the apostles except Thomas, who was late. The scene is shown in this 14th-century Byzantine mosaic.

earthly course, Mary was assumed into heavenly glory, body and soul". This is the 1950 definition given by Pope Pius XII, in a decree (*Munificentissimus Deus*) whose solemnity is apparent from the fact that it is the only ex-cathedra invocation by a pope since the doctrine of papal infallibility was established in 1870.

Pius XII's decree leaves vague the question of whether or not Mary actually died before she was raised by God into heaven. A variety of early non-scriptural accounts of the Assumption exist, some written by early saints, such as Gregory of Tours and John of Damascus.

Eastern Orthodox Catholics tend to favour more explicit stories concerning Mary's actual death, stating that she was surrounded by 11 of the apostles at the moment of her death. They refer to this death as Mary's Dormition, but believe along with Western Catholics that she was bodily assumed into heaven after her burial; the Dormition is also celebrated on 15 August. In any case, the Assumption is viewed by most Catholics as prefiguring the final redemption of all observant Catholics on the Last Day.

MOTHERLY LOVE

Despite all the unusual doctrines that surround Mary, the Catholic fascination with this figure seems to be related to something intimate and simple: her motherhood. The familiar enveloping motherly relationship and the idea that Jesus had a special fondness for Mary were illustrated when he did favours for her (turning water into wine at the wedding at Cana). Some of his last words as a living man were spoken to her as he hung from the Cross, where he appointed his apostle John to care for his mother. These actions seem to simplify Jesus' humanity into something that we can understand, even while he maintains his godliness. A simple emotion in powerful people is always resonant, and through Mary we can find this in Christ.

Above Mary rests her cheek on the head of her thriving son, whom she closely resembles. This early 16th-century Madonna and Child by Raphael emphasizes the natural maternal bond.

Marian Apparitions

APPARITIONS OF THE BLESSED VIRGIN MARY HAVE BEEN REPORTED FOR MANY CENTURIES. THE CATHOLIC CHURCH REFERS TO SUCH VISIONS AS "PRIVATE REVELATIONS".

Probably the earliest of the Marian revelations dates back to AD 40. It occurred before Mary's Assumption into heaven, when the apostle James, who was in Spain trying to spread the gospel, had a vision of the Virgin atop a marble pillar. She instructed him to build a church on the site, and that church today is said to be the first of the thousands of churches that have been dedicated to and named for the Blessed Virgin.

GUADALUPE

The three most influential Marian apparitions occurred at Guadalupe in Mexico, Lourdes in France and Fatima in Portugal. Guadalupe is notable because the visionary, Juan Diego, was an Aztec and a recent convert to Christianity. Mary appeared to him in 1531 at the site of a former temple to the Aztec gods,

and as a proof of her appearance she left her image mysteriously imprinted on Juan Diego's tilma, a type of cactus-fibre cloak. The image and the cloak have never decomposed and even today, more than four centuries later, the cloak (protected by bullet-proof glass) can still be seen at the basilica that was built in Guadalupe. Juan Diego's vision was influential in converting many indigenous Mexicans to Christianity, although these people were initially disinclined to do so because of their subjugation by the Spanish.

LOURDES AND FATIMA

Probably the best-known Marian vision occurred at Lourdes in 1858. The lady who appeared to a poverty-stricken and sickly shepherd girl said very little, mainly directing her supplicant to pray the rosary and to do penance. Yet the simple, intense, committed (and lifelong) piety and certainty of Bernadette Soubirous so impressed the clergy who examined her that Bernadette remains today the exemplary believable visionary in the eyes of the Church. Lourdes is also known for Massabielle, the spring blessed by the Virgin that has been responsible for dozens of otherwise inexplicable cures.

Fatima is remarkable for both the number of the visions and the loquacity of the Virgin Mary. Appearing six times in 1917 to three young children, Mary foretold the end of World War I but warned of a

Above Our Lady, atop a pillar carried by angels, is illustrated in a c.1629 painting by Nicolas Poussin. She appeared to the apostle James as he prayed by the banks of the Ebro River in Zaragoza, Spain.

worse war to come. She provided the children with a brief vision of hell and requested that Russia (this was during the Russian Revolution) be consecrated to her Immaculate Heart. Pope John Paul II, who felt that Our Lady of Fatima was

Left The Basilica of Guadalupe in Mexico is the most visited Catholic shrine in the world; on the feast of Our Lady of Guadalupe, millions make the pilgrimage – some on their knees.

THE PRINCIPAL REVELATIONS

At least 75 visions, or private revelations, have been reported over the centuries, but the Church has deemed "worthy of belief" perhaps 30 of them. Of these, there are nine principal, approved Marian apparitions:

Guadalupe (Mexico, 1531)
Rue du Bac (France, 1830)
La Salette (France, 1846)
Lourdes (France, 1858)
Pontmain (France, 1871)
Knock (Ireland, 1879)
Fatima (Portugal, 1917)
Beauraing (Belgium, 1932)
Banneux (Belgium, 1933)

responsible for his own survival from an assassination attempt that occurred on the feast of the Lady of Fatima, did perform such a consecration in May 1984. As a gesture toward Russia, he mentioned the nations that "particularly needed to be... consecrated" in the consecration.

THE DEPOSIT OF FAITH

The Church teaches that even the private revelations they dub "worthy of belief" do not constitute part of the "deposit of Faith" (the approved doctrines) of the Catholic Church, and that Church members are not bound to believe even the "approved" apparitions. The Church holds that the sum total of crucial Catholic revelations was given in apostolic times and, in particular, is contained in the doctrines of Christ's birth, death and Resurrection. Cardinal Ratzinger (who is now Pope Benedict XVI) commented in 2000 that the "...mystery of Christ as enunciated in the New Testament" was the utter, complete revelation of God to humanity, and that the Church neither needs nor expects anything more. There is no need for further divine manifestations. The Church feels that revelation is complete and that "secrets" revealed by visions cannot add to it.

MODERN REVELATIONS?

The attitude of the Catholic Church to Marian apparitions is cautious. The amount of attention paid to contemporary apparitions (such as the "disapproved" manifestations in Bayside, Queens, New York City) can quickly get out of hand due to the speed and widespread nature of modern publicity and ease of travel for pilgrims. The Church is concerned

Right Our Lady of Fatima asked the three shepherd children to whom she appeared to pray the rosary daily; today there are nightly candlelight processions to the shrine, where the participants pray.

Sainte Bernadette

Ton sourire divin illumine ma vie
Et lorsqu'au dernier jour vers toi prenant l'essor
Mon âme aura quitté l'exil pour la patrie
O Vierge Immaculée viens me sourire encor

that such charismatic phenomena will spread false doctrine and corrupt its magisterial authority. In essence, the devotees of particular Marian visions run the risk of developing into cultists.

Catholic doctrine also teaches that private revelation is not something to aspire to. St Teresa of Ávila

Left A personal supplication to St Bernadette of Lourdes (1844–79) is inscribed on this little holy card, together with an image of Bernadette (shown with a halo) after the pious woman entered the Sisters of Charity.

(though she herself had visions) reflected the sentiments of the Church when she said, "They desire to see; faith holds on without seeing." In other words, you should not need visions to believe. Christ himself said, "More blessed are they who have not seen and have believed."

Modern-day investigations of Marian apparitions are instituted by the bishop of the relevant diocese. If the messages being relayed by the apparition to the visionary are in any way contrary to the accepted doctrine of the Church, that alone is enough to have the apparition declared invalid. Investigations will also probe the mental, physical and spiritual health of the visionary and consider whether the messages being conveyed by the apparition are considered beneficial to the spiritual health of the faithful.

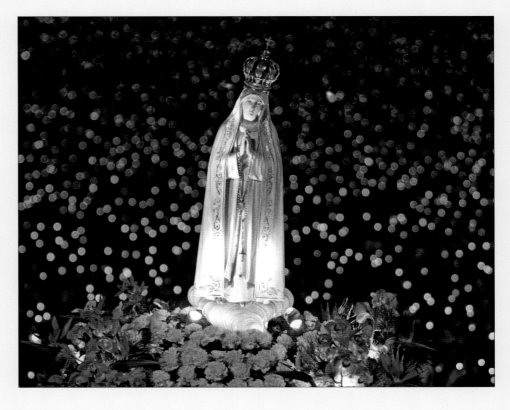

ALL SAINTS

THE MOST FAITHFUL SERVANTS OF GOD WHILE THEY WERE ON EARTH
ARE KNOWN AS SAINTS, AND CATHOLICS BELIEVE THEY ARE REWARDED
WITH A PARTICULAR INTIMACY WITH GOD IN HEAVEN.

The word "saint" comes from the Latin *sanctus*, or "holy, consecrated". In the general sense, the Catholic Church believes that anyone who has died and been accepted into heaven has earned the status of saint. However, there are also people who have been judged worthy of canonization by the Church hierarchy here on earth because of their exemplary behaviour as Christians. These saints are considered to have an especially intense beatific vision of God.

THE FIRST SAINTS

In the early centuries of Christianity, saints came from the ranks of the martyrs, those who in Roman times chose death rather than renounce their faith. After Christianity was legalized by the Edict of Milan in AD 313, the learned of the faith such as bishops or theologians ("doctors") were often considered for sainthood. Anchorites, or hermits, were also likely to achieve the designation by popular reputation. A saint chosen

Above St Matthew was stabbed in the back by a hired assassin while saying Mass in the church he built in Ethiopia. He is a saint by virtue of being an apostle and a martyr. This 14th-century illustration is from an altarpiece of St Matthew showing scenes from his life.

by reputation would be venerated by the people, who might visit the person's tomb or celebrate the day of his or her death.

After many years, the ecclesiastical authorities became involved and eventually created an official process for declaring someone a saint. The first saint for whom official canonization documents exist is St Udalricus, who was canonized in AD 973. In the early days of canonization, it was part of the practice to exhume the presumed saint's body and place it under an altar, apparently to facilitate the practices of veneration and pilgrimage that often resulted. An alternate way to express canonization is "to be

Left In this 15th-century painting, the bones of King Louis IX of France are disinterred (for reburial under an altar) by Pope Boniface VIII, who later canonized Louis.

THE LONG ROAD TO CANONIZATION

There is a set procedure to follow for a person to be made a saint. First there is The "Opening of the Cause", which occurs when the diocesan bishop agrees that there is enough evidence to initiate an investigation into the life of a deceased resident of his diocese, by popular opinion known as outstandingly holy. Usually, there is a five-year waiting period after the candidate's death, but in the case of Pope John Paul II, Pope Benedict XVI waived this waiting period. At this point the candidate can be called "a servant of God". The report that results from the investigation is sent to the Congregation for the Causes of Saints, the Vatican investigative body that vets saintly nominees. If the Vatican agrees the report profiles a saint in waiting, the candidate is called "Venerable".

A posthumous miracle, evidence of the candidate's intercessory influence with God, must be verified. After verification, the candidate is beatified. Mother Teresa was beatified in 2003. After beatification, the candidate is called "Blessed". The Congregation for the Causes of Saints must verify that a second miracle occurred after the beatification before the candidate can be called a "Saint".

Above *The widely held conviction that Pope John Paul II was an exceptionally holy man caused Pope Benedict XVI to open the cause for canonization only weeks after John Paul's death.*

raised to the full honours of the altar". Even today, saintly bodies reside under altars in some of the most surprising places – the body of St Mother Mary Frances Cabrini, for example, is under the altar of the chapel at Mother Cabrini High School in New York City.

VENERATION OR WORSHIP?

The modern Church recognizes saints as people of exemplary holiness who are worthy of veneration, which is not the same as worship. The act of worshipping a saint would violate the first commandment – "thou shalt not have strange gods before me". Catholicism is emphatically a mono-theistic religion. The Church makes a specific distinction between *latria*, or "worship", due only to God, and *dulia*, which is "honour or venera-tion", due to saints. The Blessed Mother has her own intermediate category, known as *hyperdulia* – a very high degree of veneration due only to her.

Right *St Anne's status as grandmother of the Holy Family means that she is asked to intercede on family matters. Shown here in this 17th-century French painting, she is patroness of expectant mothers, women in labour and of the sick.*

Worship and veneration can seem similar, since their practices (prayers to the worshipped or venerated, for example, or kneeling before statues, and feast days) are alike. However, the difference between worship and veneration is found in the believer's heart. When he or she worships, he or she is recognizing that the object of worship is divine. There is an element of awe rather than respect. When you venerate or honour, you are recognizing that the object of your veneration is due your respect – in the case of the Blessed Mother, the highest respect – but there is no awe and no intent to confer or recognize divinity.

Catholics who pray to saints do so not to obtain grace or favour straight from the saints themselves, but to ask the saint to intercede with God. This is because the saint is so close to God that their intercession is likely to smooth the way of the prayers of the petitioner.

A State of Grace

An individual's state of grace (whether or not he or she will receive sanctifying grace from God) depends on his or her efforts to gain salvation by turning to God through free will. Yet, one has to only briefly consider contemporary scandals that fill the newspapers' headlines to realize that humankind's sinful nature has not changed much over the centuries since early ascetic monks and doctors of the Church, such as Thomas Aquinas, created the Christian vocabulary to talk about sin. The seven "deadly" categories still apply – pride, avarice, greed, lust, gluttony, envy and sloth – leading men and women into both public and private trouble and strife. What has changed over the centuries is the emphasis that the Church places on forgiveness rather than punishment, and most particularly on the manner in which it defines not only punishment, but reward.

Also enduring is the human metaphysical longing for answers to ultimate questions and the craving to put our faith in something that is unified, peaceful and eternal. Catholicism defines this as the Trinity, the ultimate end of our seeking. The emphasis that the modern Church places on our personal relationship with God and on our eventual either beatific union with or desolate divorce from him is evidence that the Church has shifted the promise of heaven's glory and the threat of hell's fires and mutilations from the pointedly physical to the ineffably spiritual. The Church offers the heaven of rest and union with God.

Above The seven deadly sins all imply gross self-absorption. This attribute is evident in the oblivious expression and callous disregard of the child's pleas displayed by the overstuffed man in a scene depicting gluttony from Hieronymous Bosch's late 15th-century Tabletop of the Seven Deadly Sins and the Four Last Things.

Left In contrast to many paintings of the Harrowing of Hell, Giotto di Bondone portrays Christ as a tender and kind, rather than glorious and triumphant, liberator in his c.1320–5 painting, Descent into Limbo.

THE SOUL REDEEMED

CATHOLICS HAVE DISAGREED ON WHAT PEOPLE NEED TO DO TO GAIN
REDEMPTION FROM ORIGINAL SIN. IN ADDITION TO CHRIST'S SACRIFICE,
INDIVIDUALS MUST ALSO CONTRIBUTE TO THEIR OWN SALVATION.

Debates between Christians on what sinful humans need to do to attain salvation involved some of the most divisive issues of the 16th century, leading to the Protestant Reformation. Shuffled around in the debates were issues of grace, faith and the relative significance of human good works, along with the role of Christ's sacrifice on the Cross. The Catholic Magisterium, or teaching authority, and Martin Luther – the Catholic priest responsible for starting the Protestant Reformation by nailing his influential 95 Theses to the door of a church in Wittenberg – agreed on one important issue: that Christ's ultimate sacrifice on the Cross was the absolutely necessary prerequisite for human redemption.

Above Faithful Catholics pray before
The Way of the Cross, *a sculpture that
emphasizes the physical reality of Christ's
sacrifice. The weight of the Cross seems to
drive Christ into the ground, with only
the help of Simon of Cyrene keeping
him from falling.*

GOD'S GIFT

As a result of original sin, humans are viewed as helpless to effect their redemption on their own. (Pelagius, a 5th-century theologian, disagreed and thought that people could handle their redemption without God's intervention; the Catholic Church declared him a heretic.) Both Catholics and Lutherans also agreed that salvation is a gift from God. God has no obligation or need to save sinful humanity.

Fortunately, even the grievous fact of original sin was not enough to destroy God's love for humanity – his Creation – and his infinite goodness is displayed in the mystical balance of Christ's redemptive sacrifice. As the 20th-century theologian Jaroslav Pelikan has noted, Christ's obedient passion and sacrifice on the tree of the Cross undid the damage that humankind had done next to the tree of disobedience.

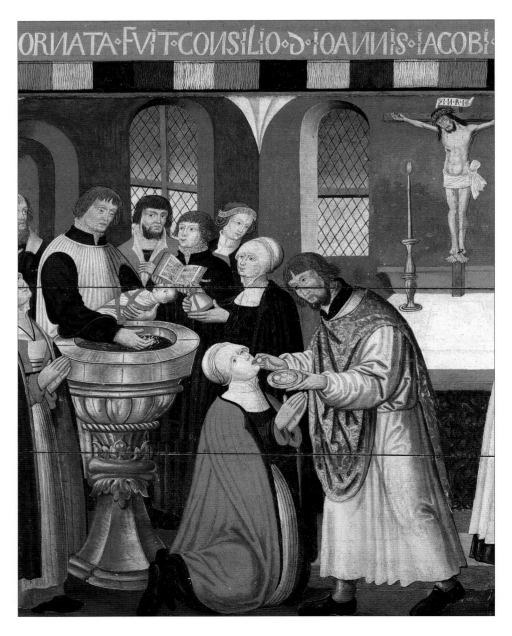

Left The Catholic Church recognizes
seven sacraments, while the Lutheran
Church practises only two – baptism and
the Eucharist. In this detail from a 1561
altar front from Torslunde, Denmark,
Martin Luther, who was once a Catholic
monk, performs both.*

HAVING FAITH

Luther believed that *sola fide* (or "faith alone") was the sole active principle in humankind's salvation. People would be saved by their faith in Christ's life, death and Resurrection. Christ basically earned redemption that is "imputed", or credited, to us if we have faith. Although Luther agreed that due to their faith in Christ, people develop a disposition to do good works, known as the process of sanctification, he thought that these human good works would never be enough to have any active effect on our redemption. Christ's sacrifice, and our faith in it, are all that matter. Luther is said to have declared, "Good works are useless."

CATHOLIC BAPTISM

In contrast, Catholicism teaches that not only can we be active contributors to our own salvation, but in fact, we must be so, in order to be saved. Faith alone will not be sufficient. Catholics view salvation as a process, so unlike Protestants they do not say, "I've been saved". Their ultimate salvation will be decided on their particular Judgement Day.

Catholicism teaches that we are redeemed through the progressive and co-operative interactions of first (and most crucially) Christ's initial sacrifice, the prerequisite that has made our personal redemption possible. Next we need to participate in a baptism, which is like our first purifying bath to cleanse us of original sin and infuse us with an initial dose of sanctifying grace. This act of baptism can be seen as an introductory step toward the process necessary for spiritual salvation.

JUSTIFICATION

Catholic theologians call what happens at baptism "initial justification". Justification is defined as making a person righteous in the eyes of God. However, to keep the spiritual introduction received at baptism

Above On the day of the final judgement, Catholic tradition declares that soul and body will be reunited. This 15th-century fresco by Giovanni Canavesio shows bodies rising from their graves on this ultimate day.

vigorous, Catholicism teaches that we need to participate actively in the Church and its sacraments, especially attendance at Mass, reception of the Eucharist and good works. Through these sincere acts of participation in the Catholic community, we become more immune to sin – and we also turn into more vigorous spiritual beings. This level of participation is known as "progressive justification".

Above The scallop shell is the traditional Catholic symbol of baptism. John the Baptist is said to have baptized Christ with water poured from a scallop shell. Here Pope John Paul II baptizes a child in the Sistine Chapel in 2001.

THE NATURE OF SIN

CATHOLICISM RECOGNIZES DIFFERENT TYPES OF SIN, FROM THE ORIGINAL SIN OF ADAM AND EVE TO THE UNFORGIVABLE SIN. IT IS OUR CHOICE TO TURN TO GOD AND NOT SIN OR TO TURN AWAY FROM HIM.

Above A 15th-century Italian illustration shows Jesus uttering the famous words, "He that is without sin among you, let him cast the first stone at her".

To understand how sin is viewed in Catholic doctrine, one needs to consider the concept of *aversio ad deo*, or "turning away from God". Sin is an insult to God, an almost unimaginable rudeness when considering that, in the Catholic view, God has offered us the most superb gift, his love. Sin is perverse, in that it says "no" to the love of God; the Catholic catechism says that sin contradicts the love of God.

Sin is the refusal to accept this priceless love and to choose instead to turn down the blind alley of self-love or toward a false attraction to worldly objects or persons. It is a disordered perception (as a result of original sin) of the value of attractions of the temporal world that we

Below Man's fallen nature leaves him vulnerable to the attractions of the temporal world, including riches, corporeal delights and secular power, shown in Jean de Gerson's 1462 Mirror of Humility.

mistakenly define as love. The more complete the degree of turning away from God, the more distance we put between ourselves and the grace we receive in his presence, and thus the more likely we are to continue to sin.

PERSONAL SIN

When we resist or turn away from God's love for us, we cannot receive his grace, and without God's grace we lose the most effective means to avoid our tendency toward personal sin. While original sin is inherited from our ancestral parents, personal sin is our own production (though we can blame Adam and Eve for the fact that we were born imperfect). Regardless of excuse, Catholic doctrine teaches that after Adam and Eve's fall from grace, humanity retained, in weakened form, its free will. Since we still have free will, even in a fallen world we can choose to "turn toward God", or *conversio ad deo*, and not sin.

VENIAL VERSUS MORTAL

Catholics classify sins as either venial or mortal (theologians break these sins down into smaller categories, but for most of us the mortal/venial distinction is sufficient). To continue the metaphor of turning away from God, a venial (from the Latin word *venia*, or "forgiveness, pardon") sin would be a slight acknowledgement, and a mortal (from Latin *mortalis*, or "death") sin would be turning one's back, which is the rudest of cuts that would sever all social ties (*see Before the Mortal Blow, opposite*). Biblical reference to the venial versus mortal sin distinction can be found in 1 John 5:16–17:

> He that knoweth his brother to sin a sin which is not to death, let him ask, and life shall be given to him, who sinneth not to death. There is a sin unto death: for that I say not that any man ask.

Venial sins (those little rudenesses to God) do not in and of themselves sever all ties and destroy our hope for eternal life with God. However, like any rudeness, they can damage the relationship between us and him and lead in time to the final rift unless

BEFORE THE MORTAL BLOW

Unconfessed and therefore unforgiven mortal sins cause the death of the soul and consign the sinner to hell – eternal punishment. However, God is fair and just, so mortal sins are not easy to commit. You cannot "accidentally" commit a mortal sin. Before you turn away from God and choose the devil, three ominous conditions must be present:

Grave Matter: The act, to any person of normal reason, would be understood as evil.

Full Knowledge: The potential sinner must know that the act is evil. A person with a mental illness, such as schizophrenia, for example, may not have full knowledge that an act he is about to commit is heinous.

Deliberate Consent: It is up to us. The choice is ours, because God endowed us with free will. We can choose to turn toward the Dark or the Light. If you hit someone with your car accidentally and kill him or her, that is not a mortal sin; but if the accident happened because you drank alcohol at a party, knowing that you planned to drive home, then the accident is a mortal sin because you acted irresponsibly.

Right St Augustine thought one of the most terrible results of the fall of man was libido dominandi, *or "the lust for dominance". Cain, son of Adam, enacts a tragic result of that lust – fratricide – in* The Killing of Abel, *a detail from the 1379–83 Grabower Altarpiece by Master Bertram of Minden.*

we mend our ways. As this particular passage makes clear, mortal sin leads to the death of the soul.

THE UNFORGIVABLE SIN

The New Testament refers to an eternal, or unforgivable, sin. In Mark 3:22–30, Christ says, "All sins will be forgiven the sons of men, and whatever blasphemies they may utter; but he who blasphemes against the Holy Spirit never has forgiveness, but is subject to eternal condemnation." Christ also refers to unforgivable sin in Matthew 12:3–32, when Pharisees, who witness Christ cast out demons, claim Christ had the power of Beelzebub (the devil).

The unforgivable sin is connected to a wilful rejection of God in the face of all the manifest good that is clearly vouchsafed to us. This sin consists of seeing good and perversely calling it evil. It blasphemes against the Holy Spirit in his role as a "convincer of sin", which is what Pope John Paul II called the Holy Spirit in the 1986 encyclical, *Dominum et Vivificantem*. John Paul pointed out that the Holy Spirit's role is to purify humankind's consciences, so that they are able to call good and evil by their proper names. When we radically reject the Holy Spirit, we are no longer able to see our good and our salvation even when they stare us in the face. This is the unforgivable sin.

Right A 14th-century biblical illumination shows the fool who said, "There is no God" (Psalm 53). The sin of apostasy, or rejecting God, is called the unforgivable sin.

THE SEVEN DEADLY SINS

SINCE THE 5TH CENTURY, CATHOLIC THEOLOGIANS HAVE DISCUSSED A LIST OF PARTICULAR SINS FOR THE FAITHFUL TO AVOID, BUT IT WAS ONLY IN THE 12TH CENTURY THAT A CREED LISTED THE SEVEN DEADLY SINS.

Although the list of the seven deadly, or cardinal, sins has traditionally been paired with a list of virtues, it is the sins that are remembered. The seven deadly sins (and the corresponding virtues), in the order of descending gravity, are: pride (humility), avarice (generosity), envy (kindness), wrath (patience), lust (chastity), gluttony (temperance) and sloth (diligence).

The Catholic catechism refers to these sins as capital vices, noting that they are capital because they produce other sins. In fact, the seven deadly sins are actually categories of sin, and

Below Hieronymus Bosch's 15th-century Tabletop of the Seven Deadly Sins and the Four Last Things *shows the deadly sins balanced with four medallions of the four last things: death, judgement, heaven and hell.*

sins falling within those categories are not always mortal. For example, eating two desserts when you really needed only one – or none – would be a sin classified as gluttony, but it would not be enough to send you to eternal punishment (unless it was a symptom of a much larger problem).

EARLY MENTIONS
The tradition of the seven deadly sins originated in the writings of John Cassian, a 5th-century monk and ascetic. In his book *Collationes*, he provided a list of eight vices that were particularly tormenting to ascetic monks, as follows: gluttony, impurity, covetousness, anger, dejection, accidia (or boredom), vainglory and pride. Pope Gregory the Great included a similar list in his book *Moralia on Job*. Cassian and Gregory

Above The virtue of flourishing generosity is seen in opposition to the deadly vice of avarice in this 1945 illustration, Allegory of Generosity and Avarice, *by Rémy Hetreau.*

may have been influenced in turn by *Psychomachia*, an allegorical poem by the 4th-century Roman Christian poet Aurelius Prudentius Clemens. His poem featured a battle between personified virtues and vices in the style of the *Aeneid*. Prudentius may have influenced later authors who made specific use of the deadly sins in their writing, in particular, Geoffrey Chaucer and Dante Alighieri. Of the church fathers, Thomas Aquinas in his *Summa Theologiae* (1265–73) paid attention to the seven deadly sins, for example, analysing multiple manifestations of gluttony, such as *studiose*, or "eating too daintily", and *laute*, or "eating too expensively".

BY COUNCIL DECREE
The wide dissemination and subsequent popularity in public discourse of the seven deadly sins can be traced back to the Church's Fourth Lateran Council (1214). One of the decrees of the council was the

In 2005, the Church published a "Compendium of the Social Doctrine of the Church", which reasserted the humanist position of the Catholic Church on all social issues. The widely publicized list of the seven "social sins" derived from this compendium. The social sins of the 21st century are:

1: Bioethical violations, such as birth control
2: Morally dubious experiments, such as stem cell research
3: Drug abuse
4: Polluting the environment
5: Contributing to the widening gap between rich and poor
6: Excessive wealth
7: Creating poverty

The compendium states that social sin falls into two categories: "On the one hand, the all-consuming desire for profit, and on the other, the thirst for power, with the intention of imposing one's will upon others." Bishop Gianfranco Girotti also stated that, "While sin used to mostly concern the individual, today it has mainly a social resonance, thanks to the phenomenon of globalization."

Above The oil industry often displays social sin. It pollutes the Earth in its desire for great wealth.

requirement that Catholics attend yearly confession. In order to make a good confession – or any confession at all – the ordinary communicant needed to be educated in the concept of sin and given a vocabulary to talk about it. Parish priests as well had to learn the language of sin. In the Lambeth Constitutions of 1281, Archbishop of Canterbury John Peckham provided the clergy with a syllabus that included the seven deadly sins (as well as the seven virtues and the seven sacraments).

THE NUMBER SEVEN
Many Christians have asked why there are only seven deadly sins and have noted some considerable

Above St Thomas Aquinas, one of the Church's most erudite theologians, provided an exhaustive analysis of the seven deadly sins in his Summa Theologiae. *This portrait of Aquinas is by Alessandro Botticelli (1445–1510).*

omissions from the list, such as cruelty to others. This is because seven was considered a number of significance in the Old Testament, starting with the creation of the world in seven days, and it has reappeared in many other guises as an important ordering principle in Scripture, in particular, in the "Book of Sevens", Revelation. Seven is generally considered a number of high sacred significance.

JUDGEMENT DAY

ACCORDING TO CATHOLICISM, EACH PERSON IS JUDGED AT DEATH (PARTICULAR JUDGEMENT). CHRIST WILL RETURN ON JUDGEMENT DAY TO JUDGE THE LIVING AND THE DEAD (GENERAL JUDGEMENT).

The Catholic vision of Judgement Day is a particularly specific one. Catholic tradition teaches that there are two separate and specific judgements: the particular and the general. The particular judgement, as the name implies, has more significance for the fate of each person, while the general judgement is the Judgement Day that will see the Second Coming of Christ and the end of the world as we know it.

AT DEATH
Particular judgement happens at the exact moment of individual death, when the soul separates from the body. Catholic sacred tradition teaches that the particular judgement is instantaneous, so that the soul will simply know, immediately, what the verdict is and go on its own in the right direction. The choices are heaven, which is reserved for the perfectly pure; Purgatory, for the vast group of the imperfectly pure

(those with venial sins that are still unconfessed and unforgiven); and hell, for the definitely not pure (those with mortal sins that remain unconfessed and unforgiven).

A PAPAL BULL
This belief in the prompt fulfilment of the sentence was a controversial one within the early Church. Some Church fathers argued that either the bliss of the beatific vision (for example, the intuitive knowledge of God) or the suffering of the tormenting fires of hell would be postponed until the general judgement. Pope Benedict XII convened a commission to decide the question, and after four months of testimony

Below During the Second Coming of Christ, saints will be rewarded with the beatific vision of Christ, implied in this early 15th-century German painting by his larger size in relation to the others and the blissful expression of the saints.

Above Aided by its guardian angel, this soul is slipping away to its judgement (fresco detail from the Last Judgement, *Voronet Monastery, Moldavia, Romania). The soul will be reunited to the body it leaves behind at the general judgement.*

from various theologians, he issued the 1336 papal bull, *Benedictus Deus*. This bull proclaimed, once and for all, that your fate was indeed determined right away.

GENERAL JUDGEMENT
The judgement that has been traditionally depicted in Western art – full of angels, demons, writhing naked bodies and a just Christ sitting on a throne with a group of saints in attendance – is known as the general judgement. It is a popular theme of medieval and Renaissance paintings.

Church tradition teaches that at the general judgement, all bodies, both the saved and the damned, will be rejoined to their immortal souls. The wicked, unfortunately, will not be happy to meet their bodies again, as noted in Revelation 9:6, "The wicked shall seek death, and shall not find it, shall desire to die, and death shall fly from them…"

Scripture specifically assigns the general judgement as a role for Christ. In John 5:28, it states, "…for the hour cometh wherein all that are in the graves shall hear the voice of the Son of God." This is why the general judgement is also referred to as Christ's Second Coming.

It will be during the general judgement that the Godhead's ultimate purpose for mankind will finally be fulfilled.

The general judgement appears to have the same function as a public trial: although a particular judgement has already been pronounced, the general judgement is needed so that all may witness the justice of the final decrees. General judgement features an aspect of public proclamation, as described in the Athanasian Creed, "at whose coming all men must rise with their bodies and are to render an account of their deeds". The general judgement is the day of public accounting and is a final judgement.

THE FINAL JUDGEMENT

Catholicism teaches its followers that when Christ returns, it will be for the final judgement and that the resulting reign will be eternal and in heaven. Over the centuries, however, Christians have held different

Below Weighing souls after death, shown in this 12th-century Catalan fresco, was an ancient belief of Egypt and Greece as well as early Christianity. Traditionally, the archangel Michael escorted souls to God on Judgement Day and weighed them.

views on what will happen during the final judgement (*see* Final Judgement and the Millennium, *below*). Pre-millennialism describes this as an actual return of Christ for a thousand years, before the final judgement. However, post-millennialism prefers to describe an achieved perfection on earth due to the preaching of the gospel, as a result of which the entire earth will be Christianized. After the thousand years of earthly Christian perfection, then Jesus returns to conduct the final judgement. Pre-millennialism posits a return and reign of Christ on earth prior to the final judgement,

Above A phalanx of saints are in attendance above, the mouth of hell gaping is on the right and delight or dismay (as applicable) are shown on earth in The Last Judgement *by Bartholomaeus Spranger (1546–1611).*

whereas post-millennialism believes in a period of achieved perfection on earth prior to the final judgement.

The Catholic Church refutes pre-millennialism and also rejects the post-millennial view that there will ever be a period of perfection on earth prior to the final judgement (this view would contradict the doctrine of original sin).

FINAL JUDGEMENT AND THE MILLENNIUM

The Book of Revelation, and Chapter 20 in particular, is problematic for Catholics. This difficult chapter describes a thousand-year period when Satan will be bound with chains in a pit, after which he will be "loosed for a little while" and emerge to deceive again. This thousand-year period when Satan will be bound is known as the millennium. There are many gradations of opinion (much of it Protestant evangelical) on the millennium, but most understand it as a thousand-year "golden age" of the triumph of Christianity, a reign of Christ himself (pre-millennialism) or of the Christian religion (post-millennialism) on earth that will be distinct from the final judgement and distinct from eternity.

VISIONS OF HEAVEN

THE WRITERS OF THE BIBLE REFERRED TO HEAVEN AS A PHYSICAL PLACE, GOD'S FIRMAMENT. HOWEVER, TODAY'S CATHOLIC CHURCH DESCRIBES HEAVEN AS A STATE OF BEING.

The Bible uses several descriptive phrases when referring to heaven, including a kingdom, a crown, the city of God, a reward and even an inheritance. This metaphorical variety on the part of biblical writers shows that the early Christians felt a certain liberty in their attempts to imagine heaven, as long as it provided a good image.

In the popular imagination, both in the past and present, heaven is often seen as being palatial, expressed in the term "pearly gates", which derives from the opulent description of heaven as the "New Jerusalem". In Revelation 21:21, its gates "are twelve pearls, one to each: and every several gate was of one pearl". In paintings and movies, heaven is

Above Orderly groups of saints approach the fortified portal of paradise in this 1480 detail from the Last Judgement, *Voronet Monastery, Moldavia, Romania.*

dreamy, awash in clouds that are often shot through with pastel rays of effulgent light. In common usage, "heavenly" is the adjective of choice for anything highly pleasurable, from pizza ("a slice of heaven") to relaxing in a hot bubble bath.

GOD'S FIRMAMENT
Despite these images, the etymology of the word "heaven" derives from words referring to "a roof or covering", confirming the majority view that heaven is above us. Genesis 7:10 describes God making the "firmament", which serves as a vast buttress that divides the elemental regions of the earth: "And God made a firmament, and divided the waters that were under the firmament, from those that were above the firmament... And God called the firmament heaven...".

Left St Augustine, in one of his most influential works, Civitate Dei, *described two opposing cities, the earthly and the heavenly. These are shown in this early 15th-century French illustration,* La Cite de Dieu, *or "City of God".*

This soaring support of the world came to be associated with the abode of God, "…a building of God, a house not made with hands, eternal in heaven" (2 Corinthians 5:1). Medieval cathedrals aspired to represent in earthly architecture the inspiring span and lofty height of heaven.

A STATE OF BEING

Catholic doctrine, however, is circumspect in describing heaven as an actual physical place. No doctrine of the Church has ever attempted to establish the latitude and longitude of heaven, and although it is the traditional concept, the modern Church is even cautious in describing heaven as the dwelling place of God. This is because by doing so, it would imply that God can be contained in a particular place.

Instead, the Church describes heaven as a state of being achieved only by those who are pure of all sin. The Catholic catechism says that when we enter into the state of being of heaven, we will have a "beatific vision" of God. Unless God makes himself open to an individual for contemplation, God cannot be seen. If this contemplation takes place, our spiritual and intellectual perceptive capacity will be unbound from its earthly limitations so that we will be able to perceive and receive God – this is a beatific vision. Such an encounter "is what the perfect happiness of heaven will consist of".

In 1336, Pope Benedict XII defined belief in the beatific vision (for those who attain heaven) as a dogma of the faith. Theologians, however, put limits on even the beatific vision. They state that while we will see God (such as in the Trinity) entirely, our vision will not have the absolute and infinite clarity with which God perceives himself. The Church also believes that there are degrees of beatitude granted to the Blessed; saints have a more extensive vision of God.

Above New residents, borne on the backs of obliging angels, are welcomed to heaven with open arms in this 15th-century work from Hastings Book of Hours.

BEING REUNITED

There is also a more homely aspect to heaven. The Church teaches that in heaven we will be reunited with our beloved family and friends who have gone there before us, and the language of some of the prayers for the dead in the Church emphasizes that heaven is the true home of the righteous and that our arrival in heaven will actually be a homecoming. In the service that is given for the dead, the Prayer of Commendation states:

May you return to [your Creator] who formed you from the dust of the earth.
May holy Mary, the angels, and all the saints come to meet you as you go forth from this life…
May you see your Redeemer face to face.

The sense is of a family's loving, eager greeting to one of its members who has been too long away. Heaven is also a homecoming in that we return to our first home, paradise, redeemed from a long sojourn in the fallen world. St Augustine said, "Thou hast made us for Thyself (O God) and our heart is troubled till it rests in Thee."

Below The Madonna and saints contentedly work, read and play in a walled garden in this c.1410 German painting, Paradise Garden. *The garden is the earthly mirror of paradise, which is from the old Persian word for "a walled garden" or "park".*

PURGATORY

CATHOLICS BELIEVE THAT AFTER DEATH THERE ARE MANY SOULS THAT
ARE NOT DESTINED FOR HELL BUT THAT ARE NOT READY TO ENTER
HEAVEN WITH GOD – THEY GO TO PURGATORY TO BE CLEANSED OF SIN.

The Catholic doctrine regarding the concept of Purgatory has developed from the Catholic belief that God is both merciful and just. Because God is merciful, sinners can atone for their non-mortal sins even after death, but because he is just, this atonement is a requirement that must be met.

Purgatory (from the Latin word *purgare*, "to make clean, to purify") is where that atonement happens. The Church teaches that Purgatory is where those who die without mortal sin on their soul, but also without making full satisfaction to God for their sins, must suffer for a time to purify their souls and to make recompense to God. Purgatory is different from hell because it is temporary. Souls suffering in Purgatory know that eventually they will be with God. In traditional teaching, Purgatory is a place; however, in more contemporary teaching it is a state of being.

A DEVELOPING CONCEPT

The early church Councils of Lyons (1274), Florence (1438–43) and Trent (1545–63) all made statements describing, with varying degrees of

Above Few theologians were as aware of the struggle between good and evil as St Augustine. In this 15th-century French woodblock print, he focuses on his work despite the clamour of demonic distractions around him.

specificity, the Church's developing concept of Purgatory. In *The City of God*, St Augustine expressed his belief that there would be temporal punishment after death, and Pope (later St) Gregory the Great, influenced by Augustine, was principally responsible for refining the idea of *purgatorius ignis*, or the "cleansing fire", into doctrine.

Going to Purgatory is not completely inevitable. The pure do not go to Purgatory, and Catholics also believe that those who, through no fault of their own, have suffered terribly in life (say an unjustly convicted prisoner), essentially pay recompense for their sins by experiencing Purgatory here on earth. However, those who have been less than pure will go to Purgatory.

PURGING OUR SINS

Purgatory is necessary, in most cases, even if you have made an appropriate confession of your sins and have been forgiven. The Catholic concept of penance is that temporal punishment is required to discharge our debt

Above Purgatorial punishments match the earthly sin. In an illustration in Le Trésor de Sapience *by Jean de Gerson (1363–1429), the prideful are pushed into the ground and trodden on, expiating their arrogance by being forced to grovel in flames.*

of sin as a necessary condition of absolution. The Church makes the point that Purgatory is necessary not because God is vengeful but because our sins, like a stain, have worked into our essence. Only the spiritually clean can truly see God, and being spiritually cleansed is difficult work, a sense expressed by the early Church father, Gregory of Nyssa, in his reflections on Purgatory:

…we may figure to ourselves the agonized struggle of that soul which has wrapped itself up in earthy material passions, when God is drawing it, his own one, to himself, and the foreign matter, which has somehow grown into its substance, has to be scraped from it by main force, and so occasions it that keen intolerable anguish.

INTERCEDING SAINTS

Catholicism also teaches that the prayers of the faithful still residing on earth can help the souls in Purgatory. The Communion of Saints refers to the belief that all faithful members of the Church, whether living or dead, are united as members of a single spiritual community and can help one another; therefore, the saints in heaven can intercede with God to help us on earth, and by offering suffrages – our prayers, fasting and works of charity on earth – we can obtain divine mercy for the souls in Purgatory, perhaps even hastening the time that they will be released into heaven.

Above Part of a larger panoramic 15th-century French painting by Enguerrand Quarton, The Coronation of the Virgin, *this detail depicts Purgatory in an unexpected location – just beneath the walled city of Rome. It includes a few fortunate penitents who have completed their time in Purgatory and are rising from the depths, with the aid of angels.*

HEAVEN SHOULD NOT BE FOR SALE

Indulgences, or remission of time spent in Purgatory, became a hot trading commodity during the early 16th century. The trade in indulgences reflected the extreme concern with the afterlife during this era when the Black Death (plague) had decimated Europe's population. Pope Leo X took advantage of this situation to enrich the Church coffers by selling indulgences – though selling them is a mortal sin (Leo, a member of the Medici family, was extremely corrupt). Leo was selling plenary indulgences, a particular type of indulgence that provides total remission of the temporal punishment (time in Purgatory).

Indulgences are legal in the Church, but because of this earlier history they are often misunderstood as being a kind of coupon for time off from Purgatory that the Church offers in exchange for cash. However, what many do not understand is that even forgiven sins may result in some time in Purgatory after death, before an individual is in acceptable spiritual shape for heaven. Plenary indulgences can free you from that prospect, but there are conditions attached. First, they should never be offered solely in exchange for money. Sins must be forgiven by confession; the person receiving the indulgence must go to confession and receive Communion for a week, and the person must perform charitable works prescribed by the Church.

Above Johann Tetzel, a Dominican prior, sells indulgences in Germany in this 18th-century woodblock print.

VISIONS OF HELL

MODERN CHURCH DOCTRINE ON HELL IS RELATIVELY TAME IN COMPARISON TO THE LURID VISION OF ETERNAL DAMNATION THAT HAS GRIPPED THE POPULAR IMAGINATION SINCE THE MIDDLE AGES.

The Scriptures contain a number of references to a hell with a fearsome aspect, describing it as a place of fire and darkness. Among these are: "pool of fire" (Revelation 19:20), "everlasting fire (Matthew 18:8; 25:41; Jude 7), "unquenchable fire" (Matthew 3:12), "furnace of fire where they will weep and gnash their teeth" (Matthew 13:42, 50), "exterior darkness" (Matthew 7:12; 22:13; 25:30) and "mist" or "storm of darkness" (2 Peter 2:17; Jude 13).

ETERNAL DAMNATION
These are all arresting descriptions, particularly when coupled with the concept of being never ending, because hell, of course, is eternal. Contemporary Catholic clergy are

Above The license allowed in portraits of Satan is evident in this 15th-century rendition, which depicts him with belled horns, wings like ribbed leaves and tusks.

unlikely to dwell for long on these descriptions. However, in medieval times and up to the Second Vatican Council (1962–5), priests and nuns often invoked the grim spectre of hell in an effort to scare their congregations into good behaviour. The Church considered meditation on the "Last Things," which are death, judgement, heaven and hell, as salutary to spiritual health.

We are indebted to the medieval period for many of our images of hell as a place of gruesome punishments and apocalyptic landscapes. The vision literature of the Middle Ages featured an entire genre of texts that recounted personal tours of hell, featuring horrible retributions that were tailor-made to suit the sin. This early vision literature influenced the great Florentine poet Dante, who in his *Inferno* described hell as a series of nine concentric circles, with limbo, the least severe, at the outer rim and Satan confined at the centre.

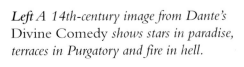

Left A 14th-century image from Dante's Divine Comedy *shows stars in paradise, terraces in Purgatory and fire in hell.*

Right A demon delivers a new soul to hell to join eternally tormented souls in this detail from a 15th-century painting by Enguerrand Quarton.

HELLFIRE

The fires of hell are supernatural: they do not require fuel and they do not consume those they burn, but blaze eternally. Traditional Catholic theology describes hellfire as *poena sensus*, meaning the "pain of sense". *Poena sensus* is considered a corporeal pain, because Scripture specifies that after the last judgement, the damned will be rejoined to their bodies. Some have noted that *poena sensus* was an appropriate pain, because mortal sin is often allied to excessive desire for physical and material pleasures.

THE CHURCH'S VIEW

The Second Vatican Council did not mention hell, but the gentling of Church rhetoric on hell dates from then. The current Catholic definition of hell, as noted by Pope John Paul II, states that the ultimate punishment for sin itself is hell, and that it is "more than a physical place". Hell represents the state of those who have chosen freely and completely to "separate themselves from God".

The Catholic catechism describes hell as a state of being where the individual chooses to reject God's love, thereby dying in mortal sin. By choosing to exclude him or herself from God, and by not repenting, he or she will be separated from God for eternity – this is hell.

To older Catholics whose lifetime spans the expositions of both the older eternal, infernal physical punishment vision of hell from before the Second Vatican Council and today's metaphysical "eternally separated from God" hell, the difference can be striking. This is a situation in which the Catholic Church has exercised its magisterial authority to interpret Scripture. Here we see the evolution of Church tradition at work.

John Paul II also went on to say that we need to understand the meanings presented by the images of hell in Scripture, which illustrate an empty and frustated life if living without accepting God. The Pope calls the scriptural words on hell "images" and says, not that they "are" hell, but that they "show" a state of being. So, heaven is unity with God and hell is separation from God. Although John Paul II did not repudiate the old concept of hell, he did go so far as to redefine the terms of the discussion.

Above The damned make their way to hell and the pure to heaven in Rogier van der Weyden's 15th-century painting of the Last Judgement.

THE PAIN OF LOSS

Poena damni, or the "pain of loss", refers to psychic pain. The Church describes *poena damni* as a real, intense pain, rooted in the loss of the beatific vision. The damned still retain the human need for God, even if they have rejected this desire, and so are tormented eternally by the unquiet described by Augustine in his *Confessions*, "...You have formed us for yourself, and our hearts are unquiet until they find rest in you." The disquiet of the damned can never be stilled, so they burn with eternal despair. It is the *poena damni* that Pope John Paul II emphasized in his definition of hell. "Damnation" comes from the Latin word *damnum*, which means "loss", emphasizing that the essence of hell is in the pain of loss.

VISIONS OF DAMNATION

THE ARTISTIC REPUTATION OF PAINTINGS OF HELL HAS ALWAYS ECLIPSED THOSE OF HEAVEN. BLISS SEEMS TO LEAVE ARTISTS AT A LOSS, BUT THEY APPEAR TO HAVE A PASSION FOR PAINTING ETERNAL PUNISHMENT.

Hell was by no means an unusual subject in religious art. Two popular themes are of "The Harrowing of Hell", when Christ descended into hell after his Crucifixion, before his Resurrection, and the Last Judgement. Numerous artists, including Giotto di Bondone (*c*.1267–1337), Fra Angelico (*c*.1387–1455), Hans Memling (*c*.1440–94) and Michelangelo (1475–1564), have depicted hell. Giotto's hell is a fiery nether region dwarfed by a conquering Christ who was enthroned in an orderly heaven with the righteous in attendance.

Memling's triptych *The Last Judgement* depicts hell as a flaming pit into which the undifferentiated bodies of the damned tumble,

Above The descent into the mouth of hell was a standard subject of medieval "doom" paintings. In a detail from Hans Memling's 15th-century version, the damned souls tumble with arms and legs extended in almost balletic poses.

superintended by colossal and well-armed demons. Jesus holds centre stage as the archangel Michael weighs the souls. The left panel shows the pure being led to heaven, while the right panel shows the damned.

Fra Angelico's hell is honey-combed with flaming caverns where bleeding, naked people are bound, speared and burnt by gleeful demons resembling diabolical monkeys, or the unfortunate occupants are eaten in great gulps by Satan himself, looking like a great ape.

THE MASTER OF HELL

Pre-eminent among all the painters of the horrors of hell is Hieronymus Bosch (*c*.1450–1516). He was an unassuming Dutchman who never travelled far from 's-Hertogenbosch, his village in the duchy of Brabant (modern-day Netherlands). In a small house on the market square, besides making devotional wood-cuts, he painted hell and its countless demons in endlessly inventive, startlingly modern, gruesome detail.

In contrast to many of the other illustrations of hell, Bosch's chaotic, brightly coloured depictions are typically overrun with life, albeit in monstrous forms: strange demons that resemble insects or sea creatures, monstrous birds, odd plants with pod-like excrescences, enormous ears, mussel shells, eggs, unusual ice skaters and odd little bathyspheres with grilles for doors. One representative Bosch monster is a fish swallowing another fish, with lobster legs and a spiny tail.

Bosch's demons tend to have long whip-like tails resembling the stingers on stingrays. The damned are not simply burnt or bound, but are

tortured in an indescribable variety of obscene manners by a wealth of phantasmagoric creatures. Hellfire burns on the outskirts of Bosch's canvases, in dark regions shot with red light; unlike the typical painting of hell, the flames are not the principle torture of the damned.

THE FIRST SURREALIST

Because he married an heiress, Bosch did not depend on the Church hierarchy for commissions of his work, unlike many other artists. Free from the need to submit his compositions to the censorship of the Church, he was able to produce beautifully painted works featuring imagery not found in any Scripture.

Bosch's technique came to him naturally: several of his relatives were also painters, including his grandfather, father, brother and three uncles. The Flemish style of slender, restrained human bodies and of

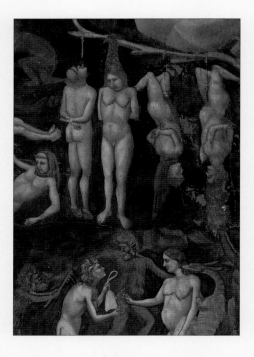

Above The damned are subjected to various forms of torture applied by tiny demons, from being suspended by the hair to the racking of bare skin, in this detail from Giotto di Bondone's *c*.1303 painting, The Last Judgement.

Right Looking at Hieronymus Bosch's imagery, such as The Garden of Earthly Delights (c.1500), it is hard to believe that he lived and painted in the 15th century. His imagery and technique still look startlingly modern today.

meticulous attention to detail is evident in his work. However, Bosch's iconography is like no other religious painter's and is a precursor in its hallucinatory specificity to the early 20th-century work of the Surrealists, artists that were hailed as "revolutionary" more than five centuries after Bosch.

A DEVOUT BROTHER

Surprisingly, the little-known story of Bosch's life suggests that he partici-pated in the conventional pious observances of society: he was a sworn member of the Society of Our Lady, a devout brotherhood founded in 1318. The society was a powerful but exclusive group, and

Bosch was allowed to become a member upon marriage because his wife was already one. The studies of the brotherhood may have contri-buted to Bosch's obsession with hell: they were said to conduct daily readings of accounts of hell.

Despite his deeply unconven-tional work, during his lifetime Bosch became enormously popular among the laity, if not the Church itself. King Philip II (1527–98), the Spanish monarch known for his collection of saintly relics, was a particular admirer of Bosch. He was a keen collector of his works and kept Bosch's painting of a wheel depicting the seven deadly sins in his bedroom at the Escorial Palace.

Left Only in the hell of Bosch would one find what resembles a penguin on ice skates, as seen in this 1503–4 detail from Die Hölle. *The horror of Bosch's hell is its complete lack of logic and reason – all the universe is askew.*

Above Fra Angelico's vision of hell exemplifies the "cooking and eating" motif, with a cauldron of unfortunates being boiled, Satan gorging on their flesh and lesser demons contemplating bodies massed for their delectation.

LIMBO

A REGION ON THE EDGE OF HELL, LIMBO WAS RESERVED FOR THOSE WHO DIED FREE FROM SERIOUS PERSONAL SIN, YET, THROUGH NO FAULT OF THEIR OWN, WERE STILL IN A STATE OF ORIGINAL SIN.

The name "limbo" derives from the Latin *limbus*, meaning "hem", "border" or "edge", reflecting its juxtaposition with hell. The concept of limbo was developed as an extension of the doctrinal importance that the Church ascribes to original sin and baptism, added to its belief that only those who are free of all vestiges of sin will be worthy of the beatific vision of God.

There are two categories of candidate that can go to limbo. These are either virtuous people who died before Jesus redeemed them from original sin, or babies who died before being baptized.

GOD'S GIFT

Original sin is an inescapable fate for all humans, with only the Virgin Mary being conceived without it. Romans 5:18 says, "Therefore, as by the offence of one, unto all men condemnation; so also by the justice of one, unto all men justification of life." This scriptural syllogism makes clear the direction of the Church's thinking: if salvation, that gift of God, is going to apply to all people, then so must the unfortunate predecessor to salvation: the hereditary stain that marks all the unbaptized as exiles from God. In other words, the unbaptized are at risk.

Above The halo over Mary in Pietro Lorenzetti's 14th-century painting, The Birth of the Virgin Mary, *is a clue that she was conceived without original sin.*

THE TWO LIMBOS

Catholic tradition originally taught that there were two limbos: *limbus patrum*, for virtuous but unbaptized adults (*patrum* refers to "fathers"), reflecting the belief that the Old Testament patriarchs – including Abraham – would go there, and *limbus infantium*, for unbaptized infants. The two limbos were required because *limbus patrum* would end with the Second Coming, whereas *limbus infantium* was permanent. The fathers could not be baptized because Jesus Christ had not yet redeemed man. The babies were not baptized because they had died before anyone had baptized them.

In fact, this is why the Church teaches that in an emergency, anyone can baptize a baby by making the sign of the cross over the infant and

Left Abraham holds the souls of the righteous in this 12th-century French manuscript. Because he lived before Jesus was born, Abraham was not redeemed before he died and went to limbo.

speaking the words, "I baptize thee (NAME) in the name of the Father and of the Son and of the Holy Spirit." Many doctors, nurses and midwives have performed such baptisms over newborns they feared would not survive.

INNOCENT BUT IN LIMBO

The ultimate fate of the innocent but unbaptized was controversial, as were so many theological issues before their applicable doctrines were established. St Augustine was the most severe: this 4th-century theologian believed that the innocently unbaptized would be punished, though more mildly than the truly damned. The theologian Peter Abelard (1070–1142) believed that the innocent but unbaptized suffered no physical pain, only the pain of the loss of God, and Pope Innocent III (1160–1216) agreed.

St Thomas Aquinas held an even more soothing concept, stating that limbo was a place of "natural happiness", but with the crucial exception that its residents were deprived of the transcendent joy of true union with God (known as

supernatural happiness). However, the Council of Florence (1438–43) seemed to backtrack, stating, "the souls of those dying in actual mortal sin or in original sin alone go down at once into hell, to be punished, however, with widely different

penalties". Yet the teaching of Aquinas remained the somewhat equivocal general Church position – crucially, it was never a definitive doctrine – right up until the 21st century and the pontificate of Pope Benedict XVI.

A 21ST-CENTURY DEBATE

Centuries of debate about limbo continue. In April 2007, the International Theological Commission, an advisory panel to the Vatican (previously headed by Cardinal Ratzinger, now Pope Benedict XVI) published a report endorsing the belief that *limbus infantium* was too limiting when it came to salvation. The report affirmed the superabundance of God's Grace over sin, noting that Christ's relationship with humankind must be stronger than any links with Adam. In a contest between original sin and salvation where no personal guilt is involved, the power of Christ's mercy vanquishes the power of Adam's sinfulness. The report, however, does not repudiate the Church's doctrine of original sin or the need for baptism. Instead, it theorizes that in the case of unbaptized infants, God can give his Grace without the need of the sacrament being given in baptism.

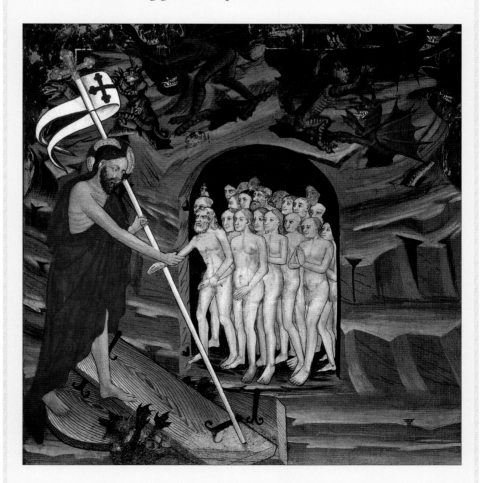

Above *In the Harrowing of Hell, between death and Resurrection, Christ went to limbo to free the just who died before him. It is depicted in this 15th-century fresco.*

Above *The theologian Peter Abelard, shown in this 19th-century engraving, supported the idea of* limbus infantium. *Pope Innocent III accepted his view.*

PRACTISING CATHOLICISM

One of the world's biggest institutions, the Catholic Church has a huge hierarchy. As leader of the Church, the pope rules from the Vatican, the centre of the Church's government. From there, the pope provides guidance to the bishops in their dioceses, the priests in their parishes, the monks and nuns in their monasteries and missionaries, and ordinary lay people in their everyday activities. People from all these walks of life seek inspiration from the Church as they practise their faith and celebrate the holy days that occur throughout the liturgical year.

The Eucharist, along with baptism and confirmation, is a sacrament of initiation into the Catholic Church. These girls are taking their first Holy Communion in Charlotte, North Carolina, in the United States.

INSTITUTIONS OF THE CHURCH

On Easter Day, tens of thousands of Roman Catholics pack into St Peter's Square in Vatican City, Rome, to hear the pope celebrate Mass and give his Easter address. The event is broadcast live around the world: the address and the Apostolic blessing that follows it are termed *Urbi et Orbi* ("to the City [of Rome] and to the World").

As spiritual leader of the Roman Catholic Church, the pope heads a vast global organization. Pope Benedict XVI's third Easter address, delivered on 23 March 2008, was televised in 57 countries, and he followed it by giving Easter greetings in no fewer than 63 languages. According to figures released by the Church hierarchy in March 2008, more than one in six people worldwide – 17.4 per cent of the global population – is Roman Catholic. This percentage is equal to around 1.13 billion people.

For these people the pope's authority is supreme. As well as being Europe's only absolute monarch, ruler of Vatican City (the world's smallest independent state), he stands at the head of the Holy See, the Church's machinery of government, and its administrative structure, the Roman Curia. He is at the peak of the great Church hierarchy of cardinals and archbishops, bishops, priests and deacons that also includes the many thousands of priests, monks, friars, nuns and religious sisters in the Church's religious orders. He is nothing less than the Vicar of Christ, his representative on earth. Yet in all these roles, the pope is called to humility and service: among his official titles is "Servant of the Servants of God", in line with the passage in St Matthew's Gospel (20:27) where Christ declares "whoever would be first among you must be your slave".

Above Standing in the central loggia of St Peter's Basilica, Pope Benedict XVI gives the Urbi et Orbi *blessing that follows the Easter Sunday Mass.*

Left A vast crowd of the Roman Catholic faithful attend open-air Mass in St Peter's Square at the Vatican on Easter Sunday.

THE HOLY FATHER

THE POPE HAS ULTIMATE AUTHORITY OVER ROMAN CATHOLICS AND OVER THE CHURCH. HE IS ONE OF A LONG SUCCESSION OF POPES, ELECTED TO THIS POSITION BY THE COLLEGE OF CARDINALS.

The title "pope" derives from the words in Late Latin (*papa*) and Greek (*pappas*) meaning "father", and his position is similar to that of a father in a patriarchal family. The pope is addressed as "Your Holiness" and "Holy Father". In addition, the pope has eight formal titles listed in the official directory of the Holy See (the central government of the Catholic Church): Bishop of Rome, Vicar of Jesus Christ, Successor of the Prince of the Apostles, Supreme Pontiff of the Universal Church, Primate of Italy, Archbishop and Metropolitan of the Roman Province, Sovereign of the State of Vatican City and Servant of the Servants of God.

SUCCESSOR OF ST PETER

Bishop of Rome and Successor of the Prince of the Apostles are two titles that reflect the fact that for Roman Catholics the pope is a spiritual descendant of the apostle St Peter. Pope Benedict XVI, who has been pope from 19 April 2005, is said to be the 265th pope in an unbroken succession of popes from St Peter.

According to biblical accounts, Christ renamed Simon, son of John, Peter, based on the Greek *petros*, or "rock", because the Church was to be built with his strength. In later tradition, Peter was recognized as the leader of the 12 disciples who established the Christian Church in Italy, becoming the first Bishop of Rome. He was also buried in Rome, in the place where the high altar in St Peter's Basilica now stands.

CHRIST'S REPRESENTATIVE

The pope is also called the Vicar of Christ, meaning his representative – a person acting in his place.

Below Under rules introduced in 1970 by Pope Paul VI, only cardinals aged 80 or below can vote for a new pope. In 2005, 117 cardinals were eligible to vote when Pope Benedict XVI was elected.

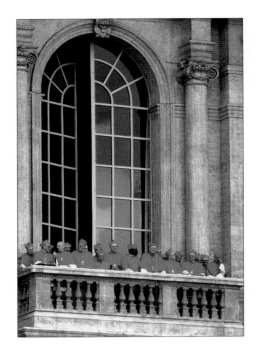

Above The name conclave comes from the Latin cum clave *("with a key"). At one time the cardinals were locked away until a new pope was elected.*

For Roman Catholics, the pope serves as Christ's officer, with supreme authority over the Church, because he occupies the place of St Peter, who was originally given the authority to serve in this way. Pope Gelasius I (served AD 492–6) was the first to assume the name "Vicar of Christ"; before his time Christians had reserved the title for the Holy Spirit and popes were referred to as "Vicar of St Peter". The other titles reinforce the pope's position as supreme ruler of both the Catholic Church and the Vatican.

Roman Catholics believe that – just as the pope is the successor of St Peter – the archbishops and bishops of the Church are the successors of the apostles. The archbishops, bishops and the pope receive from the Holy Spirit the gift of infallibility – the capacity to discern what is right, and to be free from mistakes in morals and matters of faith when they jointly proclaim a doctrine. By this remarkable gift they share a part of Christ's own infallibility. The pope as

A BURNING ISSUE

After each vote the ballot papers are burnt. Crowds gathered in St Peter's Square watch for the smoke to see the result: when a new pope has been elected white smoke is sent up, but when the vote has been unsuccessful black smoke rises. In the past, the cardinals used damp straw to colour the smoke but today they use more reliable chemicals.

leader of the bishops possesses a unique infallibility that makes it possible for him to make a definitive decree on doctrine that concerns matters of faith or morals.

RITUALS OF ELECTION

The pope is elected by the College of Cardinals in a series of closed sessions called a papal conclave, held in the Sistine Chapel in the Vatican Palace. The cardinals vote by writing the name of their preferred candidate on ballot papers beneath the words *Eligo in Summum Pontificem* ("I Elect as Supreme Pontiff"). They carry on voting until one man has the votes of two-thirds of the cardinals plus one. However, if the process becomes prolonged, the cardinals can agree to elect by simple majority.

When one name is agreed, the cardinal in question is asked if he accepts election as Supreme Pontiff. If he replies yes, he then gives the papal name by which he will be known, and the other cardinals pay him their respects.

The pope blesses the crowd and is then ceremonially installed in a service a few days later. At one time this was a grand coronation, but since the time of Pope John Paul I (served for 33 days in 1978), this has been replaced with a simpler ceremony in which the pope is invested with the papal robe, called the pallium, during a Papal Inauguration Mass.

Above During a conclave in the Sistine Chapel at the Vatican to appoint a new pope, ballot papers are placed in these ballot boxes by the cardinals.

Below Pope John Paul II greets the faithful during his first public appearance at the Vatican after his election to the papacy on 16 October 1978.

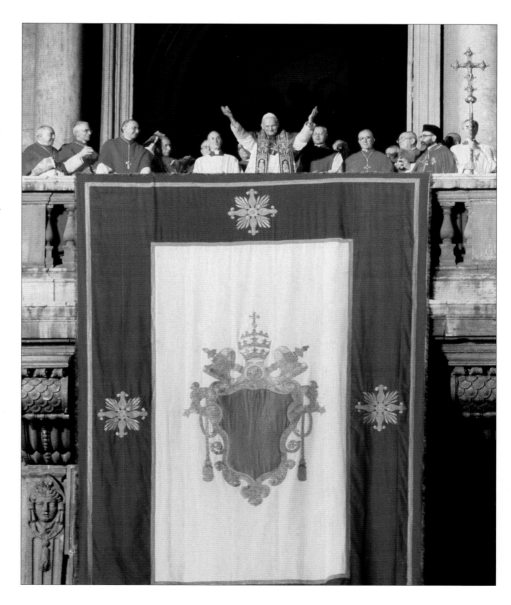

THE VATICAN: A PLACE APART

THE ROMAN CATHOLIC CHURCH'S CENTRE OF GOVERNMENT, GENERALLY KNOWN AS "THE VATICAN", IS IN VATICAN CITY. IT HAS ITS OWN MILITARY CORPS, GOVERNMENT AND INFRASTRUCTURE.

Vatican City is a city-state set within the Italian capital Rome. The world's smallest independent state, the Vatican covers about 44 hectares (109 acres) and has a population of between 800 and 1,000 people. The city-state is mostly enclosed by high stone walls that separate it from Rome. It is the sovereign territory of the Holy See (the Church's central government), and heads the Church's machinery of spiritual and pastoral rule.

While the Holy See has a history dating to the time of St Peter, Vatican City was created only in 1929 under the Lateran Treaty signed by the Kingdom of Italy and the Holy See. Its official name is *Stato della Città del Vaticano* ("the State of Vatican City").

Below St Peter's Basilica looks down on St Peter's Square. The basilica's majestic 45m (150ft)-high façade was built by Carlo Maderno in the 17th century.

Vatican City is run as an elected monarchy that is ruled by the pope. One of the pope's formal titles is Sovereign of the State of Vatican City. Roman Catholic clergymen serve as the city-state's chief functionaries. The official state flag is the yellow and white papal banner.

MOUNT VATICAN

Vatican City takes its name from the hill in north-western Rome on which it stands. This area was known as *Mons Vaticanus* ("Mount Vatican") by the Romans in the pre-Christian era. The city contains the magnificent domed church of St Peter's Basilica, which by tradition stands over the burial place of St Peter, as well as the vast Vatican Palace (also known as the Apostolic Palace). With more than 1,000 rooms, this is an impressive structure that contains the pope's apartments, the

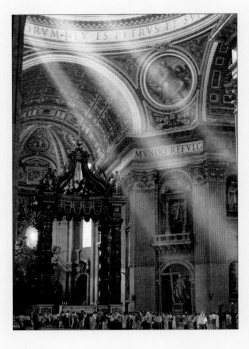

Above Indoors, the vast scale of St Peter's Basilica impresses upon worshippers the power and grandeur of God – Father, Son and Holy Spirit.

Church's government offices and several chapels, as well as the Vatican Museum and the Vatican Library.

Within the complex is the Sistine Chapel, famed for its ceiling frescoes of scenes from the book of Genesis that were painted by Michelangelo in 1508–12. It also has a papal reception suite decorated with frescoes by Raphael and the artists of his studio, from 1508 onward, and the Borgia Apartment, a suite decorated with frescoes by Pinturicchio in 1492–5 for Rodrigo Borgia, Pope Alexander VI. The Vatican Museum contains a wealth of statuary, including the ancient Roman statues of *Apollo Belvedere* (350–325 BC) and of *Laocoön and His Sons* (160–20 BC).

Adjacent to the museum, the Vatican Archive houses religious and historical documents dating back over centuries, including the report on the Church trial in 1633 of mathematician and astronomer Galileo Galilei, whose promotion of the theory that Earth and other planets revolve around the Sun was condemned by the Church on the grounds that it conflicted with Scripture. The complex also holds the Vatican Library, which has one of the world's most valuable collections of manuscripts and early books.

A number of other buildings belong to Vatican City but are situated beyond the city walls. These include the pope's summer villa in Castle Gandolfo, 24km (15 miles) south of Rome, as well as the churches of St John Lateran, St Mary Major and St Paul's Outside the Walls, all in Rome. The Church of St John Lateran is Rome's Cathedral Church and the ecclesiastical seat of the Bishop of Rome – that is, of the pope.

PROTECTING THE CITY

Vatican City has its own military corps known as the Pontifical Swiss Guard. The guardsmen, who are all Swiss and Roman Catholics, maintain a 24-hour watch over the pope and the Apostolic Palace. The Swiss Guard's role in protecting the pope dates back to the time of Pope Sixtus IV in the late 15th century. The guardsmen wear a Renaissance-style uniform that is sometimes said to have been designed by Michelangelo, but in fact was created in 1914. Technically, the Swiss Guard is a unit of the Holy See, not Vatican City.

The city has its own security and civil defence services department. It encompasses a police and security force called the Gendarme Corps of Vatican City-State, as well as its own fire brigade.

RUNNING THE CITY

The Vatican has the infrastructure and machinery of government necessary to run an independent country: a diplomatic corps; a court system; its own bank and independent postal,

Right The elaborate Vatican Library was established by Pope Nicholas V in 1448. It holds some of the most important books from the earliest days of the Church.

Above As well as protecting the pope and the Apostolic Palace, the Pontifical Swiss Guard are responsible for controlling access into and out of Vatican City.

telephone and telegraph services; its own water supply; street-cleaning and lighting; and a railway system. The railway is a stretch of track about 270m (885ft) in length, used for carrying freight. There is even a Vatican jail and a printing plant.

The Pontifical Commission for the State of Vatican City, a group of cardinals appointed by the pope, has responsibility for the state's domestic administration, while foreign relations are handled by the Secretariat of State of the Holy See.

The Vatican City newspaper *L'Osservatore Romano* (The Rome Observer) has been published since 1 July 1861. It was initially independently run, but since 1885 it has been owned by the Holy See.

HIERARCHY OF THE CHURCH

FROM PAPACY TO PARISH, THE CATHOLIC CHURCH'S HIERARCHY IS A VAST PYRAMID CONNECTING THE POPE AT ITS SUMMIT THROUGH PRIESTS AND DEACONS TO MEMBERS OF THE FAITHFUL AT THE BASE.

Above Archbishop Egan leads his first service as archbishop in St Patrick's Cathedral, New York, on 19 June 2000. Archbishops are responsible for presiding over Mass in their ecclesiastical seat.

As Vicar of Christ on Earth, the pope holds supreme and universal power over the Roman Catholic Church. As Bishop of Rome and successor to St Peter, he is foremost among, and leader of, the bishops of the Church.

THE UPPER HIERARCHY

Bishops, archbishops and cardinals are at the top of the hierarchy. The pope has ultimate authority for the appointment of bishops. With them he shares what is termed "collegiate" responsibility for leading the Church.

Below On ordination a bishop becomes a member of the College of Bishops and takes on his share of responsibility for governing the Church.

The bishops together form the College of Bishops. They are viewed as the successors of Christ's apostles and have a duty to teach the faithful.

Each bishop is in charge of an ecclesiastical area known as a diocese, which contains several individual parishes. His principal task is to care for the faithful in his area, like a shepherd cares for sheep. The main church of the diocese is known as a cathedral and is the ecclesiastical seat (base) of the bishop. In some metropolitan areas, an "ordinary bishop" is the principal bishop and is assisted by a team of auxiliary bishops.

The pope appoints some bishops as archbishops. They have control of an even larger area known as an archdiocese, which contains a number of dioceses. The pope is also responsible for appointing some senior bishops as cardinals. They form the College of Cardinals. Some care for dioceses, while others serve the pope as advisers and administrators in Rome. When a pope dies or if a pope abdicates, the cardinals meet in closed session (conclave) to elect one of their number as the next pope.

PRIESTS AND DEACONS

Beneath the bishops are two further ranks in the ordained orders: priests and deacons. Priests have the same principal responsibility as a bishop, which is to care for the faithful in the area. Priests proclaim the gospels, lead community prayer and worship, celebrate Mass and the other sacraments for their congregation and teach the faith. Some are members of religious orders, while others are diocesan priests devoted to service in a particular diocese. Most serve in parishes but some instead serve as chaplains in hospitals, universities, prisons or the armed services.

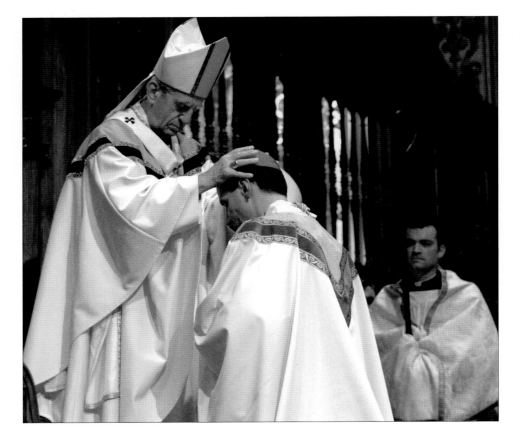

Both priests and bishops are assisted by deacons. In the early Church, deacons also held a special responsibility for charitable work, but as the role of deacon evolved, it became no more than a stage in training to become a priest. However, reforms introduced in 1967 by Pope Paul VI have re-established a group of permanent deacons in the Church. These deacons are men not called to be priests. They often have full-time jobs outside the Church, and whereas priests must be celibate, some deacons may be married.

WITHIN THE RANKS

Ecclesiastical duties are restricted by rank. Only bishops can perform ordination – that is, make others a bishop, a priest or a deacon through the sacrament of Holy Orders, which is centred on the laying on of hands and a prayer of consecration. Only bishops or priests can say Mass or hear confession.

Deacons have a special responsibility for reading the gospel in Church and for working with the poor. Deacons can preach, perform baptism and conduct marriage services – in the latter case they technically act as witnesses, because the bride and groom administer the sacrament of Holy Matrimony to one other.

CHURCH GOVERNMENT

The pope is the head of the Holy See, the Church's central machinery of government. The Holy See's administrative structures are collectively known as the Roman Curia. The Roman Curia is divided into several departments, the most important of which is the Secretariat of State, which performs political and diplomatic work for the Holy See.

Right Pope Benedict XVI presides over the Roman Curia at the Vatican. Curia (from medieval Latin) means "court" – as in "royal court".

CANON LAW

The Roman Catholic Church has its own legal system, complete with its courts, judges, lawyers and legal code. The code derives its authority from the council of bishops as descendants of the apostles and the pope as successor of St Peter and Vicar of Christ.

The code has its original source in canons (rules) adopted by Church councils, supplemented by papal decretals or letters that state legal decisions, and input from Celtic, Saxon and other legal traditions. The material was formulated as a code and promulgated by Pope Benedict XV in 1917, then revised in the 1960s to 1980s and repromulgated by Pope John Paul II in 1983.

Parts of the code were adapted from Roman Law as codified on the order of Byzantine emperor Justinian I in AD 529–34. Church courts follow the Roman law style practised in continental Europe, with panels of judges and inquisitorial or investigative proceedings, as distinct from the adversarial proceedings with a single judge and a jury followed in law courts in the United Kingdom and the United States.

Above A canon law tribunal hears a case. Roman Catholic canon law is the world's oldest continuously used legal system.

The Secretariat is split into the Section for General Affairs, which holds responsibility for appointments, documents and so on, and the Section for Relations with States.

The latter is responsible for interacting with governments of countries from around the world as well as with international bodies, such as the United Nations.

THE PATH TO PRIESTHOOD

A MAN CALLED TO THE PRIESTHOOD UNDERGOES TRAINING THAT OFTEN TAKES SEVEN OR MORE YEARS AND INCLUDES STUDY IN A SEMINARY AND PASTORAL WORK IN A PARISH.

The journey to the priesthood starts by receiving a call from God to serve as a priest. The calling is known as a vocation (from the Latin *vocatus*, which is the past participle of *vocare*, or "to call"). The call to become a priest is only one of four possible vocations that are recognized by the Roman Catholic Church.

The other three are the calls to life as a brother or sister in a religious order; the call to marriage, with husband and wife sharing faithful love; and the call to single life, embracing celibacy and living either alone, with family or with other single faithful.

These four vocations are viewed as being equal but different. Each faithful Catholic will receive a call by God to one of the four forms of life. The task is to discern the calling and then test it to be sure that a person is

Below During an ordination service, ordinands prostrate themselves to symbolize their personal unworthiness, humility and reliance on the Grace of God.

truly being called to that particular pathway. The training to become a priest is known as his formation. The details of the training vary from place to place, but the process typically encompasses several stages.

PASSING THE TEST

If a young man acts upon a calling to become a priest, he must be willing to embrace a life of celibacy and prayer. He must be ready to commit to proclaiming the gospel, teaching the Catholic faith and doing his utmost to build his faith community. This is a lifelong commitment, so first the young man will need to test his vocation during a period of enquiry and preparation.

He is expected to pray to God for guidance and to be open and patient in waiting for a response. He will discuss his vocation with his local priest and either through him or independently can make contact with the specialist vocations director of the diocese or of a religious order if he feels called to join one.

Above Young men training for the priesthood pray in a seminary chapel. The word "seminary" comes from the Latin seminarium *("bed of seeds").*

EARLY EDUCATION

If he is convinced that he has a vocation, the next stage is to apply to a seminary, a theological college specializing in training priests. A young man who wants to become a diocesan priest applies to a seminary through his local diocese. If he wants to become a priest in a religious order, such as the Franciscans, he applies directly to the order. The application process for a seminary generally includes academic assessment, interviews and psychological tests.

If the young man is accepted into the seminary, he begins his priestly education. The amount of time this takes depends on many factors, including the level of his previous education. His studies will include philosophy, theology, history and Scripture. The training will usually encompass a pre-pastoral stage of study for a year or two, followed by a pastoral stage in which the student serves in a working parish – perhaps returning to his own parish.

TRANSITIONAL DEACON

The next stage is to train as a deacon. For many years being a deacon was a stage in training to be a priest, but following Pope Paul VI's reforms there has been a return to the practice – common in the early Church – of maintaining a group of permanent deacons who are not destined to be priests. For this reason, students training to be priests who become deacons are now referred to as transitional deacons to distinguish them from permanent deacons.

After training the student is ordained a deacon. He will then serve for some time – at least six months, but often longer than that – as a transitional deacon before being ordained as a priest.

CALLED AS A PRIEST

At the completion of his training a student is called to be a priest by his bishop. If the bishop makes the decision not to call a student to become a priest, his action establishes that the young man did not truly have a vocation to the priesthood.

Young men must normally be at least 25 years old to become priests. Bishops have the authority to lower this age limit by one year, but only the Holy See can authorize the ordination of anyone younger than 24 years old.

Below A deacon assists at the Mass. Transitional deacons become familiar with the priestly functions they will perform once they have completed their ordination.

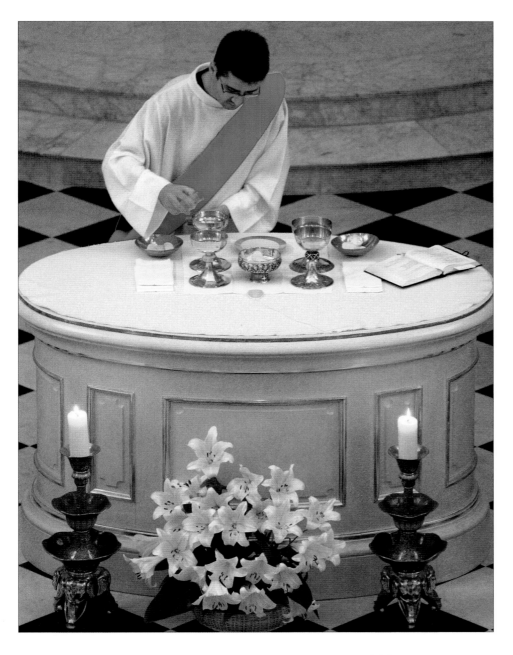

TAKING VOWS

At ordination priests take vows of celibacy and of obedience to their bishop. Priests in religious orders take a vow of poverty in addition to those of obedience and celibacy. Before they can actively serve, priests have to be "incardinated" by a bishop or certain other religious superiors, such as the head of a religious order. This word derives from the Latin word for "a hinge", and when a priest is incardinated it means he is attached to and subject to a religious superior.

In practice, the priest will promise obedience to the bishop during his ordination service. However, if the priest has already made a vow of obedience to the superior of a religious order, then he will also acknowledge this pre-existing vow during his ordination.

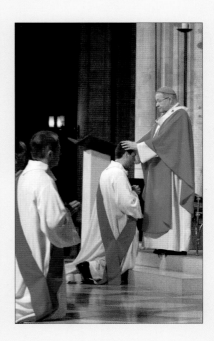

Above After a priest takes his vows of celibacy during his ordination, the bishop will practise laying on of hands – this is a symbolic gesture that has been used since the Old Testament.

MARRIED TO THE CHURCH

A PRIEST IS EXPECTED TO EMBRACE A CELIBATE LIFE. BEING CELIBATE ENABLES HIM TO AVOID WORLDLY DISTRACTIONS AND CONCENTRATE ON DEDICATING HIS LIFE TO SERVING GOD.

Roman Catholics believe that a priest's celibate life is a reflection of heaven. Priests are said to be married to the Church. The catechism declares that priests who embrace celibacy are "called to consecrate themselves with undivided heart to God…and give themselves entirely to God and to men" and that when it is accepted "with a joyous heart", "celibacy radiantly proclaims the Reign of God". Celibacy is a gift from the priest to God and to the people, to be made in a spirit of service.

The Church stresses that requiring celibacy in priests does not devalue the sacrament of marriage.

Below Both brothers and sisters in Christ make sacrifices in adapting their lives to harmonize with the Church's teachings.

Being a priest or entering married life are among the four vocations recognized by Catholics – and no one vocation is said to be superior to any of the others.

BIBLICAL JUSTIFICATION

There is a principal source often cited by the Church in support of a call for clerical celibacy, a biblical passage found in Matthew, Chapter 19. In this passage Christ gives a description of marriage as a divinely ordained union between man and woman, and declares that any man who divorces his wife on grounds other than "unchastity" and then takes another is committing adultery. The disciples then say that if this is true it is surely better not to marry. In his response Christ apparently agrees, saying "Not all men can receive this saying, but only those to whom it is given" – that is, not everyone can accept this. He then adds, in the key verse (Matthew 19:12) that is generally cited by Roman Catholics:

> *For there are eunuchs who have been so from birth, and there are eunuchs who have been made eunuchs by men, and there are eunuchs who have made themselves eunuchs for the sake of the kingdom of heaven.*
> *He who is able to receive this, let him receive it.*

By the word that is translated as "eunuchs", Christ is thought to mean men who are celibate, who have freely chosen not to have sexual relations. Priests are an example of those in Christ's third category, who are celibate "for the sake of the kingdom of heaven".

Above A priest consecrates himself to a new life and adopts celibacy, as stated in the catechism, "for the love of God's kingdom and the service of men".

Another key biblical justification for the celibacy requirement can be found in the writing of St Paul in the First Letter to Corinthians (7:32-4): "The unmarried man is anxious about the affairs of the Lord, how to please the Lord; but the married man is anxious about worldly affairs, how to please his wife, and his interests are divided." These verses clearly support the Church's position that a celibate life frees a priest to concentrate on serving God and man.

PRESSURE ON THE CHURCH

In the late 20th and early 21st centuries, critics inside and outside the Church have questioned the requirement of celibacy in priests. In an era of sexual liberation through much of Western society, the vow of celibacy has apparently made it more difficult to attract young men to the priesthood. There has been a mounting crisis in vocations, with the Church unable to replace priests who die and a number of parishes being left without priests.

THE CHURCH HOLDS FIRM

Nevertheless, the requirement of sexual abstinence by priests has been repeatedly reaffirmed by the Church hierarchy. The Second Vatican Council's Decree on the Ministry and Life of Priests in 1965 addressed the issue and claimed that celibacy was a charitable act of the priest, one that provided "a source of spiritual fruitfulness in the world".

In 1967, Pope Paul VI expressed in his encyclical *On Priestly Celibacy* that when a priest dedicates himself to God through celibacy, he can form a more profound relation with God, and this would benefit humankind. The priest would be better prepared to devote himself to his parishioners. In 1979, Pope John Paul II declared in a letter to priests that in order to serve their fellow humans, the priests must be free in their hearts – and that celibacy is a sign of this freedom.

Right Pope Paul VI called celibacy a special kind of asceticism that is more exacting than the sacrifices demanded of other Christians.

Below Pope Paul VI, enthroned, opens the Second Vatican Council in 1965. In its deliberations, the Council made notable pronouncements on celibacy.

MARRIED PRIESTS?

There are some exceptions to the strict requirement of celibacy. Certain Protestant ministers who are married and then convert to Catholicism are allowed to serve as priests while married if they are given authority by the pope. Men of mature age who are married may be ordained and serve as permanent deacons – that is, they may be deacons but may not become priests. Men who have been ordained deacons while single may not later marry.

CALLED TO SERVE

IN THE SACRAMENT OF HOLY ORDERS, CANDIDATES ARE ORDAINED AS
BISHOP, PRIEST OR DEACON. THE PROFOUND, BEAUTIFUL CEREMONIAL
CONTAINS MOMENTS OF POWERFUL VISUAL THEATRE.

There are three types of ordination: as bishop, priest or deacon. On his ordination the candidate will join the relevant order – of bishops, priests or deacons. The word "ordination" means the incorporating of an individual into an order.

Only bishops have the power to perform ordinations. The essential rite of the sacrament is when the bishop lays his hands on the head of the candidate, or ordinand, and pronounces the prayer of consecration. It is traditional, but not required, for

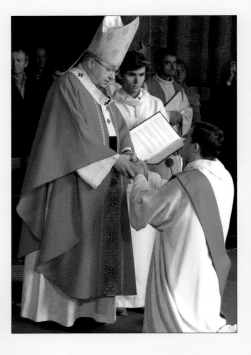

Above An ordinand puts his clasped hands between those of his bishop as a sign of faithfulness to his ecclesiastical superior.

the ordination to take place during a Mass; ordinations are often held on a Sunday in the cathedral of the presiding bishop.

THE ORDINAND'S EXAM
In the usual service of ordination, the ordinands are called forward to the altar after the reading of the gospel. The presentation follows, when the bishop asks a series of questions to establish that the candidates have passed through the necessary levels of training in their formation as priests and that they are worthy to become priests. The bishop then "elects" – that is, chooses – each candidate and offers the prayer: "We rely on the help of the Lord God and our Saviour Jesus Christ and we choose this man, our brother, for priesthood in the presbyteral order." The congregation present then signals its support by applauding.

Left Prostrating himself while the bishop prays the Litany of the Saints, the ordinand shows his reliance on the Holy Spirit and the support of the faithful.

The candidates sit while the bishop delivers a homily (sermon) on the nature of priesthood and the role of the priest. The candidates then come forward to the altar once more for the examination, in which the bishop asks whether they are willing: to discharge the office of the priesthood; to celebrate Christ's mysteries; to exercise the ministry of the Word; and to consecrate their lives to God through Christ the High Priest. They reply each time "I am".

VOW OF OBEDIENCE

Each ordinand goes forward and, putting his hands in those of the bishop, promises to respect and be obedient to the bishop and his successors. (In some forms of the ordination service, when the candidates are being ordained as priests in a religious order, rather than as diocesan priests, they instead make a vow of obedience to the superior of the religious order to which they belong.) The bishop prays, "May God who has begun the good work in you bring it to fulfilment."

Next the ordinands lie prostrate on the floor while the bishop and assembled faithful recite the Litany of the Saints. The ordinands lie face down to symbolize their unworthiness to be a priest (or bishop or deacon, depending on the service) and the fact that to take on and succeed in the job they depend on the grace of God, and the prayers both of the saints and martyrs and of the Christian Community on Earth.

LAYING ON OF HANDS

The ordinands kneel. The ordaining bishop places his hands on the head of each ordinand in silence. The already ordained priests helping at the service do likewise. The laying on

Right The laying on of hands is a principal ritual that symbolizes the granting of priestly authority and the descent of the Holy Spirit.

of hands is an ancient ritual going back to Old Testament times, when it was used by Jews to install their priests. The gesture is symbolic of the bishop's prayer to the Holy Spirit to descend on the candidate, and also of the long tradition of sacerdotal, or priestly, authority running right back to the time of the apostles.

The bishop says the Prayer of Consecration. He prays to the Holy Spirit to descend on the priest-to-be, to give him gifts needed for the ministry to which he is called.

THE NEW PRIEST

Priests who are newly ordained now put on the stole and chasuble, the vestments worn by priests when celebrating Mass. The bishop anoints the hands of each new priest with chrism (consecrated oil), which is symbolic of Christ himself as High Priest. The newly made priests then wipe the chrism from their hands on cloths. (They usually give these to their mothers in recognition of the women's sacrifice in giving their sons to the service of the Church.)

The new priests are given patens and chalices that have been brought forward by the people. The bishop prays: "Accept from the holy people of God the gifts to be offered to Him.

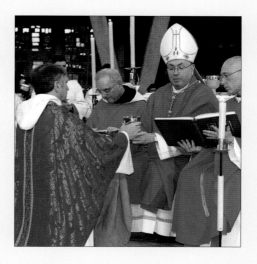

Above A newly ordained priest receives from the bishop the chalice and paten he will use to celebrate his first Mass.

Know what you are doing, and imitate the mystery you celebrate: model your life on the mystery of the Lord's Cross."

The bishop makes the sign of peace to the newly ordained priests. They then join with the bishop in celebrating the Eucharist. At the close of the Mass service the bishop will kneel before the altar and the priests will give him their blessing. The priests can now share in Christ's own eternal priesthood: they have now been ordained to serve the Church as Christ did many centuries earlier.

UNDER ORDERS

MEMBERS OF RELIGIOUS ORDERS UNDERTAKE TO FOLLOW A RELIGIOUS RULE OR WAY OF LIFE UNDER THE LEADERSHIP OF A SUPERIOR. THEY MAKE A FORMAL DEDICATION OF THEIR LIVES TO GOD.

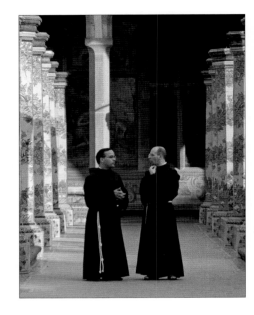

Religious orders are also known as Institutes of Consecrated Life. Their members take solemn public vows of chastity, poverty and obedience under Church law. Some members of religious orders are also ordained as priests or deacons, but if they are not they are considered to be members of the laity rather than clergy.

Within a religious order, authority is centralized in a superior or general house, which holds jurisdiction over geographically distributed dependent houses. However, a major exception to this general rule is the Order of St Benedict, in which there is no single superior house with overall authority and each of the individual abbeys is autonomous.

THE RELIGIOUS ORDERS
Some members are known as monks and nuns, or simply monastics, and live in enclosed communities. They devote their lives primarily to prayer and devotions. Others are known as friars and religious sisters, or mendicants, and live in a more open context and engage in social, medical or educational work. Historically, the monastics are self-supporting, while the mendicant orders rely on alms for their upkeep.

There is also a distinction between canons regular and clerks regular. Those known as canons regular live in either a closed community or as secular canons in open society. Although they are first and foremost monks, some of them are priests. They devote themselves primarily to the monastic life, which is centred on celebration of the liturgy and on contemplation. Conversely, clerks regular are first and foremost priests, but they choose to live in a community following a religious rule, in a similar manner to monks. Clerks regular devote themselves primarily to the ministry of the priesthood.

TAKING OF VOWS
Members of religious orders take what are known as solemn vows of obedience, chastity and poverty. Under solemn vows they renounce

Above Franciscan friars confer in the cloisters of Santa Chiara in Naples, Italy. They share the complex with nuns of the Poor Clares.

the right to own property. Members of another type of order, called religious congregations, take "simple" vows. In practice, those who swear simple vows retain the right to own material possessions, but they hand over the administration of the possessions to the congregation. Simple vows can be for a limited period, whereas solemn vows are for life. Those serving as novices, who are in the process of becoming a

---

RULE OF LIFE
The "rule of life" is a set of guidelines that govern all aspects of behaviour by members of a religious order. Major examples in the Roman Catholic tradition include:

- The Rule of St Francis of Assisi, which is followed by those in the Franciscan tradition, such as the Order of the Friars Minor
- The Rule of St Benedict, followed by the Benedictines
- The Rule of St Augustine, which is traditionally followed by the Augustinians.

Right Benedictine monks harvest flowers in the grounds of the 11th-century Abbey of Santa Maria Assunta at Praglia, near Padua, Italy.

Above Jesuits are led from Rome by the Superior General, who holds the office for life. Spanish father Adolfo Nicolas was appointed in 2008.

monk or nun, swear simple vows for a limited period before professing solemn vows for life.

There is another kind of religious community in which members do not take any vows. This is called a Society of Apostolic Life. A bishop grants this kind of society authority to operate in his diocese. An example is the Catholic Foreign Missionary Society of America.

SOCIETY OF JESUS

Jesuits are an important example of clerks regular. They are members of the Society of Jesus, which was established in the 1530s by Spaniard Ignatius Loyola in Paris. Today the society is governed from its head-quarters in Rome, the General Curia, by the Superior General (also known as Father General), who is confirmed in his position by the pope. The Father General is assisted by an advisory council in Rome;

around the world, the order is split into geographic provinces, each one led by a Father Superior.

The Society is the largest religious order of priests in the Catholic Church. About 13,500 of its 20,000 members are priests, with around 1,800 brothers, 3,000 students and almost 1,000 novices. From its early days the society combined strong central authority with mobility. Jesuits place emphasis on obedience to the pope – they are said to take a "fourth vow" (in addition to those of poverty, obedience and chastity) of particular obedience to the pope. Because Loyola had a military background, and due to this particular reverence for the papacy's authority, the Jesuits are sometimes referred to as the "Foot soldiers of the pope".

Right A statue of Father John Carroll sits in front of the Jesuit university of Georgetown. He founded the private university in 1789.

JESUIT EDUCATION

Priests and brothers engage in many kinds of evangelical work, including missions and social work in less developed countries, but they are associated with education. Their first university, the Pontifical Gregorian University, or Gregorianum, in Rome, has been providing education since its foundation in 1551.

The Jesuits staff and run many schools, colleges, seminaries, universities and theological colleges. They work in more than 112 different countries around the world, and their education work is particularly important in India and the United States. In India, the Jesuits maintain colleges and schools in Mumbai, Calcutta, Delhi and Goa. In the United States, the Jesuits run more than 50 universities, colleges and schools, including the celebrated Georgetown University, which was founded in Washington, D.C., and Fordham University, which is located in New York City.

BROTHERS IN CHRIST

ONE BRANCH OF THE RELIGIOUS ORDERS STRESSES THE SPIRITUAL BENEFITS OF COMMUNITY LIVING. MONKS FOLLOW A RELIGIOUS RULE CENTRED ON CELEBRATING THE LITURGY OF THE HOURS TOGETHER.

St Benedict of Nursia, author of the *Rule of St Benedict*, is often celebrated as being the founder of Western monasticism. Modern Benedictines are the successors of the 6th-century monks for whom Benedict, founder of the monastery at Monte Cassino in Italy, wrote his rule of life in *c*. AD 535–40.

In a prologue and 73 chapters, the *Rule of St Benedict* directs monks to divide their time mainly between common prayer, prayerful meditative reading and manual work. The monks are expected to work six hours a day with their hands. The Rule, which St Benedict calls "a school of the Lord's service", also gives detailed guidance on acceptable sleeping arrangements, food and drink, clothing and caring for the sick, as well as hospitality for guests and recruitment. Although

Below The brothers of Bec Abbey at Le Bec-Hellouin, a Benedictine abbey in France, are joined for Mass by the sisters of the nearby Monastère de Ste Françoise Romaine.

modern Benedictines do not follow the rule so strictly, they do still use it to guide their lives.

THE ORGANIZATION

From early on the Benedictines were organized to allow for local decision-making. Each monastery or "house" is autonomous, and the houses are grouped in 21 congregations. In 1893, Pope Leo XIII established the Benedictine Confederation of the Order of St Benedict, which is a confederation of the autonomous congregations, and appointed an abbot primate as its head. The abbot primate does not have direct jurisdiction in Benedictine monasteries but has a general concern for the wellbeing of Benedictines world-wide. The headquarters of the confederation is in Rome.

A LIFE GOVERNED BY VOWS

Benedictine monks take three vows: of obedience, that they promise to live according to the Rule of St Benedict; of stability, that they will endeavour to remain in the

Above St Benedict's great legacy was his inspired and moderate Rule for monastic life. He wears a plain cloak in this 15th-century illustration by Andrea di Bartolo.

Benedictine order for life; and of conversion, that they will seek to follow Christ's example in all things, and will transform their life by adopting poverty and chastity.

In a typical Benedictine house, the monk's day is structured around six church services in the Liturgy of the Hours, with intervening periods of work and private prayer with meditative reading (known as *lectio*

divina). The typical day includes four hours in liturgical prayer, five hours in private prayer and spiritual reading, six hours of labour and eight hours of sleep. The remaining hour is set aside for eating.

A monk is required to attend the liturgical services. The first service is the "night office" of matins, which is prayed while still dark, and this is followed by the "morning office" of lauds at dawn. The monks work in the morning, and meet for midday prayer. They then work again in the afternoon, and celebrate Mass together in the late afternoon. The evening services are vespers (evening prayer) and compline (night prayer), which is said and sung before the monks retire to sleep.

The monks view their times of prayer and reading as their true work, but they are also required by the Rule of St Benedict to work. It warns that idleness can be dangerous to the life of the soul and urges brothers to keep themselves busy, sometimes at manual labour and at other times, in spiritual reading. The Rule specifically calls on the monks to work with their hands, but in modern monasteries the work done varies according to circumstance. Many Benedictine houses run schools in which monks work as teachers and administrators; there is also a good deal of practical work in and around the monastery: in the gardens, kitchens and laundry. In some houses, the monks also run a parish and keep a retreat house. They also often perform social work with local people.

BECOMING A MONK
A young man who wants to become a monk typically starts by staying in the monastery for a period as a visitor, then progresses to being a

Right The Rule of St Benedict encourages brothers to work with their hands each day. A monk works prayerfully in his pottery studio.

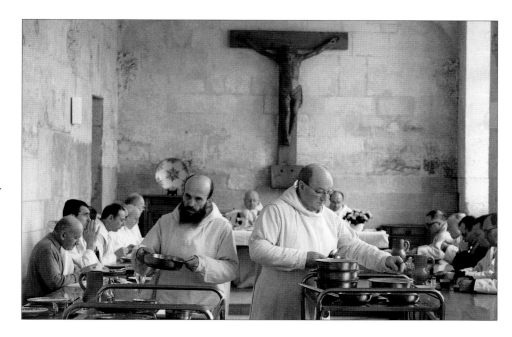

postulant. As a postulant he commits to living in the monastery alongside the monks for three to six months.

He may leave after six months, or commit to being a novice. As a novice he is "clothed": this means he is given his monk's habit or cloak. After one or two years as a novice, the young man may be asked to renew his simple (temporary) vows for three years. After three years he may take solemn (life) vows and become

Above Brothers share a meal. Their communal life is known as cenobitic monasticism, from the ancient Greek words koinos *and* bios *("common" and "life").*

a monk. He can continue as a novice for six or nine years, but after that period he must take life vows or leave the monastery. At any point when the applicant is free to leave, he may also be asked to leave if the abbot thinks he is not suited to monastic life.

DECLINING NUMBERS
Membership of the Roman Catholic Church is on the rise, but the number of those living a monastic life is in decline. Figures released in February 2008 showed that the number of members of the consecrated life fell a little under 10 per cent in 2005–6 to 945,210. There are many more nuns and sisters than brothers and friars. Of those in the consecrated life, around 750,000 are women compared to approximately 190,000 men. Today, around 8,400 men and 14,600 women live in monastic communities. They follow different rules of life.

A CONTEMPLATIVE CHRISTIANITY

IN THE TRADITION OF CONTEMPLATIVE MONASTICISM, MONKS LIVE IN AN ENCLOSED COMMUNITY AND COMMIT TO A LIFE OF SELF–DISCIPLINE AND PRAYER ON BEHALF OF THE CHURCH AND THE WORLD.

Above St Bruno was a brilliant theologian and teacher. In this detail from a 17th-century painting by Nicholas Regnier, he is receiving the order.

Contemplative monks have no active ministry in terms of pastoral or missionary work or charitable enterprises, and they have little social interaction except through prayer. They generally live under strict rules governing their interaction. They spend large parts of the day alone and endeavour to live largely in silence. They usually work to produce goods by which they wholly or partially support themselves.

Members of the Carthusian Order (or the Order of St Bruno) live a life of this kind. The order was founded by St Bruno of Cologne in 1084 and takes its name from Chartreuse in France, where Bruno established his first hermitage with six companions. Carthusian monasteries are headed by a prior. They contain a community of cloister

Below The mother house of the Carthusian Order is the remote monastery of La Grande Chartreuse, which is based in the Chartreuse Mountains of eastern France.

monks (sometimes called fathers), who commit to greater solitude, and brothers (or lay brothers), who have a less solitary life and take on the material tasks necessary to the running of the house.

In England, Carthusian monasteries are called charterhouses. The order is open to women as well as to men. There are currently 24 charterhouses worldwide – 19 monasteries, holding 370 monks, and 5 nunneries, holding 75 nuns.

LIFE IN A HERMITAGE

In a typical charterhouse, each of the cloister monks has his own hermitage, or living quarters, which usually has two storeys. Below is a workshop and wood for the wood-burning stove that is the hermitage's source of heat. The main room, above, is the cubiculum. The hermitage also has its own water supply and lavatory.

In the cubiculum, the monk prays, studies, sleeps and eats. He follows most of the Liturgy of the Hours, using full ceremony as if in

public, although three daily services are celebrated communally in the chapel attached to the monastery. The monk enters the cubiculum through a small antechamber, which is known as the Ave Maria. This symbolizes the fact that in prayer the monk comes to Christ by way of the Blessed Virgin Mary. He begins all his offices and other prayers with intercessions to the Virgin. In the workshop area, the monk performs work for at least two hours a day.

The hermitage adjoins a walled garden in which the cloister monk meditates and grows vegetables and flowers. Each of the hermitages gives

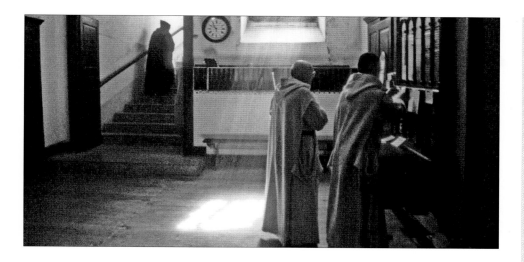

on to a communal cloister through a turnstile: food and other materials can be left in this area without disturbing the cloister monk, which allows the contemplative monk to maintain absolute solitude.

Unlike the monks, the brothers of the community spend less time in prayer and more maintaining the monastery. They are responsible for managing food and other supplies, preparing meals, organizing the library and delivering books to cloister monks, carrying out repairs around the charterhouse and so on.

SILENCE

The monks attempt to live in silence. Although they do not take a vow of silence, they try to speak only when strictly necessary. They aim by this discipline to cultivate inner serenity.

Each cloister monk leaves his hermitage three times a day for services in the main chapel. These are the night offices (matins), the morning Eucharist and vespers in the evening. Occasionally, he meets his superior for a conference. On feast days and Sundays, all the monks meet for a community meal, held in silence. Once a week the brothers participate in a four-hour walk in the countryside around the charterhouse. They are permitted to speak on the walk: they walk in pairs, and change partners every 30 minutes. Two times a year the monks join in a

Above A documentary film Into Great Silence *(2005) provided an insight into the lives of Carthusian monks at La Grande Chartreuse.*

community day of recreation and once annually they receive a visit from family.

THE SOLITARY LIFE

The Carthusian motto is the Latin *Stat crux dum volvitur orbis* ("The Cross holds steady while the world turns"). It celebrates the idea that silent contemplation and solitary prayer can create a place of sacred stillness amid change. The place of stillness serves to sanctify the wider world.

The monks endeavour to interiorize the silence amid which they live. They report that by a spiritual paradox, in solitude they can experience unity with all God's Creation. Through this experience their hearts are expanded to the dimensions of the love felt by Christ himself, for all people and all creatures.

The Carthusians live by a rule known as the Statutes. It declares that the hermitage is on holy ground and is a place where the monks can talk to God, where "earth meets heaven, and the divine meets the human". Carthusians aim to live in a state of constant and pure prayer, to exist in the presence of God and to maintain their hearts as an altar from which prayer rises constantly to God.

TRAPPIST MONKS

Another well-known group of contemplative monks is the Order of Cistercians of the Strict Observance. Its members are known as Trappists, from the name of La Grande Trappe (La Trappe Abbey) in Normandy, France, where the order was established in 1664. Trappists are contemplative monks who follow the Rule of St Benedict. Like the Cistercians, they divide their day between prayer and work. Trappist monasteries are known particularly for their production of celebrated ales, such as Chimay, which is made in Scourmont Abbey in Forges, Belgium, and Orval, made in the Abbaye Notre-Dame d'Orval monastery, also in Belgium. The order is open to women as well as to men. There are currently about 2,500 Trappist monks and 1,800 Trappist nuns (known as Trappistines) housed in about 170 monasteries worldwide.

Above A monk at La Trappe Abbey in Normandy, France, reads in front of a 1692 portrait of Father de Rancé, who was the founder of the Trappists.

WORKING IN THE WORLD

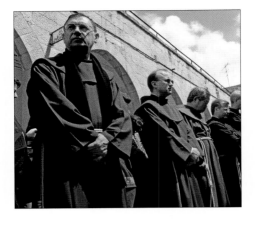

ANOTHER BRANCH OF THE RELIGIOUS ORDERS, KNOWN AS THE MENDICANTS, MAKES IT A PRIORITY TO PREACH THE WORD OF GOD AND TO PERFORM GOOD WORKS IN SOCIETY.

The mendicant orders are distinct from the monastic orders. The calling of monastic orders, such as the Benedictines or the Carthusians, is to live a life of self-disciplined routine and devotion in a monastery. While many monastic orders minister to the world through schools, parishes and retreat houses attached to their monasteries, the mendicant orders follow a call to engage directly with the wider world. They traditionally rely on the charity of others for support as they administer their work.

The mendicant orders also have a different organization. Brothers are attached to a province rather than to an individual monastery. They are answerable to a provincial superior general instead of to the abbot or prior of their own religious house.

Brothers and priests in the mendicant orders are known as friars, which distinguishes them from their counterparts in the monastic orders, who are called monks. "Friar" comes from the French *frère* and the Latin *frater* (both meaning "brother").

THE FOUR GREAT ORDERS

Of the mendicant orders, four of them in particular are referred to as the "great orders": the Franciscans, the Dominicans, the Carmelites and the Augustinians. They were recognized as the four Great Orders at the Second Council of Lyon (the Fourteenth Ecumenical Council of the Roman Catholic Church) in 1274. There are other mendicant orders, which are generally known as the lesser mendicant orders (*see Catholic Mendicant Orders, left*).

The Franciscans were founded in about 1209 by St Francis of Assisi. They are sometimes called the Friars

Above Franciscan friars gather to follow the Via Dolorosa ("Way of Grief") in Jerusalem on Good Friday. Devotions are the ground from which good works grow.

Minor because Francis called his followers *fratres minores* ("lesser brothers") to place stress on their humility. They are traditionally called the Grey Friars because they wear a grey habit. The Dominicans were established in around 1215 by St Dominic; they are often called the Black Friars because they wear a

Below A Carmelite friar from Aylesford Priory in Kent, England, leads local children in learning and worship. The priory was founded in the 13th century.

CATHOLIC MENDICANT ORDERS

The great and lesser mendicant orders are listed below, with the year they were established:

- Franciscans, founded in 1209
- Dominicans, founded *c.*1214
- Carmelites, founded *c.*1155, mendicant order from 1245
- Augustinians, founded in 1256
- Minims, founded in 1474
- Conventual Franciscans, founded in 1517
- Capuchins, founded in 1520
- Third Order Regular of St Francis, founded in 1521
- Discalced Carmelites, founded in 1568
- Discalced Trinitarians, founded in 1593
- Order of Penance, founded in 1781

Right Children orphaned by the tsunami disaster of 2004 can attend a new nursery that has been set up by the Salesians of Don Bosco in Sri Lanka.

black *cappa*, or "cloak", over a white habit. The Carmelites were founded in about 1155, originally as a contemplative order, but they became mendicants in 1245. They are also called the White Friars because they wear a white cloak over a brown habit. In 1255, the Augustinians were founded as a mendicant order from various groups of hermits by Pope Alexander IV and follow a rule based on the writings of St Augustine. They wear black garments too.

THE FRIARS' WORK

Many thousands of friars in the mendicant orders engage with needs across the world. Augustinian friars work as teachers, missionaries and also as parish priests; there are more than 2,700 Augustinian friars serving in about 40 countries. Franciscan friars work in virtually every country in the world. They have a special calling to work with the poor, in shelters, hospitals, schools and in programmes supporting justice and peace.

Dominican friars have a special calling to preach the gospel – indeed their official title is the Order of Preachers. They are also strongly committed to communal religious life, which they see as an essential support for their preaching work. According to their constitutions, they commit themselves to study assiduously, to celebrate the liturgy and especially the Eucharist together, to persevere and "to live with one mind the common life".

Dominican friars live in priories under an elected prior, where they sing the Mass and Holy Liturgy

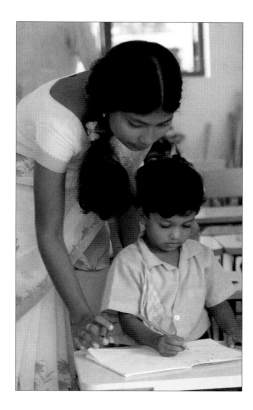

together and share their meals and times of recreation. They commit to spreading the gospel wherever their work takes them, whether it is in hospitals, prisons, universities or schools. They see publishing books and dissemination of the gospel on the Internet as part of their work. These friars aim to emulate their

founder, of whom it was said that he was always either talking to God or about God.

TEACHING ORDERS

Some religious orders are devoted particularly to teaching in schools and colleges. The De La Salle brothers, which was founded in 17th-century France by St Jean-Baptiste de La Salle, a canon at Rheims Cathedral, runs schools in 80 countries teaching more than 900,000 students.

The Salesians of Don Bosco, which was founded in 19th-century Italy by St John Bosco, are committed to working with young people in need. The Salesians number more than 16,000 priests and brothers who work with the young in 128 countries.

The Salesians run a large number of secondary or high schools, including: in London, Farnborough and Bolton in England; in Los Angeles and Richmond, California, and New Rochelle, New York, in the United States; at Imphal and Calcutta in India; and one in Hong Kong. They also run college-level educational establishments, which include DeSales University in Pennsylvania.

Right Street children from Nairobi enjoy working the land at a youth centre founded in 1994 by the Salesians of Don Bosco in Langata, Kenya.

BRIDES OF CHRIST

WOMEN ENTER RELIGIOUS ORDERS TO SERVE GOD THROUGH PRAYER, DEVOTIONS AND GOOD WORKS. WOMEN CALLED TO RELIGIOUS SERVICE ARE CALLED "BRIDES OF CHRIST".

When women commit themselves to religious life they can choose to become nuns or religious sisters. The words "nun" and "sister" are often not distinguished in common usage, but strictly speaking a nun is a woman who has taken vows, committing herself to an enclosed life of prayer and contemplative devotions within a convent, while a religious sister has chosen a much more actively engaged life of service, caring for the sick, starving, poor and otherwise needy.

LIFE IN A CONVENT
Nuns live in a monastery or a convent. A monastery is normally thought to be a community of monks

Below Sisters of contemplative orders work tirelessly and devotedly through prayer to bring peace and God's love to a troubled world.

and a convent to be a community of nuns, but some communities of monks are also called convents and some communities of nuns are referred to as monasteries, especially in the Benedictine tradition. (Religious communities of nuns were once also called nunneries, but this word is now archaic.)

Nuns live an enclosed life. They are not generally permitted to leave the convent or to receive visitors, although some do carry out teaching or other ministries as permitted by the constitution or rule of their particular community. Strictly, convents should be built so that the inner courtyards and gardens cannot be seen from without and the windows do not open on to public roads.

The convents are independent of one another, with each community headed by a Mother Superior. She is usually elected for life, but

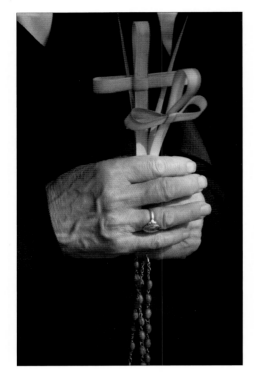

Above Today's nuns still follow the advice of the 16th-century nun St Teresa of Ávila, who taught sisters that Christ "has no hands on earth but yours".

in some constitutions the Mother Superior is subject to re-election every three years.

If the community is an abbey, she is known as an abbess, and if it is a priory she is a prioress. The distinction made between abbey and priory depends on differences in the particular religious orders and in the community's level of independence.

STEPS TO SISTERHOOD
If a young woman feels she has a calling to the religious life as a nun or sister, she becomes a postulant for six months to a year. During this time she usually lives in the community, following the life of the nuns and sisters closely, but takes no vows. If she and the order then determine that she has a vocation, she is generally given the habit (clothing) of the order and lives for one to two years as a novice; at this point she still takes no vows. The next stage is to take temporary vows for one year or

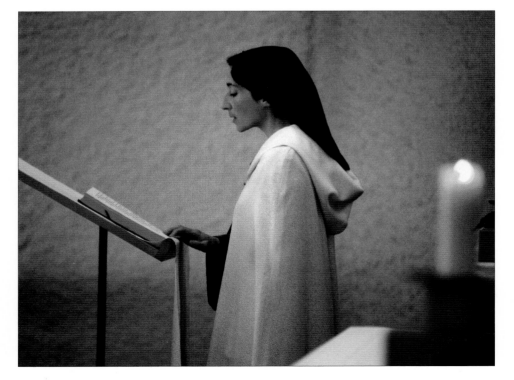

Right Work is a form of prayer for nuns, such as for these English Benedictine sisters attentively labouring over the ironing.

more, up to six years. The last stage is to take final vows and make perpetual profession.

The vows the nuns take will vary from one order to another. In the Benedictine tradition nuns, such as Trappistines and Cistercians, take a threefold vow of stability (to remain a member of the community), of obedience to the Mother Superior and of conversion of life (to adopt poverty and chastity). Franciscan and Dominican nuns take a vow of poverty, chastity and obedience. Some nuns take an extra vow specific to the kind of work they do or the character of their order.

TYPES OF ORDERS

There are contemplative orders and charitable orders. Most of the strictly enclosed congregations of nuns are members of contemplative religious orders who are devoted to seeking union with God through prayer and contemplation. The Carmelite nuns, the Redemptoristines and the Poor Clares (or Order of Poor Ladies) are all examples of contemplative orders. They sometimes undertake enclosed ministries by supporting a particular type of work through prayer in the convent: for example, the Redemptoristines pray for the work of the Redemptorist friars. They often support themselves by labour in the convent – for example, by making liturgical items, such as church candles and vestments.

Women in the charitable orders are committed to performing works of charity and mercy, teaching and caring for the sick or aged. Examples include the Little Sisters of the Poor, Ursulines and the Sisters of Charity.

THE DEVOTION OF ST THÉRÈSE

St Thérèse of Lisieux was a French Carmelite nun of the late 19th century whose spiritual autobiography, *L'histoire d'une âme* ("Story of a Soul"), published in 1898, inspired great popular devotion. She was canonized in 1925 by Pope Pius XI and in 1997 Pope John Paul II declared her a Doctor of the Universal Church. She is one of three women among the 33 Doctors of the Church.

Thérèse, who is today popularly known as "the Little Flower of Jesus", became a Carmelite novice in April 1888 at the tender age of 15, following her sisters Pauline and Marie into the order. She died of tuberculosis on 30 September 1897 when just 24 years old. Thérèse is celebrated for her "Little Way" of devotion and love, which promotes the need for trust and absolute surrender. She wrote:

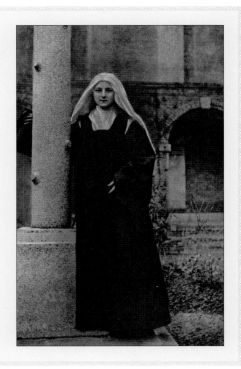

Love shows itself in deeds.... Great deeds are beyond me. The only way I can show my love is by throwing out flowers and these flowers are each a small sacrifice, each look and word, and doing of the very least thing simply for love.

Right St Thérèse was a teenage novice when she posed for this picture at the Carmelite house in Lisieux, c.1890.

LIVING FOR OTHERS

WOMEN IN THE RELIGIOUS ORDERS DEDICATE THEIR LIVES TO GOD IN
CHRIST AND TO PRAYING FOR AND SERVING THOSE IN NEED BECAUSE
OF POVERTY, SICKNESS OR IGNORANCE OF THE GOSPEL.

Whether nuns or religious sisters are members of a contemplative or charitable order, their religious life is intended to reach out to help other people. Enclosed orders seek to ease suffering in the world through devoted prayer, while charitable orders provide care, shelter, education and love to the needy.

IN AN ENCLOSED ORDER

The Poor Clares, which was established in 1212 by St Clare of Assisi and St Francis of Assisi, is an enclosed contemplative order of Franciscan nuns who are committed to a life of prayer without possessions. These nuns pray the Holy Liturgy and

Below Sisters in the Poor Clares dedicate themselves to service through prayer. Some undertake strict acts of penance, fasts and other austerities.

celebrate Mass together. They see intercessionary prayer as an important part of their calling, and they accept prayer requests from outside the convent and pray daily for the Church and the world.

Some houses keep retreat centres in the grounds of the convent. They also work in their convent to maintain the community as well as to support themselves. To this aim, they might make candles, vestments, greeting cards or religious pictures. The nuns follow a rota for cooking, gardening, cleaning, answering calls and so on.

The nuns view the enclosed life they live as a vital spiritual discipline that expresses their love for God. They leave the enclosed community only when it is absolutely necessary – perhaps to visit the doctor or dentist or to see a parent who cannot

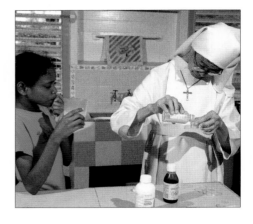

Above A sister distributes medicine at an Ursuline orphanage in Guyana, South America. The Ursulines have a special calling to education and healthcare.

travel. They are permitted to receive visits by close family members as allowed by the abbess.

CARING FOR THE POOR

Among many orders of nuns dedicated to charitable work in the world, the Missionaries of Charity, a religious order with a special calling to serve the extremely poor, is one of the most celebrated in modern times. The order was established in 1950 by Mother Teresa of Calcutta, and today it includes 4,500 nuns working in 133 countries.

These nuns care for orphans, lepers, victims of AIDS, refugees, former prostitutes, street children, the mentally ill and those suffering in the wake of famine and natural disasters. In Calcutta, the place of their foundation, they maintain no fewer than 19 homes, including ones for the dying, for lepers and a school for street children. The nuns in this order take the conventional vows of poverty, chastity and obedience. They also take a fourth vow to offer "wholehearted and free service to the poorest of the poor".

CARING FOR THE OLD

The Little Sisters of the Poor is a religious order with a particular calling to care for the elderly. The order

MOTHER TERESA

Albanian Agnes Gonxha Bojaxhiu (later Mother Teresa) was a Roman Catholic nun who went to India as a missionary and took her solemn vows in 1937. She reported that she received a call from God to work with the poor in Calcutta in 1946, and in 1950 she received permission from the Vatican to establish the Diocesan Congregation of the Calcutta Diocese, which became the Missionaries of Charity. She opened her first home for the dying in Calcutta in 1952. In the 1960s, the order expanded through India and around the world. In the 1970s, she was internationally recognized for her work and received the Nobel Peace Prize in 1979. She died on 5 September 1997 and was beatified by Pope John Paul II in 2003 under the name Blessed Teresa of Calcutta.

Right *Mother Teresa declared that her mission was to care for the hungry, destitute and those without homes, for all people who feel that others do not want or love them.*

was established in 1839 in France by Jeanne Jugan, but they have a strong presence in many cities in the United States. Today the order has approximately 4,000 sisters caring for more than 22,000 elderly people in 34 countries, including India, Hong Kong, Taiwan and the United Kingdom. In the United States alone, the Little Sisters of the Poor are responsible for running 32 homes for the elderly, including houses in San Francisco, Washington, D.C., New Orleans, Indianapolis and Pittsburgh.

The Little Sisters of the Poor put into practice their founder's instuctions to always show kindness toward others, but particularly to those who are sick. Jeanne Jugan had stressed that the calling to serve the sick was a great sign of God's Grace, and she declared that because the infirm were God's creatures, when the sisters cared for the sick they were serving God himself.

The nuns rely on charitable contributions to support their work, and they generally tour the area around their home in a "begging van", in which they collect gifts not only of food but also of medical and other important supplies.

Right *The Benedictine sisters in this early 18th-century French painting by Louise Madeleine care for the sick.*

In addition to vows of obedience, chastity and poverty, the sisters take a fourth vow of hospitality. They endeavour not just to give their residents shelter, food and comfort, but also to cater for their spiritual, psychological and social needs.

PRAYER AND DEVOTION

Sisters in charitable orders, such as the Missionaries of Charity and the Little Sisters of the Poor, anchor their active life in a routine of prayer and contemplative devotions. The Little Sisters of the Poor, for instance, will typically start the day with meditation and morning prayer, and then hold a daily Mass at the end of the morning. Residents in their homes are welcomed to this service. The sisters also take time for regular prayer throughout the day and they engage in meditative religious reading, or *lectio divina*. In addition, they meet for evening prayer at the end of the day.

THE MISSIONS

A NUMBER OF ROMAN CATHOLIC RELIGIOUS ORDERS ARE DEDICATED TO MISSIONARY WORK. THEY WORK ACROSS THE WORLD IN BOTH DEVELOPED AND DEVELOPING COUNTRIES TO SPREAD THE GOSPEL.

There are many Catholic missionary orders, but the Missionaries of the Sacred Heart, an order founded in France in 1854 by French priest Jules Chevalier, is particularly notable.

WORLDWIDE MISSION

The Sacred Heart has about 2,000 brothers and priests working around the world in more than 50 countries from Australia to Venezuela, inspired by their founder to find opportunities to serve Christ in the depths of the world's need. Chevalier was convinced that Christians could have as profound an experience of God's

Below The brothers of some missionaries are active in helping the poverty-stricken, such as these from the Missionaries of the Poor, repairing roofs in Kingston, Jamaica.

Grace in the world as they would in an enclosed religious community, and he declared that when brothers were helping the poor, the great power of God's love and of the Sacred Heart of Jesus would flow forth as needed. The greater the difficulties the brothers encountered in doing God's work, the greater the help God would provide.

Brothers still work in Papua New Guinea, where the order sent its first missionaries in 1882. They run the St Joseph Training Centre at Fissoa on the island of New Ireland, in which young men, many the sons of subsistence farmers from rural villages, study mathematics, English, music and religion while majoring in mechanics or carpentry. The young men also learn agricultural skills.

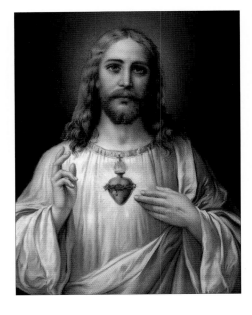

Above The Sacred Heart of Jesus provides spiritual inspiration to the brothers of the Missionaries of the Sacred Heart.

Many are given scholarships, paid from a fund set up by two of the Sacred Heart brothers.

The brothers, who are sometimes better known as MSC from the initials of their name in Latin, *Missionarii Sacratissimi Cordis*, declare that they see their work as "to be on Earth the heart of God", to meet need in whatever form they encounter it. In missions in England, Wales and Ireland, for example, they work with migrants and refugees in ecumenical interfaith initiatives and widely in education and parishes. Their motto is: "May the Sacred Heart of Jesus be everywhere loved."

On 1 September 2004, Pope John Paul II wrote to the Sacred Heart to mark its 150th anniversary, praising its founder and its work. He said that the organization's founder, Father Chevalier, established the Sacred Heart as a place for God to meet humankind, and expressed his wish that the community continue to inspire and have strength for its spiritual work. He also declared that they had a wonderful history worth remembering, but also "a great history still to be accomplished".

MARYKNOLL

Formerly known as the Catholic Foreign Missionary Society of America, Maryknoll sends more than 550 priests and brothers to work around the world, especially in Africa, Latin America, Korea, Japan and China. The order was founded in 1911 in the United States by Fathers James Anthony Walsh and Thomas Frederick Price.

In their mission statement, the brothers declare that, wherever they have travelled, they have been touched by the strength of human perseverance and greatly empowered by their experience of Christian faith in times of need. They work with them in declaring their faith in Jesus. The Maryknoll brothers commit themselves to standing in solidarity with the poor, to entering inter-religious dialogue, to serving as witnesses of Christ, to celebrating the Church's liturgy and to proclaiming the gospel and teaching the faith.

The society is linked to the Maryknoll Sisters of St Dominic, a group of religious sisters founded in 1912, in the United States. More than 700 Maryknoll Sisters work in 30 countries, including Albania, Panama, Nepal, Sudan and Taiwan. The sisters are associated with setting up convent schools. Widely known examples are Maryknoll Convent School in Kowloon Tong, Hong Kong, and Miriam College in Quezon City, Manila, the Philippines.

OTHER MISSIONS

The larger religious orders, while not formed primarily to carry out missionary outreach, do a great deal of work of this kind. Among many examples, Capuchin Franciscans maintain missions in Central America (Panama and Nicaragua) and in South Africa. In Pretoria, South Africa, for example, they run the Damietta Peacemaking Initiative to promote non-violence and peace, from Padre Pio Friary in Rietvallei.

The Jesuits spread the gospel through their outreach work in educational establishments, orphanages, hospitals and community centres as part of their overseas missions – notably in Guyana, Zimbabwe and South Africa. The Carmelites also maintain several missions, including ones in Kenya, Mozambique, Indonesia, East Timor, Burkina Faso, Cameroon and the Democratic Republic of Congo. In Kenya, for instance, the Carmelites have established an enclosed monastery in Machakos and a house of formation in Ngong diocese.

Another notable order is the Missionaries of La Salette, which was founded in 1852 in La Salette, near Grenoble, France, where a shrine to the Blessed Virgin Mary was established. The order has around 1,000 nuns, priests and lay members working in support of healing and reconciliation in North America and Europe, as well as performing missionary work in countries such as Madagascar, the Philippines, Bolivia, Myanmar, Namibia and Angola.

LAY GROUPS

THE CHURCH ENDORSES THE WORK OF SEVERAL ORGANIZATIONS THAT WERE ESTABLISHED TO HELP LAY CATHOLICS FOLLOW THE GOSPEL IN THEIR RELIGIOUS WORK AND FAMILY LIVES.

The largest lay group, Opus Dei (Latin for "God's work") is a Roman Catholic organization of predominately lay people who seek to grow closer to God and achieve sanctity through work and everyday activities, including family life. There are around 87,000 members worldwide, in 80 countries; 98 per cent are lay people and just 2 per cent priests. Approximately 30 per cent of lay members (called numeraries) are celibate and live in Opus Dei centres, while roughly 70 per cent (called supernumeraries) are married and serve God in family life.

The movement was founded in 1928 in Spain by Roman Catholic priest Josemaría Escrivá and received approval in 1950 from Pope Pius XII.

In 1982, Pope John Paul II declared the organization a personal prelature within the Church, under the name the Prelature of the Holy Cross and Opus Dei. This means that it functions like a religious order. The Church governs Opus Dei members through a prelate, who is appointed by the pope, and has a status equivalent to that of a superior general in a religious order. The members remain part of local church congregations.

As an organization, Opus Dei runs high schools, colleges, university halls of residence, business and agricultural schools, and it also does charitable work. In Spain, it founded and runs the University of Navarre at Pamplona. It also runs a university at Piura in Peru.

Above Pope John XXIII stands between St Josemaría Escrivá and Msgr Álvaro del Portillo, another leading Opus Dei figure, in 1960.

A SECULAR ROUTINE

Josemaría Escrivá encouraged people to try to "convert their work into prayer". He described a dream in which God's children could sanctify themselves although they lived as ordinary citizens. It was through regular work and the mundane routine of everyday life that people could find God's love.

Escrivá died in 1975. Pope John Paul II beatified him in 1992 and proclaimed him a saint in 2002. John Paul II declared Escrivá the "saint of ordinary life", adding that he disseminated through society the awareness that a calling to holiness is received by all, with no distinctions of culture, racial identity, social class or age.

SPIRITUALITY

Opus Dei members are expected to follow a set form of personal devotions every day, including Mass, and to attend a weekly confession. They should also attend an annual spiritual retreat of three weeks for numeraries and one week for supernumeraries.

Left The Church of Our Lady of Peace in Rome is the headquarters of Opus Dei. Many pray at the crypt of St Josemaría Escrivá.

Spiritual practice for a member of Opus Dei often includes an element of sacrifice by voluntarily offering discomfort or pain to God. This can simply involve self-sacrifice in terms of self-denial and charity in dealing with others. However, some celibate numeraries are said to practise physical mortification by either wearing a spike metal chain known as a cilice on the upper thigh or by flailing themselves with a woven cotton strap known as a discipline.

A CRITICIZED PRACTICE

Self-mortification is one of many areas in which Opus Dei has been criticized. Opponents attack the practice as being akin to masochism and even liable to undermine spiritual development by fostering

Above A statue of St Josemaría Escrivá, founder of Opus Dei, stands in an alcove of the basilica façade within the Vatican.

pride. However, defenders of the practice respond that it is a valued way of identifying with Christ's physical suffering, has been used by Christians for centuries and is more used today in the Roman Catholic Church than is generally known.

A SECRETIVE SOCIETY

Opus Dei has been accused by some of being both secretive and manipulative. They claim that a number of leading politicians around the world are members of the society, although few make public statement of their membership. Some people suggest that the organization dominates members and uses overly aggressive recruitment techniques. Opus Dei, however, states that members are not coerced into joining and people are free to leave if they want to.

OTHER LAY GROUPS

Many of the major religious orders also support lay associates: for example, the Dominican laity have their own rule, the Rule of the Lay Fraternities of St Dominic, first issued in 1285, while Franciscan lay

followers are members of the Secular Franciscan Order and follow a rule established for secular followers by St Francis himself in 1221. Secular Franciscans have a novitiate and formal profession, but they are not bound by their religious vows, and can be married and live ordinary lives in the community.

Among the other Catholic lay bodies is the Catenian Association, which is an international brotherhood of Catholic professionals and businessmen. It was established in 1908 in Manchester, England, and now has about 10,000 members in Australia, Ireland, South Africa, Malta, Zimbabwe and Zambia, as well as in the United Kingdom.

Their aims are to develop social bonds and foster brotherly love among members. The association grants bursaries to provide partial support for young Catholics who are performing community work. The Catenians also maintain a Public Affairs Committee that monitors and speaks out on any proposed legislation that would contradict Catholic teaching.

Above The Catenian Association has sponsored projects to help the needy in Mexico and Africa, such as at this children's home in Zambia.

IN RECOGNITION FOR CHRISTIAN SERVICE

The Association of Papal Orders is an organization for people who have been awarded papal knighthoods. These awards are made at five levels to people who have provided a great service to the Catholic Church. The five levels are:

- Supreme Order of Christ
- Pontifical Order of the Golden Spur
- Pontifical Order of Pius IX
- Pontifical Order of St Gregory the Great
- Pontifical Order of Pope St Sylvester.

Notable recipients of the awards include Prince Rainier III of Monaco (Pontifical Order of the Golden Spur), former German Federal Chancellor Helmut Kohl (Pontifical Order of St Gregory the Great) and the Hollywood entertainer Bob Hope (Pontifical Order of Pope St Sylvester).

LIVING THE SACRAMENTS

There are seven sacraments through which practising Catholics receive God's Grace. These are baptism, confirmation, the Eucharist, penance and reconciliation (popularly known as confession), "the anointing of the sick", holy orders and Holy Matrimony. According to the *Catechism of the Catholic Church*, the sacraments were "instituted by Christ and entrusted to the Church". They are stages in the spiritual life – from new birth as a Christian in baptism and confirmation, through to the anointing of the sick, often administered at the end of earthly life before the final journey into eternal life. The sacraments help individual Catholics make spiritual progress and grow in holiness.

Most people do not receive all seven sacraments: only some have a priestly vocation and receive holy orders, for example, and all who receive holy orders (except already married deacons) cannot receive Holy Matrimony. Individuals must be prepared to receive the sacraments. God's Grace may be blocked from working if someone is not disposed to receive it. For a sacrament to be effective, a person must have faith in it, although at the same time the sacraments in themselves strengthen and give expression to a person's faith.

Particular objects used by the clergy, including the special robes or vestments that a priest or bishop wears when celebrating the Eucharist or the Liturgy of the Hours, are termed "sacramentals". They are material things blessed or set apart to summon the respect believers should have for the sacraments of the Church – in the words of the *Baltimore Catechism* (a Catholic school text in the United States) "to excite good thoughts and increase devotion".

Above The last rites performed for a dying person include celebration of the Eucharist, depicted in Hieronymus Bosch's 15th–16th-century painting Death and Last Rites.

Left The Eucharist is central among the sacraments. All seven sacraments are connected to Christ's paschal mystery – his redemptive sacrifice that is re-enacted in the Eucharist.

GOD'S HOUSE

THE FIRST CHRISTIANS WORSHIPPED IN PRIVATE HOUSES, BUT OVER TIME CHURCHES HAVE DEVELOPED INTO SUBSTANTIAL PUBLIC BUILDINGS THAT SERVE AS THE CENTRE OF ROMAN CATHOLIC LIFE.

The earliest public churches were built after Christianity was adopted as the state religion of the Roman Empire in the 4th century AD. They were based on the Roman basilica, a large roofed public building often used as a courthouse or market. Like the basilica, the early churches had a central hall, known as the nave, with a timber roof and an aisle on each side, which were separated from the nave by a line of columns.

A wooden altar was established toward one end of the nave. In the first churches, the altar was typically at the west end of the nave, in imitation of the arrangement in the Jewish Temple in Jerusalem. The bishop or

Above The Jewish Temple in Jerusalem, shown in this c. 1728 Jewish manuscript, was an inspiration to early Christians, who based part of their church layout on it.

priest celebrating the Eucharist faced east – on the grounds that it was the direction of the heavenly Jerusalem and thus it was from this direction that Christ would return in glory – and so he always looked toward the congregation. For unknown reasons, in about the 6th century the arrangement was reversed, with the altar at the east end of the nave.

Beyond the altar was the apse, basically a semicircular or sometimes rectangular recess, usually vaulted, occupied by the bishop and priests during services. When celebrating the Eucharist, the bishop or priest, who continued to face east, looked toward the apse and away from the worshippers in the nave. The area around the altar, which was set aside for the clergy, became known as the presbytery or sanctuary.

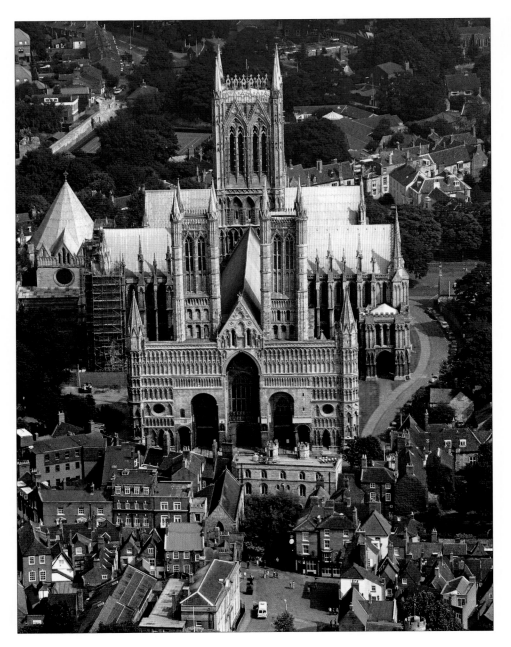

Left The west front of Lincoln Cathedral in England incorporates elements dating from 1072. The main part of the cathedral is 13th-century, in the Gothic style.

At the west end, a long entrance porch called the narthex ran across the full width of the nave and led into the nave. Unbaptized believers and penitents generally remained in the narthex, where they were separated from clergy and other believers.

THE BEMA AND THE CHOIR

There were many variations of these areas. In some churches, a wooden platform called the bema was built in the centre of the nave. The clergy sat in this area and read lessons and delivered sermons from the lectern on the bema. In some large churches, the eastern end of the nave began to be fenced off with a small railing to form an area for the choir, and sometimes the choir area was attached to the bema. This arrangement survives to this day in the Basilica di Santa Maria Maggiore (AD 430–40) in Rome. More typically, the choir area became a separate architectural feature connecting the nave and sanctuary.

CRUCIFORM PLAN

In some churches, a transept was added on a north–south axis, perpendicular to the nave, to form a church shaped like a cross. The point at which the transept cuts across the nave was known as "the crossing": the nave usually extended to the west of the crossing and the choir and sanctuary lay to the east. The arms of the crossing were called north

Above The altar stands at the centre of the Metropolitan Cathedral of Christ the King, Liverpool, England, surrounded on all sides by seats. The designer was aiming to help the congregation feel more linked to the liturgy.

transept and south transept: at each end of these, additional altars were added in honour of particular saints. Often a dome was built above the crossing. A good example of this design is the magnificent 11th-century Basilica of San Michele Maggiore in Pavia, Italy. In some cathedrals – for instance at Lincoln (built 1092–1311) and Salisbury (1220–58), both in England – a second, smaller transept was built to the east of the main one.

HALL CHURCH

In Italy in the 15th and 16th centuries, the hall church design was developed to reduce the long distance between entrance and altar. At this time, during the Counter-Reformation (the Catholic Church's response to the rise of Protestantism), Church authorities wanted to promote the importance of preaching: a pulpit was introduced halfway down the nave and large side chapels were built nearby. A fine example of this design is the Church of the Gesù in Rome, the mother church of the Society of Jesus, or Jesuits, built in around 1568 by Giacomo da Vignola and Giacomo Della Porta.

GREEK CHURCH DESIGN

From early times, many Eastern churches were built on the plan of a Greek cross – a cross with four arms of equal length. Rather than have the crossing toward one end of a long nave, these churches had four equally sized wings meeting at a central crossing. The crossing point was generally square and domed. One good example is the 6th-century Church of Hagia Sophia in Istanbul (which eventually became a mosque and is now a museum).

This design returned to relevance in Western churches of the late 20th century, many of which put the altar toward the centre of the church to symbolize the centrality of the Mass in Catholic life. Two examples include the Metropolitan Cathedral of Christ the King in Liverpool, England (1958–70), and the Cathedral of Saint Mary of the Assumption, which was built in San Francisco, California (1967–71).

THE ROOD SCREEN AND REREDOS

In many medieval churches, a wooden screen separated the faithful in the nave from the clergy and other celebrants in the choir and sanctuary. The screen consisted of a large carved cross (or "rood") with an image of Jesus upon it, often flanked by carvings of the Blessed Virgin Mary and St John looking on. The structure was called the rood screen or choir screen. Many churches also had decorated screens behind the altar in the east. This often profoundly beautiful structure was called an altar piece or reredos.

Right The intricately carved rood screen in the Gothic church of Saint-Etienne-du-Mont in Paris, France, has spiral staircases on either side.

GREAT CHURCHES

FROM ROME TO LOS ANGELES, FROM THE 4TH TO THE 21ST CENTURY, THE BASILICAS AND CATHEDRALS OF THE ROMAN CATHOLIC CHURCH ARE AMONG THE WORLD'S MOST INSPIRATIONAL BUILDINGS.

Traditionally, the apostle Peter went to Rome and became the Church's first bishop. He was martyred in Rome and was buried in a Christian cemetery on *Mons Vaticanus*, where the Vatican now stands. Emperor Constantine built a basilica on the site in AD 326–33. However, by the end of the 15th century this building was in poor condition.

ST PETER'S BASILICA
The Basilica di San Pietro di Vaticano, better known as St Peter's Basilica, was built on the same site as the original basilica over more than a century, 1506–1626, and was consecrated in 1628. Among its many architects were Donato Bramante, Michelangelo and Gian Lorenzo Bernini. It stands within Vatican City – reputedly with St Peter's grave beneath its altar – and is considered the most holy church for Catholics

worldwide. Many popes, including John Paul II in 2005, have been buried in this basilica.

MEDIEVAL CATHEDRALS
In the Middle Ages, the pope was often at odds with the Holy Roman emperor. During this time the great St Peter's Basilica in Rome was rivalled by the imperial church at Aachen (which is now part of western Germany), the most historic cathedral in northern Europe. At the heart of this church is the Palatine Chapel, which was founded by Charlemagne, King of the Franks, in 792 and consecrated to the Blessed Virgin Mary in 805 by Pope Leo III. German kings (and later emperors)

Below Filippo Brunelleschi's breathtaking dome at Florence Cathedral contains 4 million bricks. With the lantern at its top, it is 114.5m (375ft) high.

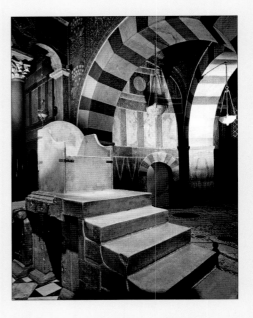

Above The throne of Charlemagne on which Holy Roman emperors were crowned stands in the upper gallery of the Palatine Chapel in Aachen, Germany.

were crowned in the Palatine Chapel for more than 600 years, between 936 and 1531.

Charlemagne himself was buried in a vault beneath the cathedral on his death in 814, and the cathedral became an attraction for pilgrims throughout the Middle Ages, when it was known as the Royal Church of St Mary at Aachen. The golden Shrine of St Mary was built in the choir in 1220–39 to contain four sacred relics: Christ's swaddling cloth, his loincloth, Mary's cloak and the beheading cloth of John the Baptist. Every seven years to the present day the relics are removed from the shrine and put on display for pilgrims.

There are other great European cathedrals of the Middle Ages and Renaissance, including the grand 13th-century Gothic cathedral of Chartres in France, celebrated for its magnificent stained-glass windows, and the Basilica di Santa Maria del Fiore, also known as Florence Cathedral, with its glorious 14th-century campanile (bell tower) partly designed by Giotto, the bronze doors of 1403–24 on the baptistery by

Above The Basilica of Our Lady of Peace in Yamoussoukro, Ivory Coast, was built with the finest Italian marble as well as 7,000sq m (75,350sq ft) of stained glass.

Lorenzo Ghiberti and the octagonal dome that was built in 1420–36 by Filippo Brunelleschi.

MODERN RIVALS

The cathedral at Florence was built to rival St Peter's Basilica in size and grandeur, and this desire survived into the late 20th century. The Basilica of Our Lady of Peace in Yamoussoukro, Ivory Coast, Africa, was modelled on St Peter's, built in 1985–90 and consecrated by Pope John Paul II on 10 September 1990. It was designed to be the greatest Catholic church in the world: it covers a slightly larger area than St Peter's – 3 hectares (7.4 acres) compared to 2.3 hectares (5.7 acres). However, critics point out that the area includes a villa and rectory, which are not part of the church, and that the Ivory Coast basilica has a smaller capacity at 18,000 people, compared with 60,000 for St Peter's.

In Liverpool, England, the Metropolitan Cathedral of Christ the King was built in the 1960s to a design by Sir Frederick Gibberd. Its

Above Light falling through the glass roof creates striking patterns in the Catedral Metropolitana Nossa Senhora Aparecida.

circular plan was drawn up in response to the call by the Second Vatican Council for increased participation by the laity in the sacred liturgy. The cathedral was consecrated on the Feast of Pentecost, 14 May 1967. Another strikingly modern, circular cathedral is the Catedral Metropolitana Nossa Senhora Aparecida in Brasilia, Brazil. It was designed by Oscar Niemeyer, built from 1958 onward and was consecrated on 31 May 1970.

OUR LADY OF THE ANGELS

The greatest Roman Catholic church dedicated in the early 21st century is surely the outwardly austere, inwardly beautiful Cathedral of Our Lady of the Angels in downtown Los Angeles, California. It was begun in 1997 to designs by Spanish architect José Rafael Moneo, and opened in September 2002. It incorporates a plaza of 1,860sq m (20,000sq ft) and a main sanctuary 100m (333ft) in length and up to 30m (100ft) high. It has superb bronze doors, created by artist Robert Graham, which pay homage across the centuries to Ghiberti's bronze doors in the Florence baptistery.

Right The Cathedral of Our Lady of the Angels is 12 storeys high and is specially designed to resist earthquake damage.

THE ALTAR OF GOD

THE ALTAR, AT WHICH THE PRIEST CELEBRATES THE EUCHARIST, IS THE FOCAL POINT OF THE SANCTUARY. IT IS REVERED BY CHRISTIANS AS THE *MENSA DOMINI* ("TABLE OF THE LORD").

The sanctuary itself is the area set aside for the priest celebrant, deacons and other ministers. It is usually raised above the rest of the church, with its area demarcated by a low rail. Within the sanctuary, the altar is the principal furnishing. The altar represents the table at which Christ shared the Last Supper with his apostles and instituted the Eucharist.

The Church teaches that the altar also stands for Jesus himself and for the Cross on which his sacrifice was made: for these reasons, it is

Above The altar stands in for the table used at the Last Supper by Christ and the apostles, which is shown in Domenico Ghirlandaio's 15th-century painting.

honoured with incense. Numbers are often symbolic to Catholics, and the five crosses carved on it represent Jesus' Five Sacred Wounds.

The table or horizontal top of the altar is normally made of natural stone because it embodies Christ, described in the First Letter of Peter as "that living stone, rejected by men but in God's sight chosen and precious" (1 Peter 2:3–4). Although the support of the tabletop can be of any material, the altar should honour Christ by being simple and beautiful.

SANCTIFIED BY RELICS

The altar stands on a raised platform called the predella. This is often made of wood. For symbolic reasons, the steps leading up to it are normally an uneven number – three, five or seven – and each about 15cm (6in) high. The steps may be of stone, wood or

Left Three steps mount to the main altar in St Patrick's Cathedral, New York City. The sanctuary was renovated in the 1930s to 1940s, when the elegant baldacchino (canopy) was added.

brick. If there are three steps, they are used to distinguish between ranks of ministers at the Eucharist: the celebrant will stand on the predella, the deacon on the second step and a subdeacon or another lower-ranking minister on the third step.

Beneath the altar is a box called the sepulchrum, used for containing a holy relic and other specific objects. The box has a gold, silver or lead reliquary to hold part of the bodily remains of a saint, together with three grains of incense and a parchment certifying that the altar has been consecrated. If possible, the relic is of the saint in whose name the church was built. The relics were traditionally placed within the altar, but they are now set beneath it. Catholics do not worship the relics or saints. The saints are honoured as men and women of great holiness, exemplars of the Christian life. The relics remind believers that the Eucharist celebrated on the altar is a source of God's Grace, the grace that enabled the saints to live such holy lives.

MARKING A CELEBRATION
For a celebration three white cloths are laid on the altar. Two candles are lighted to celebrate a Low Mass, one

Below A burning candle marks the presence of the blessed sacrament within the tabernacle (centre). Its presence further sanctifies the altar as the table of the Lord.

spoken by a priest without incense or the presence of a deacon or subdeacon; but six candles are required for a High Mass, a solemn celebration with music.

THE TABERNACLE
The gifts of the bread and the wine are consecrated during the Mass and distributed to the people. Some consecrated bread and wine – the blessed sacrament – is reserved in the tabernacle, a small carved metal container. The tabernacle is usually kept within the sanctuary, on the altar or at the side, but in some churches it is kept in a separate side chapel. It is sometimes kept beneath a small canopy or conopaeum.

A candle must always be kept burning above the tabernacle. This is called the altar lamp, or sanctuary light. The light reminds the faithful of the presence of Christ in the blessed sacrament and it embodies Christ, called in the Gospel of John "the true light that enlightens every man" (John 1:9). The light is an expression of the burning love of the faithful for their Lord. Although more than one light may be on the tabernacle, there are always uneven numbers lit: three, five, seven and so on.

GOSPEL AND SERMONS
In many churches, a raised pulpit stands at the front of the sanctuary, on the left-hand side of the church as

you face the altar. The gospel and sermons or homilies are traditionally delivered from this pulpit. On the right-hand side of the sanctuary as you face the altar is usually a lectern, from which the Epistle is generally read. Although lay people can use the lectern, only members of the clergy can use the pulpit. Some churches do not have pulpit and lectern. Instead, they have a single podium, called an ambo, in the space otherwise occupied by the pulpit.

PRIESTLY CHAIR
The sanctuary also contains a chair for the priest celebrant. Although this chair should not be grandiose, it should reflect the dignity of the priest's role in administering the sacrament of the Eucharist. In a cathedral, the bishop has a permanent chair called the cathedra and another chair is placed alongside for other priest celebrants. Additional chairs are provided for deacons and other ministers.

Above The sanctuary of the 13th-century St Asaph Cathedral in Denbighshire, North Wales, contains the bishop's seat.

VESTMENTS

WHEN CELEBRATING THE LITURGY OF THE CATHOLIC CHURCH, MEMBERS OF THE CLERGY WEAR SPECIAL ROBES OR VESTMENTS THAT SYMBOLIZE ASPECTS OF A PRIEST'S SPIRITUAL ROLE.

The celebrant's vestments distinguish him from the people and remind him of his vocation and duties, and the holiness of the acts he undertakes. The wearing of priestly vestments has historical roots going right back to the early days of Christianity – and even beyond to the Old Testament age, when the Jewish priests of Aaron wore ritual garb.

To celebrate the liturgy and in processions, clerics traditionally wear a cassock, a long, close-fitting cloak with buttons down the front, so-called from the Italian *casacca* for "greatcoat". Priests generally wear a black cassock, while bishops wear a purple one and cardinals a red one (or a black one with red piping). The pope's cassock is always white.

VESTMENTS FOR EUCHARIST

To celebrate the Eucharist, a priest also wears an alb, a cincture, a stole and a chasuble. An alb is a full-length white linen gown worn over the priest's cassock. It is a descendant of the white toga worn by the ancient Romans and takes its name from the Latin word *albus*, meaning "white". The alb's colour symbolizes purity. Around the waist the priest secures the alb with a braided linen or woollen cord called the cincture, from the Latin *cinctura*, meaning "girdle". It is usually white, like the alb. The cincture is worn to symbolize the priest's chastity.

Around his neck and across his shoulders, the priest wears a long decorated strip of material called a stole. It should be approximately 200cm (80in) long and 5–10cm (2–4in) in width. The stole generally has a cross embroidered at each end and in the middle (the part worn behind the neck); the middle cross is required because the priest must

Below Kneeling deacons wear the alb (full-length white gown), cincture (cord belt) and stole (strip across shoulder and chest).

Above Many priests still wear a black cassock for day-to-day duties, but some wear a suit with shirt and clerical collar.

kiss this when putting on the stole. Bishops wear the stole in the same manner as priests; deacons wear it over the left shoulder and diagonally across the chest.

The priest wears a decorated outer garment called the chasuble over his vestments. The chasuble is usually made of silk or velvet and often has a large cross on the back. Its name derives from the Latin *casula*, which means "little house", because the over garment provides protection or shelter for the priest. The chasuble symbolizes the yoke of Christ and the virtue of charity.

THE AMICE AND MANIPLE

Beneath the alb the priest can choose to wear an amice over his shoulders. The amice is a rectangular white cloth, marked with a cross and attached to two long ribbon-like strings, which are used to secure it. It takes its name from the Latin *amictus*, meaning "cloak" or "mantle". Wearing an amice was once compulsory for priests celebrating the Eucharist, but when liturgical reforms were introduced in 1972 wearing an amice became voluntary. Today many priests choose to wear one in honour of tradition.

The priest may also choose to wear a maniple. This is a long and narrow embroidered strip of material traditionally worn over the left arm. For most priests the maniple is an optional vestment, but those who celebrate the Extraordinary Form of the Roman Rite (the Tridentine Mass) are required to wear it when celebrating the Eucharist.

OTHER VESTMENTS

In liturgical settings other than the Mass, a priest may wear the cope, humeral veil and surplice. The cope is a very long and often heavy embroidered mantle or cloak worn over the shoulder, reaching to the ankles, and fastened at the chest with an often highly decorated clasp called a morse. The cope, which takes its name from the Latin *cappa* ("cape"), is often worn in processions and at benedictions (a service in which the blessed sacrament is exposed on the altar in a monstrance, or vessel, for the adoration of the faithful), as well as for many other solemn liturgical offices other than the Mass.

The humeral veil is also tradition-ally worn at benediction: it is a long piece of usually richly ornamented material worn over the shoulders and covering the hands of the priest. Priests also wear it when carrying sacred vessels containing the reserved sacrament in a procession.

LITURGICAL COLOURS

Priests celebrate Mass in vestments of different colours according to the season of the church year or to mark a particular saint's day or festival. The four main colours are white, red, green and purple; in addition, on more solemn days festive silver and gold vestments can also be worn – silver in place of white, and gold in place of white, red or green.

White symbolizes purity and the glory of the Resurrection and is the colour for the Easter season; it is also worn on major feast days, such as Christmas Day and Easter Day, feasts of the Blessed Virgin Mary and of saints who were confessors or virgins. Purple symbolizes repentance and is worn for Lent and Advent. Red, as the colour of blood, is worn on the feast days of saints who were martyred; as the colour of fire, it is worn on Pentecost, the festival commemorating the descent of the Holy Spirit as tongues of fire (Acts 2:3). Green is worn on ordinary days – that is, times of the year that are not part of a particular church season and not feast days. Green stands for the growth of the Church.

Above Clergy in procession at Lourdes, France, prior to a Mass for the sick wear the cope or long clerical cloak.

The surplice is basically a half-length tunic usually made of cotton or linen and sometimes featuring an embroidered hem and sleeves. It is worn over the cassock when administering sacraments other than the Eucharist and when saying the Liturgy of the Hours, as well as during processions.

Right Because this priest is celebrating the Eucharist, he is wearing a chasuble (the heavy, ornately decorated outer garment), which is worn over his alb, cincture and stole.

"GATHERED TOGETHER IN MY NAME"

IN THE FIRST PART OF THE SACRAMENT OF THE EUCHARIST, READINGS AND A HOMILY FORM THE LITURGY OF THE WORD, WHICH PREPARES THE FAITHFUL TO RECEIVE HOLY COMMUNION.

Above Pope John Paul II censes the altar during a Mass in Switzerland in 1984. He uses a thurible (metal censer).

The Catholic celebration of the Eucharist is known as the Mass, from the word *missa.* This is used as a form of dismissal at the close of the traditional Latin form of the service: *Ite, missa est* ("Go, it is finished"). The Mass is a sacramental re-enactment of the death and Resurrection of Jesus, in which bread and wine become the body and blood of Christ and are offered to God again, just as they were on the Cross. In this sacrament, the community of believers makes symbolic expression of its unity and is nourished by receiving Jesus' body and blood.

Mass was originally said in Latin, but the Second Vatican Council (1962–5) allowed conferences of bishops to make their own judgement on the extent to which English

Below The bread that Jesus broke during the Last Supper with his apostles can be seen in Girolamo di Romano's 16th-century painting The Last Supper.

or other local vernacular languages could be used. The great majority of Masses are today celebrated in approved vernacular translations, but Latin is still used occasionally and in some places is used regularly.

ENTRANCE AND GREETING

On entering, the priest kisses the altar and, when incense is used, he censes it. All present make a large sign of the Cross, using the fingertips of the open right hand to touch forehead, chest, left shoulder, then right shoulder, while the priest says "In the name of the Father, and of the Son, and of the Holy Spirit: Amen."

The priest extends both hands and, facing the people, welcomes them with one of a series of greetings based on the beginnings of the Epistles of St Paul. They respond. In the simplest form of the greeting, the priest says "The Lord be with you", and the people respond "And also with you".

ACT OF PENITENCE

The priests call on those present to take part in the act of penitence. The most common form is the Confiteor, or Mea Culpa, said by all. It begins:

> *I confess to Almighty God, and to you, my brothers and sisters, that I have sinned through my own fault in my thoughts and in my words...*

When the congregation says "through my own fault", it is customary for them to strike themselves on the chest. The act of penitence concludes with the priest praying, "May almighty God have mercy on us, forgive us our sins, and bring us to everlasting life."

All present then usually say or sing the Kyrie Eleison, either in English ("Lord have mercy, Christ have mercy, Lord have mercy") or the original Greek (*Kyrie Eleison, Christe Eleison, Kyrie Eleison*). The threefold repetition is in veneration of the Trinity of Father, Son and Holy Spirit. Afterward, all join in singing or saying the ancient hymn of *Gloria in Excelsis Deo*, which begins "Glory to God in the highest, and peace to his people on earth..."

LITURGY OF THE WORD

The priest invites all to pray and after a period of silent prayer, he reads the set collect (a collection of short prayers) for the day. Biblical readings follow with three on Sundays and solemn occasions, two on other days. The first is from the Old Testament and is usually followed by a psalm. The second is from the New Testament, generally one of the Epistles to early Christians. On both occasions, the reader declares on finishing "This is the Word of the Lord" and the congregation responds "Thanks be to God".

THE HOLY GOSPEL

The third reading is from the Holy Gospel. This is read by a deacon, or by the priest if no deacon is present. Before the Gospel an hallelujah, or expression of praise to God, is sung or said. The deacon or priest declares "The Lord be with you", to which the people respond, "And also with you"; he announces "A reading from the Holy Gospel according to..." and makes a sign of the cross over the Bible and on his own forehead, lips and chest; the people do likewise and make the response "Glory to you, Lord". When incense is used, the priest or deacon censes the book. At the end of the reading he declares "This is the Gospel of the Lord", and the congregation responds "Praise to you, Lord Jesus Christ". The priest or deacon then kisses the book.

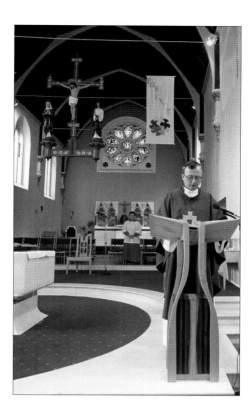

Left As the high point of the liturgy of the Word, a priest delivers a reading from the Holy Gospel.

ENDING WITH A PRAYER

A bishop, priest or deacon usually delivers a homily or sermon, then all present recite the Nicene Creed, which begins: "We believe in one God, the Father, the Almighty..." The liturgy of the Word concludes with the Prayers of the Faithful: a deacon, cantor or member of the congregation leads all in prayer requests before the priest declaims a concluding prayer.

HOLY WATER

On Sundays, and especially during the Easter season, the rite of asperges — the blessing and sprinkling of holy water — is sometimes used in place of the act of penitence and the Kyrie. The priest explains that the water is to remind all present of their baptism.

One of several prayers available includes the phrase "Lord in your mercy give us living water, always springing up as a fountain of salvation: free us, body and soul, from every danger...". The priest then takes the aspergil (silver water sprinkler) and sprinkles first himself, then the other clergy and then the people present with the holy water. While he does this, an antiphon or hymn is sung.

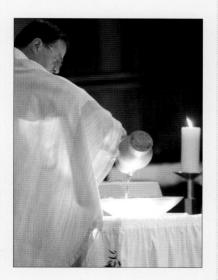

Above A priest pours out water prior to blessing and sprinkling it in the rite of asperges.

Left Priests sing "We praise Thee, We bless Thee, We worship Thee, We glorify Thee" as they lead the gloria during Mass.

THE MOST HOLY SACRAMENT OF THE ALTAR

THE SECOND PART OF THE MASS IS THE LITURGY OF THE EUCHARIST, IN WHICH THE BREAD AND WINE ARE CONSECRATED AND DISTRIBUTED TO THE COMMUNICANTS AS THE BODY AND BLOOD OF JESUS CHRIST.

In the first section of the liturgy, the bread and wine that will be used in the Eucharist are brought to the altar, usually by members of the congregation in a formal procession. They usually sing an offertory hymn.

The priest prays over the gifts of bread and wine. He places the bread on a small silver or gold plate called the paten and mixes water and wine in a precious cup, referred to as the chalice. When incense is being used, the priest censes the offerings and the altar, and a deacon or other minister censes the priest and the people. The priest then washes his hands, symbolizing his desire for inner purification.

Above At the sacred climax of the Eucharist, a bishop holds the consecrated Host aloft to show it to the congregation.

EUCHARISTIC PRAYER

The Eucharistic Prayer leads the congregation through the sacred climax of the Eucharist, in which the bread and the wine are consecrated and become Christ's body and blood. There are variations of the prayer. The key elements, found in all versions, are when making a sign of the Cross over the bread and the wine, the priest blesses the offerings on the altar and recalls how Christ instituted the Eucharist at the Last Supper.

The priest copies Christ's actions as he recounts how Christ took the bread in his sacred hands, looked to heaven, gave thanks and praise to God the Father, and then broke the bread, giving it to his disciples, and said, "Take this, all of you, and eat it", then referring to it as his body, "which will be given up for you". At this point, the bread is made holy and becomes the consecrated Host, the very body of Christ. An acolyte often rings a bell to signal the holy moment, and if incense is being used

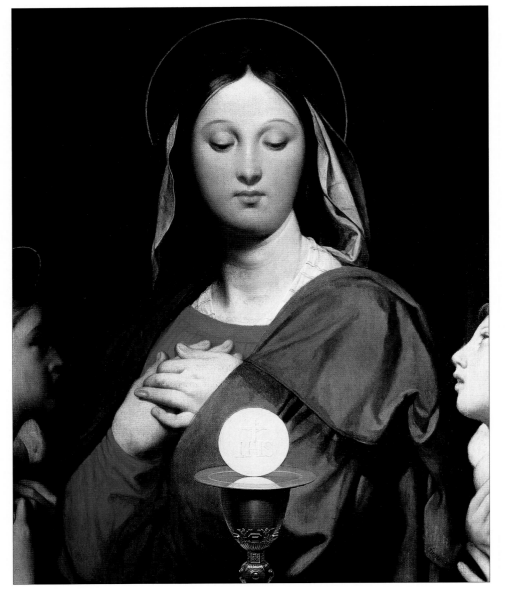

Left In Ingres' 1866 painting, Virgin of the Eucharist, *the Blessed Virgin Mary contemplates the divine mystery of her son's presence in the Host.*

he censes the priest and the paten. The priest lifts the Host and then places it back on the paten on the altar and kneels in adoration.

The priest raises the chalice and recounts Christ's actions in taking a cup of wine, giving thanks and praise to the Father in heaven, then giving it to the disciples, stating, "Take this all of you and drink from it". The priest refers to the contents in the cup as "the blood of the new and everlasting covenant" and continues by stating that blood was shed for humankind so that its sins will be forgiven. At this point, an acolyte once again rings a bell to signal the moment of consecration, and if incense is being used, he will cense the priest and chalice.

COMMUNION RITE
Before the congregation receives the Eucharist, all join in repeating the Lord's Prayer, then they share a sign of peace according to local custom. The priest breaks the Host and puts a piece in the chalice in what is called the rite of fraction, and prays: "May this mingling of the body and blood of our Lord Jesus Christ bring eternal life to all who receive it."

Below In today's Mass, communicants receive the consecrated Host when the priest places it on the tongue.

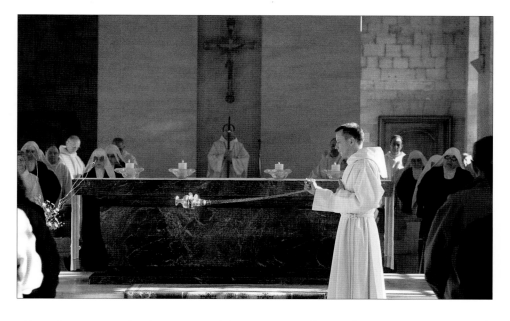

Above Incense signifies the sanctity of the altar and of the gifts of bread and wine that become the Lord's body and blood.

The priest says a prayer of personal devotion, then presents the Host (consecrated bread) to the congregation with the words, "This is the Lamb of God who takes away the sins of the world. Happy are those who are called to his supper." All present respond with the words, "Lord I am not worthy to receive you" and finish off with "say the word and I shall be healed".

The priest receives Communion himself and distributes it to other ministers and deacons, and then to the congregation, who usually come forward in procession. Each communicant bows, then receives the Host on the tongue (in the past it was sometimes received in the hand); the priest declares "the body of Christ" and the communicant responds "Amen". The communicant is offered the chalice and the priest declares "the blood of Christ".

It is possible for communicants to receive only the Host, and for the priest to dip the Host into the wine and present it in that form, laying it on the communicant's tongue; this is called intinction. Usually, the congregation sings a Communion song throughout this period.

Afterward, the chalice, paten and other vessels are washed and dried and placed on the altar and the priest declaims a prayer after Communion. At this point notices are read out, then the priest gives one of a choice of blessings on the people and pronounces one of a choice of dismissals. All include the phrase "Go in peace"; the variant based on the original Latin dismissal (*Ite, missa est*), which gives the Mass its name, is "The Mass is ended. Go in peace". The congregation responds, "Thanks be to God." Then the priest kisses the altar, makes a customary reverence with other ministers and leaves. A hymn is often sung at the close of the service.

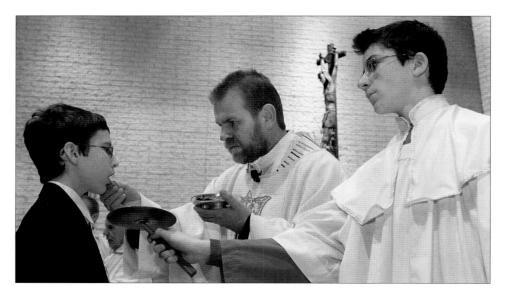

BAPTISM

IN THE SACRAMENT OF BAPTISM, AN INDIVIDUAL IS REBORN AS A CHRISTIAN AND GAINS A SANCTIFYING GRACE THAT ENABLES HIM OR HER TO SHARE IN THE LIFE OF GOD – FATHER, SON AND HOLY SPIRIT.

Most Catholics are baptized as infants, but those who convert to Catholicism can be baptized as an adult if they have not previously been baptized in another Christian denomination. With confirmation and Holy Communion, baptism is listed as one of three sacraments of initiation that prepares an individual for life as a Christian.

According to the *Catechism of the Catholic Church*, baptism is the backbone of the complete Christian life, "the gateway to life in the spirit"; through baptism people are united with Christ and are "incorporated

Below *Our Lord explains the necessity of being "born of water and the Spirit" to Nicodemus, depicted in this 17th-century painting by Crijn Hendricksz Volmarijn.*

into the Church and made sharers in Her mission". In baptism, people join the priesthood of believers.

A NEW BIRTH

One of the key biblical texts that supports baptism is from Jesus' words to Nicodemus, "Truly, truly, I say to you, unless one is born of water and the Spirit, he cannot enter the kingdom of God" (John 3:5). Baptism is a symbolic rebirth: and only through baptism can believers come to the other sacraments of Christian life.

According to Catholic doctrine, baptism frees an individual from original sin (the mark of human sinfulness with which all are tainted, and which derives from the disobedience to God's commandments of the first

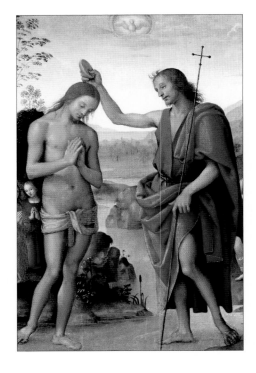

Above *When Jesus was baptized by John the Baptist, the Holy Spirit descended upon him. Perugino captured the scene in this c.1500 painting,* Baptism of Christ in the Jordan.

people, Adam and Eve, in the Garden of Eden). For this reason, practising Catholics believe they must baptize their children as infants; should the children die unbaptized, they would remain tainted by original sin and their salvation would be prevented. Baptism also liberates people from their own sins and from any punishment deriving from these.

RITE OF BAPTISM

In normal circumstances, the rite of baptism involves friends or relatives of the child's parents as "godparents"; they hold a responsibility to help the parents in raising the baptized child as a Christian. The bishop, priest or deacon greets both the parents and godparents and reminds them of the responsibilities attendant on bringing an infant to baptism, which include training the infant "in the practice of the faith" and keeping God's commandments "as Christ taught us, by loving God and our

Above An infant is baptized by Pope Benedict XVI. The catechism teaches that by being baptized "we are freed from sin and reborn as sons of God".

neighbour". He then leads the parents (and godparents if desired) in tracing the Cross of Christ on the infant's forehead.

Readings from the Holy Gospel and a homily or sermon follow. The celebrant leads the prayer of the faithful that calls on God to "bathe this child in light" and give the child "new life of baptism" and asks that the child is welcomed into the holy Church. The prayers also call on God to "renew the grace of our baptism in each one of us".

The celebrant invokes the Blessed Virgin and the saints, and proceeds to a prayer of exorcism and anointing before baptism in which he calls on God to free the child from original sin and "make him (or her) a temple of your glory". He then anoints the infant with oil in Christ's name.

SACRED WATERS

At the font, the celebrant recites an introductory prayer. The priest blesses the water in the font, then once again reminds the parents and godparents of their responsibility to raise the infant in the Catholic faith. He asks them to make three professions of their faith: in God the Father; in Jesus Christ; and in the Holy Spirit. As he says this he refers to the Catholic Church and the communion of saints, as well as Jesus' Resurrection and everlasting life. All present then announce their belief in these things: "This is our faith. This is the faith of the Church." They then declare that they are proud of their profession.

Then the celebrant baptizes the infant, saying the child's name and declaring, "I baptize you in the name of the Father and of the Son and of the Holy Spirit." At each naming of God, he either pours water over

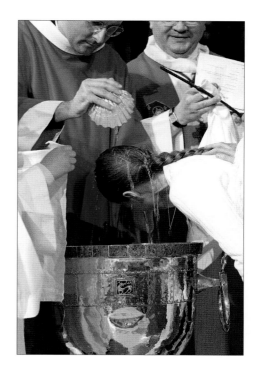

Above A Catholic convert leans over a font as she is baptized in the Cathedral of Notre-Dame de Paris – the celebrant is using a traditional scallop shell.

the infant's forehead or immerses the child in the water of the font. The celebrant anoints the infant with chrism, or holy oil, and clothes him or her in a white garment as an "outward sign of Christian dignity". The baptism usually concludes with the celebrant reaffirming that the infant has been reborn in baptism, leading the congregation in the Lord's Prayer, then giving a blessing.

SYMBOLIC WATER

When the main baptism takes place at the font, the celebrant's introductory prayer identifies water as a symbol of God's grace and a "wellspring of holiness". The waters of baptism are likened to those that existed before the Creation and on which God breathed, to those of Noah's flood, to the waters of the Red Sea that parted as the Israelites were led out of Egypt, to those of the Jordan in which Christ himself was baptized and to the waters mixed with blood that flowed from his side on the Cross.

Right A font holds holy water used for baptism – this 12th-century Belgian font depicts Jesus' own baptism.

CONFIRMATION

PEOPLE WHO RECEIVE THE SACRAMENT OF CONFIRMATION ARE ANOINTED WITH HOLY OIL. THE RITE CONFIRMS AND STRENGTHENS THE GRACE THEY DERIVED FROM BAPTISM.

Confirmation is the second of the three sacraments of initiation, and is traditionally delivered after baptism and before the Eucharist. In the early Church and the Eastern Church today, these three sacraments are delivered in a single occasion in early childhood, but in the Western Church (in the Latin Rite) confirmation is delayed until late childhood, at a time when the recipient can understand the significance of the sacrament. When adults are baptized, they usually receive the three sacraments at the same time and in the traditional order.

In most cases in the Western Church, only a bishop can administer the sacrament of confirmation, but priests have been authorized to confirm adult converts and children who are at risk of death; the priest uses chrism or holy oil blessed by the

Below The laying on of hands is a key part of confirmation. As descendants of the apostles, bishops perform the rite.

bishop. The chrism is blessed in a special service, the Chrism Mass, on Holy Thursday during Easter Week.

THE GIFT OF THE SPIRIT
The Church places an emphasis on the connection between confirmation and the Feast of Pentecost, when the Holy Spirit descended on Christ's apostles. Bishops, as successors to the apostles, administer confirmation. There is also a biblical precedent for the practice of bishops imparting the Holy Spirit to others through the laying on of hands. Acts 8:15–17 describes when the apostles Peter and John went to the Christians in Samaria and "prayed for them that they might receive the Holy Spirit, for it had not yet fallen upon any of them; they had only been baptized in the name of the Lord Jesus. Then they laid hands on them and they received the Holy Spirit."

In the Latin Rite used by the Western Catholic Church, the confirmation service begins with those

Above A bishop anoints candidates for confirmation with chrism, signifying the mark of the Holy Spirit, in this 15th-century painting by Rogier van der Weyden.

ready for confirmation, known as confirmands, renewing their baptismal vows and professing their faith. The bishop extends his hands over them and prays: "All-powerful God, Father of our Lord Jesus Christ, by water and the Holy Spirit you freed your sons and daughters from sin and gave them new life…". Then he anoints each confirmand with chrism. The bishop says, "Be sealed with the gift of the Holy Spirit." The anointing is accompanied by a laying on of hands by the bishop. The phrase "be sealed" signifies that the newly confirmed belongs to Christ in God. The seal marks the Christian as being enrolled in Christ's service and also provides a promise of divine protection. At the close of the service the bishop makes the sign of peace over the newly confirmed Christians.

In the Eastern Catholic Church, a priest generally administers the sacraments of baptism, confirmation

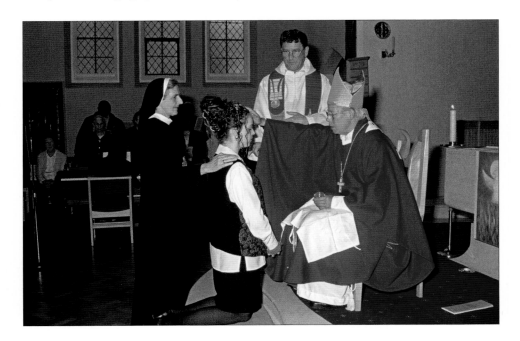

206

(usually referred to as Chrismation) and Communion in a single ceremony. The priest will use chrism blessed by the bishop, anointing the recipient on the forehead, eyes, nose, ears, lips, breast, back, hands and feet, each time, declaring "The seal of the gift that is the Holy Spirit".

ITS BENEFITS

The sacrament is called confirmation in the Western Church because it confirms, completes, strengthens and deepens the grace imparted by baptism. In confirmation, according to the catechism, baptized members of the faithful are "more perfectly bound to the Church", "enriched with a special strength of the Holy Spirit" and thereby "more strictly obliged to spread and defend the faith by word and deed".

The sacrament connects believers "more firmly to Christ" and unites the faithful in "divine filiation" (the condition of being a child of God). While baptism brings Christians into the priesthood of believers, confirmation perfects this priesthood and, according to St Thomas Aquinas, "The confirmed person receives the power to profess faith in Christ publicly and as it were officially (*quasi ex officio*)."

FIRST COMMUNION

In the Western Church, the occasion on which a young person receives Holy Communion (when he or she participates in the Eucharist) for the first time, is often celebrated with a family party. Especially in the United States and Ireland, these celebrations can be lavish: boys dress in a suit and girls wear a special white dress with a veil and gloves. In some countries, a girl wears a dress handed down from her mother or sister; in others, she will take First Communion in school uniform plus veil and gloves. In many Latin American countries, boys dress in a uniform with military-style aigullettes (braided cords) for the ceremony.

CONFIRMATION AFTER FIRST COMMUNION

The traditional order in which the three sacraments of initiation were received was: baptism, confirmation, Communion. However, in the early 20th century, Pope Pius X encouraged Catholics to allow children to receive the Eucharist as soon as they reached the age of reason (generally understood to be about the age of seven years). As a result, many young people received Communion before they were confirmed. However, in the late 20th and early 21st centuries, there has been a return to the traditional order.

Above Girls wear white dresses, sometimes with veils and gloves, for first Communion. The colour symbolizes their purity.

It is also traditional for the young person to receive a present to mark the occasion – perhaps a prayer book, icon or rosary.

Below The Eastern Catholic Church emphasizes the Christian initiation by delivering baptism, Chrismation (confirmation) and the Eucharist together.

HOLY MATRIMONY

THE SACRAMENT OF HOLY MATRIMONY GIVES A COUPLE THE DIVINE GRACE THEY NEED TO ACHIEVE HOLINESS IN THEIR MARRIED LIFE. THE "AUTHOR" OF THE MARRIAGE IS GOD.

In marriage, husband and wife receive the Holy Spirit, which helps the married couple to keep their vows. As the *Catechism of the Catholic Church* puts it, "The Holy Spirit is the seal of their covenant, the ever available source of their love and the strength to renew their fidelity."

WITNESS TO THE UNION

In the Latin Rite of the Western Church, the wedding ceremony takes place before a priest and at least two witnesses: strictly speaking, the ministers of Christ's Grace in this sacrament are the husband and wife, and the priest is a witness. However,

Above In the Eastern Catholic Church, the sacrament is called the "Crowning". The crowns worn by bride and bridegroom are a sign of the marriage covenant.

in the Eastern Catholic Church, the minister of the sacrament will be the presiding bishop or priest, who crowns husband and wife. There are two variants of the Latin Rite Catholic marriage ceremony: one with Mass, lasting about one hour, and one without Mass, which lasts around 20 minutes.

RITE OF MARRIAGE

When both husband and wife are Catholics, they are encouraged by the Church to have a wedding Mass. The priest usually meets the couple at the door of the church and leads them to the altar. The next stage is to celebrate the liturgy of the Word, in the course of which the priest delivers a homily on the mystery of marriage, the responsibilities of husband and wife and the dignity of love between a married couple.

Then the priest begins the rite of marriage. He addresses the couple: "You have come together in this church so that the Lord may seal and strengthen your love in the presence of the Church's minister and this community." He will question the

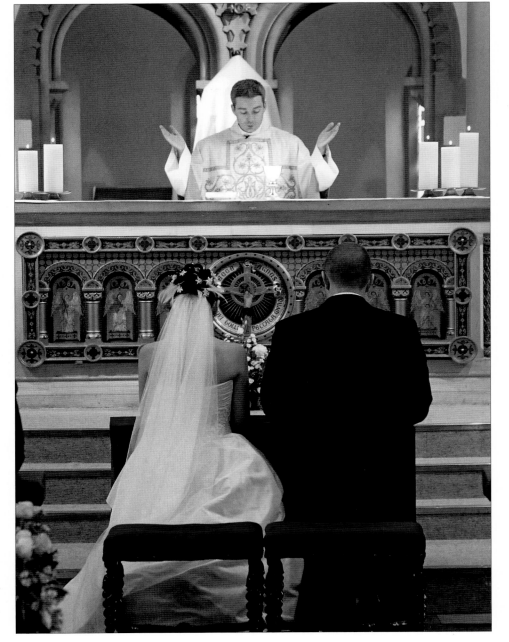

Left Catholic marriages are usually celebrated during Holy Mass. In their marriage, bride and bridegroom are inspired by Jesus' self-sacrifice. They become one body in Christ.

couple's condition and intentions, asking them to confirm that they are joining "freely and without reservations", that they will "love and honour each other as man and wife for the rest of [their] lives" and that they will accept children from God and bring them up in the law of Christ and his Church.

Then the couple exchange vows, each promising "to be true…in good times and in bad, in sickness and in health" and declaring, "I will love and honour you all the days of my life". The words of the vows may vary. The priest blesses the couple, asking Jesus to strengthen their consent and fill them with blessings. The priest then blesses the rings and the couple exchange rings, which are worn as a sign of mutual love and fidelity.

NUPTIAL BLESSING

The service proceeds by way of general intercessions into the liturgy of the Eucharist. After the Lord's

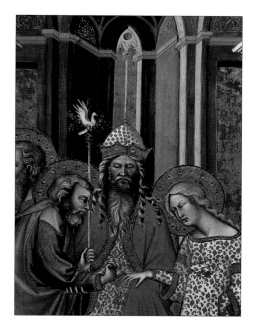

Above Joseph and Mary exchange rings in this 14th-century detail of Wedding of the Virgin Mary *by Bartolo di Fredi. From early on, the Catholic Church has taught that couples should love with a "supernatural…and fruitful love".*

Below God blesses married love; its purpose is for procreation. A married couple receive a child from God in this 15th-century French miniature.

Prayer the priest proclaims the nuptial blessing, calling on Jesus to bless bride and groom individually and as a couple joined in a holy bond and married in Christ to one another. The priest reminds all that marriage is a holy mystery that symbolizes the marriage of Christ to his Church, the one blessing of those given to Adam and Eve that was not "forfeited by original sin or washed away in the flood", and asks that the husband trust his wife and recognize that "she is his equal and heir with him to the life of grace". The priest prays, if the woman is of childbearing age, that the couple be blessed with children and have a long life, and after happy old age achieve fullness of life with the saints in heaven.

Then the couple receive Holy Communion. At the end of the service the priest blesses them once more before husband and wife kiss. All sing a hymn as the couple process out of the church. When a couple chooses a marriage service without Holy Communion it largely follows the outline above, but omits the celebration of the Eucharist.

SPECIAL DISPENSATION

Those who come forward for marriage should normally be baptized Catholics. However, a dispensation, usually granted by the priest himself, is possible for a "mixed marriage" between a Catholic and a baptized non-Catholic (a Christian of another denomination) as long as the couple have chosen freely to marry, have the intention of remaining together for life and being faithful to one another, and are planning to have children if the bride has not passed the childbearing age. If one partner is Catholic and the other is not baptized (perhaps a non-Christian or a person of no religion), a church dispensation for disparity of cult is required from the local bishop.

"WHAT GOD HAS JOINED…"

FOR CATHOLICS, HOLY MATRIMONY CREATES A PERMANENT AND INDISSOLUBLE BOND BETWEEN HUSBAND AND WIFE. GOD CREATED MARRIAGE AS THE FULFILMENT OF LIFE FOR MOST MEN AND WOMEN.

Above A blessing is given to both man and woman in this 15th-century detail from Engagement of the Virgin *by Michael Pacher. Both must freely give their consent to be married.*

As part of the blessing of the married couple during the sacrament of Holy Matrimony, the priest may state, "What God has joined together, let no man put asunder", which is a direct quotation from Christ's own teaching on marriage (Mark 10:9). The *Catechism of the Catholic Church* is also unequivocal, stating that once a marriage between a baptized couple has been consummated, it "can never be dissolved".

Like the other sacraments, Holy Matrimony has both outward and inward signs: the outward sign is the marriage contract, which is the agreement made verbally between both husband and wife when they exchange vows before the priest and witnesses; the inward sign is the grace it delivers. The Church's teaching accepts that marriage can bring many challenges; however, it also stresses that God's Grace is sufficient to help husbands and wives overcome their difficulties.

DIVINE INSTITUTION

The Church teaches that God created man and woman for one another and that married love is in the image of God's love. Christ attended the wedding at Cana in Galilee, where he performed the first of the many signs that confirmed his status as the Son of God by turning water into wine (John 2:1–11). The Church interprets this event as confirmation of the goodness of marriage and a proclamation that marriage is a sign of Christ's presence.

For Catholics, marriage is both a natural and a divine institution. It is a natural institution because it has existed in the form of a lifelong union between a man and a woman in all societies and cultures through history. Yet it is also a divine institution created by God, sanctified by Christ at Cana, and sealed through the sacrament of Holy Matrimony by the action of the Holy Spirit.

IN PREPARATION

The Church instructs that both parties to a marriage must have a clear understanding of what they are doing when they take their marriage vows. Husband and wife are required to attend preparatory meetings with the priest who will witness their marriage. These meetings are known as pre-Cana meetings – a reference to the wedding at Cana.

A course of pre-Cana meetings can be held over a single weekend or be spread over six months or so.

Below By participating in the wedding at Cana in Galilee, shown in this 14th-century painting, The Marriage Feast at Cana, *by Duccio di Buoninsegna, Jesus confirmed the holiness of the marriage bond.*

ANNULMENT OF A MARRIAGE

The key condition for a marriage is that husband and wife give their consent to be married freely and are free to give their consent. In cases where the parties to a marriage can show that either of these conditions were not met, a Church tribunal can grant an annulment of the marriage. Annulment is not the same as divorce: the judgement does not dissolve the marriage, for marriage is an indissoluble bond; it determines that the marriage did not ever take place.

The two parties must understand what they are doing and must have given the matter some consideration; they must have a genuine intention to keep the vows they swear – to form a permanent and faithful union, inclusive of sexual acts intended for the purpose of procreation. Various impediments to the marriage are grounds for annulment. Examples include husband and wife being close blood relatives, one partner being already married at the time of the wedding or one partner being in a psychological state that precludes an ability to give free consent.

Right Henry VIII's wife Catherine of Aragon is shown in The Divorce of Henry VIII, *by Eugene Deveria. Theirs was one of several marriages Henry had annulled.*

The priest and the married couple discuss the sanctity of marriage, their faith and life in the Church, plans for children and so on; they may be asked about financial matters. Nearer to the time, husband and wife, if both are baptized Catholics, are expected to receive the sacrament of penance and reconciliation in preparation for their wedding. With these preparations, both husband and wife should enter marriage prepared to maintain their vows – married life should present no surprises.

WHEN A MARRIAGE FAILS

The Church recognizes that in some cases a marriage can deteriorate so badly that husband and wife can no longer live together. In this situation, they should live separately and the members of the Church should help them live as best they can in a Christian fashion. The estranged husband and wife are not free to divorce or remarry, and they should remember that the preferred solution in the eyes of the Catholic Church would be for the couple to reconcile their differences.

If a Catholic divorces and makes a second (civil) marriage, the Church views the person as committing adultery against the first marriage partner. He or she is in contravention of God's law and cannot receive the Eucharist. Nevertheless, that person should be welcomed to church if he or she wants to come: priests and the whole Church community should be attentive toward that person.

Right God intends man and woman to join permanently in marriage; once joined, they should not seek separation. A 19th-century engraving, The Ages of Life, *shows how a married couple honour their vows throughout life.*

THE SANCTITY OF LIFE

CHURCH TEACHINGS ON MARRIAGE, SEX AND CONTRACEPTION, ABORTION AND HOMOSEXUALITY ARE UNDERPINNED BY BELIEF IN THE SANCTITY OF ALL LIVES CREATED BY GOD.

The Catholic faithful believe that sex has a divinely ordained place within a couple's marriage: its purpose and function is for the procreation of children. Married love is blessed by God and meant to be fruitful. This teaching is based on verses in Genesis, Chapter 1:

> So God created man in his own
> image, in the image of God he
> created him; male and female
> he created them. And God blessed
> them, and God said to them,
> "Be fruitful and multiply, and
> fill the earth and subdue it."
> (Genesis 1:26–29).

AT THE SERVICE OF LIFE

Parents are called not only to procreate but also to educate: having brought children into the world, they must give them instruction in moral and spiritual matters. Parents should serve their children in love. The *Catechism of the Catholic Church* states

Below The pope holds a fatherly position to Catholics. Married couples entrust their children to the care of God and his Church.

that one of the main functions of marriage and family is "to be at the service of life".

There are some married couples who have not had children, but this does not devalue their marriage in any way. They can still aim to live a life of service through hospitality, self-sacrifice and charity. Other people are called to chastity. This does not devalue marriage, either. The vocation to chastity and the vocation to married life both come from God, and both should be equally valued. The two ways of life reinforce one another.

CONTRACEPTION

The Church's teachings on contraception arise from the understanding that Catholics should only have sex within marriage and that the main function of sex is for procreation. Using contraceptives, such as a condom or the contraceptive pill, is directly against Catholic teaching. This is because these methods interfere with the natural law of God's Creation and split sex from its proper procreative role.

However, Catholics are allowed to use natural methods of birth control – chiefly by having sex only when the wife is at a low-fertility part of her cycle. Natural birth control is allowed because it is in harmony with the natural law of God's Creation and uses God-given powers, such as self-control, rather than chemical interference (as with the pill) or a physical barrier (such as a condom). Catholics must be responsible and correctly motivated in using this method: for example, it would be acceptable to use the method to space out children in a

Above In this 14th-century detail from The Creation of Adam *by Master Bertram of Minden, God is shown instructing Adam about his duty to procreate and father children.*

HOMOSEXUALITY

The Church recognizes that some men and women have deep-seated homosexual tendencies: the catechism calls these tendencies "intrinsically disordered" and "contrary to natural law". Sexual relations between people of the same sex are not approved because they "close the sexual act to the gift of life" and "do not proceed from a genuine affective and sexual complementarity". The Church believes that homosexual people are called to chastity: they are required to develop self-mastery and they are expected to pray for support. In these circumstances, they can rely on God's sacramental grace to help them reach Christian perfection.

Right Catholic parents bring their children to Christ in Lucas Cranach the Elder's Christ Blessing the Children *(c.1540). Parents are responsible for teaching their children the Catholic faith.*

family, but to do so to avoid having children in order to have more spending money would be immoral.

The Church also teaches that sex has a unifying function – it brings the husband and wife into a close spiritual, mental and physical union. By using artificial contraception, according to the teaching, the couple are violating this function and preventing themselves from giving completely to each other.

In addition, according to the Church, the use of contraception has a number of negative effects. Among these it promotes immoral behaviour, damages marriage as an institution, makes men respect women less, and gives people the idea that they can achieve total control over bodily processes of reproduction when this control rightly belongs to God.

Opponents of the Church's position argue that contraception has benefits for people both as individuals and collectively. The Church's response is that using contraception is evil and that it is never the correct approach to do evil, even if you believe good may come of it.

RIGHT TO LIFE

The Church takes a very strong position against the use of abortion. Catholics believe that a new life begins at the moment in which a woman's egg is fertilized by a sperm. The fertilized egg is a human being independent of mother and father. According to Pope John Paul II in his 1995 encyclical *Evangelum Vitae* ("The Gospel of Life"), abortion is

Right The catechism teaches that God's Grace helps married couples "attain holiness in their married life and in welcoming and educating their children".

"a grave moral disorder" because it involves the intentional killing of an innocent person. Church teaching states that every individual, including a foetus, has an inalienable right to life – and this right extends from the moment of conception until the person's physical death. In canon law, a person who procures an abortion is excommunicated.

PENANCE AND RECONCILIATION

DURING THE SACRAMENT OF PENANCE AND RECONCILIATION, WHICH IS OFTEN REFERRED TO AS CONFESSION, CATHOLICS CONFESS ANY WRONGDOINGS TO THEIR PRIEST AND RECEIVE ABSOLUTION.

Confession provides spiritual healing for people who have been distanced from God by their sins and restores to them the Grace of God. The sacrament has two effects or aspects: outer and inner – the outer aspect is that the penitent believer receives absolution from his priest, either by remission of sin or the punishment due to sin; the inner aspect is that through repentance and confession the believer is reconciled to God.

In addition to being known as confession, penance and reconciliation can also be called the sacrament of conversion (because, according to the *Catechism of the Catholic Church*, it

Below After his Resurrection, Christ tells his disciples that they have the power to forgive sins, as seen in this 14th-century panel by Duccio di Buoninsegna.

"makes sacramentally present Jesus' call to conversion") and the sacrament of forgiveness. Along with the anointing of the sick, confession is one of two sacraments of healing. Through these two sacraments, according to the catechism, the Church continues Christ's work of "healing and salvation, even among Her own members".

Christ instituted the sacrament of confession on Easter Day, when after rising from the dead following his Crucifixion he appeared to the apostles and said, "Receive the Holy Spirit. If you forgive the sins of any, they are forgiven; if you retain the sins of any, they are retained" (John 20:22–23).

There is another biblical precedent for this sacrament, found in the episode described in the Gospel of

Above The penitent admits any wrongdoing, but also humbly confesses (acknowledges and honours) God's profound holiness and great mercy.

Matthew (9:2–8) in which Jesus publicly forgave the sins of a paralytic man brought to him for healing and cured him of his paralysis.

WHEN TO CONFESS

Catholics must receive the sacrament of confession when they are aware that they have committed a mortal sin and in any case at least once a year. They are encouraged to go to confession once a month. (Mortal sins are distinct from venial sins. Mortal sins are those that condemn a soul to hell because they cannot be forgiven without repentence; lesser venial sins, if unconfessed and so not absolved, cause separation from God but not eternal damnation.)

Catholics are also required to receive the sacrament of confession before they receive the Eucharist for the first time. In Lent, the Church urges believers to receive the sacrament of confession as part of their preparation for Easter. Catholics are generally keen to receive confession

Right Sin is straying from God, while penance, such as the confession shown in this 15th-century painting by Domenico di Niccolò dei Cori, is a return to the Father.

because, as one of the seven sacraments instituted by Christ, it delivers God's Grace to those who receive it and so is a vital aid in living a good Christian life.

There are four key elements to the sacrament. Firstly, penitent individuals are required to be contrite; that is, to feel sincere remorse for their sins. They must have a genuine intention not to commit the sins again. Secondly, they must confess the number and kind of their sins to a priest. Thirdly, they need to receive absolution from the priest. Lastly, they must perform satisfaction or the acts of penance that were prescribed by the priest.

ABSOLUTION FROM SIN

A priest (or bishop) does not himself have the power to forgive sins. However, he exercises the power on behalf of Christ through the sacrament of penance if he is ordained validly and has proper jurisdiction over the penitent who makes confession. In administering the sacrament, the priest acts in *persona Christi* ("in the person of Christ").

Below In delivering absolution, a priest acts on Christ's behalf. As well as receiving God's pardon, the penitent is reconciled with the Church.

The priest hears the confessions of his parishioners or other members of the faithful at set times, and the normal form of confession is for the penitent individual to say, "Bless me Father for I have sinned" and then to specify the period that has elapsed since his or her last confession. The penitent has to confess all mortal sins committed in that period and is encouraged to confess venial sins, too. The prayer of confession begins, "O My God I am heartily sorry…"

The priest then delivers absolution. One form describes a merciful God, who "through the death and resurrection of his Son" has become reconciled to humankind and has sent the Holy Spirit among people "for the forgiveness of sins". It goes on to state that through the Church's ministry God may pardon the person and give him or her peace. The priest ends by absolving the person from his or her sins in the three names of the Holy Trinity.

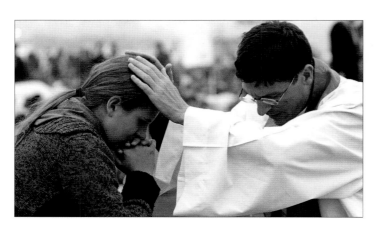

SEAL OF THE CONFESSIONAL

The priest is bound by the absolutely inviolable seal of the confessional – he cannot reveal what he has been told in confession, even under threat of death. A priest who does so is automatically excommunicated from the Church. In criminal matters, for example, if a person admits to murder in the confessional, the priest cannot tell the police or other authorities, but he can encourage the penitent to give himself or herself up and can withhold absolution as a means of leverage.

ANOINTING OF THE SICK AND THE LAST RITES

GOD'S GRACE IS DELIVERED TO THE SEVERELY ILL THROUGH THE ANOINTING OF THE SICK AND LAST RITES, WHICH HELP THEM COPE WITH SICKNESS OR DEATH AND RESIST THE FEELING OF DISCOURAGEMENT.

In the sacrament of the anointing of the sick, a priest anoints a seriously ill Catholic person with holy oil. Along with penance and reconciliation (or confession), the anointing of the sick is one of the Catholic Church's two sacraments of healing. Through the anointing of the sick, an ill person is united with the suffering of Christ, and even permitted to share in the redemptive work performed by Christ's Passion. The sacrament will bring spiritual and sometimes physical healing – and also forgiveness of sins.

All the sacraments draw on biblical precedent. The central text in support of the anointing of the sick is in James 5:14–15:

Below The sacrament delivers grace to strengthen the ill person, bringing courage, peace of mind and, subject to God's will, physical healing.

Is any among you sick? Let him call for the elders of the Church, and let them pray over him, anointing him with oil in the name of the Lord; and the prayer of faith will save the sick man, and the Lord will raise him up; and if he has committed sins, he will be forgiven.

RECEIVING THE SACRAMENT

Only a priest or bishop can administer the sacrament of the anointing of the sick. According to canon law, he can give the sacrament to any member of the faithful who has reached the age of reason and is in danger of death either though illness or old age. If a person receives the sacrament when close to death, then recovers, he or she can receive this sacrament a second time if the illness strikes again. Equally, a person can receive the sacrament a second time

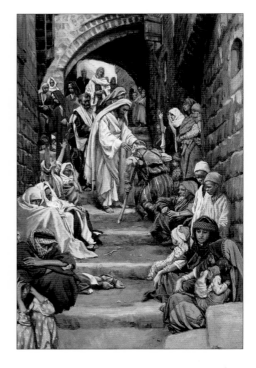

Above Christ comforted and healed the sick, as illustrated by James Tissot in his 19th-century painting, In the Villages the Sick Were Brought unto Him.

if a continuing illness worsens. A person about to have serious surgery can also receive the sacrament.

The priest can also use his pastoral judgement to determine whether or not it is appropriate to administer the sacrament a second time or even more often when a person is chronically ill or very old and weak. He can administer the sacrament to a person at home, during Mass or while in a hospital and may give it to a group of the seriously ill if desired.

ADMINISTERING THE SACRAMENT

The priest uses olive or vegetable oil that has been blessed by the bishop in the Chrism Mass on Holy Thursday (the Thursday of Holy Week). In the Latin Rite of the Western Church, the priest usually anoints the sick person on the forehead, marking the shape of the Cross, and says: "Through this holy anointing may the Lord in his love and mercy help you with the grace of the Holy Spirit. May the

Above A priest visiting a seriously ill person will carry all the equipment he needs to perform anointing and to celebrate the Eucharist.

Lord who frees you from sin save you and raise you up." He may anoint other parts of the body, without using the verbal formula.

LAST RITES

When the sick person is in immediate danger of death the anointing is considered to be one of the "last rites", which also includes penance and reconciliation and the Eucharist. The normal procedure is for the priest to hear the person's confession, then anoint him or her, before giving him or her the Eucharist. In some cases, when a person is too ill to confess, the priest can pronounce absolution – but this is believed to be effective only if the dying person inwardly feels contrition for the sins.

The Eucharist given to a seriously ill person is called *viaticum*, a Latin word meaning "provision for the voyage" and referring to the final journey of this earthly life – through death into eternal life. In the words of the *Catechism of the Catholic Church*, "As the sacrament of Christ's Passover, the

Eucharist should always be the last sacrament of the earthly journey, the *viaticum* for 'passing over' to eternal life." The sacrament of the anointing of the sick is also called *sacramentum exeuntium* ("the sacrament of those departing"). It is the last of the holy anointings of the Christian life, and follows on from the anointings of baptism and confirmation. "This last anointing," according to the catechism, "fortifies the end of our earthly life like a solid rampart for the final struggles before entering the Father's house."

> ### EXTREME UNCTION
> When given among the last rites, the anointing of the sick was traditionally known as extreme unction, meaning "a last anointing". In the modern Church, the sacrament is called the anointing of the sick, but some traditional Catholics, who usually adhere to the practice and terminology in use before the Second Vatican Council (1962–5), still use the name extreme unction.

Right In addition to anointing, those near to death confess their sins and receive the Eucharist, as in this 15th-century painting by Rogier van der Weyden.

DUST TO DUST

WHEN A PERSON DIES, CATHOLICS GIVE THANKS FOR THE GRACE OF GOD EVIDENCED IN HIS OR HER LIFE. CATHOLIC FUNERAL SERVICES COMPRISE A VIGIL, A MASS AND A BURIAL OR COMMITTAL.

The three forms of funeral service have been authorized in the *Ordo exsequiarum* ("Order of Christian Funerals") of the Catholic Church's Roman Rite. Each form has its proper place: the vigil is usually held at home; the funeral or requiem Mass in the Church; and the committal in the cemetery. All three forms express what the catechism calls the "paschal character" of death. This refers to a Catholic's understanding of death in terms of Easter, in the light of Jesus' death and Resurrection.

VIGIL, MASS, COMMITTAL

The vigil is a gathering for prayers and biblical readings, with a sermon, that is held before the day of the funeral Mass and committal, often at the home of the deceased person. One or more eulogies on the dead person's life are shared. These should not praise the individual but concentrate on the workings of God's Grace in his or her life. The vigil is often held as part of a wake.

Below After the funeral Mass, a priest blesses the coffin before it is transported to the cemetery for the committal.

The funeral Mass is often called a requiem Mass. Those gathered pray for the forgiveness of sins and the salvation of the soul of the departed. The service takes the name *requiem* from the Latin wording at the beginning of the first section, the Introit: *Requiem aeternam dona eis, Domine, et lux perpetua luceat eis* ("Grant them unending rest, O Lord, and may light perpetual fall on them"). Requiem Masses can also be held as a memorial for a deceased person and to mark an anniversary of a person's death.

The rite of committal consists of prayers and Bible readings as the body is buried in a cemetery, or before cremation. In the committal the faithful bid farewell to the deceased person; the Church commends him or her to the care of God.

FULFILMENT OF A LIFE

Catholic teaching views death as the end and fulfilment of a devout person's sacramental life. His or her religious life has been structured to lead to this end: death is the fulfilment of the new birth of baptism, of the new life that was confirmed and strengthened by the anointing

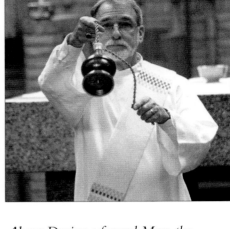

Above During a funeral Mass, the presiding priest censes and blesses the coffin as the Church expresses its communion with the departed.

of the Holy Spirit at confirmation, and the participation in the heavenly feast anticipated every time he or she received the Eucharist. During the funeral, the Church, which has carried the devout person through life, like a mother would care for a growing child, now offers him or her to God the Father, in Christ.

The liturgy and ceremonial of the requiem Mass generally follows that of the standard Mass, but omits its more joyful expressions, including the gloria and the Creed and certain doxologies, or hymns of praise. A key element of the Mass in this setting is the funeral homily, which must be delivered by a bishop, priest or deacon, and which explicates the meaning of death in the context of Christ's own death and his triumphant Resurrection.

Celebrating Mass is central to the funeral because the Eucharist lies at the very heart of a Catholic's understanding of death. In the Eucharist, a member of the faithful will have communion with Christ and with the departed person. The gathered faithful will then pray for the forgiveness of the deceased person's sins, and ask that he or she enjoy the heavenly feast to which the Eucharist looks forward: in doing this, and in

Right The funeral, followed by burial or cremation, is illuminated by belief in "the resurrection of the dead, and the life of the world to come".

receiving the Eucharist, the faithful at the Mass will learn to exist in communion with the departed.

ATTITUDE TO CREMATION

For many centuries the Catholic Church did not allow cremation because it held the practice to be counter to belief in the resurrection of the body. The official position was that cremation was a pagan practice. However, in 1963 the Vatican began to permit the use of cremation as long as the reason for choosing it did not go against Catholic beliefs.

The initial requirement was that all funeral services had to be carried out in the presence of the dead body, which would then be cremated afterward. This was changed in 1997 and since then the funeral liturgy can be used in the presence of cremated remains of the body. The Church does not permit the scattering of ashes after cremation; it teaches that the ashes should be entombed in a grave or mausoleum.

DRESSED FOR A MASS

Bishops or priests that celebrate requiem Masses were traditionally expected to wear black vestments and ornaments. Black is considered to be the colour of the most profound grief, and is also worn for services on Good Friday. Today, clergy often wear white to symbolize the glory of the Resurrection.

MUSICAL HERITAGE

Requiem Masses are often sung, and there is a very rich heritage of musical settings of requiem Masses, including works by the notable composers Wolfgang Amadeus Mozart, Hector Berlioz and Gabriel Fauré.

The revised form of the Latin Rite for the requiem Mass, which was introduced following the Second Vatican Council (1962–5) and is used generally today, does away with a number of elements of the traditional requiem that are familiar to people who know the service chiefly through these magnificent musical settings.

One example is the sequence beginning *Dies irae, dies illa, Solvet sæclum in favilla* ("Day of anger, day when the world turns to ashes…"). This is a powerful part of classical requiems by Mozart and Verdi, but was made optional and then dropped from the requiem Mass following the Second Vatican Council as part of changes designed to tone down elements suggestive of despair and fear of judgement while emphasizing hope and belief in the Resurrection. The *Dies irae* was part of the requiem Mass in the Roman Missal 1962 (prior to the Second Vatican Council) and so is still heard in churches that celebrate the Tridentine liturgy in use before the Council.

Left A memorial Mass for Pope John Paul II was held in the Church of the Holy Sepulchre (the church in which Jesus is traditionally believed to be buried), in Jerusalem, on 6 April 2005. Latin Patriarch Michel Sabbah presided, and some 200 heads of state, heads of government and royalty gathered to attend the pope's funeral.

PRAYER

IN PRAYER, CATHOLICS CAN COMMUNICATE WITH THEIR CREATOR. BELIEVERS CAN BUILD AND MAINTAIN A LIVING AND PERSONAL RELATIONSHIP WITH GOD THE FATHER, SON AND HOLY SPIRIT.

Prayer can be public or private: it can be a shared communal experience or a personal and solitary formal rite, spoken aloud or a more fluid, silent interior activity. Public forms of prayer include the Mass and the Liturgy of the Hours. Among private forms are the use of the rosary and the practice of *Lectio Divina*, which is a meditative reading of the Scriptures developed as a form of devotion by medieval monastics. The Catholic Church teaches that the chief sources of and inspirations to prayer are the Word of God in the Bible, the liturgy of the Church and the virtues of faith, hope and charity.

HOW TO PRAY

Catholic authorities stress that it is essential to pray but that the kind of prayer does not matter. Pope John Paul II, in writing about how to pray, said that it was a simple thing to do and recommended that you pray "any way you like, so long as you do pray". Prayer may be a very personal outpouring. The catechism quotes St Thérèse of Lisieux:

> For me prayer is a surge of the heart; it is a simple look turned towards heaven, it is a cry of recognition and of love, embracing both trial and joy.

Prayer is not just self-expression. Elsewhere, the catechism states that prayer is not something to be turned into a "spontaneous outpouring of interior impulse". The Holy Spirit instructs the faithful in how to pray through "a living transmission" (Sacred Tradition) within the Church.

Above *In Jacob Cornelisz van Oostsanen's 1523 painting,* Adoration of the Trinity, *a Christian (right) prays with hands clasped together.*

Prayers of all kinds must be made in the name of Jesus, for these have access to God the Father through Christ. The Holy Spirit teaches believers to pray to God the Father through the Son, and that through the many different kinds of prayer the one Holy Spirit acts.

BENEFITS OF PRAYER

The Church teaches that prayer leads the faithful away from sin toward salvation. In prayer, a believer turns to God and receives direction from the Holy Spirit; without this guidance the believer is trapped in sin. According to the Church, people who pray with eagerness and call on God cannot sin, therefore they are saved; those who do not pray are trapped in sin and are in the way of damnation.

Praying by repeating the name of Jesus in the Jesus Prayer has the effect of summoning Christ within the believer. Whereas in the Old Testament, the Jews were forbidden

---

THE JESUS PRAYER

The catechism states, "There is no other way of Christian prayer than Christ." St Paul exhorted Christians to "pray constantly" (1 Thessalonians 5:17), to attempt to keep one's life in God's presence and under his eye: a favoured way of doing this is through "prayer of the heart". One example used for centuries by Christians in both the Eastern and Western Churches is the Jesus Prayer, an invocation based on repetition of the Lord's name. The Jesus Prayer developed in a variety of forms, the most common of which is "Lord Jesus Christ, Son of God, have mercy on us sinners". Praying this prayer while being active in the world sanctifies every action.

Above *Catholics are encouraged to pray in Jesus' name, who spread the Word, as shown in this 17th-century Greek icon.*

to utter the name of God, in Jesus, God adopted human form and delivered his name to humanity: the name Jesus contains the divine presence. The catechism explains: "The name 'Jesus' contains all: God and man and the whole economy of creation and salvation…whoever invokes the name of Jesus is welcoming the Son of God who loved him [or her] and who gave himself up for him [or her]."

PRIVATE PRAYER

The Church also teaches that private meditative prayer complements and sustains the public prayer of the liturgy. In his apostolic letter *Rosarium Virginis Mariae* ("Rosary of the Virgin Mary"), which was witten on 16 October 2002, Pope John Paul II described the rosary as a good introduction and an accurate echo of Church liturgy. He added that praying the words of the rosary as taught by the Church involves carrying on an inner meditation on

the glories and hidden meanings of Christ's life and this lets the believer take part in a deep study of Christian mystery that amounts to a profound and practical training for a holy life.

Above A prayer book, shown in this 16th-century detail from Portrait of the Artist's Sister in the Garb of a Nun *by Sofonisba Anguissola, is an indispensable aid for some Catholics devoted to private prayer.*

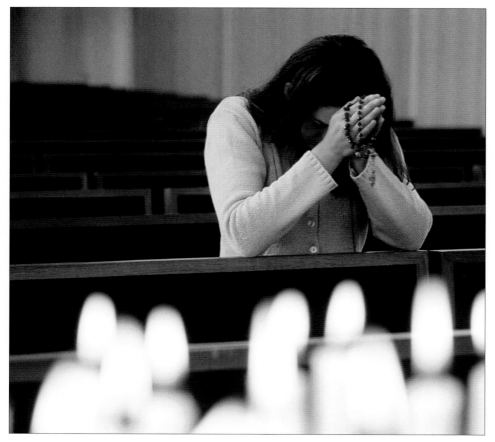

Pope Benedict XVI emphasized the fact that private prayer, contemplation and religious devotions do not distract from loving service in the world but in fact provide an essential underpinning and support for that service. He used the example of Mother Teresa of Calcutta and the work of her order, the Missionaries of Charity, as an example. In his first encyclical, *Deus Caritas Est*, written in December 2005, he declared that the example of Teresa of Calcutta illustrates the fact that when we devote time to God in private or public prayer, it does not distract us from serving our neighbours in love, but rather is a limitless source of loving service.

Left In prayer, the believer reaches out to God. The Church teaches that calling on the name of Jesus summons his presence within us.

THE SACRED HEART

CATHOLICS USE THE SACRED HEART OF JESUS AS A FOCUS FOR THEIR INTENSE DEVOTIONS IN WHICH THEY SEEK TO MAKE REPARATIONS TO JESUS FOR THE SINS OF HUMANKIND.

The Sacred Heart of Jesus is a symbol of God's love for humanity. God's love was expressed in Christ's suffering, and the Sacred Heart is pierced by human sins. Through prayer and contemplation, Catholics can consecrate themselves to the Sacred Heart.

In Catholic art, the Sacred Heart is usually shown to be aflame and shining with light, injured by the lance

Below The apostles showed human frailty when they failed to keep watch with Jesus. They are asleep in Barna da Siena's 14th-century painting, Christ in the Garden of Gethsemane.

that stabbed Jesus' side on the Cross, with a crown of thorns around it and blood falling from it. This image is often superimposed on Jesus' chest, with his wounded hands pointing to the heart. The light and flames represent the power of divine love.

DEVOTION TO THE HEART

Those who want to express their devotion to the Sacred Heart usually seek to receive Communion often. They commit to establish a "first Friday" routine – to go to confession and then receive the Eucharist on the first Friday of the month for

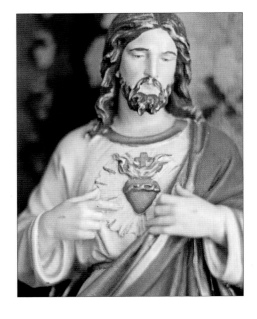

Above Many Catholic homes, churches and other institutions contain Sacred Heart statues to remind the faithful of Jesus' profound love and suffering.

nine months consecutively. They also partake of Holy Hour devotions on Thursdays. The Holy Hour is an hour-long prayer vigil, usually conducted in the presence of the Holy Sacrament. It is intended to make amends to Jesus for the hour in the garden of Gethsemane when he prayed alone, and returning to his disciples found them asleep. He reproached Peter: "So, could you not watch with me one hour? Watch and pray that you may not enter into temptation; the spirit indeed is willing, but the flesh is weak" (Matthew 26:40–41).

Sometimes the devout partake in a ceremony at home known as the enthronement of the Sacred Heart. A priest visits the home to set up ("enthrone") an image or statue of Jesus bearing his Sacred Heart: it reminds those living in the house that they have been consecrated to the Sacred Heart.

PAPAL TEACHINGS

In his encyclical *Annum Sacrum* (On Consecration to the Sacred Heart) of 25 May 1899, Pope Leo XIII

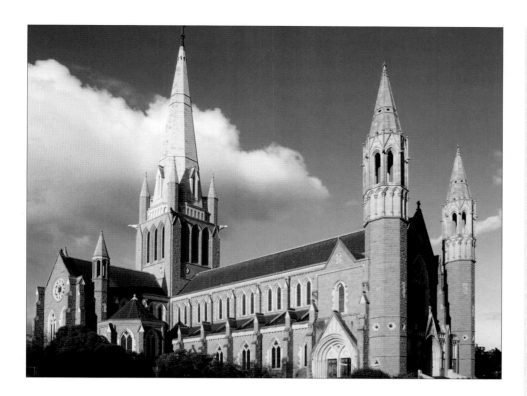

Medieval mystics were the first to develop the practice of revering Jesus' heart. The devotion then became popular among the Jesuits during the 16th and 17th centuries. The modern form of the devotion derives in particular from the 17th-century French mystic and nun St Marguerite Marie Alacoque, who had several revelations of the Sacred Heart in 1673–5. She declared that Jesus called on believers to offer prayers of expiation for his suffering, to take Communion frequently, especially on the first Friday of the month, and to observe the Holy Hour.

consecrated all humans to the Sacred Heart of Jesus. He described the Sacred Heart as a comprehensible symbol of Christ's endless love and declared that it was right that Catholics should dedicate themselves to the Sacred Heart; when the faithful do this, he added, they offer and bind themselves to Jesus. Many Catholic organizations, including churches, colleges and missionary and teaching orders, are dedicated to the Sacred Heart.

Pope Pius XII delivered a teaching on the mystical aspects of revering the heart of Jesus in his encyclical *Haurietis Aquas* (On Devotion to the Sacred Heart) in 1956. He declared the heart of Jesus to be a symbol of God's threefold love in the Father, Son and Holy Spirit; he wrote that believers should look devoutly upon the divine Redeemer's heart as an image of Jesus' love and a witness of our salvation in the events of Easter, and as a kind of mystical pathway along which we climb upward to be embraced by our Saviour.

Pius XII also declared in this letter that devotion to Jesus' Sacred Heart was the foundation on which

Above The Sacred Heart Cathedral at Bendigo in Victoria, Australia, is one of many Catholic institutions named after the Sacred Heart.

individual believers, their families and whole nations could construct the kingdom of God.

FEAST DAY
The feast of the Sacred Heart was established in the church calendar in 1856 by Pope Pius IX and is celebrated 19 days after Pentecost. Because Pentecost falls on a Sunday, the feast of the Sacred Heart takes place on a Friday. On this feast day, devout Catholics will meditate on the devotional aspects of the Sacred Heart of Jesus.

They say the prayers laid out in the Act of Reparation to the Sacred Heart, which begins "Most sweet Jesus, whose overflowing charity for men is requited by so much forgetfulness, negligence and contempt, behold us prostrate before Thee, eager to repair by a special act of homage the cruel indifference and injuries to which Thy loving Heart is everywhere subject…"

Above As a nun, St Marguerite Marie Alacoque had an intense mystical experience of Christ's suffering, captured in this 1888 painting, Beatified Marguerite Marie Alacoque's Vision of Jesus' Heart, *by Antonio Ciseri.*

STATIONS OF THE CROSS

THE STATIONS OF THE CROSS IS A SET OF 14 PENITENTIAL MEDITATIONS ON CHRIST'S PASSION, WHICH ARE OFTEN PERFORMED DURING LENT, ESPECIALLY ON FRIDAY EVENINGS.

The 14 meditations are each linked to a specific scene that illustrates one of the series of events that included Christ's condemnation to death, passage to Calvary and his Crucifixion. They are performed before paintings or statuary that represent the scene in question. The paintings or statues are usually carefully arranged around the walls of a church or chapel; however, they can also be laid out as a series of images along a pathway, for example, near a shrine.

By praying at the Stations of the Cross, the Catholic believer can make a spiritual pilgrimage. The Church teaches that the prayers and meditations before the Stations of the Cross should be performed in a spirit of reparation – in an attempt to clear away humanity's sins.

In 1928, Pope Pius XI wrote in his encyclical *Miserentissimus Redemptor* that Catholics had a duty to offer reparation to Christ for the sins that have been committed against him. In 2000, in a letter marking the 50th anniversary of the Benedictine Sisters of Reparation of the Holy Face, Pope John Paul II called the effort to make reparation for the sins committed every day against Jesus an attempt to place oneself alongside the infinite number of crosses on which the son of God is still crucified. The meditations made at these Stations often seek to focus on the positive effects of the acts of atonement that Christ performed, as well as consider the grave sins of humankind that have been the reason for Christ's suffering.

Above Pope John Paul II bears a cross during the first part of the Stations of the Cross in the Colosseum in Rome on 5 April 1996.

Above The 5th station: Jesus is judged by Pilate. These images are from a fresco by an unknown artist of the 15th century.

Above The 6th station: Jesus is mocked, beaten, blindfolded and crowned with thorns by enemies.

THE OLD SEQUENCE

The traditional sequence of the Stations of the Cross was used by Catholics for centuries. It was as follows: Jesus is condemned to death (1), is given the Cross (2), then falls for the first time under the weight of the Cross (3); Jesus encounters his mother, the Blessed Virgin Mary (4), and Simon of Cyrene is forced to carry the Cross (5); Veronica (Berenice), a pious Jerusalem woman, gives Jesus her veil to wipe his face (6); Jesus falls down for a second time (7); he addresses the daughters of Jerusalem (8); he falls for a third time (9), then he is stripped of his garments (10); Jesus is nailed to the Cross (11); Jesus dies on the Cross (12); his body is removed from the Cross and laid in the arms of his mother (13), and then laid in the tomb (14).

This sequence was altered by Pope John Paul II in 1991 because the traditional sequence included six scenes (3, 4, 6, 7, 9 and 13) not backed by Scripture. The first five of these do not appear at all in biblical accounts, while station 13 – the scene of Jesus laid in his mother's arms, represented so famously and beautifully in the many Pietà statues of art history – is a misrepresentation, for in biblical accounts Joseph of Arimathea was working alone when he took down Jesus' body and laid it in a tomb.

THE REVISED SEQUENCE

John Paul II devised a new (though not obligatory) sequence called the Scriptural Way of the Cross. The 14 scenes of this sequence are as follows: Jesus prays in the Garden of Gethsemane (1), then is betrayed by Judas Iscariot and arrested (2); he is condemned by the Jewish judicial body, the Sanhedrin (3); St Peter denies Jesus (4), then Jesus is judged by Pontius Pilate (5) and is whipped and given a crown of thorns (6); Jesus takes the Cross (7), then Simon of Cyrene carries it (8); Jesus speaks to the women of Jerusalem (9); he is crucified (10); he promises the "good thief" being crucified with him, "Truly, I say to you, today you will be with me in Paradise" (11), entrusts his mother to his disciple John with the words, "Woman, behold, your son!" and to the disciple, "Behold your mother!" (12); he dies on the Cross (13); his body is put in the tomb (14).

GOOD FRIDAY

Catholics are generally encouraged to pray and meditate at the Stations of the Cross on Good Friday. John Paul II made a practice of performing public devotions at Stations of the Cross set up in the Colosseum, Rome, each Good Friday. In 1991 and thereafter, he prayed the new scriptural sequence outlined above. Initially, the Holy Father himself carried the Cross from station to station, but in later life his age made it necessary for him to watch the devotions from a stage while others carried the Cross. In 2007, Pope Benedict XVI approved the new sequence of the Stations of the Cross for use by Catholics.

Above The 10th station: Jesus is bound and nailed to the Cross during his Crucifixion.

Above The 14th station: Jesus' body is placed in the tomb with the help of Joseph of Arimathea.

THE ROSARY

FOR CENTURIES DEVOTED CATHOLICS HAVE USED THE ROSARY — A ROUND OF PRAYERS THAT ARE CENTRED ON THE BLESSED VIRGIN MARY — IN BOTH PUBLIC AND PRIVATE DEVOTIONS.

The rosary is also a physical object that enables believers to keep track of their prayers. It consists of a small crucifix on a circular string with a medal and a series of beads of various numbers. The beads are divided into groups of ten beads called decades, each group preceded by an individual bead set apart slightly from the others. It is used to say the prayers that form the rosary. The central prayer of the rosary is the Hail Mary:

Hail Mary, full of Grace, the Lord is with thee; blessed art thou amongst women, and blessed is the fruit of thy womb, Jesus. Holy Mary, Mother of God, pray for us sinners now and at the hour of our death.

The other key prayers used in the rosary to complement the Hail Mary are the Lord's Prayer beginning "Our Father, who art in Heaven…" and the Apostles' Creed beginning "I believe in God, the Father Almighty, creator of heaven and earth…"

PRAYING THE ROSARY

The usual pattern of prayers is an introduction, then five decades of the rosary and a conclusion. During the introduction, believers hold the crucifix as they pray the dedication "In the Name of the Father, and of the Son and of the Holy Spirit: Amen" and the Apostles' Creed. Then they progress along the four beads after the crucifix, saying one Our Father and three Hail Marys.

Then they begin on the five decades. At each bead they say one Our Father and at each decade one Hail Mary. At the conclusion they hold the medal as they pray one of many other prayers to Mary, then return to the dedication "In the Name of the Father, and of the Son and of the Holy Spirit: Amen".

THE MYSTERIES

While praying the decades of the rosary, believers meditate inwardly on the mysteries of the lives of the Virgin Mary and Jesus. These

Above A Luminous Mystery: Peter, James and John see Jesus in his true light in Pietro Perugino's 15th–16th century The Transfiguration.

meditations were divided into three groups of five: the Joyful Mysteries (of Jesus' birth), the Sorrowful Mysteries (of Jesus' Crucifixion) and the Glorious Mysteries (of Jesus' Resurrection). However, in 2002 Pope John Paul II proposed a new set of mysteries, the Mysteries of Light, or Luminous Mysteries, following key events in Christ's ministry.

In each group, one mystery is aligned to one decade of the rosary, so when praying the entire rosary once, believers can meditate on one set of five mysteries. There is a pattern for meditating on the mysteries: the Joyful Mysteries are considered on Monday and Saturday, the Sorrowful Mysteries on Tuesday and Friday, the Glorious Mysteries on Wednesday and Sunday and the Luminous Mysteries are optional for Thursdays.

Left Pope John Paul II declared that the rosary prayer encompasses in its words the depth of the Holy Gospel's message.

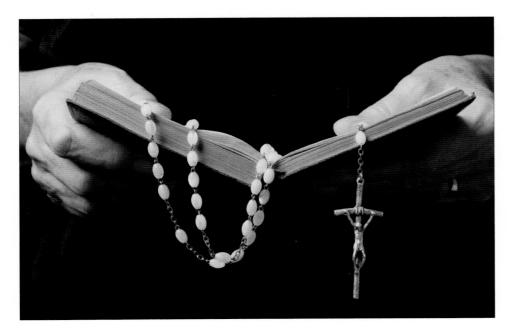

Right A Glorious Mystery: The Virgin is carried to heaven and crowned in this c.1500 Flemish illustration, Assumption and Coronation of the Virgin.

ORIGINS AND REVIVAL

The Hail Mary is also known as the Ave Maria, which comes from its first words in Latin *Ave Maria, gratia plena, Dominus tecum.* The prayer combines three main parts, the first being the salutation delivered by the archangel Gabriel to the Blessed Virgin at the Annunciation. The second part, "Blessed is the fruit of thy womb, Jesus", derives the greeting of Elizabeth to Mary (Luke 1:42); and the third part, the prayer "Holy Mary, Mother of God…" was, according to the *Catechism of the Catholic Church,* developed by the Church.

By tradition, the rosary was developed by St Dominic when combating the heresies of the dualist Cathars in 13th-century France. It has been refined over many years, but it reached its modern form by the 15th century when the Dominican

Below A Joyful Mystery: the Virgin Mary gives her consent to God's planned Incarnation at the Annunciation in Melchior Broederlam's 14th-century Annunciation and Visitation.

preacher Alan de la Roche promoted its use. In 1520, Pope Leo X gave the rosary his official papal backing.

In 1858 in Lourdes, France, Marie-Bernarde Soubirous (St Bernadette) saw apparitions of the Blessed Virgin Mary, who urged her to say her rosary, and to tell others to pray, perform penances and say the rosary for the salvation of sinners. Lourdes is now a centre of pilgrimage for Catholics.

THE WORDS OUR SAVIOUR GAVE US

Also known as the paternoster and the Our Father from its initial words in English and Latin, the Lord's Prayer is based on the one taught by Jesus to the apostles. According to the accounts in Matthew 6:9–15 and Luke 11:2–4, it runs:

Our Father who art in heaven,
Hallowed be thy name.
Thy kingdom come,
Thy will be done,
On earth as it is in heaven.
Give us this day our daily bread.
And forgive us our trespasses,
As we forgive those who
  trespass against us.
And lead us not into temptation,
  but deliver us from evil.

The Catholic version does not include the doxology or hymn of praise "For the kingdom the power and the glory are yours, now and forever" that appears in some other versions.

THE BLESSING

THERE ARE CENTURIES OF TRADITION AND LAYERS OF SYMBOLISM BEHIND CATHOLIC PRACTICES, SUCH AS THE BLESSING GIVEN BY THE CLERGY, MAKING THE SIGN OF THE CROSS AND USING HOLY WATER.

When Roman Catholic priests are ordained, their hands are anointed with chrism, holy oil that has been blessed by a bishop. After receiving the sacrament of Holy Orders through this and other related rituals, priests are able to share in Christ's own priesthood: their hands have the power to bless people and objects. In the act of blessing, the clergy can sanctify both people and objects, and dedicate them to God's service.

Above Jesus gave numerous blessings, as shown in Fernando Gallego's 15th-century Christ Blessing, *and with a gesture of his hands worked many miracles.*

The long-held practice of sanctifying both people and objects through the act of blessing has many biblical precedents. God blessed his Creation and after the Flood blessed Noah, while priests of the Jewish faith delivered blessings on their people. Christ himself and the apostles gave blessings to the sick and needy and to their followers. The Church teaches that blessing is the chief sacramental, a rite or object through and with which the sacraments are administered.

THE POWER TO BLESS
In general, only bishops and priests can deliver blessings, except in one exception under which a deacon is empowered to bless the paschal candle on Holy Saturday. Certain types of blessing are reserved for more senior clergy. Only the pope

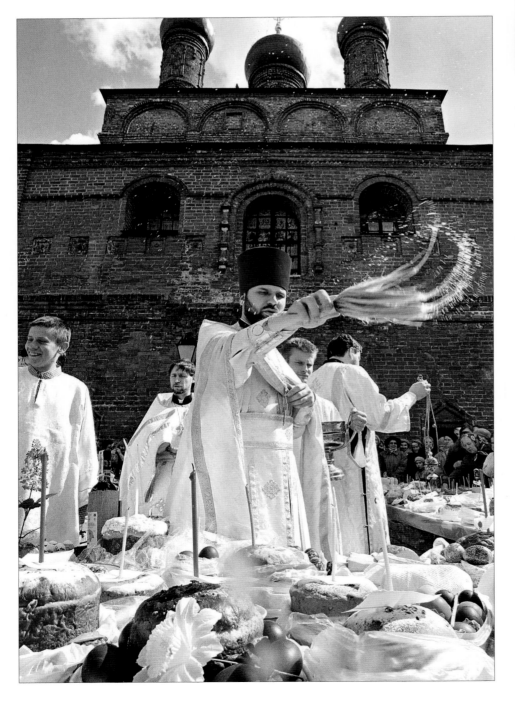

Left In Moscow, a priest of the Eastern Catholic Church blesses cakes and coloured eggs with holy water as part of the Easter celebrations. By blessing these objects, he is removing original sin from them.

can deliver some blessings – for example, those to which are attached an indulgence or remission of temporal punishment due to sin.

The pope's *Urbi et Orbi* blessing to the city of Rome and to the world, which is delivered every year on Easter and Christmas, has an indulgence attached for all Catholics who hear it in person, on television or on radio. Only bishops can deliver another class of blessings – for example, blessings on churches, cemeteries, chalices and vestments.

PRIESTLY BLESSINGS

There is a wide range of blessings that can be made by priests. They include blessings for the sick or for women due to deliver a baby and for people at various stages of Church life. There are also blessings for sanctifying objects used in religious devotions, such as crosses, images of Jesus, bells,

Above Pope Benedict XVI delivers the papal Urbi et Orbi *blessing. He prays that God's blessing should settle on the listening faithful and be with them always.*

medals, candles, rosaries and so forth. There are blessings for animals, food, buildings, such as schools or hospitals, and public objects, such as bridges, ships, stores, planes and so on.

The Church teaches that blessing is necessary and efficacious because people, animals and objects are all part of the Creation touched by sin after the Fall and therefore vulnerable to evil spirits. The blessings counter this effect by invoking the name of God, Father, Son and Holy Spirit and usually also by using the sign of the cross, a symbol of God's mercy and of Christ's victory over sin.

THE SIGN OF THE CROSS

When Catholics make the sign of the cross, they are honouring the Cross of Calvary and the redemptive sacrifice of Jesus. The Cross is a symbol of both God's mercy and his victory through Christ over sin.

Individual believers make the sign of the Cross on their own bodies as an expression of devotion. The most common form is to touch forehead, breastbone or stomach, left shoulder and then right shoulder in sequence. Usually the believer prays "In the Name of the Father" when touching the forehead, "And of the Son" when touching the stomach, "And of the Holy Spirit" when touching the left and right shoulders in sequence.

HOLY WATER

Sometimes a person will touch his fingers in holy water before making the sign of the Cross. When the faithful arrive at church for Mass, they dip their fingers in the bowl of holy water that is kept in a font near the entrance and make the sign of the Cross on head and torso.

The holy water has been blessed by a priest, and in this action the faithful bring to mind their baptismal promises as they seek to purify themselves before preparing to receive the Eucharist. Holy water is sometimes used to bless the faithful by sprinkling them with an aspergil (silver water sprinkler) during the Mass, especially during the Easter season. It is also used in blessings to sanctify places, objects and people.

DIMINUTIVE CROSSES

A variant form of the ritual is to use the thumb to make a small sign of the Cross three times over forehead, lips and chest, sometimes while praying quietly "May Christ's words be in my mind, on my lips and in my heart". This is the normal usage when the gospel is proclaimed during Mass. A third kind of Cross made by the clergy is a small sign, traced with the thumb, for example, on the forehead of a baby in the sacrament of baptism or on the Holy Gospel during the liturgy of the Word in the Mass.

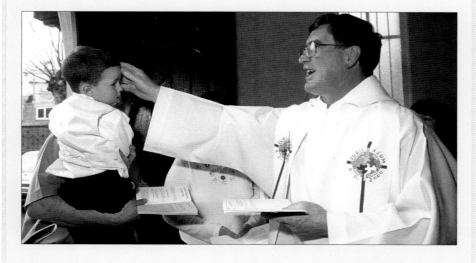

Above A priest makes the sign of the Cross on a child's forehead using his thumb. The sign assures the child of God's protection.

THE CATHOLIC YEAR

The Catholic liturgical year has been shaped by events in the life of Christ. Although the actual historical dates of these events are uncertain, over the centuries a chronology has evolved that reflects the principal milestones of Christ's life as described in the Scriptures. However, at the same time it considers the manner in which human progress through time has fluctuated with the seasonal cycles. Thus "Christ our Light" was born after the deep night of the winter solstice, and our redemption from despair and damnation came in spring, after the full moon of the equinox. In the Catholic calendar, these natural cycles have assumed a religious dimension as they are allied to the life of the God–man who Catholics believe died for humankind's eternal salvation.

Just as in the life of each individual, "ordinary time" is also a component of the liturgical year. During ordinary time, no specific events in Christ's life are celebrated, although holy days of obligation such as All Saints' and the Assumption of Mary do fall within ordinary time. Strictly speaking, "ordinary" here refers to ordinal, or numbered, time; it encompasses the period from the evening of Candlemas (2 February) until Shrove Tuesday, and again from the Monday after Pentecost until vespers the night before Advent. Ordinary time pays homage to the simpler days that Christ spent on earth and reminds us to consider, even now, how we go about our normal daily lives.

Above Mary presides over ranks of saints in this fresco in the baptistery dome of Padua Cathedral, with her eminence emphasized by an enveloping golden aureole.

Left Youthful Christians bear a massive wooden cross in Jerusalem's Church of the Holy Sepulchre, built at the site of Christ's Crucifixion. The original 4th-century church was built by Constantine; the present structure dates from the Crusades of the 12th century.

HOLY DAYS

ROMAN CATHOLICS CONSECRATE EACH DAY OF THE YEAR TO
REMEMBRANCE OF AN EVENT IN THE LIFE OF CHRIST OR THE BLESSED
MOTHER, OR TO ONE OF THE SAINTS.

There are around 10,000 Catholic saints, and in the Catholic year, which is known as the liturgical year, each day has some sacred significance relating to a saint. Catholics nourish their spiritual consciousness by meditating on the particular virtues and mysteries that are invoked by the history of the saint on each new feast or saint's day.

THE FIRST HOLY DAYS

The tradition of saints' days dates back to the first centuries of the Catholic Church during the Roman persecutions. The first saints were the Christian martyrs, and early Christians often honoured their sacrifice by celebrating the day of their death, also known as their "birthday into heaven". During the Middle Ages, saints' days were a common method of dating, so "St Martin's Tide", or "Martinmas", referred to a date near 11 November, the feast day of St Martin of Tours; "Bartholomew Tide" meant a date

Below Farm labourers, such as the one in this 15th-century image from the Historia Naturalis, *often stopped working on the many holy days in medieval times, so holy days were unpopular among landowners.*

in the waning days of summer, on about 24 August (commemorating St Bartholomew, patron of printers).

The Church classifies the daily liturgical observations as solemnities, feasts, memorials and commemorations. Solemnities, as their name implies, are the most important, but of the 13 yearly solemnities, only 6 are classified as holy days of obligation in the United States and 10 in Europe. (This group of six does not include ordinary Sundays, when Catholics are obliged to attend Mass each week, in honour of the day Christ rose from the dead.)

The Catholic Church mandates that Catholics must attend Mass on holy days of obligation, and refrain from "unnecessary servile work", often defined as physical labour. This prohibition is the genesis of today's word "holiday", which is an obvious contraction of "holy day". In feudal times serfs were freed on holy days of obligation so they could attend Mass.

MEDIEVAL HOLY DAYS

By the Middle Ages, holy days were so numerous and engrained in the observances of society that in some quarters they came to be considered a nuisance. The prohibition against servile work was taken up by the populace with enthusiasm, and soon medieval lawmakers found themselves having to issue stern decrees to make "exemptions" from the command not to work on holy days so that crucial work, such as harvesting, did not come to a standstill. The *Catholic Encyclopedia* notes that from the 13th to the 18th century, some dioceses observed more than 100 feast days – days in which no work was done. Celebrations of the

Above St Bartholomew is associated with books, as in this 14th-century illustration by Andre Beauneveu, because of a printers' celebration, the Wayzgoose. It is held on 24 August, the time of year printers began to work by candlelight.

"octaves" of major Catholic holy days, such as Easter, could cause work to stop for more than a week. Complaints reached a crescendo in

EARLY "FAIRS"

Not all Catholics abstaining from work on holy days were involved in reverent contemplation. The Latin *feria*, meaning "religious holiday", evolved to become "fair", a word that is still used to refer to a leisure activity, not to religious observance. One prelate suggested that while holy days gave Catholics a chance to "...receive the food of the Word of God, which they sorely need", they were instead using their holy days to relax or set up impromptu markets – and some of these were held within the churchyards themselves.

the 16th century, and finally in 1642 Pope Urban VIII bowed to the inevitable and issued an encyclical, *Universa per Orbem*, that reduced the number of holy days to 36 (not including Sundays).

Even priests are subject to normal human nature, and in 1858 Pope Pius IX had to issue a second encyclical – this time to order priests to offer Mass on the "suppressed" holy days. This was issued because some priests had decided to take a holiday of their own and had ceased to celebrate Mass on feasts that were no longer holy days of obligation, although to do so was still their responsibility.

EUROPEAN HOLY DAYS

Holy days of obligation vary from country to country and year to year. In Europe, holy days are often celebrated with opulence. In Rome, for example, the Feast of Sts Peter and Paul (29 June) is a general holiday for the entire city, marking the day in AD 64 when both saints were martyred for their faith (Peter by being crucified upside down and Paul by beheading). Today, Romans observe the holy day with extravagant decoration of the 4th-century basilicas dedicated to each saint, and each year the pope presents palliums (from the Latin for "stole") to the city's bishops. The palliums are newly woven from wool shorn from lambs, and they symbolize the lamb carried over the shoulders of the good shepherd, reminding the bishops they are the shepherds of their pastoral flock, just as was Peter, Rome's first bishop.

AMERICAN HOLY DAYS

The holy days of obligation in the USA are fewer than in Europe. This is, in part, because the tradition of their celebration is shorter than in many European countries, where Catholicism has been the majority religion for many centuries. In the early years of the United States,

Catholics were a minority, widely scattered in a vast country, and victims of prejudice. Puritans did not celebrate holy days because they had been offended by the excesses that they had observed in Europe. American bishops took such realities into account and reduced the number of holy days.

In the United States, if All Saints' Day or Ascension falls on a Saturday or Monday, the obligation to attend Mass is rescinded. The American Conference of Bishops has also suppressed certain holy days that are still active in Europe: the observances for Epiphany (6 January), Corpus Christi (the Thursday after Trinity Sunday), St Joseph (19 March) and the apostles Sts Peter and Paul (29 June) have been moved to the next following Sundays.

American holy days of obligation, with the exception of Christmas, are normally celebrated in a low-key manner simply by going to Mass. However, in certain American ethnic enclaves, old traditions of celebration on a saint's day still endure; for example, the feast of San Gennaro is usually celebrated with a street fair in Manhattan's Little Italy.

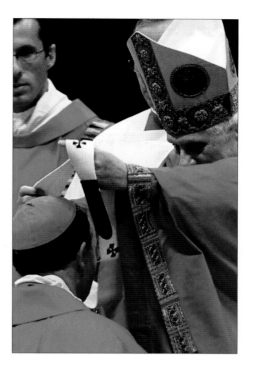

Above On the feast of Sts Peter and Paul in Rome, Pope Benedict XVI drapes a pallium made of new woven wool over the shoulders of an archbishop.

Below The September feast of San Gennaro, here celebrated in New York's Little Italy neighbourhood, home of many Italian-Americans, honours the 4th-century martyrdom of Januarius, the patron saint of Naples.

THE FESTIVE CALENDAR

THE FEASTS OF THE CATHOLIC CALENDAR HAVE MARKED THE DAYS OF THE YEAR FOR CENTURIES. SOME FEASTS OCCUR ON THE SAME DAY EACH YEAR, BUT OTHERS MOVE DEPENDING ON THE LUNAR CYCLE.

Like the saints that they honour, Catholic feast days have been ranked and classified. Solemnity is the highest ranking of the holy days, but depending on the country it is not always a holy day of obligation. A feast day is the next highest rank of holy days, with celebrations that honour Jesus, Mary and the saints. A memorial is the lowest rank of holy days, a way of honouring saints without giving them fully fledged feast days. Below is a key to symbols that indicate if the feast has a fixed or moveable date, and when a day of obligation is celebrated by most countries or only those in Europe.

KEY
✧ moveable feast
⌘ fixed feast
○ Holy Day of Obligation
❖ Additional European Holy Day of Obligation

Above A calendar of saints' days from a 14th-century French Bible highlights the numerous days that were celebrated.

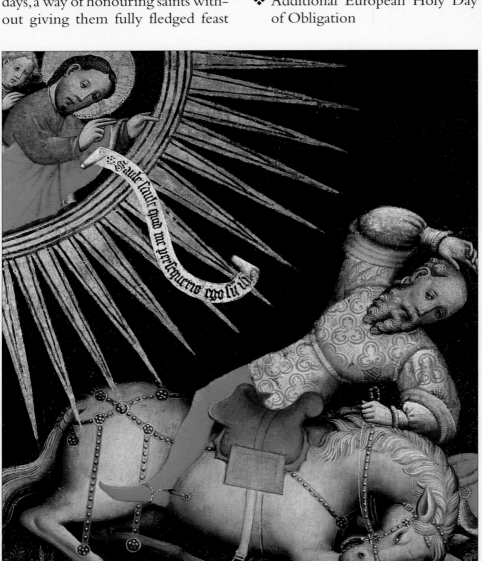

JANUARY
1 Solemnity of Mary Mother of God ⌘○
6 Solemnity of Epiphany ⌘❖
13 Feast of Baptism of Jesus ⌘
25 Feast of the Conversion of St Paul ⌘

FEBRUARY
2 Feast of Candlemas (Presentation) ✧⌘
5 Shrove Tuesday ✧
6 Ash Wednesday ✧

MARCH
2 Laetare Sunday ✧
16 Palm Sunday ✧
19 Spy Wednesday ✧
19 St Joseph ✧
20 Maundy Thursday ✧
21 Good Friday ✧
23 Easter ✧
25 Solemnity of the Annunciation ⌘

Left St Paul's conversion to Christianity, captured in this 15th-century painting by Hildesheim, is celebrated on 25 January.

Above Many feast days celebrate Jesus and the Virgin Mary, depicted together in this Byzantine painting.

MAY
1   Ascension ✧○
11 Pentecost ✧
18 Feast of Trinity Sunday ✧
22 Solemnity of Corpus Christi ✧❖
30 Sacred Heart of Jesus ✧
31 Immaculate Heart of Mary ✧

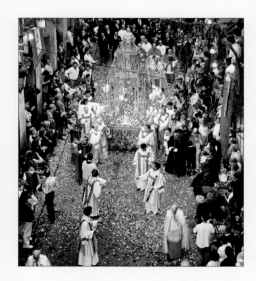

Above In Valencia, Spain, the feast of Corpus Christi is marked with processions of rocas, *carts decorated with holy statues.*

JUNE
29 Solemnity of Sts Peter and Paul ❖

AUGUST
15 Solemnity of Assumption of Mary ⌘○

SEPTEMBER
18 Birth of the Virgin Mary ⌘
29 Mass of archangels Michael, Raphael and Gabriel ⌘

NOVEMBER
1   All Saints' Day ⌘○
2   All Souls' Day ⌘
23 Feast of Christ the King ⌘
30 First Sunday of Advent ✧

DECEMBER
7   Second Sunday of Advent ✧
8   Feast of the Immaculate Conception ⌘○
14 Gaudete Sunday (Third Sunday of Advent) ✧
21 Fourth Sunday of Advent ✧
25 Christmas Day ⌘○
28 Solemnity of the Holy Family ✧

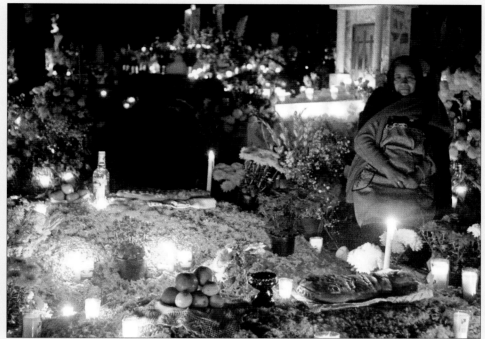

Above The holy days of All Saints and All Souls are celebrated in Mexico with graveside offerings, including pan de muertos – *bread made for the dead.*

Above Michael, Raphael and Gabriel, the only archangels in the Scriptures, share a feast day in September. They are shown in this 15th-century image by Domenico di Michelino with Tobias, an encounter described in the Book of Tobit.

Left Christmas in midwinter, lights against the darkness – despite the debate and uncertainty about the true date of Christ's birth, it is celebrated around the world on 25 December.

A CHILD IS BORN

CHRISTMAS, A SEASON THAT CATHOLICS DEVOTE TO THE CELEBRATION OF JESUS' BIRTH, ENCOMPASSES TWO PERIODS IN THE CATHOLIC CHURCH: ADVENT AND CHRISTMASTIDE.

Advent is a season of preparation that is about four weeks long, although it is sometimes a little shorter, depending on the day of the week the 25th falls on. It will always include four Sundays. Christmastide is the period from Christmas Day to the feast of the Epiphany on 6 January – the traditional 12 days of Christmas.

Above The Magi, probably Persian kings, visited Christ when he was nearly a year old – not in the stable, as some traditions suggest. Gerard David captured the visit in his Adoration of the Kings, c. 1515.

CELEBRATING ADVENT

Like the secular Christmas, the Catholic Christmas (from Old English *Cristes Maesse*, or "Mass of Christ") involves weeks of preparation. However, unlike the frenzied weeks of shopping promoted by the worldly media, the four weeks of Advent (from the Latin *Adventus*, or "coming") involve steady spiritual preparation, marked by a certain amount of sober sacrifice and longing in the beginning, but as Christmas Day approaches, a mounting sense of joy. On the third Sunday of Advent, known as Gaudete (or "Rejoice") Sunday, the heightened anticipation is symbolized by a change in the colour of the priest's vestments from purple to rose.

Celebration of Advent originated in the 5th century, when Bishop Perpetuus of Tours decreed a fast, known as "St Martin's Lent", from St Martin's Day (11 November) to Christmas. In the 6th century, Pope Gregory the Great shortened Advent to four weeks, its modern duration, and strict fasting gave way to a less rigorous abstinence from meat and dairy. The liturgy of Advent emphasizes that preparation for Christ's first coming at his birth prefigures the preparations that Christians should make for his Second Coming.

THE NATIVITY

One of the most widely known and beloved stories is that of Christ's Nativity. The tradition of the divine birth in a primitive stable in the

DOMESTIC RITUALS

The domestic rituals of Advent evolved as expressions of the longing and expectation that characterize the season. The colourful family ceremonies are particularly attractive to children, helping them to focus on the spiritual rather than the commercial meaning of the season. The Advent wreath is a circular wreath of evergreens with four evenly spaced candles, three violet and one rose, to represent the four weeks of Advent. The violet symbolizes penitence, and the rose, lit on the third Sunday known as Gaudete Sunday, represents joy at the imminent approach of the Nativity. Families gather at a weekly Sunday dinner to light the candles, a new candle as each week passes, and dine by their light in the December evening. Some modern wreaths also include a white candle, symbolic of Jesus, that is lit on Christmas Eve. The familial ritual reminds Catholics of the intimate scene of the Holy Family within the snug stable.

Nativity scenes are usually small enough to fit on a table or mantelpiece. Some are simple and homemade, others are heirloom sets crafted by old world-artisans. The stable, the barn animals and the manger are arranged before Christmas, and Mary and Joseph are allowed to set up housekeeping, but the infant Jesus and the Magi must await the day appointed for their arrival in Scripture. Meanwhile, each day children add a few wisps of straw to the manger. By Christmas Eve, the manger will be comfortable for the infant figure, who arrives on time and with ceremony – gently placed in the manger at midnight on Christmas Eve. On Epiphany, the royal visitors from the East arrive, and the three kings are added to the stable scene.

Right The weekly ritual of lighting the Advent wreath in church or at home helps children understand the spiritual significance of the Advent season.

Right *Although born in a humble setting, the Christ child seems to transfix the gaze of all in this 15th-century illustration by Rosello Franchi and Filippo Torelli.*

depth of winter concentrates the sense of mystery and delight that Catholics experience during this season. However, despite the hold that the Nativity story has on the popular imagination, the date of Jesus' birth is still unknown, and the only gospel to describe the Nativity is Luke, Chapter 2, in just a few words that have echoed down the centuries:

And she brought forth her first born son and wrapped him in swaddling clothes and laid him in a manger: because there was no room for them in the inn.

Around this quiet description, combined with the telling in Matthew, Chapter 2 of the wise men from the East who saw the star of the King of the Jews and travelled to seek and adore him, has arisen the vast tradition of the Christian Nativity in story and especially in art.

A DATE IN QUESTION

In the early centuries of the Church, Christmas was not celebrated; some early theologians, such as Origen (AD 185–254), viewed celebrating the birthday of Christ with disfavour, calling it a pagan custom. The actual date of Christ's birth was also much disputed. Scriptural evidence for the date of the Nativity is inconclusive, and many scholars have argued that shepherds would not have kept their flocks in the fields at night in winter. The choice of 25 December was a compromise. Because the Church identified Christ with the coming of the light of redemption, it seemed most natural to celebrate the birth of "Christ Our Light" at a time when light was reborn after the solstice on 21 December. The date also takes advantage of a deep-rooted human

urge to celebrate at this time; the Roman holiday of *Sol Invictus*, or the birth of the Unconquered Sun, and the birthday of Mithras, the Persian God of Light, were both celebrated in December. By the 4th century, Christ's birth was celebrated in Rome on 25 December; early celebrations of Christmas were often combined with the older celebrations of Epiphany on 6 January.

Right *The birth of Christ Our Light, after the winter solstice, reached its fruition at the Transfiguration, when Christ shone before his apostles. Fra Angelico painted the scene in* The Transfiguration, *1436–45.*

237

CARNIVAL!

THE MOST JUBILANT OF ALL OF THE CATHOLIC FESTIVALS, CARNIVAL IS INEXTRICABLY LINKED TO LENT, THE MOST AUSTERE. CARNIVAL HAS BEEN CELEBRATED BY CATHOLICS FOR SEVERAL CENTURIES.

As the predecessor to Lent in Catholic countries, carnival is a riotous indulgence of role reversal and licentious behaviour that has occurred for centuries. The word "carnival" probably derives from the medieval Latin phrase *carnem levare*, meaning "to remove meat". The linking of carnival and Lent in the calendar expresses an apparently innate human desire for cycles of feast and famine.

Some historians suggest that the Catholic Church was aware that carnival, which originated in southern European countries, was simply the ancient Roman pagan festival of Saturnalia under another name, yet tolerated the festival in order to smooth the transition from old pagan observances to those of the new religion. However, it is also true that the Catholic Church, especially when compared to the more sober Christian sects, such as Puritans or Quakers, has always had an appreciation of festival and pageantry.

EARLY CELEBRATIONS

Contemporary carnivals are often associated with Rio de Janeiro – which mixes the European tradition with native American and African cultures: Venice, New Orleans and the Caribbean – and they almost always include vast costume parades with elaborate floats. However, carnival celebrations in Catholic countries have a long history – the Venetian carnival is mentioned in documents from 1092. In ancient times, carnival is said to have begun just after Epiphany (6 January) and lasted until Shrove Tuesday (*see* Shrove Tuesday, *below*), but in Rome the carnival was permitted to last for eight days, from the Monday of the week before Lent until Shrove Tuesday.

Above Like carnival, the Roman festival of Saturnalia was officially approved and served as an antidote to a more solemn time – Saturnalia was held in mid-winter; and carnival before Lent.

THE POPE AND CARNIVAL

Right up through the 19th century, Rome held a famous carnival that was supported, sometimes implicitly and sometimes explicitly, by the popes. No Roman carnival could begin without a papal edict, and depending on the reigning pope, that edict might be withheld.

Some popes, such as the 15th-century Pope Paul II, were involved in planning for carnival. Paul II ordered the Jewish people of Rome to pay a yearly tax of 1,130 gold

SHROVE TUESDAY

The British version of carnival, which is held on the day before the first day of Lent, is Shrove Tuesday. It takes its name from the verb "to shrive", meaning to absolve of sin and give penance. Medieval custom was to confess and receive penance just before Lent in order to approach the austere week in a state of penitent purity.

A more whimsical name for Shrove Tuesday is Pancake Day because fasting was practised during Lent, and pancakes were a convenient way to use up any remaining eggs, milk and butter. This particular Tuesday has many aliases and is also known as Mardi Gras, which is French for another common name, Fat Tuesday. New Orleans is renowned for its Mardi Gras, its carnival celebrations that culminate on Fat Tuesday.

Right A 19th-century vignette by Basile de Loose shows the making of pancakes, enjoyed by young and old.

Above The pre-Lenten celebration of carnival reaches its apotheosis in Rio de Janeiro's sambodrome, a custom-built parade ground for carnival extravaganzas.

florins (the 30 added to recall Judas and the 30 pieces of silver), and the money was spent on carnival. Paul II also paid, straight from the papal treasury, for races for the elderly, children, asses and bulls. Conversely, Pope Sixtus V (elected in 1585) directed that gibbets and whipping posts be erected on the piazzas as a warning not to let carnival licentiousness to verge to the criminal.

In the 16th century, the Church attempted to steal carnival's thunder by holding a 40-hour prayer service on Monday and Shrove Tuesday – however, the 40 hours of prayer did not have a lasting negative effect on carnival's popularity.

RACES AND CANDLES

The high points of the Roman carnival, popular from the 17th century onward, were the race of Berber horses and the Race of the Candles, both held in the Via del Corso. The riderless horses were released, wearing balls full of sharp pins hanging from their sides to goad them on down the crowded Corso. In 1882, 15 people were killed when the horses charged into the crowd, and that put an end to this tradition.

The Festa dei Moccoletti (candles) was held on the last night of carnival, when the people dressed in costume, and carrying candles and lanterns, swarmed through the streets trying to put out others' candles while keeping their own lit. The custom also ended in the 19th century, but children in Rome still celebrate it by going to school in costume.

Above The Race of the Candles involved three wooden pillars – representing Sts George, Ubaldo and Anthony – raced to the basilica. They seem ready to topple in this 19th-century Italian illustration.

ASH WEDNESDAY AND LENT

LENT IS AN AUSTERE PERIOD OF SPIRITUAL PREPARATION LEADING UP TO EASTER. IT STARTS ON ASH WEDNESDAY, AND DEVOUT CATHOLICS FAST DURING THIS 40-DAY PERIOD.

Lent is a period of penitence and self-denial. It developed as an adaptation of an ascetic period of study and prayer followed by early postulants converting to Christianity. They undertook this period before being baptized on Easter eve. Pre-baptism instruction in these early centuries also included exorcism; descriptions of such initiation preparations are found in the 3rd-century *Apostolic Tradition*, a written collection of early Christian practices attributed to St Hippolytus. The word "Lent" derives from Middle English *Lenten*, or "spring", and is related to the German root for "long", because the days in spring get longer.

Below A 16th-century Flemish artist has portrayed carnival as a corpulent figure among revellers. He is armed with a spitted fowl, ready to do battle with the opposing force of Lent, who thrusts a baker's paddle bearing fish toward him.

THE PERIOD OF LENT

Lent lasts for a total of 40 days, in imitation of the number of days Christ was in the wilderness, fasting and withstanding the temptations of Satan (Matthew 4:1–2, Mark I:12–13, Luke 4:1–2). Until the 600s, Lent always began on Quadragesima Sunday, 40 days before Easter, but Pope Gregory the Great moved the start to Ash Wednesday to achieve 40 days without counting Sundays, which are feast days, when fasting is relaxed. During Lent, fasting was general: law courts were closed (in AD 380, the Roman emperor Gratian decreed that all legal proceedings be suspended for 40 days); theatres were shuttered; and hunting and military manoeuvres were all forbidden.

THE START OF LENT

On Ash Wednesday, priests smear the foreheads of penitents with ash (made by burning the palms used in

Above Jesus' 40-day fast in the desert, when he was tempted by the devil, is captured in this 19th-century painting by Ivan Nikolaevich Kramskoy. It is the model for the 40-day period of Lent.

the previous year's Palm Sunday celebration) in the shape of a cross, saying "Remember that you are dust, and to dust you shall return" (Genesis 3:19), a reminder to those who have revelled in the excesses of Mardi Gras. Expressing penitence by using ashes is a custom inherited from ancient Jewish observance. In the Old Testament, Job expresses penitence to God with the words, "Therefore I despise myself and repent in dust and ashes" (Job 42:6).

Right Lent's sobriety is represented by this stark composition of ash and palm, invoking the two celebrations of Ash Wednesday and Palm Sunday.

In the early days of Christianity, ashes were used for those who had declared serious sins and asked to be shriven; the penance imposed began on Ash Wednesday and exiled the penitents from society for the 40 days of Lent; this custom is the genesis of the word "quarantine". The ashes were not smeared in a cross but sprinkled on the heads of the sinners. Over time, a public display of humility and penitence by the mark of the ashen cross became widespread.

FASTING DURING LENT

Lent has always been associated with fasting; there is a scriptural basis for this, as in Matthew 9:15, Christ, when questioned why his disciples, unlike the Pharisees, did not fast, commented, "Days will come, when the bridegroom shall be taken away from them, and then they shall fast." It was after Jesus' departure that Christians began fasting. By the 12th century, St Bernard of Clairvaux noted that Lenten fasting was general: "kings, and princes, clergy and laity…" all fasted. When King Wenceslaus of Bohemia needed to eat meat during Lent due to ill health, he first sought dispensation from the pope. The "Black Fast" referred to one meal, taken in the evening, consisting of bread, herbs and water. Rules for fasting have become more lenient over time, but devout Catholics will still fast on Lenten Fridays.

MODERN FASTING

For today's Catholics, 40 days of Lenten fasting in imitation of Christ's trial and temptation in the wilderness can be a particularly instructive experience, as we are so accustomed to relative plenty. A strict fast today is defined as only one meal, with two smaller meals that taken together would not equal a full meal. Animal foods, except fish, are avoided. As Christ lay in the tomb for 40 hours, the devout undertake a total fast for 40 hours just prior to Easter.

Catholics often undertake fasting as a family affair (although children under 14, according to canon law, are not required to fast), with the entire family choosing to give up meat, dessert, television or video games, then donating the money saved by this abstinence to charity, following the ancient Lenten tradition of alms-giving. Catholics are also encouraged to allow a sort of spiritual plenty to fill the space no longer occupied by temporal delights – Lent is a time of prayer and meditation. For this little time, Catholics follow the rigorous practice of monks, hoping to achieve some of the same religious insight.

Participating in fasting and other forms of abstinence are understood to be physical self-control that mirrors spiritual discipline. The Catholic catechism describes fasting as an "interior penance" and "spiritual preparation" that prepares Catholics for the arrival of Christ in the Eucharist, at his Resurrection and at the Second Coming.

Below On Ash Wednesday, the first of Lent's 40 days, Catholics wear a cross of ash on the forehead, a symbol of penitence since Old Testament times.

HOLY WEEK

THE WEEK LEADING UP TO EASTER IS A PERIOD IN WHICH CATHOLICS REMEMBER AND MOURN THE SUFFERING OF JESUS, WHEN HE WAS SACRIFICED ON THE CROSS TO REDEEM HUMANKIND.

The week before Easter begins with Palm Sunday and extends to the vigil of Easter at sunset on Holy Saturday; it is known as Holy Week. During Holy Week devout Catholics follow along with Christ in a respectful attempt to take on the burden of the agony that he accepted as the price for their redemption.

Before the agony in the garden, anticipating the trial about to come, Christ said to Peter and the sons of Zebedee, "I am sorrowful even unto death....Stay you here and watch with me" (Matthew 26:38). The apostles, though, fell asleep, leaving Christ alone; he reproached them with, "Could you not watch one hour with me?" (Matthew 26:40). The liturgy and customs of Holy Week draw Catholics along with Christ's Passion, so that they "watch" with Christ and try to make reparation for that original abandonment.

IN MOURNING

The stark and mournful tone of Holy Week is marked in many churches by obscuring all statues and crucifixes in purple veiling. The custom derives from the European tradition of hiding the altar crucifix behind a

Above Judas was paid 30 pieces of silver to betray Christ. He is shown with the apostles' money bag in this 16th-century fresco by Eglise St Sébastien Plampinet.

hanging that would be dropped to the ground during Palm Sunday, and reading from Matthew 27:51: "And behold the veil of the temple was rent in two from the top even to the bottom." This was one of the cataclysms that followed Christ's death. The liturgical atmosphere is of a community in mourning: the altar is not decorated with flowers, and the Te Deum and gloria are not sung.

FROM PALM SUNDAY

In Scripture, Holy Week begins with the entry of Jesus into Jerusalem, his way strewn with palms and lauded with the Hosannas of the multitude, an event described by all four Evangelists. However, the triumph was short-lived; by Friday, Jesus would hang from the Cross. Today the entry into Jerusalem is commemorated as Palm Sunday. Palms are distributed at Mass, and some palms are saved to burn to make ashes for the next year's Ash Wednesday, symbolically linking

Left After the Last Supper, Christ washed the apostles' feet. The ritual of washing feet, shown in Giovanni Agostino da Lodi's painting, 1500, symbolizes repentance.

triumph (palms) and penitence and death (ash). Wednesday of Holy Week is also known as "Spy Wednesday", referring to Judas and his agreement to betray Christ for 30 pieces of silver.

THE HEART OF THE WEEK

Easter Triduum (*triduum* is Latin for "three days") refers to the three days at the heart of Holy Week: Maundy Thursday, Good Friday and Holy Saturday. In Anglo-Saxon times, the Triduum was called "The Still Days", referring to the sorrow Catholics feel at this time, as well as to the time Christ lay in the tomb.

Maundy Thursday has tremendous significance for the Catholic Church, because it is on this day, at the paschal meal of the Last Supper, that Christ instituted the Eucharist. "Maundy" from the Latin *Mandatum*, or "commandment", refers to Christ's injunction to the apostles at the Last Supper, "A new commandment I give unto you, That ye love one another; as I have loved you" (John 13:34).

In John's Gospel, there is also a description of Christ humbly washing the apostles' feet on this day, and some churches commemorate Holy Thursday by a ritual in which the diocesan bishop washes the feet of 12 parishioners. In monasteries, the tradition was for the abbot to wash the feet of an ordinary monk.

After Thursday evening Mass, known as the Mass of the Lord's Supper, the altar is stripped of all cloths and candles, and the Eucharist in its chalice is removed from the tabernacle on the central altar and set in an unobtrusive side altar, known as the "altar of repose". The central altar remains bare and desolate of the sacred presence for all of Good Friday, the day marking Christ's Crucifixion and his death. Many churches remain open so that their parishioners can stay and pray quietly, "watching" with Christ in his time of need.

Above A cross is borne through the streets in Corsica, France, on Good Friday.

No masses are celebrated on Good Friday – the only day of the liturgical year on which it is forbidden to celebrate the Mass. Good Friday observances often include the Way of the Cross. Parishioners and clergy assemble in the late afternoon (Scripture notes that Christ died at the ninth hour, or 3 p.m.) at some public meeting place outdoors and carry a large cross in procession through the streets, stopping at designated points along the route to recite the Stations of the Cross. This public ritual is another example of the effort Catholics make during Holy Week to share and make reparation for the agony that Christ experienced for their sake.

THE TENEBRAE SERVICE

Although the events commemorated by Holy Week occurred around 2,000 years ago, the Tenebrae is designed to help Catholics bridge the emotional distance and experience Christ's Passion as though they were there. "Tenebrae" means "shadows or darkness", and the service makes its participants feel as though a dark cloud has just passed over the sun.

The elements of the Tenebrae date from the 5th century. The original Tenebrae services were held in monasteries in the earliest morning hours. Today the service is held on either Maundy Thursday or Good Friday, usually at dusk. The church is in semi-darkness, the only light source a triangular candelabra known as the hearse, from the Middle English *herse*, or "harrow" (the two were similar in shape). As the service of sorrowful psalms, chants and lamentations is read, the candles are extinguished one by one until only a single lit candle remains. Then the celebrants, making no sound, leave the altar, marooning the congregation in the dark, silent church. Suddenly, a rough, clattering noise, known as the *strepitus* (Latin for "wild din" or "crash") is heard. It represents the convulsion of the earth at Christ's death. The congregation file from the church in silence, their way lit only by a few candles as they depart.

Right Since the 13th century, the hearse has held candles during the Tenebrae service. "Hearse" later came to refer to a candle frame over a coffin, and from that to the vehicle that carries a coffin.

THE RESURRECTION AND EASTER

AFTER THE SOMBRE HOLY WEEK, CATHOLICS AROUND THE WORLD CELEBRATE EASTER, A JOYOUS OCCASION COMMEMORATING THE RESURRECTION OF CHRIST OUR LIGHT.

To Catholics, Easter is the greatest Catholic celebration and completes the meaning of all that came before and all that followed and is to come in Christian history. Without Easter, Catholic doctrine has no point, but all of Christianity is enlivened by the Resurrection of Christ on Easter.

The name "Easter" in Germanic languages is derived from old English and Germanic root words referring to the East and dawn. *Eastre* or *Ostara* was also the Anglo-Saxon Teutonic goddess of spring and fertility. In France, Easter is known as *Pâques*, and all Romance language names for Easter are from *Pascha*, for "Passover".

HE IS RISEN

The Easter story can be simply told: two days after Christ was placed in the tomb of Joseph of Arimathea and a big stone rolled across the entrance, Mary Magdalene, Mary, the mother of James and Salome, and "the other women" (the gospels differ on who was with Mary Magdalene) visited the tomb to anoint the body with spices, only to find the stone rolled away and the sepulchre empty. An angel sitting on the stone informed them that Jesus had risen (*see Easter: The Quem Quaeritis, opposite*).

A DATE IN DISPUTE

Easter was first known as "Pasch", and the earliest references to it date from the 2nd century. Easter is a moveable feast, meaning that its date varies each year according to the lunar calendar (all of the other major Christian holidays follow the solar calendar). During the first centuries of Christianity, the correct date was disputed, but the First Council of Nicaea in AD 325 finally decreed that

Above *The unleavened bread of Passover has become in Catholicism the unleavened bread transubstantiated into the Eucharist. The bread is being made in this 15th-century detail from the Schocken Bible.*

Easter was to be celebrated the first Sunday after the 14th day of the moon (approximately the full moon) following the date of the spring equinox (assumed to be 21 March). Therefore, Easter can come as early as 22 March or as late as 25 April. The dates of other holy days, such as Pentecost, depend on the Easter date. Easter's date is linked to the Jewish celebration of Passover, because the Last Supper, three days before Christ's Resurrection, was a Passover Seder.

CHRIST OUR LIGHT

After the darkness of the events of Holy Week, Catholics express their jubilation at the Resurrection in the traditional Easter vigil service. Near midnight on Easter eve, Catholics gather in a dimly lit church, symbolizing the darkness of Christ's tomb, and wait. Outside the church, a new fire is kindled and blessed. At midnight, priests light the paschal candle, marked with the Cross and the alpha and omega, symbols of Christ, from the new fire and process

Left *Andrea Mantegna's dramatic 15th-century painting of Christ's Resurrection is scripturally inaccurate – according to the Bible no man or woman witnessed Christ coming forth from the tomb.*

EASTER: THE QUEM QUAERITIS

Four lines of dialogue beginning in Latin *Quem Quaeritis*, or "Whom do you seek?" were the genesis of the theatrical tradition of miracle and mystery plays that began in the 10th century. The Quem Quaeritis is a trope, or elaboration, of the part of the Easter liturgy that describes Mary Magdalene and "the other women" finding Jesus' tomb empty, with an angel sitting on the great stone.

> *Whom do ye seek in the sepulchre, O followers of Christ?*
> *Jesus of Nazareth, the Crucified, O heavenly ones.*
> *He is not here; he is risen, just as he foretold.*
> *Go, announce that he is risen from the sepulchre.*

The original adapted dialogue has come down to us in manuscripts from the monks at the 10th-century Abbey of St Gall and in actual stage directions written *c.*AD 965 by Bishop Ethelwold for Benedictine monks at Winchester. The original four-line vignette was performed, in Latin, by priests in the church sanctuary. Such dramatic renditions by the clergy of parts of the Easter liturgy were so popular that the subject matter was expanded to dramatize episodes from the New Testament and the lives of the saints. Responsibility for productions was removed from the clergy and taken over by the guilds of medieval towns, who performed the plays in English, with non-reverent elements.

Above Mystery plays, adaptations of biblical scenes, were produced in public squares on moveable stages known as pageant wagons, as depicted in this 16th-century English illustration.

into the dark Church, symbolizing the Resurrection of Christ our Light. Easter is also traditionally associated with the baptism of new converts to Christianity, and Easter vigil services often incorporate baptisms of new Catholics on this auspicious day. The custom of wearing new clothes at Easter derives from the fresh white robes worn by the newly baptized.

The association of light with Christ's Resurrection is also the symbolic basis of the sunrise services, a variation of the Easter vigil. Often held on a hilltop, the faithful wait to see the new light of dawn pierce the dim sky; after dawn, a mass is celebrated outdoors. Joyful Catholics may be greeted by their priest with the ancient traditional Easter greeting, "Christ is risen indeed!" The one greeted then replies with "And hath appeared unto Simon!"

Right An Easter vigil opens with the kindling of a new paschal candle, a large white candle symbolizing the return of the light of Christ, which is relit throughout the year to mark sacred rites.

CHRONOLOGY OF POPES

SINCE ST PETER, THE FIRST POPE, THERE HAS BEEN AN ALMOST CONTINUOUS SUCCESSION OF POPES. THE FOLLOWING IS A CHRONOLOGICAL LISTING OF ALL THE POPES WHO HAVE HEADED THE ROMAN CATHOLIC CHURCH.

c.32–66 Peter
c.66–78 Linus
c.79–91 Anacletus
c.91–101 Clement I
c.101–109 Evaristus
c.109–16 Alexander I
c.116–25 Sixtus I
c.125–36 Telesphorus
c.138–42 Hyginus
c.142–55 Pius I
c.155–66 Anicetus
c.166–74 Soter
c.174–89 Eleutherus
c.189–98 Victor I
c.198–217 Zephyrinus
217–22 Callistus I
222–30 Urban I
230–5 Pontian
235–6 Anterus
236–50 Fabian
251–3 Cornelius
253–4 Lucius I
254–7 Stephen I
257–8 Sixtus II

260–8 Dionysius
269–74 Felix I
275–83 Eutychian
283–96 Caius
296–304 Marcellinus
c.306–8 Marcellus I
c.310 Eusebius
311–14 Miltiades
314–35 Silvester I
336 Mark
337–52 Julius I
352–66 Liberius
366–84 Damasus I
384–99 Siricius
399–401 Anastasius I
401–17 Innocent I
417–18 Zosimus
418–22 Boniface I
422–32 Celestine I
432–40 Sixtus III
440–61 Leo I
461–8 Hilarius
468–83 Simplicius
483–92 Felix III
492–6 Gelasius I
496–8 Anastasius II
498–514 Symmachus
514–23 Hormisdas
523–26 John I
526–30 Felix IV
530–2 Boniface II
533–5 John II
535–6 Agapetus I
536–7 Silverius
537–55 Vigilius
556–61 Pelagius I
561–74 John III
575–9 Benedict I
579–90 Pelagius II
590–604 Gregory I
604–6 Sabinian
607 Boniface III
608–15 Boniface IV
615–18 Adeodatus I
619–25 Boniface V
625–38 Honorius I

638–40 Severinus
640–2 John IV
642–9 Theodore I
649–53 Martin I
654–7 Eugene I
657–72 Vitalian
672–6 Adeodatus II
676–8 Donus
678–81 Agatho
682–3 Leo II
684–5 Benedict II
685–6 John V
686–7 Conon
687–701 Sergius I
701–5 John VI
705–7 John VII
708 Sisinnius
708–15 Constantine
715–31 Gregory II
731–41 Gregory III
741–52 Zachary
752 Stephen II
752–7 Stephen III
757–67 Paul I
768–72 Stephen IV
772–95 Hadrian I
795–816 Leo III
816–17 Stephen V
817–24 Paschal I
824–7 Eugene II
827 Valentine
827–44 Gregory IV
844–7 Sergius II
847–55 Leo IV
855–8 Benedict III
858–67 Nicholas I
867–72 Hadrian II

Above St Peter, the first pope, was traditionally supposed to have been crucified upside down, as in this fresco by Leonhard von Brixen, 1470.

872–82 John VIII
882–4 Marinus I
884–5 Hadrian III
885–91 Stephen VI
891–6 Formosus
896 Boniface VI
896–7 Stephen VII
897 Romanus
897 Theodore II
898–900 John IX
900–3 Benedict IV
903 Leo V
904–11 Sergius III
911–13 Anastasius III
913–14 Lando

Above St Francis of Assisi presents the regulations of his new order to Pope Innocent IV in this 18th-century painting by Niccolo Ricciolini. Innocent IV was a strong pope, affirming papal authority.

Right Pope Clement V was responsible for moving the papacy to a new seat in Avignon, France, in 1305. This statue tops his tomb in Bordeaux's St André Cathedral.

Above Pope Clement VII suffered being taken prisoner in 1527. Giuliano Bugiardini's portrait, c.1532, shows him six years later, in more dignified times.

914–28 John X
928 Leo VI
928–31 Stephen VIII
931–5 John XI
936–9 Leo VII
939–42 Stephen IX
942–6 Marinus II
946–55 Agapetus II
955–63 John XII
963–5 Leo VIII
964 Benedict V (deposed)
965–72 John XIII
973–4 Benedict VI
974–83 Benedict VII
983–4 John XIV
985–96 John XV
996–9 Gregory V
999–1003 Sylvester II
1003 John XVII
1003–9 John XVIII
1009–12 Sergius IV
1012–24 Benedict VIII
1024–32 John XIX
1032–44; 1045; 1047–8
  Benedict IX
1045 Sylvester III
1045–6 Gregory VI
1046–7 Clement II
1048 Damasus II
1049–54 Leo IX
1055–7 Victor II
1057–8 Stephen X

1058–61 Nicholas II
1061–73 Alexander II
1073–85 Gregory VII
1086–7 Victor III
1088–99 Urban II
1099–1118 Paschal II
1118–19 Gelasius II
1119–24 Callistus II
1124–30 Honorius II
1130–43 Innocent II
1143–4 Celestine II
1144–5 Lucius II
1145–53 Eugene III
1153–4 Anastasius IV
1154–9 Hadrian IV
1159–81 Alexander III
1181–5 Lucius III
1185–7 Urban III
1187 Gregory VIII
1187–91 Clement III
1191–8 Celestine III
1198–1216 Innocent III
1216–27 Honorius III
1227–41 Gregory IX
1241 Celestine IV
1243–54 Innocent IV
1254–61 Alexander IV
1261–4 Urban IV
1265–8 Clement IV
1271–6 Gregory X
1276 Innocent V
1276 Hadrian V
1276–7 John XXI
1277–80 Nicholas III
1281–5 Martin IV
1285–7 Honorius IV
1288–92 Nicholas IV
1294 Celestine V
1294–1303 Boniface VIII
1303–4 Benedict XI
1305–14 Clement V
1316–34 John XXII
1334–42 Benedict XII
1342–52 Clement VI
1352–62 Innocent VI
1362–70 Urban V
1370–8 Gregory XI
1378–89 Urban VI
1389–1404 Boniface IX
1404–6 Innocent VII
1406–15 Gregory XII
1417–31 Martin V
1431–47 Eugene IV

Right Pope Urban VIII was a temporal leader as well as a spiritual ruler, with his own coinage. This gold coin was produced in Avignon, France.

1447–55 Nicholas V
1455–8 Callistus III
1458–64 Pius II
1464–71 Paul II
1471–84 Sixtus IV
1484–92 Innocent VIII
1492–1503 Alexander VI
1503 Pius III
1503–13 Julius II
1513–21 Leo X
1522–3 Hadrian VI
1523–34 Clement VII
1534–49 Paul III
1550–5 Julius III
1555 Marcellus II
1555–9 Paul IV
1559–65 Pius IV
1566–72 Pius V
1572–85 Gregory XIII
1585–90 Sixtus V
1590 Urban VII
1590–1 Gregory XIV
1591 Innocent IX
1592–1605 Clement VIII
1605 Leo XI
1605–21 Paul V
1621–3 Gregory XV
1623–44 Urban VIII

1644–55 Innocent X
1655–67 Alexander VII
1667–9 Clement IX
1670–6 Clement X
1676–89 Innocent XI
1689–91 Alexander VIII
1691–1700 Innocent XII
1700–21 Clement XI
1721–4 Innocent XIII
1724–30 Benedict XIII
1730–40 Clement XII
1740–58 Benedict XIV
1758–69 Clement XIII
1769–74 Clement XIV
1775–99 Pius VI
1800–23 Pius VII
1823–9 Leo XII
1829–30 Pius VIII
1831–46 Gregory XVI
1846–78 Pius IX
1878–1903 Leo XIII
1903–14 Pius X
1914–22 Benedict XV
1922–39 Pius XI
1939–58 Pius XII
1958–63 John XXIII
1963–78 Paul VI
1978 John Paul I
1978–2005 John Paul II
2005– Benedict XVI

Left Pope Benedict XVI, who was elected pope after one of the shortest conclaves in Catholic history, must face the challenge of giving leadership to the world's Catholics in an age of increasing secularism.

RELIGIOUS ORDERS

THERE ARE A GREAT MANY DIFFERENT ORDERS WITHIN THE CATHOLIC CHURCH. BELOW IS A LIST OF THE MAJOR RELIGIOUS ORDERS AND THEIR FOUNDERS, ARRANGED CHRONOLOGICALLY.

BENEDICTINES
The first great order of monks, founded by St Benedict of Nursia in 529.

CARTHUSIANS
Enclosed order, including both monks and nuns, established by St Bruno of Cologne, 1084.

CISTERCIANS
Reformist monastic order, founded by Robert of Molesme in 1098 and greatly expanded by St Bernard of Clairvaux.

CARMELITES
The Brothers (and Sisters) of Our Lady of Mount Carmel, founded in the 12th century on Mount Carmel, Israel.

TRINITARIANS
Order of the Holy Trinity, an order of priests, monks and nuns that was founded by St John de Matha in France in 1198.

FRANCISCANS
Friars (Mendicant Brothers), founded by St Francis of Assisi in 1209.

POOR CLARES
The Order of Poor Ladies, founded in Assisi, Italy, by St Clare with the help of St Francis in 1212.

DOMINICANS
Friars, predominantly a teaching order; established by St Dominic in southern France in *c.*1215.

AUGUSTINIANS
A group of monastic orders, incorporated as a "Grand Union" in 1256.

CAPUCHINS
The Order of Friars Minor Capuchin, following a back-to-first-principles re-foundation of the Franciscans, started by Matteo di Bascio in 1520.

THEATINES
The Congregation of Clerks Regular of the Divine Providence, known as the Theatines from their foundation in Chieti (Theate), Italy, founded in 1524 by St Cajetan.

Above St Benedict of Nursia can be seen teaching his Rule to his monks in this 13th-century French illustration.

JESUITS
The Society of Jesus, founded by St Ignatius Loyola in 1534.

URSULINES
Order of nuns, devoted mainly to the teaching of girls, established in Italy by Ste Angela de Merici in 1535.

SISTERS OF LORETO
Order of nuns founded by Mary Ward, an Englishwoman in French exile, in 1609.

Above St Bruno, founder of the Carthusian order, prays in the wilderness at Chartreuse, France, in this 17th-century painting by Nicolas Mignard.

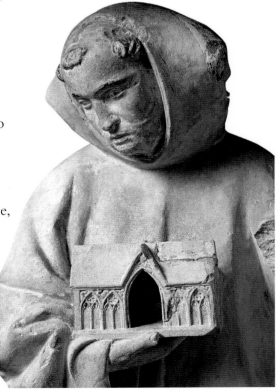

Right A 14th-century sculpture shows St Bernard of Clairvaux, a leading Cistercian, carrying the chapel of Clairvaux, the abbey that he founded.

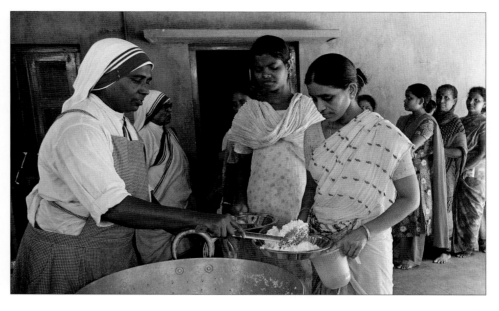

Above St Ignatius Loyola presented the rule book for his newly established Society of Jesus to Pope Paul III (1534–49), shown in this anonymous painting.

CONGREGATION OF THE MISSION

Also known as the Lazarists or Vincentians, this order of priests was established by St Vincent de Paul in 1624.

DAUGHTERS OF CHARITY

Often referred to as Sisters of Charity, a congregation of nuns formed by St Vincent de Paul in 1633.

TRAPPISTS

An order of monks and nuns, a Cistercian offshoot named for France's La Trappe Abbey, where their famous rule of silence was first introduced in 1664.

LOVERS OF THE HOLY CROSS

Order of nuns, founded in 1670 in Vietnam and centred in the Far East.

REDEMPTORISTS

The Congregation of the Most Holy Redeemer, who are missionaries to the poor; the order was founded in Italy by St Alphonsus of Ligouri in 1732.

CONGREGATION OF CHRISTIAN BROTHERS

Commonly known as Christian Brothers, a congregation of lay brothers within the Roman Catholic Church, dedicated to educating poor boys worldwide; it was established by Edmund Ignatius Rice in Waterford, Ireland in 1808.

Above Trappist monks perform their religious office at the Abbey Notre-Dame d'Aiguebelle, France. Prayer is an important part of their routine.

Above An Indian nun from the Missionaries of Charity ministers to Calcutta's poor. Founder Mother Teresa won international renown for the charity's work with the destitute.

SOCIETY OF MARY

The Marist Fathers (the Marist Brothers are an offshoot), an order of teachers and workers dedicated to the poor, founded by William Joseph Chaminade in France, 1817.

LITTLE SISTERS OF THE POOR

Order of nuns dedicated to the care of the poor – especially the elderly – founded in France by Jeanne Jugan in 1839.

SOCIETY OF AFRICAN MISSIONS

Founded by Melchior de Marion Brésillac in 1850.

WHITE FATHERS

More formally, the Society of the Missionaries of Africa, founded in Algeria by the French cardinal Charles Lavigerie in 1868.

MISSIONARIES OF CHARITY

An order of nuns established in 1950 by Mother Teresa of Calcutta to help the poor.

GLOSSARY

ABSOLUTION The power of forgiveness that can be exercised by a priest during the sacrament of penance (confession).

ANATHEMA From the Greek word originally meaning an offering to a god, but subsequently coming to mean despised, hated and accursed; excommunicated from or condemned by the Church.

ANNUNCIATION A festival celebrated on 25 March to commemorate the announcement by the archangel Gabriel to Mary of Jesus' coming birth.

ANTICHRIST From the New Testament, the ultimate enemy of Christ who will oppose Christ's teachings and substitute himself for Christ.

APOSTASY A total rejection of the Christian faith by a baptized person.

APOSTLE A messenger with the purpose of spreading the Christian message; specifically, the name given by Jesus to 12 of his faithful followers, who were given the task to spread the Word by preaching the gospels.

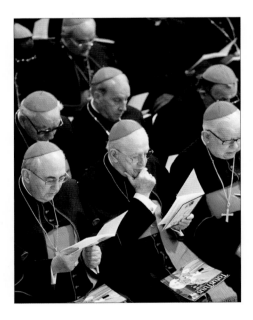

Above Pope John Paul II moved a step closer to sainthood when he was beatified after a dossier was presented to the Vatican.

APOSTLES' CREED A 1st-century AD formula of Church teachings established by the first pope, St Peter.

APOSTOLIC FATHERS Writers of the Christian faith in the 1st and 2nd centuries AD, thought to have known or been personally influenced by the apostles and their writings.

ASCENSION The elevation of Christ to heaven on the 40th day after his Resurrection, celebrated as a feast day that falls 40 days after Easter.

ASSUMPTION OF MARY The entrance of the body and soul of Mary to heaven after her death, commemorated on 15 August.

ATHANASIAN CREED A formula of Catholic faith, probably drawn up in the 4th or 5th century AD in response to various heretical theories on the nature of Christ.

BAPTISM A sacramental rite involving water that cleanses a person of sin; in Catholic doctrine, due to original sin, baptism is a necessary requirement to gain entry into heaven.

BEATITUDES The blessings due to followers of Christianity listed by Jesus at the beginning of the Sermon on the Mount, recorded in Matthew (5:3–12) and Luke (23:42).

BEATIFICATION A papal declaration of a deceased person as officially "blessed", a stage in the process of canonization.

CANONIZATION The process by which a deceased person who has previously been beatified is formally declared a saint.

CATECHISM An exposition of the doctrines of Catholicism taught in a catechistic, or question and answer, form.

COMMUNION The act of celebrating the Eucharist (thanksgiving) through partaking of bread and wine

Above St Matthew the Evangelist, shown in this 12th-century Byzantine evangelistary, was one of the four apostles responsible for the gospels.

that Catholicism states are the true body and blood of Jesus Christ.

CONFESSION The sacrament of penance, or admission of sins committed after baptism, to a priest in order to obtain forgiveness.

COUNTER-REFORMATION A period of Catholic revival from *c.*1522 to 1648, during which time attempts were made to stem the rise of Protestantism through reforms in the Catholic Church.

CULT OR CULTUS A system of beliefs and religious observances surrounding a particular saint.

DEUTEROCANONICALS Also known as the Apocrypha, certain Old Testament books and passages that are present in the Catholic Bible but that are not part of the Jewish or Protestant canon.

DOCTRINE An authoritative set of beliefs taught by the Church.

DOGMA Church doctrine that has been revealed by God and therefore is deemed to be indisputable, belief in which is said by the Catholic Church to be necessary for salvation.

EVANGELIST Someone who aims to convert others to their cause; specifically the authors of the four Gospels, Sts Matthew, Mark, Luke and John.

EXCOMMUNICATION The suspension of a person from the possibility of redemption by revoking their membership of the Church community.

FEAST DAY A fixed or movable holy festival designated for giving special honour to God, members of the Holy Family or saints, often commemorating specific events.

HERESY A belief or set of beliefs at variance with the official or orthodox doctrine of the Church.

INCARNATION The union of the divine and human natures of the Son of God in the person of Jesus Christ.

INDULGENCES The remittance of temporal punishments given to a sinner after the sin has been confessed and absolved, dispensed by the Church.

JUDGEMENT DAY The time at which a final judgement and trial of all mankind will take place after Armageddon, where each person will be rewarded or punished according to his or her merits.

LAST SUPPER The last meal eaten by Jesus before his Crucifixion, where he asked that bread and wine be shared by those at the meal in memory of him, and when he gave his final instructions to his followers.

LIMBO The destination of righteous but unbaptized souls, such as infants who die without baptism or those who died before Christ.

MAGISTERIUM The teaching office or authority of the Catholic Church embodied in the pope and bishops, who are the representatives of the Church.

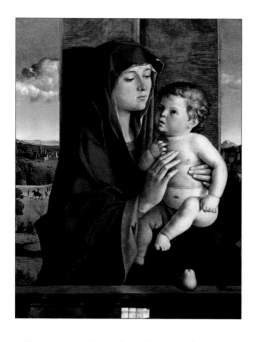

Above Some feast days honour the Madonna and child, shown in this 15th-century painting by Giovanni Bellini.

MASS The church service during which Eucharist is celebrated, which is the central act of worship in Catholic liturgy.

MORTAL SIN A deadly sin that revolts against God and deprives the sinner of their right to enter heaven.

NICENE CREED A formulation of Catholic doctrine first released in AD 325 and revised in AD 381, which outlines the nature of Christ in response to the Arian heresy.

ORIGINAL SIN The state of sin that all of humankind are born into as a result of the fall from grace of Adam and Eve, and which is cleansed through baptism.

PURGATORY The temporary destination for those who have died in a state of grace, where they can atone for their sins before they can enter heaven.

REDEMPTION The salvation of humanity through Jesus Christ, who gave his life in return for the expiation of humanity's debt of sin.

REFORMATION A period of religious, social and political unrest from 1517 to 1648, which resulted in the formation of Protestantism.

RESURRECTION The miracle of Christ's return to life three days after his death and burial, followed by his Ascension to heaven.

REVELATION The disclosure by God of himself and his plan to humanity, for example, through private revelation in the form of visions of the Virgin Mary.

SACRAMENT A formal religious ceremony, during which a specific grace is conferred upon those who receive it, such as Communion and confession.

TRANSUBSTANTIATION The process by which Catholics believe that bread and wine become the body and blood of Christ during the celebration of the Eucharist.

TRINITY, THE HOLY The name used to represent the three distinct persons present in the Christian God: the Father, the Son and the Holy Spirit.

VENIAL SIN A pardonable sin that offends against God but does not on its own deprive the sinner of his or her right to enter heaven.

Above Limbo is shown in this 14th-century panel from an altarpiece in Santo Sepulchro, a convent in Zaragoza.

INDEX

Page numbers in bold denote illustrations.

Above Noli me Tangere *by the Master
of the Lehman Crucifixion, 1370–5.*

Above A demon tempts a woman on the exterior of Chartres Cathedral, France.

Above Spaniards and Mexicans celebrate Mass in this 16th-century painting, Lienzo de Tlaxcala, *printed in* Antigüendas Mexicana.

Above *The seven pilgrim churches of Rome, seen from above in this 1575 copper engraving by Antonio Lafreri.*

This edition is published by
Lorenz Books
an imprint of Anness Publishing Ltd
Hermes House, 88-89 Blackfriars Road,
London SE1 8HA
Tel. 020 7401 2077; fax 020 7633 9499

www.lorenzbooks.com;
www.annesspublishing.com

© Anness Publishing Ltd 2009

Anness Publishing has a new picture
agency outlet for images for publishing,
promotions or advertising. Please visit
our website www.practicalpictures.com
for more information.

UK agent: The Manning Partnership Ltd,
tel. 01225 478444; fax 01225 478440;
sales@manning-partnership.co.uk
UK distributor: Grantham Book Services
Ltd, tel. 01476 541 080; fax 01476
541061; orders@gbs.tbs-ltd.co.uk
North American agent/distributor:
National Book Network, tel. 301 459
3366; fax 301 429 5746;
www.nbnbooks.com

Australian agent/distributor:
Macmillan Australia, tel. 1300 135 113;
fax 1300 135 103;
customer.service@macmillan.com.au
New Zealand agent/distributor:
David Bateman Ltd, tel. (09) 415 7664;
fax (09) 415 8892

ETHICAL TRADING POLICY
Because of our ongoing ecological
investment programme, you, as our
customer, can have the pleasure and
reassurance of knowing that a tree is
being cultivated on your behalf to
naturally replace the materials used to
make the book you are holding. For
further information about this scheme,
go to www.annesspublishing.com/trees

Anness Publishing Ltd:
Publisher: Joanna Lorenz
Editorial Director: Helen Sudell

Produced for Lorenz Books by
Toucan Books:
Managing Director: Ellen Dupont
Editor: Theresa Bebbington
Project Manager: Hannah Bowen
Designer: Elizabeth Healey
Picture Researcher: Marian Pullen
Proofreader: Marion Dent
Indexer: Michael Dent
Cartography by Cosmographics, UK

Endpaper: St Benedict of Nursia prays
with his monks, fresco by Giovanni-
Antonio Bazzi.

The publishers have made every effort to trace
the photograph copyright owners. Anyone we
have failed to reach is invited to contact Toucan
Books, 89 Charterhouse Street, London EC1M
6HR, United Kingdom.
Abbreviations ADO: Alfredo Dagli Orti; BL:
British Library, London; GDO: Gianni Dagli
Orti; Priv Coll: Private Collection; V&A:
Victoria & Albert Museum, London.
akg-images 1m, 5bml, 9bl, 13t, 19tl, 21br,
25b, 26tr, 33bl, 36tr, 37br, 38b, 39tr, 39bm, 40tr,
42-43, 44tr, 48bl, 49tl, 60bl, 61bl, 62tr, 65tr, 70tr,
71l, 72tr, 75tr, 78b, 80tr, 81l, 81br, 82tr, 83tm,
90tr, 90bl, 91tr, 100tr, 118tr, 119bl, 122tr, 126tr,
126bl, 129bl, 133bl, 138-139, 143br, 146tr,
147bl, 149tm, 150bl, 151br, 154tr, 154bl, 155bl,
156bl, 186tr, 192tr, 193br, 204tr, 204b, 214bl,
223br, 235tl, 246br, 247tl, 255t. **Alamy** Front
Cover b, 82b, 87tm, 103br, 111tm, 158-159,
165br, 170bl, 174tr and 174br, 180t, 181b, 183tr,
183br, 184t, 185t, 186bl, 192bl, 193tm, 195bl,
196bl, 197br, 198bl, 199rm, 201bl, 203bl, 208tr,
208bl, 213br, 214tr, 216bl, 218tr, 218bl, 223t,
226b, 229bl, 238tr, 243t, 243br, 245tr.
Ancient Art & Architecture 15b.
ArkReligion.com Back Cover mt, 169br,
172t, 172bl, 173tr, 178, 180br, 182bl, 195tl,
197bl, 201tm, 202tr, 206bl, 207br, 236bm.
The Art Archive Front Cover mt, tmr, b,

inside flap, Back Cover tm, t, b, bmr, spine, 2, 3t,
3, 4bml, 4bm, 5bm, 5b, 6t, 8tm, 8tl, 9bl, 9b, 10-
11, 12-1, 14br, 17b, 18tr, 20tr, 22t, 22m, 22b,
23tr, 23b, 24tr, 24b, 25t, 27t, 28bl, 29, 30tr, 30b,
31t, 31b, 33, 35t, 35b, 35br, 37b, 38tr, 40bl,
42tm, 43tm, 44bl, 45b, 45b, 47bl, 51b, 52try, 55b,
58t, 58bl, 59br, 62b, 63, 64t, 64bl, 65b, 66tr, 66bl,
68tr, 69br, 70bl, 71r, 73br, 74tr, 76tr, 76bl, 77tl,
77br, 78tr, 79tr, 79br, 80bl, 84tr, 85tr, 86tr, 89,
91bm, 92tr, 92br, 93tm, 94bl, 96bl, 97tm, 98bl,
99br, 104tr, 117tm, 118b, 119tr, 120bl, 121br,
123tm, 123bl, 124tr, 124, 125tm, 130bl, 131br,
133b, 136bl, 137br, 139tm, 140bl, 141tr, 142bl,
144tr, 148tr, 149br, 150tr, 152t, 155br, 156tr,
157b, 157br, 191tm, 194tr, 195tr, 200bl, 202bl,
206tr, 209tm, 209br, 210bl, 211tr, 211br, 213t,
217b, 220bm, 224bl, br and 225bl, br, 227tr,
227b, 228tr, 231tm, 234tr, 234bm, 236tr, 237b,
239b, 242tr, 244tr, 244bl, 246tr, 246bl, 247tr,
248bl, 248br, 249tl, 250t, 251t, 252bl, 254b, 256,
Endpaper. **The Bridgeman Art Library**
Front Cover tr and Back Cover b, Back Cover
tm, 4bl, 5bl, 15, 16t, 18, 19b, 20bl, 21, 27b, 29tr,
34tr, 36bl, 46t, 47tr, 50t, 52b, 53t, 53, 56-5, 57t,
59t, 60t, 63tr, 67b, 67br, 68b, 68br, 69tr, 73tr,
74b, 75br, 77bm, 83br, 84b, 85br, 87bl, 87br, 88-
89, 94bl, 95bl, b, 96tr, 97br, 101bl, 116-11, 120tr,
122b, 125b, 127bl, 128t, 129b, 130t, 131tr, 132b,
134tr, 136tr, 142tr, 143t, 144bl, 145t, 146b, 147t,

151t, 152b, 153t, 153b, 155tr, 176tr, 185br, 196t,
212tr, 215tr, 220ty, 221tr, 222b, 226t, 232t, 232b,
235mr, 237tr, 238by, 240t, 242bl, 251br, 253b,
189br. **Corbis** Front Cover tl and Back Cover
bl, mtl and Back Cover bm, m, Back Cover ta,
Back Cover Inside Flap, 4br, 14tr, 16bl, 17, 32b,
55tr, 72bl, 86b, 99bl, 102t, 103tl, 104b, 105tm,
106b, 107bl, 107br, 108t, 108bl, 110tr, 113br,
114-115, 132tr, 134bl, 135tm, 135br, 137tr,
140tr, 141br, 145br, 148b, 162b, 163tr, 164bl,
165tr, 166tr, bl, 169bl, 170tr, 175br, 176bl,
177tr and bm, 178tr, 179br, 190-191, 199br,
200tr, 201b, 203tr, 205tr, 207tr, 210tr, 216tr,
219bl, 224tr, 229tm, 230-231, 233br, 240, 241t,
247br, 250bl. **Getty Images** 51tl, 98tr, 102bl,
105bl, 106tr, 109tr, 110bl, 111bl, 112tr, 112bl,
113tr, 121tr, 128br, 161tm, 162tr, 163br, 166bl,
167mr, 167br, 171tr, 171bl, 173br, 175tl, 188tr,
188bl, 189tm, 205tl, 212bl, 215bl, 221bl, 228bl,
233tr, 235tr, 241br, 245br, 249tr. **Courtesy
Hayes & Finch** 198tr. **Heritage-Images**
48tr, 50br, 61br. **Kobal Collection** 179tr.
Photoshot 249bm. **Photolibrary** 7, 160-
161, 6181t, 184bl, 194bl, 219tm, 222tr, 235bl,
239t. **Rex Features** 101br, 109br. **Robert
Harding** 54tr, 164tr, 182br, 205br, 235br.
Sonia Halliday Photographs 26bl, 28tr,
54bl. **TopFoto** 34bl, 100tr, 127br, 187tr and br.
Courtesy Vanpoulles Ltd 217tl.